English
Novel
Explication

Supplement I

Compiled by

Peter L. Abernethy
Christian J. W. Kloesel
Jeffrey R. Smitten

THE SHOE STRING PRESS, INC.   1976

Library of Congress Cataloguing in Publication Data (Revised)

Palmer, Helen H.
   English novel explication.

Supplements The English novel, 1578-1956, by I. F. Bell
and D. Baird.—Cf. Supplement I.

————Supplement I.
Most of the citations are to material published 1972-1974.

1. English fiction—History criticism—Bibliography—
Indexes. I. Dyson, Anne, 1912-   joint author. II. Bell,
Inglis Freeman, 1917-   The English novel, 1578-1956.   III.
Abernethy, Peter L.   IV. Kloesel, Christian J. W.   V. Smit-
ten, Jeffery R.   VI. Title.
Z2014.F5P26Suppl   016.823'03   73-410 √

   ISBN 0-208-01464-0

© 1976 by The Shoe String Press, Inc.
Hamden, Connecticut 06514

CONTENTS

PREFACE

The present bibliography is intended to supplement and update *English Novel Explication: Criticisms to 1972* compiled by Helen H. Palmer and Anne Jane Dyson (1973), which itself was a supplement to *The English Novel, 1578-1956: A Checklist of Twentieth-Century Criticism* (1958) complied by Inglis F. Bell and Donald Baird. The chronological boundaries of our compilation are not rigid. On the one hand, we have included such 1975 publications as we could locate; on the other, we have added many books and articles omitted from Palmer-Dyson, as well as a few from Bell-Baird. Still, our bibliography does not claim to be a systematic or complete revision of these earlier works. Our primary responsibility was to examine and gather material published from 1972 through 1974.

Although departing from Palmer-Dyson in some matters, our bibliography maintains continuity with the earlier work in two important respects. First, we too have accepted a very broad definition of the term "novel." With so much confusion and contradiction over definition of the genre, we felt that the less restrictive our definition, the more useful our bibliography. The range of works which we admit as novels is based primarily on Ernest A. Baker's comprehensive *History of the English Novel* with the exception that we include nothing in verse (Chaucer's *Troilus and Criseyde*, for example). Consequently, in addition to the "standard" English novels, the user of this supplement will find listings for their more or less distant relations, such as *Le Morte Darthur*, the *Arcadia*, *Pilgrim's Progress*, *Gulliver's Travels*, *Rasselas*, *News From Nowhere*, *Orlando*, and *Down and Out in Paris and London*.

Second, we have also accepted a broad definition of what constitutes "explication." This critical term was originally closely associated with New Criticism, especially during the 1940's and 1950's. In fact, the Bell-Baird volume was conceived as a companion to George Arms and Joseph M. Kuntz's *Poetry Explication* (1950), a checklist of criticism designed to solidify the forces of the New Critics at an early moment in their development. In accordance with this history of "explication," we have included all studies which discuss aspects of fiction stressed by New Criticism, including theme, structure, symbolism, imagery, and diction. But, as David Daiches said some years ago, "a poem or a play or a novel can be very many things at the same time—a reflection of the cultural climate of its age, a document in the mental history of its author, a carefully patterned arrangement of words, ideas, images and situations, a fable, a piece of rhetoric, and the communication of a unique insight into an aspect of human experience through one or several of these means." The development of literary criticism since the 1950's has more than borne out Daiches's view: the ranks of the New Critics have been augmented by yet newer critics drawing on Neo-Aristotelians, on structuralism, phenomenology, and the history of ideas, and on Marxism, existentialism, and many other fields and movements. Given this fact, to limit our bibliography to the

v

original definition of "explication" would be hidebound. We have there-
fore taken explication to mean an interpretation of the meaning of a novel
regardless of the methodology employed to arrive at that interpretation.
In practice, this means simply the omission of studies which are exclu-
sively devoted to sources and influence, critical reception, biography, or
bibliography.

Despite these broad areas of agreement, our bibliography differs from
Palmer-Dyson on a number of more specific points of scope and format.
For convenience, these may be enumerated.

1. We have excluded all book reviews, dissertations, and abstracts of
dissertations. Since there are published indexes for these, little would be
gained by listing them here. Like Palmer-Dyson, we have (regretfully) not
listed reprints of books and articles. We hope that this important gap can
be filled in a future supplement or revised edition.

2. We have included no short novels that are listed in Warren S. Walker's
Twentieth-Century Short Story Explication (for example, *Animal Farm,
St. Mawr,* or *Heart of Darkness*). However, since Walker tends not to list
criticism of short fiction written before 1800, we have included it, although
the works in question are not of "regular" novel length. Many early
readers would have called these short pieces "novels"; accordingly, they
have a significant place in the development of the more modern English
novel.

3. We have defined "English novelist" to be a writer born in England,
Scotland, Ireland, Wales, or the Commonwealth who has lived in Great
Britain during some significant portion of his creative years. This definition excludes writers like Henry James and Brian Moore and includes
others like Doris Lessing, Malcolm Lowry, and P. G. Wodehouse.

4. We have included a very brief section of ANONYMOUS NOVELS
at the end of the bibliography.

5. The form of our entries differs in several respects from Palmer-
Dyson's. (a) Virtually all book titles have been abbreviated. The reader
desiring the full title and publication information should consult the
LIST OF BOOKS INDEXED. (b) Citations of essays in collections have
been arranged so as to give the individual essay's author and title as well
as the collection's editor and title. All collections are listed in the LIST
OF BOOKS INDEXED by the editor's name. (c) Page numbers refer only
to those sections of a work which explicate a particular novel. If several
novels are discussed concurrently, page numbers for the entire discussion
are given. Books for which no page citation is provided refer *in toto* to
the novel in question. (d) Journal entries have been given in full, although
journal subtitles are almost never used. In the case of journals with identical or very nearly identical titles, the place of publication is given in
parentheses following the title. We saw no need for a LIST OF JOURNALS
INDEXED, because full bibliographical journal information may be easily
obtained from the *Union List of Serials*.

6. The dates of publication following the novel titles are the dates of first
publication in book form in Great Britain. In the rare instances in which a

novel was published only in serial form or only outside Great Britain, the date of first publication is given. The dates of novel publication and the dates of authors' lives included in the INDEX have been obtained from such standard reference sources as the *New Cambridge Bibliography of English Literature* and *Contemporary Authors.*

Inevitably in a work of this scope human frailty will cause many errors and omissions. In addition, circumstances will often conspire against the makers of bibliographies. Particularly troublesome for us were library binding schedules and the slow arrival of very recent books and journals, both of which made this bibliography less complete than it might have been. Consequently, we would appreciate notice of errors and omissions so that they may be corrected in future supplements or revised editions.

We would like to thank Mrs. Gloria Lyerla and the staff of the Inter-library Loan Department of the Texas Tech University Library for their patience and diligence in securing books for us. We are similarly grateful to Mrs. Billie Osborne and Miss Teresa Thomas for typing speedily a long and difficult manuscript.

P.L.A.
C.J.W.K.
J.R.S.

Lubbock, Texas
September 1975

WILLIAM HARRISON AINSWORTH

Cardinal Pole, 1863

Ligocki, Llewellyn. "Ainsworth's Tudor Novels: History as Theme." *Studies in the Novel*, 4 (1972), 364-377.

The Constable of the Tower, 1861

Ligocki, Llewellyn. "Ainsworth's Tudor Novels: History as Theme." *Studies in the Novel*, 4 (1972), 364-377.

The Fall of Somerset, 1877

Ligocki, Llewellyn. "Ainsworth's Tudor Novels: History as Theme." *Studies in the Novel*, 4 (1972), 364-377.

Jack Sheppard, 1839

Hollingsworth, Keith. *The Newgate Novel*. 1963. Pp. 131-148.

Worth, George J. "Early Victorian Criticism of the Novel and Its Limitations: *Jack Sheppard*, a Test Case," in Harold Orel and George J. Worth, eds., *The Nineteenth-Century Writer and His Audience*. 1969. Pp. 52-59.

Rookwood, 1834

Hollingsworth, Keith. *The Newgate Novel*. 1963. Pp. 98-109.

Tower Hill, 1871

Ligocki, Llewellyn. "Ainsworth's Tudor Novels: History as Theme." *Studies in the Novel*, 4 (1972), 364-377.

The Tower of London, 1840

Ligocki, Llewellyn. "Ainsworth's Tudor Novels: History as Theme." *Studies in the Novel*, 4 (1972), 364-377.

Windsor Castle, 1843

Ligocki, Llewellyn. "Ainsworth's Tudor Novels: History as Theme." *Studies in the Novel*, 4 (1972), 364-377.

RICHARD ALDINGTON

Very Heaven, 1937

Vickery, John B. "Mythopoesis and Modern Literature," in Melvin J. Friedman and John B. Vickery, eds., *The Shaken Realist*. 1970. Pp. 220-223.

BRIAN ALDISS

Barefoot in the Head, 1969

Blish, James. *More Issues at Hand*. 1970. Pp. 138-145.

KINGSLEY AMIS

The Anti-Death League, 1966

Bičanič, Sonia. "Cats, Birds and Freedom." *Studia Romanica et Anglica Zagrabiensia*, 29-32 (1970-1971), 515-522.

Haimart, S. M. "Kingsley Amis: *Lucky Jim* ou la tunique de Nessus." *Etudes Anglaises*, 25 (1972), 380-383.

I Like It Here, 1958

Voorhees, Richard J. "Kingsley Amis: Three Hurrahs and a Reservation." *Queen's Quarterly*, 79 (1972), 40-46.

Lucky Jim, 1954

Haimart, S. M. "Kingsley Amis: *Lucky Jim* ou la tunique de Nessus." *Etudes Anglaises*, 25 (1972), 369-374.

Macleod, Norman. "*This Familiar Regressive Series*: Aspects of Style in the Novels of Kingsley Amis," in A. J. Aitken, Angus McIntosh, and Hermann Pálsson, eds., *Edinburgh Studies in English and Scots*. 1971. Pp. 123-136.

Meckier, Jerome. "Looking Back in Anger: The Success of a Collapsing Stance." *Dalhousie Review*, 52 (1972), 47-58.

Schleussner, Bruno. *Der neopikareske Roman*. 1969. Pp. 123-128.

Voorhees, Richard J. "Kingsley Amis: Three Hurrahs and a Reservation." *Queen's Quarterly*, 79 (1972), 40-46.

One Fat Englishman, 1963

Haimart, S. M. "Kingsley Amis: *Lucky Jim* ou la tunique de Nessus." *Etudes Anglaises*, 25 (1972), 378-380.

Kelly, Edward. "Satire and Word Games in Amis's *Englishman.*" *Satire Newsletter*, 9 (1972), 132-138.

Take a Girl Like You, 1960

Haimart, S. M. "Kingsley Amis: *Lucky Jim* ou la tunique de Nessus." *Etudes Anglaises*, 25 (1972), 375-378.

Macleod, Norman. "*This Familiar Regressive Series*: Aspects of Style in the Novels of Kingsley Amis," in A. J. Aitken, Angus McIntosh, and Hermann Pálsson, eds., *Edinburgh Studies in English and Scots*. 1971. Pp. 130-136.

That Uncertain Feeling, 1955

Macleod, Norman, "*This Familiar Regressive Series*: Aspects of Style in the Novels of Kingsley Amis," in A. J. Aitken, Angus McIntosh, and Hermann Pálsson, eds., *Edinburgh Studies in English and Scots*. 1971. Pp. 127-136.

Voorhees, Richard J. "Kingsley Amis: Three Hurrahs and a Reservation," *Queen's Quarterly*, 79 (1972), 40-46.

WILLIAM DELAFIELD ARNOLD

Oakfield, 1853

Goonetilleke, D. C. R. A. "Forgotten Nineteenth-Century Fiction: William Arnold's *Oakfield* and William Knighton's *Forest Life in Ceylon*." *Journal of Commonwealth Literature*, 7 (1972), 14-18.

DAISY ASHFORD

The Young Visiters, 1919

Starkey, Penelope Schott. "*The Young Visiters* Revisited in Light of Virginia Woolf." *Research Studies*, 42 (1974), 161-166.

PENELOPE AUBIN

The Life of Madam de Beaumont, 1721

Richetti, John J. *Popular Fiction*. 1969. Pp. 221-227.

JANE AUSTEN

Emma, 1816

Aers, Lesley. "Jane Austen and the Social Revolution." *Use of English*, 24 (1973), 313-317.

Beer, Patricia. *Reader, I Married Him*. 1974. Pp. 49-82.

Bennett, James R. "'Doating on You, Faults and All': Mr. George Knightley." *Studies in the Novel*, 5 (1973), 248-250.

Bradbury, Malcolm. *Possibilities*, 1973. Pp. 59-66.

Brown, Lloyd W. *Bits of Ivory*. 1973. Pp. 44-47, 61-65, 73-76, 96-99, 128-136, 193-198, 220-222.

Burgan, Mary Alice. "Feeling and Control: A Study of the Proposal Scenes in Jane Austen's Major Novels," in George Goodin, ed., *The English Novel*. 1972. Pp. 39-44.

Bush, Douglas. *Jane Austen*. 1975. Pp. 137-167.

Corwin, Laura J. "Character and Morality in the Novels of Jane Austen." *Revue des Langues Vivantes*, 38 (1972), 366-367, 377-378.

Halperin, John. *Egoism and Self-Discovery*. 1974. Pp. 12-29.

Halperin, John. *The Language of Meditation*. 1973. Pp. 28-46.

Harding, D. W. "Two Aspects of Jane Austen's Development." *Theoria* (Natal), 35 (1970), 10-15.

Kestner, Joseph A., III. "The 'I' Persona in the Novels of Jane Austen." *Studies in the Novel*, 4 (1972), 6-15.

Kestner, Joseph A., III. "Silence and Shyness in the Novels of Jane Austen: 'The Quietness of It Does Me Good.'" *Descant*, 16 (1971), 43-44, 46.

Kroeber, Karl. *Styles in Fictional Structure*. 1971. Pp. 15-26, 75-79, 151-180.

Lauber, John. "Heroes and Anti-Heroes in Jane Austen's Novels." *Dalhousie Review*, 51 (1971-1972), 489-503.
Lauber, John. "Jane Austen's Fools." *Studies in English Literature, 1500-1900*, 14 (1974), 520-523.
Lerner, Laurence. *The Truthtellers*. 1967. Pp. 72-74, 96-102, 144-145.
McMaster, Juliet. "Surface and Subsurface in Jane Austen's Novels." *Ariel*, 5:2 (1974), 20-23.
Mansell, Darrel. *The Novels of Jane Austen*. 1973. Pp. 146-184.
Matache, Liliana. "Metoda narativa oblica si stilul indirect liber in romanul *Emma* de Jane Austen." *Analele Universitatii Bucuresti: Literatura Universala si Comparata*, 18:2 (1969), 63-69.
Mews, Hazel. *Frail Vessels*. 1969. Pp. 61-62.
Moers, Ellen. "Woman's Lit: Profession and Tradition," *Columbia Forum*, 1 (1972), 31-33.
Morgan, Alice. "On Teaching *Emma*." *Journal of General Education*, 24 (1972), 103-108.
Moynahan, Julian. "Pastoralism as Culture and Counter-Culture in English Fiction, 1800-1928." *Novel*, 6 (1972), 26-27.
Nardin, Jane. *Those Elegant Decorums*. 1973. Pp. 109-128.
Page, Norman. *The Language of Jane Austen*. 1972. Pp. 42-48.
Pikoulis, John. "Jane Austen: The Figure in the Carpet." *Nineteenth-Century Fiction*, 27 (1972), 51-60.
Pinion, F. B. *A Jane Austen Companion*. 1973. Pp. 114-122.
Rauter, Herbert. "Austen: *Emma*," in Franz K. Stanzel, ed., *Der englische Roman*. 1969. Vol. II, 9-38.
Rubinstein, E. "Jane Austen's Novels: The Metaphor of Rank." *Literary Monographs*, 2 (1969), 153-172.
Steig, Michael. "Psychological Realism and Fantasy in Jane Austen: *Emma* and *Mansfield Park*." *Hartford Studies in Literature*, 5 (1973), 127-128.
Stoll, John E. "Psychological Dissociation in the Victorian Novel." *Literature and Psychology*, 20 (1970), 64-67.
Tave, Stuart M. *Some Words of Jane Austen*. 1973. Pp. 205-255.
Watts, Mary. "God and Jane Austen." *New Blackfriars*, 53 (1972), 15-22.
Williams, Ioan. *The Realist Novel*. 1974. Pp. 12-24.
Wolff, Cynthia Griffin. "The Problem of Eighteenth-Century Secular Heroinism." *Modern Language Studies*, 4 (1974), 39-41.

Lady Susan, 1871

Brown, Lloyd W. *Bits of Ivory*. 1973. Pp. 145-155.
Brown, Lloyd W. "Jane Austen and the Feminist Tradition." *Nineteenth-Century Fiction*, 28 (1973), 334-335.
Pinion, F. B. *A Jane Austen Companion*. 1973. Pp. 68-72.

Love and Friendship, 1922

Brissenden, R. F. *Virtue in Distress*. 1974. Pp. 279-283.
Brown, Lloyd W. *Bits of Ivory*. 1973. Pp. 18-21, 141-145, 206-210.

Brown, Lloyd W. "Jane Austen and the Feminist Tradition." *Nineteenth Century Fiction*, 28 (1973), 332-334.

Pinion, F. B. *A Jane Austen Companion*. 1973. Pp. 55-57.

Mansfield Park, 1814

Ames, Carol. "Fanny and Mrs. Norris: Poor Relations in *Mansfield Park*." *Dalhousie Review*, 54 (1974), 491-498.

Amis, Kingsley. *What Became of Jane Austen?* 1971. Pp. 13-17.

Anderson, Walter E. "The Plot of *Mansfield Park*." *Modern Philology*, 71 (1973), 16-27.

Beer, Patricia. *Reader, I Married Him*. 1974. Pp. 63-82.

Brown, Lloyd W. *Bits of Ivory*. 1973. Pp. 48-51, 81-96, 124-129, 229-234.

Brown, Lloyd W. "Jane Austen and the Feminist Tradition." *Nineteenth-Century Fiction*, 28 (1973), 337.

Burgan, Mary Alice. "Feeling and Control: A Study of the Proposal Scenes in Jane Austen's Major Novels," in George Goodin, ed., *The English Novel*. 1972. Pp. 33-39.

Bush, Douglas. *Jane Austen*. 1975. Pp. 108-135.

Corwin, Laura J. "Character and Morality in the Novels of Jane Austen." *Revue des Langues Vivantes*, 38 (1972), 367-370.

Donovan, Robert Alan. *The Shaping Vision*. 1966. Pp. 140-172.

Fleishman, Avrom. *A Reading of "Mansfield Park*." 1967. Pp. 19-81.

Fowler, Marian E. "The Courtesy-Book Heroine of *Mansfield Park*." *University of Toronto Quarterly*, 44 (1974), 31-46.

Friebe, Freimut. "Von Marianne Dashwood zu Anne Elliott: Empfindsame Motive bei Jane Austen." *Anglia*, 91 (1973), 315-341.

Gould, Gerald L. "The Gate Scene at Sotherton in *Mansfield Park*." *Literature and Psychology*, 20 (1970), 75-78.

Hummel, Madeline. "Emblematic Charades and the Observant Woman in *Mansfield Park*." *Texas Studies in Literature and Language*, 15 (1973), 251-265.

Kestner, Joseph A., III. "The 'I' Persona in the Novels of Jane Austen." *Studies in the Novel*, 4 (1972), 6-15.

Kestner, Joseph A., III. "Silence and Shyness in the Novels of Jane Austen: 'The Quietness of It Does Me Good.'" *Descant*, 16 (1971), 41-43, 45.

Kroeber, Karl. *Styles in Fictional Structure*. 1971. Pp. 72-74, 124-130.

Lauber, John. "Heroes and Anti-Heroes in Jane Austen's Novels." *Dalhousie Review*, 51 (1971-1972), 489-503.

Lauber, John. "Jane Austen's Fools." *Studies in English Literature, 1500-1900*, 14 (1974), 518-520.

Lerner, Laurence. *The Truthtellers*. 1967. Pp. 147, 149, 157-160.

McMaster, Juliet. "Surface and Subsurface in Jane Austen's Novels." *Ariel*, 5:2 (1974), 10-15.

Mansell, Darrel. *The Novels of Jane Austen*. 1973. Pp. 108-145.

Mews, Hazel. *Frail Vessels*. 1969. Pp. 57-60.

Nardin, Jane. *Those Elegant Decorums.* 1973. Pp. 82-108.
Page, Norman. *The Language of Jane Austen.* 1972. Pp. 34-42.
Pikoulis, John. "Jane Austen: The Figure in the Carpet." *Nineteenth-Century Fiction*, 27 (1972), 54-57.
Pinion, F. B. *A Jane Austen Companion.* 1973. Pp. 101-113.
Rubinstein, E. "Jane Austen's Novels: The Metaphor of Rank." *Literary Monographs*, 2 (1969), 133-153.
Steig, Michael. "Psychological Realism and Fantasy in Jane Austen: *Emma* and *Mansfield Park.*" *Hartford Studies in Literature*, 5 (1973), 128-134.
Tave, Stuart M. *Some Words of Jane Austen.* 1973. Pp. 158-204.
Trilling, Lionel. *Sincerity and Authenticity.* 1972. Pp. 75-80.
Watts, Mary. "God and Jane Austen." *New Blackfriars*, 53 (1972), 15-22.
Weinsheimer, Joel C. "*Mansfield Park*: Three Problems." *Nineteenth-Century Fiction*, 29 (1974), 185-205.

Northanger Abbey, 1818

Beer, Patricia. *Reader, I Married Him.* 1974. Pp. 66-77.
Brown, Lloyd W. *Bits of Ivory.* 1973. Pp. 112-118, 172-177, 210-217.
Brown, Lloyd W. "Jane Austen and the Feminist Tradition." *Nineteenth-Century Fiction*, 28 (1973), 335-336.
Bush, Douglas. *Jane Austen.* 1975. Pp. 57-70.
Fleishman, Avrom. "The Socialization of Catherine Morland." *ELH*, 41 (1974), 649-66/.
Hennedy, Hugh L. "Acts of Perception in Jane Austen's Novels." *Studies in the Novel*, 5 (1973), 25-30.
Kestner, Joseph A., III. "The 'I' Persona in the Novels of Jane Austen." *Studies in the Novel*, 4 (1972), 6-15.
Kiely, Robert. *The Romantic Novel in England.* 1972. Pp. 118-135.
Lauber, John. "Jane Austen's Fools." *Studies in English Literature, 1500-1900*, 14 (1974), 512-513.
Lerner, Laurence. *The Truthtellers.* 1967. Pp. 241-242.
Levy, Maurice. *Le Roman "gothique" anglais.* 1968. Pp. 506-510.
Mansell, Darrel. *The Novels of Jane Austen.* 1973. Pp. 1-45.
Mews, Hazel. *Frail Vessels.* 1969. Pp. 55-57.
Nardin, Jane. *Those Elegant Decorums.* 1973. Pp. 62-81.
Page, Norman. *The Language of Jane Austen.* 1972. Pp. 15-20.
Pinion, F. B. *A Jane Austen Companion.* 1973. Pp. 76-83.
Pirani, Alix. "*Northanger Abbey* and the New Fifth." *Use of English*, 24 (1972), 117-121, 126.
Rothstein, Eric. "The Lessons of *Northanger Abbey.*" *University of Toronto Quarterly*, 44 (1974), 14-30.
Rubinstein, E. "Jane Austen's Novels: The Metaphor of Rank." *Literary Monographs*, 2 (1969), 107-111.
Tave, Stuart M. *Some Words of Jane Austen.* 1973. Pp. 36-73.

Persuasion, 1818

Auerbach, Nina. "O Brave New World: Evaluation and Revolution in *Persuasion*." *ELH*, 39 (1972), 112-128.

Beer, Patricia. *Reader, I Married Him.* 1974. Pp. 45-82.

Bradbury, Malcolm. *Possibilities.* 1973. Pp. 67-78.

Brown, Lloyd W. *Bits of Ivory.* 1973. Pp. 39-43, 55-59, 99-107.

Brown, Lloyd W. "Jane Austen and the Feminist Tradition." *Nineteenth-Century Fiction*, 28 (1973), 324-327.

Burgan, Mary Alice. "Feeling and Control: A Study of the Proposal Scenes in Jane Austen's Major Novels," in George Goodin, ed., *The English Novel.* 1972. Pp. 44-50.

Bush, Douglas. *Jane Austen.* 1975. Pp. 169-186.

Corwin, Laura J. "Character and Morality in the Novels of Jane Austen." *Revue des Langues Vivantes*, 38 (1972), 365-366, 372-374, 378-379.

Friebe, Freimut. "Von Marianne Dashwood zu Anne Elliot: Empfindsame Motive bei Jane Austen." *Anglia*, 91 (1973), 314-341.

Hennedy, Hugh L. "Acts of Perception in Jane Austen's Novels." *Studies in the Novel*, 5 (1973), 30-36.

Inglis, Fred. *An Essential Discipline.* 1968. Pp. 212-224.

Kestner, Joseph A., III. "The 'I' Persona in the Novels of Jane Austen." *Studies in the Novel*, 4 (1972), 6-15.

Kroeber, Karl. *Styles in Fictional Structure.* 1971. Pp. 79-84.

Lauber, John. "Jane Austen's Fools." *Studies in English Literature, 1500-1900*, 14 (1974), 523-524.

Lerner, Laurence. *The Truthtellers.* 1967. Pp. 166-172.

McMaster, Juliet. "Surface and Subsurface in Jane Austen's Novels." *Ariel*, 5:2 (1974), 15-20.

Mansell, Darrel. *The Novels of Jane Austen.* 1973. Pp. 185-221.

Mews, Hazel. *Frail Vessels.* 1969. Pp. 62-66.

Nardin, Jane. *Those Elegant Decorums.* 1973. Pp. 129-154.

Page, Norman. *The Language of Jane Austen.* 1972. Pp. 48-53.

Pikoulis, John. "Jane Austen: The Figure in the Carpet." *Nineteenth-Century Fiction*, 27 (1972), 57-60.

Pinion. F. B. *A Jane Austen Companion.* 1973. Pp. 123-129.

Rackin, Donald. "Jane Austen's Anatomy of Persuasion," in George Goodin, ed., *The English Novel.* 1972. Pp. 52-80.

Rubinstein, E. "Jane Austen's Novels: The Metaphor of Rank." *Literary Monographs*, 2 (1969), 172-186.

Tave, Stuart M. *Some Words of Jane Austen.* 1973. Pp. 256-287.

Watts, Mary. "God and Jane Austen." *New Blackfriars*, 53 (1972), 15-22.

Wiesenfarth, Joseph. "*Persuasion:* History and Myth." *Wordsworth Circle*, 2 (1971), 160-168.

Pride and Prejudice, 1813

Beer, Patricia. *Reader, I Married Him*. 1974. Pp. 47-75.

Brown, Lloyd W. *Bits of Ivory*. 1973. Pp. 31-39, 65-67, 121-124, 161-166, 186-190.

Brown, Lloyd W. "Jane Austen and the Feminist Tradition." *Nineteenth-Century Fiction*, 28 (1973), 330-332.

Burgan, Mary Alice. "Feeling and Control: A Study of the Proposal Scenes in Jane Austen's Major Novels," in George Goodin, ed., *The English Novel*. 1972. Pp. 29-33.

Bush, Douglas. *Jane Austen*. 1975. Pp. 91-107.

Corwin, Laura J. "Character and Morality in the Novels of Jane Austen." *Revue des Langues Vivantes*, 38 (1972), 364-365, 375-377.

Halperin, John. *Egoism and Self-Discovery*. 1974. Pp. 4-12.

Halperin, John. *The Language of Meditation*. 1973. Pp. 19-28.

Harding, D. W. "Two Aspects of Jane Austen's Development." *Theoria* (Natal), 35 (1970), 4-10.

Kestner, Joseph A., III. "The 'I' Persona in the Novels of Jane Austen." *Studies in the Novel*, 4 (1972), 6-15.

Kroeber, Karl. *Styles in Fictional Structure*. 1971. Pp. 68-72.

Lauber, John. "Heroes and Anti-Heroes in Jane Austen's Novels." *Dalhousie Review*, 51 (1971-1972), 489-503.

Lauber, John. "Jane Austen's Fools." *Studies in English Literature, 1500-1900*, 14 (1974), 516-518.

Lemon, Lee T. "The Hostile Universe: A Developing Pattern in Nineteenth-Century Fiction," in George Goodin, ed., *The English Novel*. 1972. Pp. 2-5.

Lerner, Laurence. *The Truthtellers*. 1967. Pp. 149-150, 153-155.

Mansell, Darrel. *The Novels of Jane Austen*. 1973. Pp. 78-107.

Mews, Hazel. *Frail Vessels*. 1969. Pp. 52-55.

Nardin, Jane. *Those Elegant Decorums*. 1973. Pp. 47-61.

Otten, Kurt, *Der englische Roman*. 1971. Pp. 94-98.

Page, Norman. *The Language of Jane Austen*. 1972. Pp. 24-34.

Pikoulis, John. "Jane Austen: The Figure in the Carpet." *Nineteenth-Century Fiction*, 27 (1972), 38-51.

Pinion, F. B. *A Jane Austen Companion*. 1973. Pp. 92-100.

Prescott, Orville, Jan Struther, and Lyman Bryson. *"Pride and Prejudice,"* in George D. Crothers, ed., *Invitation to Learning*, 1966. Pp. 71-79.

Rubinstein, E. "Jane Austen's Novels: The Metaphor of Rank." *Literary Monographs*, 2 (1969), 121-133.

Tave, Stuart M. *Some Words of Jane Austen*. 1973. Pp. 116-157.

Walcutt, Charles Child. *Man's Changing Mask*. 1966. Pp. 71-90.

Weinsheimer, Joel. "Chance and the Hierarchy of Marriages in *Pride and Prejudice*." *ELH*, 39 (1972), 404-419.

Sanditon, 1925

Bush, Douglas. *Jane Austen*. 1975. Pp. 187-193.
Lauber, John. "*Sanditon:* The Kingdom of Folly." *Studies in the Novel*, 4 (1972), 353-363.
Lock, F. P. " 'The Neighborhood of Tombuctoo': A Note on *Sanditon*." *Notes and Queries*, 19 (1972), 97-99.
Pinion, F. B. *A Jane Austen Companion*. 1973. Pp. 130-134.
Rubinstein, E. "Jane Austen's Novels: The Metaphor of Rank." *Literary Monographs*, 2 (1969), 187-190.

Sense and Sensibility, 1811

Brissenden, R. F. *Virtue in Distress*. 1974. Pp. 273-276.
Brown, Lloyd W. *Bits of Ivory*. 1973. Pp. 21-31, 118-121, 157-160, 177-185, 218-220.
Bush, Douglas. *Jane Austen*. 1975. Pp. 78-88.
Corwin, Laura J. "Character and Morality in the Novels of Jane Austen." *Revue des Langues Vivantes*, 38 (1972), 368-372.
Harding, D. W. "Two Aspects of Jane Austen's Development." *Theoria* (Natal), 35 (1970), 1-7.
Kestner, Joseph A., III. "The 'I' Persona in the Novels of Jane Austen." *Studies in the Novel*, 4 (1972), 6-15.
Kroeber, Karl. *Styles in Fictional Structure*. 1971. Pp. 65-68.
Lauber, John. "Heroes and Anti-Heroes in Jane Austen's Novels." *Dalhousie Review*, 51 (1971-1972), 489-503.
Lauber, John. "Jane Austen's Fools." *Studies in English Literature, 1500-1900*, 14 (1974), 513-515.
Lerner, Laurence. *The Truthtellers*. 1967. Pp. 137-139, 160-166.
Mansell, Darrel. *The Novels of Jane Austen*. 1973. Pp. 46-77.
Mews, Hazel. *Frail Vessels*. 1969. Pp. 48-52, 132-134.
Nardin, Jane. *Those Elegant Decorums*. 1973. Pp. 24-46.
Page, Norman. *The Language of Jane Austen*. 1972. Pp. 20-24.
Pinion, F. B. *A Jane Austen Companion*. 1973. Pp. 84-91.
Rubinstein, E. "Jane Austen's Novels: The Metaphor of Rank." *Literary Monogrnphs*, 2 (1969), 107-117.
Tave, Stuart M. *Some Words of Jane Austen*. 1973. Pp. 74-115.

The Watsons, 1871

Bush, Douglas. *Jane Austen*. 1975. Pp. 71-76.
Pinion, F. B. *A Jane Austen Companion*. 1973. Pp. 72-75.
Rubinstein, E., "Jane Austen's Novels: The Metaphor of Rank." *Literary Monographs*, 2 (1969), 117-121.

ROBERT BAGE

Man As He Is, 1792

Vooys, Sijna de. *The Psychological Element*. 1966. Pp. 17-20.

JAMES GRAHAM BALLARD

The Crystal World, 1966

Perry, Nick, and Roy Wilkie. "The Undivided Self: J. G. Ballard's *The Crystal World.*" *Riverside Quarterly*, 5 (1973), 268-277.

SABINE BARING-GOULD

Mehalah, 1880

Benedikz, B. S. "The Fury of the Marshes: Baring-Gould's *Mehalah*," in B. S. Benedikz, ed., *On the Novel.* 1971. Pp. 179-187.

JANE BARKER

Exilius, 1715

Richetti, John J. *Popular Fiction.* 1969. Pp. 231-236.

EATON STANNARD BARRETT

The Heroine, 1813

Lévy, Maurice. *Le Roman "gothique" anglais.* 1968. Pp. 500-506.

JAMES MATTHEW BARRIE

Auld Licht Idylls, 1888

Chapple, J. A. V. *Documentary and Imaginative Literature.* 1970. Pp. 55-58.

Farewell, Miss Julie Logan, 1932

Geduld, Harry M. *Sir James Barrie.* 1971. Pp. 69-70.

The Little Minister, 1891

Geduld, Harry M. *Sir James Barrie.* 1971. Pp. 39-45.

The Little White Bird, 1902

Geduld, Harry M. *Sir James Barrie.* 1971. Pp. 53-70.

Margaret Ogilvy, 1896

Geduld, Harry M. *Sir James Barrie.* 1971. Pp. 25-31, 37.

Peter and Wendy, 1911

Geduld, Harry M. *Sir James Barrie.* 1971. Pp. 65-69.

Peter Pan in Kensington Gardens, 1906

Geduld, Harry M. *Sir James Barrie.* 1971. Pp. 59-62.

Sentimental Tommy, 1896

Geduld, Harry M. *Sir James Barrie*. 1971. Pp. 45-49.

Tommy and Grizel, 1900

Geduld, Harry M. *Sir James Barrie*. 1971. Pp. 45-46, 49-52.

When A Man's Single, 1888

Geduld, Harry M. *Sir James Barrie*. 1971. Pp. 31-36.

A Window in Thrums, 1889

Geduld, Harry M. *Sir James Barrie*. 1971. Pp. 36-39.

SAMUEL BECKETT

How It Is, 1964

Abbott, H. Porter. *The Fiction of Samuel Beckett*. 1973. Pp. 138-146.
Alvarez, A. *Samuel Beckett*. 1973. Pp. 66-74.
Cohn, Ruby. *Samuel Beckett*. 1962. Pp. 182-207.
Cornwell, Ethel F. "Samuel Beckett: The Flight From Self." *Publications of the Modern Language Association*, 88 (1973), 48-50.
Federman, Raymond. *Journey to Chaos*. 1965. Pp. 3-12.
Hassan, Ihab. *The Dismemberment of Orpheus*. 1971. Pp. 234-237.
Hayward, Susan. "Le Rôle du monologue intérieur dans les romans de Samuel Beckett." *Language and Style*, 7 (1974), 187-190.
Janvier, Ludovic. *Pour Samuel Beckett*. 1966. Pp. 133-145.
Kenner, Hugh. *A Reader's Guide to Samuel Beckett*. 1973. Pp. 136-146.
Schwartz, Paul J. "Life and Death in the Mud: A Study of Beckett's *Comment c'est*." *International Fiction Review*, 2 (1975), 43-48.
Scott, Nathan A. *Samuel Beckett*. 1965. Pp. 74-79.
Tindall, William York. *Samuel Beckett*. 1964. Pp. 37-39.

The Lost Ones, 1971.

Federman, Raymond. "The Impossibility of Saying the Same Old Thing the Same Old Way: Samuel Beckett's Fiction Since *Comment c'est*." *L'Esprit Créateur*, 11:3 (1971), 39-43.
Finney, Brian H. "*since how it is*." 1972. Pp. 11-16, 36, 40-41.
Janvier, Ludovic. "Peupler dépeupler c'est écrire." *Critique* (Paris), No. 288 (1971), 432-445.
Vercier, Bruno. "Samuel Beckett: *Le Dépeupler*." *Nouvelle Revue Française*, No. 221 (1971), 107-110.

Malone Dies, 1956

Abbott, H. Porter. *The Ficton of Samuel Beckett*. 1973. Pp. 110-123.
Alvarez. A. *Samuel Beckett*. 1973. Pp. 52-57.
Barrett, William. *Time of Need*. 1972. Pp. 257-261.

Cohn, Ruby. *Samuel Beckett.* 1962. Pp. 116-168.

Conely, James. "*Arcana; Molloy, Malone Dies, The Unnamable:* A Brief Comparison of Forms." *Hartford Studies in Literature,* 4 (1972), 187-196.

Cornwell, Ethel F. "Samuel Beckett: The Flight From Self." *Publications of the Modern Language Association,* 88 (1973), 45.

Dobrez, Livio. "Samuel Beckett's Irreducible." *Southern Review* (Adelaide), 6 (1973), 214-215.

Fletcher, John. *The Novels of Samuel Beckett.* 1964. Pp. 151-176.

Hassan, Ihab. *The Dismemberment of Orpheus.* 1971. Pp. 229-232.

Hoffman, Frederick J. "The Elusive Ego: Beckett's M's," in Melvin J. Friedman, ed., *Samuel Beckett Now.* 1970. Pp. 50-54.

Iser, Wolfgang. *The Implied Reader.* 1974. Pp. 167-170, 266-267.

Jacobsen, Josephine, and William R. Mueller. *The Testament of Samuel Beckett.* 1964. Pp. 46-47, 88-89.

Janvier, Ludovic. *Pour Samuel Beckett.* 1966. Pp. 64-73.

Kenner, Hugh. *A Reader's Guide to Samuel Beckett.* 1973. Pp. 100-108.

Kenner, Hugh. *Samuel Beckett.* 1961. Pp. 79-81, 91-93, 176-177.

Marissel, André. *Samuel Beckett.* 1963. Pp. 49-70.

Scott, Nathan A. *Samuel Beckett.* 1965. Pp. 64-66.

Seltzer, Alvin J. *Chaos in the Novel.* 1974. Pp. 194-210.

Silver, Sally Thrum. "Satire in Beckett: A Study of *Molloy, Malone Dies* and *The Unnamable.*" *Essays in French Literature,* No. 10 (1973), 86-87, 89-95.

Szanto, George H. *Narrative Consciousness.* 1972. Pp. 90-92.

Tindall, William York. *Samuel Beckett.* 1964. Pp. 26-29.

Varela Jácome, Benito. *Renovación de la novela.* 1967. Pp. 374-377.

Walcutt, Charles Child. *Man's Changing Mask.* 1966. Pp. 339-346.

Wicker, Brian. "Samuel Beckett and the Death of the God-Narrator." *Journal of Narrative Technique,* 4 (1974), 64-69.

Mercier et Camier, 1970

Abbott, H. Porter. *The Fiction of Samuel Beckett.* 1973. Pp. 75-91.

Cohn, Ruby. *Samuel Beckett.* 1962. Pp. 95-98.

Federman, Raymond. *Journey to Chaos.* 1965. Pp. 135-176.

Fletcher, John. *The Novels of Samuel Beckett.* 1964. Pp. 110-118.

Janvier, Ludovic. *Pour Samuel Beckett.* 1966. Pp. 39-43.

Kenner, Hugh. *A Reader's Guide to Samuel Beckett.* 1973. Pp. 83-91.

Kenner, Hugh. *Samuel Beckett.* 1961. Pp. 70-77.

Molloy, 1955

Abbott, H. Porter. *The Fiction of Samuel Beckett.* 1973. Pp. 92-109.

Alvarez, A. *Samuel Beckett.* 1973. Pp. 46-52.

Bajomée, Danielle. "Beckett devant dieu." *Lettres Romanes,* 25 (1971), 350-357.

Barrett, William. *Time of Need.* 1972. Pp. 255-257.

Boisdeffre, Pierre de. *Où va le roman?* 1972. Pp. 269-272.

Boulais, Véronique. "Samuel Beckett: Une écriture en mal de je." *Poétique*, 17 (1974), 114-125.

Cohn, Ruby. *Samuel Beckett*. 1962. Pp. 115-168.

Conely, James. "*Arcana; Molloy, Malone Dies, The Unnamable*: A Brief Comparison of Forms." *Hartford Studies in Literature*, 4 (1972), 187-196.

Cornwell, Ethel F. "Samuel Beckett: The Flight From Self." *Publications of the Modern Language Association*, 88 (1973), 43-45.

Dobrez, Livio. "Samuel Beckett's Irreducible." *Southern Review* (Adelaide), 6 (1973), 213-214.

Federman, Raymond. "Beckettian Paradox: Who Is Telling the Truth?", in Melvin J. Friedman, ed., *Samuel Beckett Now*. 1970. Pp. 103-107, 110-112.

Fletcher, John. "Interpreting *Molloy*," in Melvin J. Friedman, ed., *Samuel Beckett Now*. 1970. Pp. 157-170.

Fletcher, John. *The Novels of Samuel Beckett*. 1964. Pp. 119-150.

Goodrich, Norma Lorre. "Molloy's Musa Mater," in Wolodymyr T. Zyla, ed., *From Surrealism to the Absurd*. 1970. Pp. 31-53.

Hassan, Ihab. *The Dismemberment of Orpheus*. 1971. Pp. 225-229.

Hayman, David. "*Molloy* or the Quest for Meaninglessness: A Global Interpretation," in Melvin J. Friedman, ed., *Samuel Beckett Now*. 1970. Pp. 134-156.

Hayward, Susan. "Le Rôle du monologue intérieur dans les romans de Samuel Beckett." *Language and Style*, 7 (1974), 182-185.

Hoffman, Frederick J. "The Elusive Ego: Beckett's M's," in Melvin J. Friedman, ed., *Samuel Beckett Now*. 1970. Pp. 44-50.

Iser, Wolfgang. *The Implied Reader*. 1974. Pp. 164-167, 264-266.

Jacobsen, Josephine, and William R. Mueller. *The Testament of Samuel Beckett*. 1964. Pp. 40-46.

Janvier, Ludovic. *Pour Samuel Beckett*. 1966. Pp. 48-61.

Kenner, Hugh. *A Reader's Guide to Samuel Beckett*. 1973. Pp. 92-100.

Kenner, Hugh. *Samuel Beckett*. 1961. Pp. 82-83, 107-110, 117-132, 177-180.

Kern, Edith. "Ironic Structure in Beckett's Fiction." *L'Esprit Créateur*, 11:3 (1971), 9-10.

Marissel, André. *Samuel Beckett*. 1963. Pp. 49-70.

Rose, Gilbert J. "On the Shores of Self: Samuel Beckett's *Molloy*—Irredentism and the Creative Impulse." *Psychoanalytic Review*, 60 (1973-1974), 587-604.

Scott, Nathan A. *Samuel Beckett*. 1965. Pp. 61-64.

Seltzer, Alvin J. *Chaos in the Novel*. 1974. Pp. 169-194.

Sherzer, Dina. "Quelques manifestations du narrateur-créateur dans *Molloy* de Samuel Beckett." *Language and Style*, 5 (1972), 115-121.

Silver, Sally Thrum. "Satire in Beckett: A Study of *Molloy, Malone Dies* and *The Unnamable*." *Essays in French Literature*, No. 10 (1973), 83-86, 89-95.

Spraggins, Mary. "Beckett's *Molloy*: As Detective Novel." *Essays in Literature* (Denver), 2 (1974), 11-33.
Szanto, George H. *Narrative Consciousness*. 1972. Pp. 85-90.
Tindall, William York. *Samuel Beckett*. 1964. Pp. 21-26.
Wicker, Brian. "Samuel Beckett and the Death of the God-Narrator." *Journal of Narrative Technique*, 4 (1974), 64-69.
Zéraffa, Michel. *Personne et personnage*. 1969. Pp. 397-402.

Murphy, 1938

Abbott, H. Porter. *The Fiction of Samuel Beckett*. 1973. Pp. 37-55.
Alvarez, A. *Samuel Beckett*. 1973. Pp. 25-32.
Cohn, Ruby. *Samuel Beckett*. 1962. Pp. 45-64.
Cornwell, Ethel F. "Samuel Beckett: The Flight From Self." *Publications of the Modern Language Association*, 88 (1973), 41-43.
Dobrez, Livio. "Samuel Beckett's Irreducible." *Southern Review* (Adelaide), 6 (1973), 207-211.
Federman, Raymond, *Journey to Chaos*. 1965. Pp. 56-93.
Fletcher, John. *The Novels of Samuel Beckett*. 1964. Pp. 38-55.
Hoffman, Frederick J. "The Elusive Ego: Beckett's M's," in Melvin J. Friedman, ed., *Samuel Beckett Now*. 1970. Pp. 31-38.
Iser, Wolfgang. *The Implied Reader*. 1974. Pp. 262-264.
Jacobsen, Josephine, and William R. Mueller. *The Testament of Samuel Beckett*. 1964. Pp. 25-32, 67-72, 79-82, 118-121.
Janvier, Ludovic. *Pour Samuel Beckett*. 1966. Pp. 25-31.
Kenner, Hugh. *A Reader's Guide to Samuel Beckett*. 1973. Pp. 57-71.
Kenner, Hugh. *Samuel Beckett*. 1961. Pp. 49-52.
Rabinovitz, Rubin. "Style and Obscurity in Samuel Beckett's Early Fiction." *Modern Fiction Studies*, 20 (1974), 399-406.
Scott, Nathan A. *Samuel Beckett*. 1965. Pp. 41-46.
Seltzer, Alvin J. *Chaos in the Novel*. 1974. Pp. 156-162.
Steinberg, S. C. "The External and Internal in *Murphy*." *Twentieth-Century Literature*, 18 (1972), 93-110.
Szanto, George H. *Narrative Consciousness*. 1972. Pp. 78-81.
Tindall, William York. *Samuel Beckett*. 1964. Pp. 13-21.

The Unnamable, 1958

Abbott, H. Porter. *The Fiction of Samuel Beckett*. 1973. Pp. 124-137.
Alvarez, A. *Samuel Beckett*. 1973. Pp. 57-65.
Bajomée, Danielle. "Beckett devant dieu." *Lettres Romanes*, 25 (1971), 350-357.
Barrett, William. *Time of Need*. 1972. Pp. 257-262.
Boisdeffre, Pierre de. *Où va le roman*? 1972. Pp. 272-274.
Boulais, Véronique. "Samuel Beckett: Une écriture en mal de je." *Poétique*, 17 (1974), 125-132.
Coetzee, J. M. "Samuel Beckett and the Temptations of Style." *Theoria* (Natal), 41 (1973), 45-50.
Cohn, Ruby. *Samuel Beckett*. 1962. Pp. 117-168.

Conely, James. *"Arcana; Molloy, Malone Dies, The Unnamable*: A Brief Comparison of Forms." *Hartford Studies in Literature*, 4 (1972), 187-196.

Cornwell, Ethel F. "Samuel Beckett: The Flight From Self." *Publications of the Modern Language Association*, 88 (1973), 45-48.

Dobrez, Livio. "Samuel Beckett's Irreducible." *Southern Review* (Adelaide), 6 (1973), 215-218.

Fletcher, John. *The Novels of Samuel Beckett*. 1964. Pp. 179-194.

Garzilli, Enrico. *Circles Without Center*. 1972. Pp. 20-27, 47-52.

Hassan, Ihab. *The Dismemberment of Orpheus*. 1971. Pp. 232-233.

Hayward, Susan. "Le Rôle du monologue intérieur dans les romans de Samuel Beckett." *Language and Style*, 7 (1974), 185-187.

Hoffman, Frederick J. "The Elusive Ego: Beckett's M's," in Melvin J. Friedman, ed., *Samuel Beckett Now*. 1970. Pp. 54-58.

Iser, Wolfgang. *The Implied Reader*. 1974. Pp. 170-174, 267-268.

Janvier, Ludovic. *Pour Samuel Beckett*. 1966. Pp. 74-81.

Kawin, Bruce F. *Telling It Again and Again*. 1972. Pp. 140-146.

Kenner, Hugh. *A Reader's Guide to Samuel Beckett*. 1973. Pp. 108-115.

Kenner, Hugh. *Samuel Beckett*. 1961. Pp. 84-86, 128-129.

Kern, Edith. "Ironic Structure in Beckett's Fiction." *L'Esprit Créateur*, 11:3 (1971), 11-13.

Marissel, André. *Samuel Beckett*. 1963. Pp. 49-70.

Mood, John J. "Samuel Beckett's Impasse-Lessness." *Ball State University Forum*, 14 (1973), 74-80.

Scott, Nathan A. *Samuel Beckett*. 1965. Pp. 66-67.

Seltzer, Alvin J. *Chaos in the Novel*. 1974. Pp. 211-235.

Silver, Sally Thrum. "Satire in Beckett: A Study of *Molloy, Malone Dies* and *The Unnamable*." *Essays in French Literature*, No. 10 (1973), 87-88, 89-95.

Szanto, George H. *Narrative Consciousness*. 1972. Pp. 92-94.

Tindall, William York. *Samuel Beckett*. 1964. Pp. 29-32.

Wicker, Brian. "Samuel Beckett and the Death of the God-Narrator." *Journal of Narrative Technique*, 4 (1974), 64-69.

Watt, 1953

Abbott, H. Porter. *The Fiction of Samuel Beckett*. 1973. Pp. 56-74.

Alvarez, A. *Samuel Beckett*. 1973. Pp. 32-38.

Cohn, Ruby, *Samuel Beckett*. 1962. Pp. 65-94.

Dobrez, Livio. "Samuel Beckett's Irreducible." *Southern Review* (Adelaide), 6 (1973), 211-213.

Federman, Raymond. *Journey to Chaos*. 1965. Pp. 94-132.

Fletcher, John. *The Novels of Samuel Beckett*. 1964. Pp. 59-89.

Glicksberg, Charles I. *The Ironic Vision*. 1969. Pp. 237-241.

Hartung, Rudolf. *"Watt."* *Neue Rundschau*, 82 (1971), 163-167.

Harvey, Lawrence E. *Samuel Beckett: Poet and Critic*. 1970. Pp. 350-397.

Hoffman, Frederick, J. "The Elusive Ego: Beckett's M's," in Melvin J. Friedman, ed., *Samuel Beckett Now*. 1970. Pp. 39-44.

Jacobsen, Josephine, and William R. Mueller. *The Testament of Samuel Beckett*. 1964. Pp. 73-76, 82-84.

Janvier, Ludovic. *Pour Samuel Beckett*. 1966. Pp. 31-39.

Kawin, Bruce F. *Telling It Again and Again*. 1972. Pp. 131-142, 166-169.

Kenner, Hugh. *A Reader's Guide to Samuel Beckett*. 1973. Pp. 72-82.

Kenner, Hugh. *Samuel Beckett*. 1961. Pp. 58-60, 86-88, 98-104.

Kern, Edith. "Ironic Structure in Beckett's Fiction." *L'Esprit Créateur*, 11:3 (1971), 8-9.

Kern, Edith. "Reflections on the Castle and Mr. Knott's House: Kafka and Beckett," in Wolodymyr T. Zyla, ed., *Franz Kafka*. 1971. Pp. 97-111.

Law, Richard A. "Mock Evangelism in Beckett's *Watt*." *Modern Language Studies*, 2 (1972), 68-82.

Mood, John J. "The Personal System—Samuel Beckett's *Watt*." *Publications of the Modern Language Association*, 86 (1971), 255-265.

Rabinovitz, Rubin. "Style and Obscurity in Samuel Beckett's Early Fiction." *Modern Fiction Studies*, 20 (1974), 399-406.

Scott, Nathan A. *Samuel Beckett*. 1965. Pp. 48-58.

Seltzer, Alvin J. *Chaos in the Novel*. 1974. Pp. 162-169.

Skerl, Jennie. "Fritz Mauthner's 'Critique of Language' in Samuel Beckett's *Watt*." *Contemporary Literature*, 15 (1974), 474-487.

Smith, Frederik N. "The Epistemology of Fictional Failure: Swift's *Tale of a Tub* and Beckett's *Watt*." *Texas Studies in Literature and Language*, 15 (1973), 649-672.

Szanto, George H. *Narrative Consciousness*. 1972. Pp. 81-85.

Tindall, William York. *Samuel Beckett*. 1964. Pp. 17-21.

WILLIAM BECKFORD

Vathek, 1786

Graham, Kenneth W. "Beckford's *Vathek*: A Study in Ironic Dissonance." *Criticism*, 14 (1972), 243-252.

Kiely, Robert. *The Romantic Novel in England*. 1972. Pp. 43-64.

Sena, John F. "Drawing From Blots: The Landscapes of *Vathek* and the Paintings of Alexander Cozens." *Etudes Anglaises*, 26 (1973), 212-215.

Solomon, Stanley J. "Subverting Propriety as a Pattern of Irony in Three Eighteenth-Century Novels: *The Castle of Otranto, Vathek*, and *Fanny Hill*." *Erasmus Review*, 1 (1971), 114-115.

The Vision, 1930

Siniscalchi, Marina Maymone. "*The Vision* di Beckford e il simbolismo della pia filosofia." *English Miscellany*, 22 (1971), 147-154.

MAX BEERBOHM

Zuleika Dobson, 1911

Felstiner, John. *The Lies of Art.* 1972. Pp. 169-186.
McElderry, Bruce R., Jr. *Max Beerbohm.* 1972. Pp. 101-108.

BRENDAN BEHAN

Borstal Boy, 1959

Boyle, Ted E. *Brendan Behan.* 1969. Pp. 102-110.

The Scarperer, 1964

Boyle, Ted E. *Brendan Behan.* 1969. Pp. 119-124.

APHRA BEHN

The History of the Nun, 1689

Link, Frederick M. *Aphra Behn.* 1968. Pp. 143-145.

Love Letters Between a Nobleman and His Sister, 1684

Link, Frederick M. *Aphra Behn.* 1968. Pp. 130-135.

Oroonoko, 1688

Böker, Uwe. "Sir Walter Ralegh, Daniel Defoe und die Namengebung in Aphra Behns *Oroonoko.*" *Anglia*, 90 (1972), 96-99, 102-104.
Echeruo, M. J. C. "The 'Savage Hero' in English Literature of the Enlightenment." *English Studies in Africa*, 15 (1972), 6-8, 11-13.
Guffey, George. "Aphra Behn's *Oroonoko*: Occasion and Accomplishment," in *Two English Novelists.* 1975. Pp. 3-41.
Link, Frederick M. *Aphra Behn.* 1968. Pp. 139-142.
Sebbar-Pignon, Leila. "Le Mythe du bon nègre, ou l'idéologie coloniale dans la production romanesque du XVIIIe siècle." *Temps Modernes*, 29 (1974), 2352-2369.

HILAIRE BELLOC

Emmanuel Burden, 1904

Kellogg, Gene. *The Vital Tradition.* 1970. Pp. 96-100.

ARNOLD BENNETT

Anna of the Five Towns, 1902

Hall, James. *Arnold Bennett.* 1959. Pp. 32-39.

Clayhanger, 1910

> Barker, Dudley. *Writer by Trade*. 1966. Pp. 163-170.
> Bellamy, William. *The Novels of Wells, Bennett, and Galsworthy*. 1971. Pp. 150-161.
> Hall, James. *Arnold Bennett*. 1959. Pp. 84-105.
> Hepburn, James G. *The Art of Arnold Bennett*. 1963. Pp. 81-94.

The Glimpse, 1909

> Hepburn, James G. *The Art of Arnold Bennett*. 1963. Pp. 65-75.

Hilda Lessways, 1911

> Hall, James. *Arnold Bennett*. 1959. Pp. 106-114.

Imperial Palace, 1930

> Hepburn, James G. *The Art of Arnold Bennett*. 1963. Pp. 151-174.

Leonora, 1903

> Hall, James. *Arnold Bennett*. 1959. Pp. 39-42.

Lord Raingo, 1926

> Hall, James. *Arnold Bennett*. 1959. Pp. 139-151.
> Hepburn, James G. *The Art of Arnold Bennett*. 1963. Pp. 44-50.

A Man From the North, 1898

> Bellamy, William. *The Novels of Wells, Bennett, and Galsworthy*. 1971. Pp. 71-87.

The Old Wives' Tale, 1908

> Goetsch, Paul. *Die Romankonzeption in England*. 1967. Pp. 301-310.
> Hall, James. *Arnold Bennett*. 1959. Pp. 47-83.
> Hepburn, James G. *The Art of Arnold Bennett*. 1963. Pp. 17-32, 55-65, 143-149.
> Siegel, Paul N. "Revolution and Evolution in Bennett's *The Old Wives' Tale*." *Clio*, 4 (1975), 159-172.
> Swinden, Patrick. *Unofficial Selves*. 1973. Pp. 137-148.

The Pretty Lady, 1918

> Hepburn, James G. *The Art of Arnold Bennett*. 1963. Pp. 132-142.

The Price of Love, 1914

> Hepburn, James G. *The Art of Arnold Bennett*. 1963. Pp. 98-118.

Riceyman Steps, 1923

> Barker, Dudley. *Writer by Trade*. 1966. Pp. 215-218.
> Hall, James. *Arnold Bennett*. 1959. Pp. 130-138.
> Hepburn, James G. *The Art of Arnold Bennett*. 1963. Pp. 34-44.

Sacred and Profane Love, 1905

Hall, James. *Arnold Bennett.* 1959. Pp. 42-46.

These Twain, 1915

Barker, Dudley. *Writer by Trade.* 1966. Pp. 186-189.
Hall, James. *Arnold Bennett.* 1959. Pp. 115-129.

WALTER BESANT

All Sorts and Conditions of Men, 1882

Keating, P. J. *The Working Classes.* 1971. Pp. 96-99, 106.

Children of Gibeon, 1886.

Keating, P. J. *The Working Classes.* 1971. Pp. 96-102.

RICHARD D. BLACKMORE

Lorna Doone, 1869

Sutton, Max Keith. "The Mythic Appeal of *Lorna Doone.*" *Nineteenth-Century Fiction*, 28 (1974), 435-449.

JAMES BENJAMIN BLISH

A Case of Conscience, 1958

Bradham, Jo Allen. "The Case in James Blish's *A Case of Conscience.*" *Extrapolation*, 16 (1974), 67-80.

GEORGE BORROW

Lavengro, 1851

Maxwell, Ian R. " 'But the Fight! With Respect to the Fight, What Shall I Say?' " *AUMLA*, No. 37 (1972), 18-36.

ELIZABETH BOWEN

The Death of the Heart, 1938

Austin, Allan E. *Elizabeth Bowen.* 1971. Pp. 59-66.
Coles, Robert. *Irony in the Mind's Life.* 1974. Pp. 107-153.
Kenney, Edwin J., Jr. *Elizabeth Bowen.* 1975. Pp. 53-65.
Parrish, Paul A. "The Loss of Eden: Four Novels of Elizabeth Bowen." *Critique* (Atlanta), 15 (1973), 93-96.
Sharp, Sister M. Corona, O.S.U. "The House as Setting and Symbol in Three Novels by Elizabeth Bowen." *Xavier University Studies*, 2 (1963), 98-103.

Eva Trout, 1969

> Austin, Allan E. *Elizabeth Bowen*. 1971. Pp. 87-91.
> Kenney, Edwin J., Jr. *Elizabeth Bowen*. 1975. Pp. 95-104.
> Parrish, Paul A. "The Loss of Eden: Four Novels of Elizabeth Bowen." *Critique* (Atlanta), 15 (1973), 96-100.

Friends and Relations, 1931

> Austin, Allan E. *Elizabeth Bowen*. 1971. Pp. 49-53.

The Heat of the Day, 1949

> Austin, Allan E. *Elizabeth Bowen*. 1971. Pp. 69-75.
> Davenport, Gary T. "Elizabeth Bowen and the Big House." *Southern Humanities Review*, 8 (1974), 33-34.
> Gill, Richard. *Happy Rural Seat*. 1972. Pp. 187-189.
> Kenney, Edwin J., Jr. *Elizabeth Bowen*. 1975. Pp. 67-76.
> Rupp, Richard H. "The Post-War Fiction of Elizabeth Bowen." *Xavier University Studies*, 4 (1965), 56-59.

The Hotel, 1927

> Austin, Allan E. *Elizabeth Bowen*. 1971. Pp. 31-37.

The House in Paris, 1935

> Austin, Allan E. *Elizabeth Bowen*. 1971. Pp. 53-59.
> Kenney, Edwin J., Jr. *Elizabeth Bowen*. 1975. Pp. 46-53.
> Parrish, Paul A. "The Loss of Eden: Four Novels of Elizabeth Bowen." *Critique* (Atlanta), 15 (1973), 89-93.
> Sharp, Sister M. Corona, O.S.U. "The House as Setting and Symbol in Three Novels by Elizabeth Bowen." *Xavier University Studies*, 2 (1963), 95-98.

The Last September, 1929

> Austin, Allan E. *Elizabeth Bowen*. 1971. Pp. 37-41.
> Davenport, Gary T. "Elizabeth Bowen and the Big House." *Southern Humanities Review*, 8 (1974), 29-32.
> Gill, Richard. *Happy Rural Seat*. 1972. Pp. 181-183.
> Kenney, Edwin J., Jr. *Elizabeth Bowen*. 1975. Pp. 32-37.
> Parrish, Paul A. "The Loss of Eden: Four Novels of Elizabeth Bowen." *Critique* (Atlanta), 15 (1973), 87-89.
> Sharp, Sister M. Corona, O.S.U. "The House as Setting and Symbol in Three Novels by Elizabeth Bowen." *Xavier University Studies*, 2 (1963), 93-95.

The Little Girls, 1964

> Austin, Allan E. *Elizabeth Bowen*. 1971. Pp. 82-87.
> Kenney, Edwin J., Jr. *Elizabeth Bowen*. 1975. Pp. 86-95.
> Rupp, Richard H. "The Post-War Fiction of Elizabeth Bowen." *Xavier University Studies*, 4 (1965), 64-66.

To the North, 1932

    Austin, Allan E. *Elizabeth Bowen*. 1971. Pp. 41-46.
    Kenney, Edwin J., Jr. *Elizabeth Bowen*. 1975. Pp. 41-46.

A World of Love, 1955

    Austin, Allan E. *Elizabeth Bowen*. 1971. Pp. 75-82.
    Gill, Richard. *Happy Rural Seat*. 1972. Pp. 189-191.
    Kenney, Edwin J., Jr. *Elizabeth Bowen*. 1975. Pp. 77-86.
    Rupp, Richard H. "The Post-War Fiction of Elizabeth Bowen." *Xavier University Studies*, 4 (1965), 59-64.

JOHN BOWEN

A World Elsewhere, 1966

    White, John J. *Mythology in the Modern Novel*. 1971. Pp. 175-182.

JOHN BRAINE

The Crying Game, 1966

    Alayrac, Claude. "Inside John Braine's Outsider." *Caliban*, 8 (1971), 115-138.

The Jealous God, 1965

    Alayrac, Claude. "Inside John Braine's Outsider." *Caliban*, 8 (1971), 119-138.
    Lee, James W. *John Braine*. 1968. Pp. 95-107.

Life at the Top, 1962

    Alayrac, Claude. "Inside John Braine's Outsider." *Caliban*, 8 (1971), 118-138.
    Kahrmann, Bernd. *Die idyllische Szene*. 1969. Pp. 73-75.
    Lee, James W. *John Braine*. 1968. Pp. 82-94.
    Meckier, Jerome. "Looking Back in Anger: The Success of a Collapsing Stance." *Dalhousie Review*, 52 (1972), 47-58.

Room at the Top, 1957

    Alayrac, Claude. "Inside John Braine's Outsider." *Caliban*, 8 (1971), 113-138.
    Hermes, Liesel. "Ein Vorschlag zur Romanbehandlung im Englischunterricht der Sekundarstufe II." *Die Neueren Sprachen*, 73 (1974), 551-556.
    Kahrmann, Bernd. *Die idyllische Szene*. 1969. Pp. 75-79, 98-101.
    Lee, James W. *John Braine*. 1968. Pp. 52-68.
    Meckier, Jerome. "Looking Back in Anger: The Success of a Collapsing Stance." *Dalhousie Review*, 52 (1972), 47-58.
    Schleussner, Bruno. *Der neopikareske Roman*. 1969. Pp. 146-153.

The Vodi, 1959

Alayrac, Claude. "Inside John Braine's Outsider." *Caliban*, 8 (1971), 117-138.

Lee, James W. *John Braine*. 1968. Pp. 69-81.

ANNE BRONTË

The Tenant of Wildfell Hall, 1848

Hannah, Barbara. *Striving Towards Wholeness*. 1971. Pp. 177-189.

Meier, T. K. "*The Tenant of Wildfell Hall*: Morality as Art." *Revue des Langues Vivantes*, 39 (1973), 59-62.

Mews, Hazel. *Frail Vessels*. 1969. Pp. 135-139.

CHARLOTTE BRONTË

Jane Eyre, 1847

Aldrich, John W., Margaret Webster, and Lyman Bryson. "*Jane Eyre*," in George D. Crothers, ed., *Invitation to Learning*. 1966. Pp. 109-117.

Beer, Patricia. *Reader, I Married Him*. 1974. Pp. 86-126.

Benvenuto, Richard. "The Child of Nature, the Child of Grace, and the Unresolved Conflict of *Jane Eyre*." *ELH*, 39 (1972), 620-638.

Blom, M. A. "Charlotte Brontë: Feminist *Manquée*." *Bucknell Review*, 21 (1973), 88-91, 101-102.

Blom, M. A. "*Jane Eyre*: Mind as Law Unto Itself." *Criticism*, 15 (1973), 350-364.

Burkhart, Charles. *Charlotte Brontë*. 1973. Pp. 63-77.

Eagleton, Terry. "Class, Power and Charlotte Brontë." *Critical Quarterly*, 14 (1972), 225-235.

Halperin, John. *Egoism and Self-Discovery*. 1974. Pp. 45-61.

Hardy, Barbara. *The Appropriate Form*. 1964. Pp. 61-70.

Kroeber, Karl. *Styles in Fictional Structure*. 1971. Pp. 86-89.

Langford, Thomas A. "Prophetic Imagination and the Unity of *Jane Eyre*." *Studies in the Novel*, 6 (1974), 228-235.

Oldfield, Jennifer. " 'The Homely Web of Truth': Dress as the Mirror of Personality in *Jane Eyre* and *Villette*." *Brontë Society Transactions*, 16 (1973), 178-181.

Peters, Margot. *Charlotte Brontë*. 1973. Pp. 131-154.

Petit, J.-P. "Temps et récit dans *Jane Eyre* et *Wuthering Heights*," in *Récit et roman*. 1972. Pp. 38-46, 51-52.

Simpson, Jacqueline. "The Function of Folklore in *Jane Eyre* and *Wuthering Heights*," *Folklore*, 85 (1974), 47-51.

Sullivan, Paula. "Rochester Reconsidered: *Jane Eyre* in the Light of the Samson Story." *Brontë Society Transactions*, 16 (1973), 192-198.

Wagner, Geoffrey. *Five for Freedom*. 1972. Pp. 124-137.
Wilson, F. A. C. "The Primrose Wreath: The Heroes of the Brontë Novels." *Nineteenth-Century Fiction*, 29 (1974), 42-46.
Yeazell, Ruth Bernard. "More True Than Real: Jane Eyre's 'Mysterious Summons.'" *Nineteenth-Century Fiction*, 29 (1974), 127-143.

The Professor, 1857

Beer, Patricia. *Reader, I Married Him*. 1974. Pp. 101-105.
Burkhart, Charles. *Charlotte Brontë*. 1973. Pp. 45-62.
Mews, Hazel. *Frail Vessels*. 1969. Pp. 73-75.
Wilson, F. A. C. "The Primrose Wreath: The Heroes of the Brontë Novels." *Nineteenth-Century Fiction*, 29 (1974), 46-47.

Shirley, 1849

Beer, Patricia. *Reader, I Married Him*. 1974. Pp. 84-124.
Bentley, Phyllis. *The English Regional Novel*. 1966. Pp. 14-17.
Blom, M. A. "Charlotte Brontë: Feminist *Manquée*." *Bucknell Review*, 21 (1973), 91-96, 100-102.
Burkhart, Charles. *Charlotte Brontë*. 1973. Pp. 78-95.
Cazamian, Louis. *The Social Novel in England*. 1973. Pp. 232-235.
Eagleton, Terry. "Class, Power and Charlotte Brontë." *Critical Quarterly*, 14 (1972), 225-235.
Kroeber, Karl. *Styles in Fictional Structure*. 1971. Pp. 132-134.
Mews, Hazel. *Frail Vessels*. 1969. Pp. 75-77, 184-185.
Wilson, F. A. C. "The Primrose Wreath: The Heroes of the Brontë Novels." *Nineteenth-Century Fiction*, 29 (1974), 47-48.

Villette, 1853

Beer, Patricia. *Reader, I Married Him*. 1974. Pp. 87-126.
Blom, M. A. "Charlotte Brontë: Feminist *Manquée*." *Bucknell Review*, 21 (1973), 96-100, 102.
Burkhart, Charles. *Charlotte Brontë*. 1973. Pp. 96-121.
Kroeber, Karl. *Styles in Fictional Structure*. 1971. Pp. 89-94, 109-112, 151-180.
Mews, Hazel. *Frail Vessels*. 1969. Pp. 77-80.
Oldfield, Jennifer. "'The Homely Web of Truth': Dress as the Mirror of Personality in *Jane Eyre* and *Villette*." *Brontë Society Transactions*, 16 (1973), 181-193.
Schwartz, Roberta C. "The Ambiguities of *Villette*." *North Dakota Quarterly*, 42 (1974), 40-52.
Wilson, F. A. C. "The Primrose Wreath: The Heroes of the Brontë Novels." *Nineteenth-Century Fiction*, 29 (1974), 48-49.

EMILY BRONTË

Wuthering Heights, 1847

Arnold, J. V. "George Sand's *Mauprat* and Emily Brontë's *Wuthering Heights*." *Revue de Littérature Comparée*, 46 (1972), 211-218.

Burns, Wayne. "In Death They Were Not Divided: The Moral Magnificence of Unmoral Passion in *Wuthering Heights*." *Hartford Studies in Literature*, 5 (1973), 135-159.

Burns, Wayne. "On *Wuthering Heights*." *Recovering Literature*, 1 (Fall 1972), 5-25.

Carson, Joan. "Visionary Experience in *Wuthering Heights*." *Psychoanalytic Review*, 62 (1975), 131-151.

Daley, A. Stuart. "The Moons and Almanacs of *Wuthering Heights*." *Huntington Library Quarterly*, 37 (1974), 337-353.

Daniel-Rops. "Le Romancier et ses paysages." *Revue Générale*, 3 (1970), 61-65.

Dingle, Herbert. "The Origin of Heathcliff." *Brontë Society Transactions*, 16 (1972), 131-138.

Donoghue, Denis. "Emily Brontë: On the Latitude of Interpretation," in Morton W. Bloomfield, ed., *The Interpretation of Narrative*. 1970. Pp. 124-133.

Gose, Elliott B., Jr. *Imagination Indulged*. 1972. Pp. 54-71.

Guerard, Albert J. "The Illuminating Distortion." *Novel*, 5 (1972), 103-105.

Hannah, Barbara. *Striving Towards Wholeness*. 1971. Pp. 201-202, 208-257.

Heilbrun, Carolyn G. *Towards a Recognition of Androgyny*. 1973. Pp. 80-82.

Hewish, John. *Emily Brontë*. 1969. Pp. 109-155.

Hewitt, Douglas. *The Approach to Fiction*. 1972. Pp. 123-126.

Horne, Harriet van, Walter Allen, and George D. Crothers. "*Wuthering Heights*," in George D. Crothers, ed., *Invitation to Learning*. 1966. Pp. 117-124.

Junkin-Hill, Margaret. "Myths and Fallacies in *Wuthering Heights*." *Lakehead University Review*, 3 (1970), 46-55.

Keppler, C. F. *The Literature of the Second Self*. 1972. Pp. 135-138.

Kiely, Robert. *The Romantic Novel in England*. 1972. Pp. 233-251.

Kühnelt, Harro H. "Brontë: *Wuthering Heights*," in Franz K. Stanzel, ed., *Der englische Roman*. 1969. Vol. II, 39-70.

Lavers, Norman. "The Action of *Wuthering Heights*." *South Atlantic Quarterly*, 72 (1973), 43-52.

Lemon, Lee T. "The Hostile Universe: A Developing Pattern in Nineteenth-Century Fiction," in George Goodin, ed., *The English Novel*. 1972. Pp. 5-8.

Madden, William A. "*Wuthering Heights*: The Binding of Passion." *Nineteenth-Century Fiction*, 27 (1972), 127-154.

Mitchell, Giles. "Incest, Demonism, and Death in *Wuthering Heights*." *Literature and Psychology*, 23 (1973), 27-35.

Moynahan, Julian. "Pastoralism as Culture and Counter-Culture in English Fiction, 1800-1928." *Novel*, 6 (1972), 27-29.

Otten, Kurt. *Der englische Roman.* 1971. Pp. 136-140.

Patterson, Charles I., Jr. "Empathy and the Daemonic in *Wuthering Heights*," in George Goodin, ed., *The English Novel.* 1972. Pp. 81-96.

Petit, J.-P. "Temps et récit dans *Jane Eyre* et *Wuthering Heights*," in *Récit et roman.* 1972. Pp. 39-52.

Pittock, Malcolm. "*Wuthering Heights* and Its Critics." *Critical Survey*, 5 (1971), 146-154.

Roberts, Mark. *The Tradition of Romantic Morality.* 1973. Pp. 158-197.

Scrivner, Buford, Jr. "The Ethos of *Wuthering Heights*." *Dalhousie Review*, 54 (1974), 451-462.

Shunami, Gideon. "The Unreliable Narrator in *Wuthering Heights*." *Nineteenth-Century Fiction*, 27 (1973), 449-468.

Simpson, Jacqueline. "The Function of Folklore in *Jane Eyre* and *Wuthering Heights*." *Folklore*, 85 (1974), 51-61.

Sucksmith, H. P. "The Theme of *Wuthering Heights* Reconsidered." *Dalhousie Review*, 54 (1974), 418-428.

Tough, A. J. "*Wuthering Heights* and *King Lear*." *English*, 21 (1972), 1-5.

Van de Laar, Elisabeth Th. M. *The Inner Structure of "Wuthering Heights*." 1969.

Van Ghent, Dorothy. "Dark 'Otherness' in *Wuthering Heights*," in Miriam Allott, ed., *Emily Brontë.* 1970. Pp. 177-182.

Visick, Mary. "The Genesis of *Wuthering Heights*," in Miriam Allott, ed., *Emily Brontë.* 1970. Pp. 207-227.

Viswanathan, Jacqueline. "Point of View and Unreliability in Brontë's *Wuthering Heights*, Conrad's *Under Western Eyes* and Mann's *Doktor Faustus*." *Orbis Litterarum*, 29 (1974), 42-59.

Wagner, Geoffrey. *Five for Freedom.* 1972. Pp. 106-124.

Widdowson, Peter. "Emily Brontë: The Romantic Novelist." *Moderna Sprak*, 66 (1972), 1-19.

Williams, Gordon. "The Problem of Passion in *Wuthering Heights*." *Trivium*, No. 7 (1972), 41-53.

Wilson, F. A. C. "The Primrose Wreath: The Heroes of the Brontë Novels." *Nineteenth-Century Fiction*, 29 (1974), 50-57.

HENRY BROOKE

The Fool of Quality, 1764-1770

Gassenmeier, Michael. *Der Typus des "man of feeling."* 1972. Pp. 103-123.

OLIVER MADOX BROWN

Gabriel Denver, 1873

>   Fredeman, William E. "Pre-Raphaelite Novelist Manqué: Oliver Madox Brown." *Bulletin of the John Rylands Library*, 51 (1968), 49-54.

JOHN BUCHAN

The Thirty-Nine Steps, 1915

>   Voorhees, Richard J. "Flashman and Richard Hannay." *Dalhousie Review*, 53 (1973), 116-120.

EDWARD BULWER-LYTTON

The Coming Race, 1871

>   Seeber, Hans Ulrich. "Gegenutopie und Roman: Bulwer-Lyttons *The Coming Race* (1871)." *Deutsche Vierteljahresschrift*, 45 (1971), 150-180.
>   Seeber, Hans Ulrich. *Wandlungen der Form*. 1970. Pp. 207-214.
>   Wolff, Robert Lee. *Strange Stories*. 1971. Pp. 323-333.

The Disowned, 1828

>   Hollingsworth, Keith. *The Newgate Novel*. 1963. Pp. 44-47.

Eugene Aram, 1832

>   Hollingsworth, Keith. *The Newgate Novel*. 1963. Pp. 82-98.

Lucretia, 1846

>   Hollingsworth, Keith. *The Newgate Novel*. 1963. Pp. 182-202.

Night and Morning, 1841

>   Hollingsworth, Keith. *The Newgate Novel*. 1963. Pp. 170-174.

Paul Clifford, 1830

>   Cazamian, Louis. *The Social Novel in England*. 1973. Pp. 45-50.
>   Hollingsworth, Keith. *The Newgate Novel*. 1963. Pp. 65-82.

Pelham, 1828

>   Hollingsworth, Keith. *The Newgate Novel*. 1963. Pp. 38-41.

A Strange Story, 1862

>   Wolff, Robert Lee. *Strange Stories*. 1971. Pp. 265-322.

Zanoni, 1842

    Wolff, Robert Lee. *Strange Stories*. 1971. Pp. 159-232.

JOHN BUNYAN

The Life and Death of Mr. Badman, 1680

    Talon, Henri A. *John Bunyan*. 1956. Pp. 31-33.

The Pilgrim's Progress, 1678

    Adeney, Elizabeth. "Bunyan: A Unified Vision?" *Critical Review* (Melbourne), No. 17 (1974), 97-109.

    Blondel, Jacques. "Bunyan et la Bible dans *The Pilgrim's Progress*." *Langues Modernes*, 67 (1973), 58-66.

    Colwell, C. Carter. *The Tradition of British Literature*. 1971. Pp. 198-202.

    Fish, Stanley E. "Progress in *The Pilgrim's Progress*." *English Literary Renaissance*, 1 (1971), 261-293.

    Fish, Stanley E. *Self-Consuming Artifacts*. 1972. Pp. 224-264.

    Genotiva, David A. "Mythic Patterns in John Bunyan's *Pilgrim's Progress*." *Silliman Journal*, 21 (1974), 327-334.

    Göller, Karl Heinz. *"Romance" und "novel."* 1972. Pp. 135-143.

    Greaves, Richard Lee. *John Bunyan*. 1969. Pp. 27-160.

    Hardin, Richard F. "Bunyan, Mr. Ignorance, and the Quakers." *Studies in Philology*, 69 (1972), 496-508.

    Howell, Elmo. "Bunyan's Two Valleys: A Note on the Ecumenic Element in *Pilgrim's Progress*." *Tennessee Studies in Literature*, 19 (1974), 1-7.

    Iser, Wolfgang. *The Implied Reader*. 1974. Pp. 1-28.

    Knott, John R., Jr. "Bunyan's Gospel Day: A Reading of *The Pilgrim's Progress*." *English Literary Renaissance*, 3 (1973), 443-461.

    Otten, Kurt. *Der englische Roman*. 1971. Pp. 43-46.

    Rutherford, Anna. "Quest Patterns in English, American and Australian Literature." *Revue des Langues Vivantes*, 38 (1972), 381-382.

    Shenk, Robert. "John Bunyan: Puritan or Pilgrim?" *Cithara*, 14 (1974), 77-93.

    Southall, Raymond. *Literature and the Rise of Capitalism*. 1973. Pp. 133-143.

    Stürzl, Erwin. "Bunyan: *The Pilgrim's Progress*," in Franz K. Stanzel, ed., *Der englische Roman*. 1969. Vol. I, 85-107.

    Talon, Henri A. *John Bunyan*. 1956. Pp. 19-31.

    White, Alison. "*Pilgrim's Progress* as a Fairy-Tale." *Children's Literature: The Great Excluded*, 1 (1972), 42-45.

    Wolff, Erwin. *Der englische Roman*. 1968. Pp. 12-24.

ANTHONY BURGESS

Beds in the East, 1959

DeVitis, A. A. *Anthony Burgess*. 1972. Pp. 57-64.

A Clockwork Orange, 1962

Aggeler, Geoffrey. "Pelagius and Augustine in the Novels of Anthony Burgess." *English Studies*, 55 (1974), 51-54.

Bergonzi, Bernard. *The Situation of the Novel*. 1971. Pp. 182-187.

Cullinan, John. "Anthony Burgess' *A Clockwork Orange*: Two Versions." *English Language Notes*, 9 (1972), 287-292.

DeVitis, A. A. *Anthony Burgess*. 1972. Pp. 104-112.

Evans, Robert O. "The *Nouveau Roman*, Russian Dystopias, and Anthony Burgess." *Studies in the Literary Imagination*, 6 (Fall 1973), 34-37.

Fitzpatrick, William P. "Anthony Burgess' Brave New World: The Ethos of Neutrality." *Studies in the Humanities,* 3 (1972), 32-33.

Fulkerson, Richard P. "Teaching *A Clockwork Orange*." *CEA Critic*, 17 (1974), 8-10.

Isaacs, Neil D. "Unstuck in Time: *Clockwork Orange* and *Slaughterhouse-Five.*" *Literature/Film Quarterly*, 1 (1973), 124-127.

McCracken, Samuel. "Novel into Film, Novelist into Critic: *A Clockwork Orange* . . . Again." *Antioch Review*, 32 (1973), 427-436.

Morris, Robert K. *The Consolations of Ambiguity*. 1971. Pp. 55-75.

Plank, Robert. "The Place of Evil in Science Fiction." *Extrapolation*, 14 (1973), 100-111.

Stinson, John J. "The Manichee World of Anthony Burgess." *Renascence*, 26 (1973), 41-44.

Devil of a State, 1961

DeVitis, A. A. *Anthony Burgess*. 1972. Pp. 86-95.

Morris, Robert K. *The Consolations of Ambiguity*. 1971. Pp. 37-42.

The Doctor Is Sick, 1960

DeVitis, A. A. *Anthony Burgess*. 1972. Pp. 79-86.

Enderby, 1968

Morris, Robert K. *The Consolations of Ambiguity*. 1971. Pp. 75-89.

Enderby Outside, 1968

DeVitis, A. A. *Anthony Burgess*. 1972. Pp. 130-133.

Hoffmann, Charles G., and A. C. Hoffmann. "Mr. Kell and Mr. Burgess: Inside and Outside Mr. Enderby," in Melvin J. Friedman and John B. Vickery, eds., *The Shaken Realist*. 1970. Pp. 300-310.

The Enemy in the Blanket, 1958

   DeVitis, A. A. *Anthony Burgess*. 1972. Pp. 49-57.

The Eve of St. Venus, 1964

   DeVitis, A. A. *Anthony Burgess*. 1972. Pp. 148-153.

Honey for the Bears, 1963

   DeVitis, A. A. *Anthony Burgess*. 1972. Pp. 134-141.
   Fitzpatrick, William P. "Black Marketeers and Manichees: Anthony
      Burgess' Cold War Novels." *West Virginia University Bulletin:
      Philological Papers*, 21 (1974), 80-84.
   Morris, Robert K. *The Consolations of Ambiguity*. 1971. Pp. 49-55.

Inside Mr. Enderby, 1963

   DeVitis, A. A. *Anthony Burgess*. 1972. Pp. 124-130.

The Long Day Wanes, 1965

   Morris. Robert K. *The Consolations of Ambiguity*. 1971. Pp. 21-31.
   Morris, Robert K. *Continuance and Change*. 1972. Pp. 71-91.

MF, 1971

   Aggeler, Geoffrey. "Incest and the Artist: Anthony Burgess's *MF* as
      Summation." *Modern Fiction Studies*, 18 (1972-1973), 529-543.

Nothing Like the Sun, 1964

   DeVitis, A. A. *Anthony Burgess*. 1972. Pp. 141-148.
   Stinson, John J. "The Manichee World of Anthony Burgess." *Re-
      nascence*, 26 (1973), 44-46.

One Hand Clapping, 1961

   DeVitis, A. A. *Anthony Burgess*. 1972. Pp. 119-124.

The Right to an Answer, 1960

   DeVitis, A. A. *Anthony Burgess*. 1972. Pp. 70-79.
   Morris, Robert K. *The Consolations of Ambiguity*. 1971. Pp. 42-49.

Time for a Tiger, 1956

   DeVitis, A. A. *Anthony Burgess*. 1972. Pp. 40-49.

Tremor of Intent, 1966

   DeVitis, A. A. *Anthony Burgess*. 1972. Pp. 153-163.
   Fitzpatrick, William P. "Black Marketeers and Manichees: Anthony
      Burgess' Cold War Novels." *West Virginia University Bulletin:
      Philological Papers*, 21 (1974), 84-90.
   Morris, Robert K. *The Consolations of Ambiguity*. 1971. Pp. 15-21.

A Vision of Battlements, 1965

> DeVitis, A. A. *Anthony Burgess*. 1972. Pp. 29-39.
> Morris, Robert K. *The Consolations of Ambiguity*. 1971. Pp. 9-15.

The Wanting Seed, 1962

> Aggeler, Geoffrey. "Pelagius and Augustine in the Novels of Anthony Burgess." *English Studies*, 55 (1974), 47-50.
> Chalpin, Lila. "Anthony Burgess's Gallows Humor in Dystopia." *Texas Quarterly*, 16 (Autumn 1973), 73-84.
> Cullinan, John. "*The Wanting Seed*: Epilogue, Chapter 4." *Explicator*, 31 (1973), No. 51.
> DeVitis, A. A. *Anthony Burgess*. 1972. Pp. 112-118.
> Evans, Robert O. "The *Nouveau Roman*, Russian Dystopias,. and Anthony Burgess." *Studies in the Literary Imagination*, 6 (Fall 1973), 34-37.
> Ftizpatrick, William P. "Anthony Burgess' Brave New World: The Ethos of Neutrality." *Studies in the Humanities*, 3 (1972), 33-36.
> Morris, Robert K. *The Consolations of Ambiguity*. 1971. Pp. 55-75.
> Murdoch, Brian. "The Overpopulated Wasteland: Myth in Anthony Burgess' *The Wanting Seed*." *Revue des Langues Vivantes*, 39 (1973), 208-217.

The Worm and the Ring, 1961

> Aggeler, Geoffrey. "A Wagnerian Affirmation: Anthony Burgess's *The Worm and the Ring*." *Western Humanities Review*, 27 (1973), 401-410.
> DeVitis, A. A. *Anthony Burgess*. 1972. Pp. 96-103.

FRANCES HODGSON BURNETT

The Secret Garden, 1911

> White, Alison. "Tap-Roots into a Rose Garden." *Children's Literature: The Great Excluded*, 1 (1972), 74-76.

FANNY BURNEY

Camilla, 1796

> Adelstein, Michael E. *Fanny Burney*. 1968. Pp. 96-104.
> Mews, Hazel. *Frail Vessels*. 1969. Pp. 36-38, 127-129.

Cecilia, 1782

> Adelstein, Michael E. *Fanny Burney*. 1968. Pp. 64-73.
> Mews, Hazel. *Frail Vessels*. 1969. Pp. 33-36.

Evelina, 1778

> Adelstein, Michael E. *Fanny Burney*. 1968. Pp. 28-44.
> Mews, Hazel. *Frail Vessels*. 1969. Pp. 32-33.
> Rubenstein, Jill. "The Crisis of Identity in Fanny Burney's *Evelina*."
> *New Rambler*, No. 109 (Spring 1972), 45-50.

The Wanderer, 1814

> Adelstein, Michael E. *Fanny Burney*. 1968. Pp. 121-129.
> Mews, Hazel. *Frail Vessels*. 1969. Pp. 38-41.

SAMUEL BUTLER

Erewhon, 1872

> Bisanz, Adam John. "Samuel Butler's 'Colleges of Unreason.'" *Orbis*
> *Litterarum*, 28 (1973), 9-22.
> Bisanz, Adam John. "Samuel Butler: A Literary Venture into Atheism
> and Beyond." *Orbis Litterarum*, 29 (1974), 316-336.
> Bisanz, Adam John. "Swiftian Patterns of Narrative in Samuel
> Butler's *Erewhon*." *Sprachkunst*, 3 (1972), 313-326.
> Brever, Hans-Peter. "The Source of Morality in Butler's *Erewhon*."
> *Victorian Studies*, 16 (1973), 317-328.
> Seeber, Hans Ulrich. *Wandlungen der Form*. 1970. Pp. 139-145.

Erewhon Revisited, 1901

> Bisanz, Adam John. "The 'Grand-Inquisitor' Motif in Samuel Butler's
> *Erewhon Revisited*." *Revue de Littérature Comparée*, 47 (1973),
> 369-383.
> Bisanz, Adam John. "Samuel Butler: A Literary Venture into Atheism
> and Beyond." *Orbis Litterarum*, 29 (1974), 316-336.

The Way of All Flesh, 1903

> Buckley, Jerome Hamilton. *Season of Youth*. 1974. Pp. 119-139.
> Fadiman, Clifton, William Y. Tindall, and Lyman Bryson. "*The Way*
> *of All Flesh*," in George D. Crothers, ed., *Invitation to Learning*.
> 1966. Pp. 154-162.
> Furbank, P. N. *Samuel Butler*. 1948. Pp. 10-15, 17-18.
> Otten, Kurt. *Der englische Roman*. 1971. Pp. 171-175.
> Wiley, Paul L. "Butler: The Counterplay of Recollection." *Tamkang*
> *Review*, 1 (October 1970), 141-153.

LEWIS CARROLL

Alice's Adventures in Wonderland, 1865

> Arnoldi, Richard. "Parallels Between *Our Mutal Friend* and the Alice
> Books." *Children's Literature: The Great Excluded*, 1 (1972), 54-57.

Auerbach, Nina. "Alice and Wonderland: A Curious Child." *Victorian Studies*, 17 (1973), 31-47.

Blake, Kathleen. *Play, Games, and Sport*. 1974. Pp. 108-131.

Cixous, Hélène. "Au sujet de Humpty Dumpty toujours déjà tombé," in Henri Parisot, ed., *Lewis Carroll*. 1971. Pp. 11-16.

Eagleton, Terry. "Alice and Anarchy." *New Blackfriars*, 53 (1972), 447-455.

Etienne, Luc. "Les Jeux de langage chez Lewis Carroll," in Henri Parisot, ed., *Lewis Carroll*. 1971. Pp. 30-34.

Flescher, Jacqueline. "The Language of Nonsense in *Alice*." *Yale French Studies*, 43 (1969), 128-144.

Gattegno, Jean. "Pour Lewis Carroll," in Henri Parisot, ed., *Lewis Carroll*. 1971. Pp. 35-40.

Graham, Neilson. "Sanity, Madness and Alice." *Ariel*, 4:2 (1973), 80-89.

Henkle, Roger B. "The Mad Hatter's World." *Virginia Quarterly Review*, 49 (1973), 100-106, 111-117.

Johnson, Paula. "Alice Among the Analysts." *Hartford Studies in Literature*, 4 (1972), 114-122.

Jorgens, Jack J. "Alice Our Contemporary." *Children's Literature: The Great Excluded*, 1 (1972), 152-161.

Kibel, Alvin C. "Logic and Satire in *Alice in Wonderland*." *American Scholar*, 43 (1974), 605-629.

Kincaid, James R. "Alice's Invasion of Wonderland." *Publications of the Modern Language Association*, 88 (1973), 92-99.

Martin, Jean Paul. "Alice chez Polysème," in Henri Parisot, ed., *Lewis Carroll*. 1971. Pp. 51-57.

Mayoux, Jean-Jacques. "Le Dialogue d'Alice: Confrontations, contestations, humour," in Henri Parisot, ed., *Lewis Carroll*. 1971. Pp. 58-66.

Otten, Terry. "Steppenwolf and Alice—In and Out of Wonderland." *Studies in the Humanities*, 4 (1974), 28-34.

Sapire, D. "*Alice in Wonderland*: A Work of Intellect." *English Studies in Africa*, 15 (1972), 53-62.

Walters, Jennifer R. "The Disquieting Worlds of Lewis Carroll and Boris Vian." *Revue de Littérature Comparée*, 46 (1972), 284-294.

Sylvie and Bruno, 1889

Blake, Kathleen. *Play, Games, and Sport*. 1974. Pp. 150-172.

Toubeau, Hélène. "L'Esprit et la lettre." *Critique* (Paris), No. 309 (1973), 131-135.

Sylvie and Bruno Concluded, 1893

Blake, Kathleen. *Play, Games, and Sport*. 1974. Pp. 150-172.

Through the Looking-Glass, 1871

Arnoldi, Richard. "Parallels Between *Our Mutual Friend* and the Alice Books," *Children's Literature: The Great Excluded*, 1 (1972), 54-57.

Auerbach, Nina. "Alice and Wonderland: A Curious Child." *Victorian Studies*, 17 (1973), 31-47.

Blake, Kathleen. *Play, Games, and Sport*. 1974. Pp. 132-148.

Brocas, Françoise. "L'Immatérialisme Berkeleyen dans les deux Alice," in Henri Parisot, ed., *Lewis Carroll*. 1971. Pp. 110-117.

Henkle, Roger B. "The Mad Hatter's World." *Virginia Quarterly Review*, 49 (1973), 107-111.

Johnson, Paula. "Alice Among the Analysts." *Hartford Studies in Literature*, 4 (1972), 114-122.

Jorgens, Jack J. "Alice Our Contemporary." *Children's Literature: The Great Excluded*, 1 (1972), 152-161.

Otten, Terry. "Steppenwolf and Alice—In and Out of Wonderland." *Studies in the Humanities*, 4 (1974), 28-34.

JOYCE CARY

The African Witch, 1936

Bloom, Robert. *The Indeterminate World*. 1962. Pp. 52-54.
Echeruo, Michael J. C. *Joyce Cary*. 1973. Pp. 74-113.
Mahood, M. M. *Joyce Cary's Africa*. 1965. Pp. 145-166.

Aissa Saved, 1932

Bloom, Robert. *The Indeterminate World*. 1962. Pp. 46-48.
Echeruo, Michael J. C. *Joyce Cary*. 1973. Pp. 28-43.
Mahood, M. M. *Joyce Cary's Africa*. 1965. Pp. 105-124.

An American Visitor, 1933

Bloom, Robert. *The Indeterminate World*. 1962. Pp. 48-52.
Echeruo, Michael J. C. *Joyce Cary*. 1973. Pp. 44-73, 114-115.
Mahood, M. M. *Joyce Cary's Africa*. 1965. Pp. 125-144.

Castle Corner, 1938

Bloom, Robert. *The Indeterminate World*. 1962. Pp. 66-72.
Mahood, M. M. *Joyce Cary's Africa*. 1965. Pp. 192-195.
Simmons, James. "Joyce Cary in Ireland," in B. S. Benedikz, ed., *On the Novel*. 1971. Pp. 141-155.

Charley Is My Darling, 1940

Bloom, Robert. *The Indeterminate World*. 1962. Pp. 59-63.
Webb, Bernice Larson. "Animal Imagery and Juvenile Delinquents in Joyce Cary's *Charley Is My Darling*." *South Central Bulletin*, 32 (1972), 240-242.

Except the Lord, 1953

> Bloom, Robert. *The Indeterminate World*. 1962. Pp. 139-169.
> Friedman, Alan Warren. "Joyce Cary's Cubistic Morality." *Contemporary Literature*, 14 (1973), 78-96.

A Fearful Joy, 1949

> Bloom, Robert. *The Indeterminate World*. 1962. Pp. 77-83.

Herself Surprised, 1941

> Bloom, Robert. *The Indeterminate World*. 1962. Pp. 84-90.
> Friedman, Alan Warren. "Joyce Cary's Cubistic Morality." *Contemporary Literature*, 14 (1973), 78-96.
> Kahrmann, Bernd. *Die idyllische Szene*. 1969. Pp. 56-58, 79-80.
> Mitchell, Giles. *The Art Theme*. 1971. Pp. 23-41.
> Reed, Peter J. " 'The Better the Heart': Joyce Cary's Sara Monday." *Texas Studies in Literature and Language*, 15 (1973), 357-370.

The Horse's Mouth, 1944

> Bloom, Robert. *The Indeterminate World*. 1962. Pp. 96-105.
> Friedman, Alan Warren. "Joyce Cary's Cubistic Morality." *Contemporary Literature*, 14 (1973), 78-96.
> Messenger, Ann P. "A Painter's Prose: Similes in Joyce Cary's *The Horse's Mouth*." *Re: Arts and Letters*, 3 (1970), 16-27.
> Mitchell, Giles. *The Art Theme*. 1971. Pp. 78-112.
> Seltzer, Alvin J. "Speaking Out of Both Sides of *The Horse's Mouth*: Joyce Cary vs. Gulley Jimson." *Contemporary Literature*, 15 (1974), 488-502.

A House of Children, 1941

> Bloom, Robert. *The Indeterminate World*. 1962. Pp. 63-66.
> Simmons, James. "Joyce Cary in Ireland," in B. S. Benedikz, ed., *On the Novel*. 1971. Pp. 155-160.

Mister Johnson, 1939

> Bloom, Robert. *The Indeterminate World*. 1962. Pp. 54-59.
> Echeruo, Michael J. C. *Joyce Cary*. 1973. Pp. 121-139.
> Mahood, M. M. *Joyce Cary's Africa*. 1965. Pp. 169-186.

The Moonlight, 1946

> Bloom, Robert. *The Indeterminate World*. 1962. Pp. 72-77.

Not Honour More, 1955

> Bloom, Robert. *The Indeterminate World*. 1962. Pp. 170-200.
> Friedman, Alan Warren. "Joyce Cary's Cubistic Morality." *Contemporary Literature*, 14 (1973), 78-96.

Prisoner of Grace, 1952

> Bloom, Robert. *The Indeterminate World*. 1962. Pp. 108-138.
> Friedman, Alan Warren. "Joyce Cary's Cubistic Morality." *Contemporary Literature*, 14 (1973), 78-96.

To Be a Pilgrim, 1942

> Bloom, Robert. *The Indeterminate World*. 1962. Pp. 90-96.
> Friedman, Alan Warren. "Joyce Cary's Cubistic Morality." *Contemporary Literature*, 14 (1973), 78-96.
> Gill, Richard. *Happy Rural Seat*. 1972. Pp. 202-205, 206-211.
> Mitchell, Giles. *The Art Theme*. 1971. Pp. 42-77.

G. K. CHESTERTON

The Ball and the Cross, 1910

> Clipper, Lawrence J. *G. K. Chesterton*. 1974. Pp. 132-134.
> Hollis, Christopher. *The Mind of Chesterton*. 1970. Pp. 93-95.

The Flying Inn, 1914

> Hollis, Christopher. *The Mind of Chesterton*. 1970. Pp. 140-147.

The Man Who Was Thursday, 1908

> Barker, Dudley. *G. K. Chesterton*. 1973. Pp. 176-180.
> Clipper, Lawrence J. *G. K. Chesterton*. 1974. Pp. 129-132.
> Hollis, Christopher. *The Mind of Chesterton*. 1970. Pp. 56-60.

The Napoleon of Notting Hill, 1904

> Barker, Dudley. *G. K. Chesterton*. 1973. Pp. 140-144.
> Clipper, Lawrence J. *G. K. Chesterton*. 1974. Pp. 126-129.
> Hollis, Christopher. *The Mind of Chesterton*. 1970. Pp. 107-111.

The Return of Don Quixote, 1927

> Clipper, Lawrence J. *G. K. Chesterton*. 1974. Pp. 138-140.

HENRY CHETTLE

Piers Plainnes, 1595

> Davis, Walter R. *Idea and Act*. 1969. Pp. 203-210.

AGATHA CHRISTIE

The Murder at the Vicarage, 1930

> Ercoli, Emma. "Agatha Christie." *Nuova Antologia*, 109 (1974), 245-248.

Murder in Mesopotamia, 1936

Ludwig, Hans-Werner. "Der Ich-Erzähler im englisch-amerikanischen Detektiv-und Kriminalroman." *Deutsche Vierteljahresschrift*, 45 (1971), 438-441.

JOHN CLELAND

Fanny Hill, 1748

Bradbury, Malcolm. *Possibilities*. 1973. Pp. 41-54.

Braudy, Leo. "*Fanny Hill* and Materialism." *Eighteenth-Century Studies*, 4 (1970), 21-40.

Copeland, Edward W. "*Clarissa* and *Fanny Hill*: Sisters in Distress." *Studies in the Novel*, 4 (1972), 343-352.

Emrich, Wilhelm. *Polemik*. 1968. Pp. 249-262.

Epstein, William H. *John Cleland*. 1974. Pp. 85-107.

Neumann, Peter Horst. "Der kleine Heilsweg der Fanny Hill: Zum ideologischen Charakter pornographischer Romane." *Neue Rundschau*, 86 (1975), 80-90.

Shinagel, Michael. "*Memoirs of a Woman of Pleasure*: Pornography and the Mid-Eighteenth-Century Novel," in Paul J. Korshin, ed., *Studies in Change and Revolution*. 1972. Pp. 211-234.

Solomon, Stanley J. "Subverting Propriety as a Pattern of Irony in Three Eighteenth-Century Novels: *The Castle of Otranto, Vathek,* and *Fanny Hill.*" *Erasmus Review*, 1 (1971), 112-114.

Taube, Myron. "Fanny and the Lady: The Treatment of Sex in *Fanny Hill* and *Lady Chatterley's Lover.*" *Lock Haven Review*, 15 (1974), 37-40.

Memoirs of a Coxcomb, 1751

Epstein, William H. *John Cleland*. 1974. Pp. 121-127.

The Woman of Honor, 1768

Epstein, William H. *John Cleland*. 1974. Pp. 155-160.

MORTIMER COLLINS

Marquis and Merchant, 1871

Melada, Ivan. *The Captain of Industry*. 1970. Pp. 185-187.

WILKIE COLLINS

Antonina, 1850

Marshall, William H. *Wilkie Collins*. 1970. Pp. 29-31.

Armadale, 1866

  Marshall, William H. *Wilkie Collins*. 1970. Pp. 71-76.

Basil, 1852

  Marshall, William H. *Wilkie Collins*. 1970. Pp. 31-34.

The Black Robe, 1881

  Marshall, William H. *Wilkie Collins*. 1970. Pp. 103-104.

The Dead Secret, 1857

  Marshall, William H. *Wilkie Collins*. 1970. Pp. 36-39.

The Haunted Hotel, 1879

  Marshall, William H. *Wilkie Collins*. 1970. Pp. 110-111.

Heart and Science, 1883

  Marshall, William H. *Wilkie Collins*. 1970. Pp. 104-105.

Hide and Seek, 1854

  Marshall, William H. *Wilkie Collins*. 1970. Pp. 34-36.

Jezebel's Daughter, 1880

  Marshall, William H. *Wilkie Collins*. 1970. Pp. 102-103.

The Law and the Lady, 1875

  Marshall, William H. *Wilkie Collins*. 1970. Pp. 99-102.

The Legacy of Cain, 1889

  Marshall, William H. *Wilkie Collins*. 1970. Pp. 106-108.

Man and Wife, 1870

  Marshall, William H. *Wilkie Collins*. 1970. Pp. 85-91.

The Moonstone, 1868

  Marshall, William H. *Wilkie Collins*. 1970. Pp. 77-85.
  Reed, John R. "English Imperialism and the Unacknowledged Crime
    of *The Moonstone*." *Clio*, 2 (1973), 281-290.

The New Magdalen, 1873

  Marshall, William H. *Wilkie Collins*. 1970. Pp. 96-99.

No Name, 1862

  Marshall, William H. *Wilkie Collins*. 1970. Pp. 66-71.

Poor Miss Finch, 1872

  Marshall, William H. *Wilkie Collins*. 1970. Pp. 93-96.

The Woman in White, 1860

   Marshall, William H. *Wilkie Collins.* 1970. Pp. 56-66.

MARY COLLYER

Letters from Felicia to Charlotte, 1744

   Gassenmeier, Michael. *Der Typus des "man of feeling."* 1972. Pp. 14-36.

IVY COMPTON-BURNETT

Brothers and Sisters, 1929

   Baldanza, Frank. *Ivy Compton-Burnett.* 1964. Pp. 43-46.
   Bałutowa, Bronisława. "The Group Dynamics in the Plots of Ivy Compton-Burnett." *Zagadnienia Rodzajow Literackich*, 13 (1970), 81-82.
   Liddell, Robert. *The Novels of I. Compton-Burnett.* 1955. Pp. 37-39.
   Nevius, Blake. *Ivy Compton-Burnett.* 1970. Pp. 9-10.

Darkness and Day, 1951

   Baldanza, Frank. *Ivy Compton-Burnett.* 1964. Pp. 83-86.
   Nevius, Blake. *Ivy Compton-Burnett.* 1970. P. 40.

Daughters and Sons, 1937

   Baldanza, Frank. *Ivy Compton-Burnett.* 1964. Pp. 58-61.
   Ginger, John. "Ivy Compton-Burnett." *London Magazine*, 9:10 (1970), 63-65.
   Liddell, Robert. *The Novels of I. Compton-Burnett.* 1955. Pp. 26-28, 30-31, 42.
   Nevius, Blake. *Ivy Compton-Burnett.* 1970. Pp. 29-31.

Dolores, 1911

   Liddell, Robert. *The Novels of I. Compton-Burnett.* 1955. Pp. 15-17, 24.
   Nevius, Blake. *Ivy Compton-Burnett.* 1970. Pp. 4-6.

Elders and Betters, 1944

   Baldanza, Frank. *Ivy Compton-Burnett.* 1964. Pp. 69-72.
   Balutowa, Bronislawa. "The Group Dynamics in the Plots of Ivy Compton-Burnett." *Zagadnienia Rodzajow Literackich*, 13 (1970), 83-92.
   Liddell, Robert. *The Novels of I. Compton-Burnett.* 1955. Pp. 44-45, 59-61.
   Nevius, Blake. *Ivy Compton-Burnett.* 1970. Pp. 34-37.

A Family and a Fortune, 1939

   Baldanza, Frank. *Ivy Compton-Burnett*. 1964. Pp. 61-65.
   Ginger, John. "Ivy Compton-Burnett." *London Magazine*, 9:10 (1970), 61-63, 66-71.
   Liddell, Robert. *The Novels of I. Compton-Burnett*. 1955. Pp. 31-34.
   Nevius, Blake. *Ivy Compton-Burnett*. 1970. Pp. 31-33.

A Father and His Fate, 1957

   Baldanza, Frank. *Ivy Compton-Burnett*. 1964. Pp. 93-96.

A God and His Gifts, 1963

   Baldanza, Frank. *Ivy Compton-Burnett*. 1964. Pp. 102-105.
   Nevius, Blake. *Ivy Compton-Burnett*. 1970. Pp. 44-45.

A Heritage and Its History, 1959

   Baldanza, Frank. *Ivy Compton-Burnett*. 1964. Pp. 96-99.
   Iser, Wolfgang. *The Implied Reader*. 1974. Pp. 152-163, 234-256.

A House and Its Head, 1935

   Baldanza, Frank. *Ivy Compton-Burnett*. 1964. Pp. 53-56.
   Liddell, Robert. *The Novels of I. Compton-Burnett*. 1955. Pp. 25-26, 43-44, 77-78.
   Nevius, Blake. *Ivy Compton-Burnett*. 1970. Pp. 28-29.

Manservant and Maidservant, 1947

   Baldanza, Frank. *Ivy Compton-Burnett*. 1964. Pp. 72-76.
   Liddell, Robert. *The Novels of I. Compton-Burnett*. 1955. Pp. 40-42, 61-62.
   Nevius, Blake. *Ivy Compton-Burnett*. 1970. Pp. 37-38.

Men and Wives, 1931

   Baldanza, Frank. *Ivy Compton-Burnett*. 1964. Pp. 46-49.
   Bałutowa, Bronisława. "The Group Dynamics in the Plots of Ivy Compton-Burnett." *Zagadnienia Rodzajow Literackich*, 13 (1970), 82-83.
   Liddell, Robert. *The Novels of I. Compton-Burnett*. 1955. Pp. 28-29, 39-42, 74-77.
   Nevius, Blake. *Ivy Compton-Burnett*. 1970. Pp. 23-25.

The Mighty and Their Fall, 1961

   Baldanza, Frank. *Ivy Compton-Burnett*. 1964. Pp. 99-102.

More Women Than Men, 1933

   Baldanza, Frank. *Ivy Compton-Burnett*. 1964. Pp. 50-53.
   Liddell, Robert. *The Novels of I. Compton-Burnett*. 1955. Pp. 29-30, 42.
   Nevius, Blake. *Ivy Compton-Burnett*. 1970. Pp. 27-28.

Mother and Son, 1955

>   Baldanza, Frank. *Ivy Compton-Burnett*. 1964. Pp. 89-92.
>   Nevius, Blake. *Ivy Compton-Burnett*. 1970. Pp. 42-43.

Parents and Children, 1941

>   Baldanza, Frank. *Ivy Compton-Burnett*. 1964. Pp. 65-69.
>   Nevius, Blake. *Ivy Compton-Burnett*. 1970. Pp. 33-34.

Pastors and Masters, 1925

>   Liddell, Robert. *The Novels of I. Compton-Burnett*. 1955. Pp. 24-25,
>   37, 72-73.
>   Nevius, Blake. *Ivy Compton-Burnett*. 1970. Pp. 7-9.

The Present and the Past, 1953

>   Baldanza, Frank. *Ivy Compton-Burnett*. 1964. Pp. 86-89.
>   Liddell, Robert. *The Novels of I. Compton-Burnett*. 1955. Pp. 42-43,
>   46-47.
>   Nevius, Blake. *Ivy Compton-Burnett*. 1970. Pp. 40-42.

Two Worlds and Their Ways, 1949

>   Baldanza, Frank. *Ivy Compton-Burnett*. 1964. Pp. 76-79.
>   Nevius, Blake. *Ivy Compton-Burnett*. 1970. Pp. 39-40.

WILLIAM CONGREVE

Incognita, 1692

>   Novak, Maximillian E. *William Congreve*. 1971. Pp. 62-75.

JOSEPH CONRAD

Almayer's Folly, 1895

>   Boyle, Ted E. *Symbol and Meaning*. 1965. Pp. 16-37.
>   Braun, Andrzej. *Sladami Conrada*. 1972. Pp. 39-42, 347-351, 386-
>   389, 466-470, 478-481, 483-486, 490-494, 503-507, 512-515, 517-521.
>   Palmer, John A. *Joseph Conrad's Fiction*. 1968. Pp. 51-56.
>   Ryf, Robert S. *Joseph Conrad*. 1970. Pp. 12-13.
>   Voytovich, Edward R. "The Problem of Identity for Conrad's Wom-
>   en." *Essays in Literature* (Denver), 2:2 (1974), 53-54.
>   Watt, Ian. "*Almayer's Folly*: Memories and Models." *Mosaic*, 8
>   (Fall 1974), 171-182.
>   Yelton, Donald C. *Mimesis and Metaphor*. 1967. Pp. 152-154.

The Arrow of Gold, 1919

>   Begnal, Michael H. "The Ideals of Despair: A View of Joseph Conrad's
>   *The Arrow of Gold*." *Conradiana*, 3:3 (1971-1972), 37-40.

Coolidge, Olivia. *The Three Lives*. 1972. Pp. 192-194.
Palmer, John A. *Joseph Conrad's Fiction*. 1968. Pp. 249-253.
Yelton, Donald C. *Mimesis and Metaphor*. 1967. Pp. 202-205.

Chance, 1913

Cox, C. B. *Joseph Conrad*. 1974. Pp. 118-125.
Friedman, Alan W. "Conrad's Picaresque Narrator: Marlow's Journey From 'Youth' Through *Chance*," in Wolodymyr T. Zyla and Wendell M. Aycock, eds., *Joseph Conrad*. 1974. Pp. 32-37.
Gurko, Leo. *The Two Lives*. 1965. Pp. 174-178.
Lombardo, Agostino. *Ritratto di Enobarbo*. 1971. Pp. 274-286.
Palmer, John A. *Joseph Conrad's Fiction*. 1968. Pp. 198-221.

Lord Jim, 1900

Andreach, Robert J. *The Slain and Resurrected God*. 1970. Pp. 58-66.
Bellis, George. "Fidelity to a Higher Ideal: A Study of the Jump in Conrad's *Lord Jim*." *Erasmus Review*, 1 (1971), 63-71.
Boyle, Ted E. *Symbol and Meaning*. 1965. Pp. 60-84.
Braun, Andrzej. *Sladami Conrada*. 1972. Pp. 66-69, 580-587, 589-593.
Bruss, Paul S. "Marlow's Interview with Stein: The Implications of the Metaphor." *Studies in the Novel*, 5 (1973), 491-503.
Burstein, Janet. "On Ways of Knowing in *Lord Jim*." *Nineteenth-Century Fiction*, 26 (1972), 456-468.
Cox, C. B. *Joseph Conrad*. 1974. Pp. 19-44.
Cox, C. B. "Joseph Conrad and the Question of Suicide." *Bulletin of the John Rylands Library*, 55 (1973), 298-299.
Cox, C. B. "The Metamorphosis of Lord Jim." *Critical Quarterly*, 15 (1973), 9-31.
Deurbergue, Jean. "*Lord Jim*, roman du nebuleux?" *Etudes Anglaises*, 25 (1972), 148-161.
Deurbergue, Jean. "Récit et roman dans deux oeuvres de Conrad: *Lord Jim* et *Nostromo*," in *Récit et roman*. 1972. Pp. 64-74.
Engelberg, Edward. *The Unknown Distance*. 1972. Pp. 172-185.
Epstein, Harry S. "*Lord Jim* as a Tragic Action." *Studies in the Novel*, 5 (1973), 229-247.
Fichter, Andrew. "Dramatic Voice in *Lord Jim* and *Nostromo*." *Thoth*, 12 (Spring/Summer 1972), 3-13.
Friedman, Alan W. "Conrad's Picaresque Narrator: Marlow's Journey From 'Youth' Through *Chance*," in Wolodymyr T. Zyla and Wendell M. Aycock, eds. *Joseph Conrad*. 1974. Pp. 20-24, 27-32.
Garmon, Gerald M. "*Lord Jim* as Tragedy." *Conradiana*, 4:1 (1972), 34-40.
Garrett, Peter K. *Scene and Symbol*. 1969. Pp. 172-180.
Goetsch, Paul. *Die Romankonzeption in England*. 1967. Pp. 334-338, 347-350.
Gose, Elliott B., Jr. *Imagination Indulged*. 1972. Pp. 141-166.
Gurko, Leo. *The Two Lives*. 1965. Pp. 129-131.

Hodges, Robert R. *The Dual Heritage.* 1967. Pp. 158-164.

Jacobs, Robert G. "*Gilgamesh*: The Sumerian Epic That Helped *Lord Jim* to Stand Alone." *Conradiana*, 4:2 (1972), 23-32.

Keppler, C. F. *The Literature of the Second Self.* 1972. Pp. 86-91.

Martin, Joseph J. "Edward Garnett and Conrad's Reshaping of Time." *Conradiana*, 6 (1974), 98-102.

Miller, J. Hillis. "The Interpretation of *Lord Jim*," in Morton W. Bloomfield, ed., *The Interpretation of Narrative*. 1970. Pp. 211-228.

Mroczkowski, Przemysław. *Conradian Commentaries.* 1970. Pp. 49-136.

Müllenbrock, Heinz-Joachim. *Literatur und Zeitgeschichte.* 1967. Pp. 28-31.

Nelson, Carl. "The Ironic Allusive Texture of *Lord Jim*: Coleridge, Crane, Milton, and Melville." *Conradiana*, 4:2 (1972), 47-59.

Palmer, John A. *Joseph Conrad's Fiction.* 1968. Pp. 20-23, 26-45.

Paris, Bernard J. *A Psychological Approach.* 1974. Pp. 215-274.

Rogers, Robert. *A Psychoanalytic Study.* 1970. Pp. 45-46.

Ryf, Robert S. *Joseph Conrad.* 1970. Pp. 21-24, 37-38, 40-41.

Saveson, John E. "The Intuitionist Hero of *Lord Jim*." *Conradiana*, 4:3 (1972), 34-47.

Saveson, John E. *Joseph Conrad.* 1972. Pp. 37-53, 65-83, 89-107, 137-161, 165-178.

Schwarz, Daniel R. "The Journey to Patusan: The Education of Jim and Marlow in Conrad's *Lord Jim*." *Studies in the Novel*, 4 (1972), 442-458.

Seltzer, Alvin J. *Chaos in the Novel.* 1974. Pp. 80-91.

Sherry, Norman. "The Essential Conrad," in Wolodymyr T. Zyla and Wendell M. Aycock, eds., *Joseph Conrad*. 1974. Pp. 142-144.

Stegmaier, E. "The 'Would-Scene' in Joseph Conrad's *Lord Jim* and *Nostromo*." *Modern Language Review*, 67 (1972), 517-523.

Steinmann, Theo. "Lord Jim's Progression Through Homology." *Ariel*, 5:1 (1974), 81-93.

Widmer, Kingsley. "Conrad's Pyrrhonistic Conservatism: Ideological Melodrama Around 'Simple Ideas.'" *Novel*, 7 (1974), 136-137.

Wolff, Erwin. "Conrad: *Lord Jim*," in Franz K. Stanzel, ed., *Der englische Roman*. 1969. Vol. II, 289-316.

Yelton, Donald C. *Mimesis and Metaphor.* 1967. Pp. 162-174.

The Nigger of the "Narcissus," 1897

Bloch, Tuvia. "The Wait-Donkin Relationship in *The Nigger of the 'Narcissus.'*" *Conradiana*, 4:2 (1972), 62-66.

Bonney, William W. "Semantic and Structural Indeterminacy in *The Nigger of the 'Narcissus'*: An Experiment in Reading." *ELH*, 40 (1973), 564-583.

Boyle, Ted E. *Symbol and Meaning.* 1965. Pp. 38-59.

Burgess, C. F. "Of Men and Ships and Mortality: Conrad's *The Nigger of the 'Narcissus.'*" *English Literature in Transition*, 15 (1972), 221-231.

Daleski, H. M. "Hanging On and Letting Go: Conrad's *The Nigger of 'Narcissus.'*" *Hebrew University Studies in Literature*, 2 (1974), 171-196.

Goetsch, Paul. *Die Romankonzeption in England*. 1967. Pp. 340-343.

Gose, Elliott B., Jr. *Imagination Indulged*. 1972. Pp. 131-137.

Gurko, Leo. *The Two Lives*. 1965. Pp. 114-117.

Hodgson, John A. "Left-Right Opposition in *The Nigger of the 'Narcissus.'*" *Papers on Language and Literature*, 8 (1972) 207-210.

Michael, Marion C. "Currents in Conrad Criticism: A Symposium." *Conradiana*, 4:3 (1972), 13-15.

Michael, Marion C. "James Wait as Pivot: Narrative Structure in *The Nigger of the 'Narcissus,'*" in Wolodymyr T. Zyla and Wendell M. Aycock, eds., *Joseph Conrad*. 1974. Pp. 89-102.

Palmer, John A. *Joseph Conrad's Fiction*. 1968. Pp. 67-74.

Pinsker, Sanford. "Joseph Conrad and the Language of the Sea." *Conradiana*, 3:3 (1971-1972), 18-21.

Pinsker, Sanford. "Selective Memory, Leisure and the Language of Joseph Conrad's *The Nigger of the 'Narcissus.'*" *Descant*, 15:4 (1971), 38-48.

Ryf, Robert S. *Joseph Conrad*. 1970. Pp. 14-16, 36-37.

Saveson, John E. *Joseph Conrad*. 1972. Pp. 109-115, 187-195.

Steinmann, Theo. "The Perverted Pattern of *Billy Budd* in *The Nigger of the 'Narcissus.'*" *English Studies*, 55 (1974), 239-246.

Wiley, P. L. "Two Tales of Passion." *Conradiana*, 6 (1974), 189-193.

Yelton, Donald C. *Mimesis and Metaphor*. 1967. Pp. 154-162.

Nostromo, 1904

Andreach, Robert J. *The Slain and Resurrected God*. 1970. Pp. 66-76.

Boyle, Ted E. *Symbol and Meaning*. 1965. Pp. 154-185.

Chapple, J. A. V. *Documentary and Imaginative Literature*. 1970. Pp. 197-201.

Cooper, Christopher. *Conrad and the Human Dilemma*. 1970. Pp. 105-148.

Cox, C. B. *Joseph Conrad*. 1974. Pp. 60-82.

Deurbergue, Jean. "Récit et roman dans deux oeuvres de Conrad: *Lord Jim* et *Nostromo*," in *Récit et roman*. 1972. Pp. 64-74.

Emmett, Victor J., Jr. "The Aesthetics of Anti-Imperialism: Ironic Distortions of the Vergilian Epic Mode in Conrad's *Nostromo*." *Studies in the Novel*, 4 (1972), 459-472.

Fichter, Andrew. "Dramatic Voice in *Lord Jim* and *Nostromo*." *Thoth*, 12 (Spring/Summer 1972), 13-18.

Friedman, Alan. "The Novel," in C. B. Cox and A. E. Dyson, eds., *The Twentieth-Century Mind*. 1972. Vol. I, 424-428.

Garrett, Peter K. *Scene and Symbol*. 1969. Pp. 160-163.

Goetsch, Paul. *Die Romankonzeption in England*. 1967. Pp. 350-356.

Gurko, Leo. *The Two Lives*. 1965. Pp. 139-144.

Haltresht, Michael. "The Gods of Conrad's *Nostromo.*" *Renascence*, 24 (1972), 207-212.

Kartiganer, Donald M. "Process and Product: A Study of Modern Literary Form." *Massachusetts Review*, 12 (1971), 792-800.

King, William E. "Conrad's *Weltanschauung* and the God of Material Interests in *Nostromo.*" *Conradiana*, 3:3 (1971-1972), 41-45.

Marten, Harry. "Conrad's Skeptic Reconsidered: A Study of Martin Decoud." *Nineteenth-Century Fiction*, 27 (1972), 81-94.

Mroczkowski, Przemysław. "Joseph Conrad's International World of Men." *Kwartalnik Neofilologizny*, 21 (1974), 181-187.

Müllenbrock, Heinz-Joachim. *Literatur und Zeitgeschichte*. 1967. Pp. 79-82.

Mueller, William R. *Celebration of Life*. 1972. Pp. 77-97.

Palmer, John A. *Joseph Conrad's Fiction*. 1968. Pp. 139-165.

Pitol, Sergio. "Conrad en Costaguana." *Cuadernos Hispanoamericanos*, No. 256 (1971), 64-73.

Rosenfield, Claire. *Paradise of Snakes*. 1967. Pp. 43-78.

Ryf, Robert S. *Joseph Conrad*. 1970. Pp. 24-27, 38, 41.

Saunders, William S. "The Unity of *Nostromo.*" *Conradiana*, 5:1 (1973), 27-36.

Stegmaier, E. "The 'Would-Scene' in Joseph Conrad's *Lord Jim* and *Nostromo.*" *Modern Language Review*, 67 (1972), 517-523.

Tartella, Vincent P. "Symbolism in Four Scenes in *Nostromo.*" *Conradiana*, 4:1 (1972), 63-70.

Voytovich, Edward R. "The Problem of Identity for Conrad's Women." *Essays in Literature* (Denver), 2:2 (1974), 62-65.

Widmer, Kingsley. "Conrad's Pyrrhonistic Conservatism: Ideological Melodrama Around 'Simple Ideas.'" *Novel*, 7 (1974), 139-141.

Yelton, Donald C. *Mimesis and Metaphor*. 1967. Pp. 175-181.

The Rescue, 1920

Geddes, Gary. *"The Rescue*: Conrad and the Rhetoric of Diplomacy." *Mosaic*, 7 (Spring 1974), 107-125.

Howarth, Herbert. "Conrad and Imperialism: The Difference of *The Rescue.*" *Ohio Review*, 13 (Fall 1971), 62-72.

Liljegren, S. Bodvar. *Joseph Conrad*. 1968. Pp. 3-54.

Ryf, Robert S. *Joseph Conrad*. 1970. Pp. 33-34.

The Rover, 1923

Laine, Michael. "Conrad's *The Rover*: The Rejection of Despair." *Queen's Quarterly*, 80 (1973), 246-255.

Lippincott, H. F. "Sense of Place in Conrad's *The Rover.*" *Conradiana*, 6 (1974), 106-112.

Palmer, John A. *Joseph Conrad's Fiction*. 1968. Pp. 253-257.

Yelton, Donald C. *Mimesis and Metaphor*. 1967. Pp. 205-209.

The Secret Agent, 1907

Andreach, Robert J. *The Slain and Resurrected God.* 1970. Pp. 76-86.

Boyle, Ted E. *Symbol and Meaning.* 1965. Pp. 186-194.

Chapple, J. A. V. *Documentary and Imaginative Literature.* 1970. Pp. 152-156.

Cooper, Christopher. *Conrad and the Human Dilemma.* 1970. Pp. 18-61.

Cox, C. B. *Joseph Conrad.* 1974. Pp. 83-101.

Cox, C. B. "Joseph Conrad's *The Secret Agent*: The Irresponsible Piano." *Critical Quarterly*, 15 (1973), 197-212.

Gurko, Leo. *The Two Lives.* 1965. Pp. 149-155.

Haltresht, Michael. "Disease Imagery in Conrad's *The Secret Agent.*" *Literature and Psychology*, 21 (1971), 101-105.

Haltresht, Michael. "The Dread of Space in Conrad's *The Secret Agent.*" *Literature and Psychology*, 22 (1972), 89-96.

Hartsell, Robert L. "Conrad's Left Symbolism in *The Secret Agent.*" *Conradiana*, 4:1 (1972), 57-59.

Langbaum, Robert. "Thoughts for Our Time: Three Novels on Anarchism." *American Scholar*, 42 (1973), 236-243.

Miller, J. Hillis. *Poets of Reality.* 1966. Pp. 39-67.

Nettels, Elsa. "The Grotesque in Conrad's Fiction." *Nineteenth-Century Fiction*, 29 (1974), 154-157.

Palmer, John A. *Joseph Conrad's Fiction.* 1968. Pp. 103-121.

Rosenfield, Claire. *Paradise of Snakes.* 1967. Pp. 79-122.

Ryf, Robert S. *Joseph Conrad.* 1970. Pp. 27-30.

Saveson, John E. "Conrad, *Blackwood's,* and Lombroso." *Conradiana*, 6 (1974), 57-62.

Saveson, John E. *Joseph Conrad.* 1972. Pp. 117-136.

Shadoian, Jack. "Irony Triumphant: Verloc's Death." *Conradiana*, 3:2 (1971-1972), 82-86.

Sherry, Norman. "The Essential Conrad," in Wolodymyr T. Zyla and Wendell M. Aycock, eds., *Joseph Conrad.* 1974. Pp. 146-149.

Smitten, Jeffrey R. "Flaubert and the Structure of *The Secret Agent*: A Study in Spatial Form," in Wolodymyr T. Zyla and Wendell M. Aycock, eds., *Joseph Conrad.* 1974. Pp. 151-166.

Sullivan, Walter. "The Dark Beyond the Sunrise: Conrad and the Politics of Despair." *Southern Review* (Baton Rouge), 8 (1972), 510-519.

Sullivan, Walter. "Irony and Disorder: *The Secret Agent.*" *Sewanee Review*, 81 (1973), 124-131.

Voytovich, Edward R. "The Problem of Identity for Conrad's Women." *Essays in Literature* (Denver), 2:2 (1974), 55-58.

Widmer, Kingsley. "Conrad's Pyrrhonistic Conservatism: Ideological Melodrama Around 'Simple Ideas.'" *Novel*, 7 (1974), 137-139.

Yelton, Donald C. *Mimesis and Metaphor.* 1967. Pp. 182-190.

Under Western Eyes, 1911

Adams, Barbara Block. "Sisters Under Their Skins: The Women in the Lives of Raskolnikov and Razumov." *Conradiana*, 6 (1974), 113-124.

Andreach, Robert J. *The Slain and Resurrected God*. 1970. Pp. 86-96.

Boyle, Ted E. *Symbol and Meaning*. 1965. Pp. 195-217.

Cooper, Christopher. *Conrad and the Human Dilemma*. 1970. Pp. 62-104.

Cox, C. B. *Joseph Conrad*. 1974. Pp. 102-117.

Fries, Maureen. "Feminism-Antifeminism in *Under Western Eyes.*" *Conradiana*, 5:2 (1973), 56-65.

Gurko, Leo. *The Two Lives*. 1965. Pp. 162-166.

Martin, W. R. "Compassionate Realism in Conrad and *Under Western Eyes.*" *English Studies in Africa*, 17 (1974), 89-100.

Nettels, Elsa. "The Grotesque in Conrad's Fiction." *Nineteenth-Century Fiction*, 29 (1974), 157-161.

Palmer, John A. *Joseph Conrad's Fiction*. 1968. Pp. 124-138.

Rosenfield, Claire. *Paradise of Snakes*. 1967. Pp. 123-172.

Ryf, Robert S. *Joseph Conrad*. 1970. Pp. 30-31.

Saveson, John E. "The Moral Discovery of *Under Western Eyes.*" *Criticism*, 14 (1972), 32-48.

Sullivan, Walter. "The Dark Beyond the Sunrise: Conrad and the Politics of Despair." *Southern Review* (Baton Rouge), 8 (1972), 507-519.

Viswanathan, Jacqueline. "Point of View and Unreliability in Brontë's *Wuthering Heights*, Conrad's *Under Western Eyes* and Mann's *Doktor Faustus.*" *Orbis Litterarum*, 29 (1974), 42-59.

Voytovich, Edward R. "The Problem of Identity for Conrad's Women." *Essays in Literature* (Denver), 2:2 (1974), 60-62.

Yelton, Donald C. *Mimesis and Metaphor*. 1967. Pp. 190-202.

Victory, 1915

Andreach, Robert J. *The Slain and Resurrected God*. 1970. Pp. 96-107.

Boyle, Ted E. *Symbol and Meaning*. 1965. Pp. 218-238.

Butler, Richard E. "Jungian and Oriental Symbolism in Joseph Conrad's *Victory.*" *Conradiana*, 3:2 (1971-1972), 36-54.

Cox, C. B. *Joseph Conrad*. 1974. Pp. 125-136.

Hollahan, Eugene. "Beguiled into Action: Silence and Sound in *Victory.*" *Texas Studies in Literature and Language*, 16 (1974), 349-362.

Kennard, Jean E. "Emerson and Dickens: A Note on Conrad's *Victory.*" *Conradiana*, 6 (1974), 215-219.

Keppler, C. F. *The Literature of the Second Self*. 1972. Pp. 45-50.

Page, Norman. "Dickensian Elements in *Victory.*" *Conradiana*, 5:1 (1973), 37-42.

Palmer, John A. *Joseph Conrad's Fiction*. 1968. Pp. 166-197.

Roberts, Mark. *The Tradition of Romantic Morality*. 1973. Pp. 259-287.

Ryf, Robert S. *Joseph Conrad*. 1970. Pp. 32, 41-43.

Saveson, John E. "Conrad's Acis and Galatea: A Note on *Victory.*" *Modern Language Studies*, 2 (1972), 59-62.

Voytovich, Edward R. "The Problem of Identity for Conrad's Women." *Essays in Literature* (Denver), 2:2 (1974), 58-60.

Walcutt, Charles Child. *Man's Changing Mask*. 1966. Pp. 265-280.

JOSEPH CONRAD AND FORD MADOX FORD

The Inheritors, 1901

Andreach, Robert J. *The Slain and Resurrected God*. 1970. Pp. 5-16.

Hoffmann, Charles G. *Ford Madox Ford*. 1967. Pp. 24-26.

Mizener, Arthur. *The Saddest Story*. 1971. Pp. 464-466.

Ohmann, Carol. *Ford Madox Ford*. 1964. Pp. 13-18.

The Nature of a Crime, 1924

Hoffmann, Charles G. *Ford Madox Ford*. 1967. Pp. 30-32.

Romance, 1903

Andreach, Robert J. *The Slain and Resurrected God*. 1970. Pp. 9-16.

Hoffmann, Charles G. *Ford Madox Ford*. 1967. Pp. 26-30.

Rose, Charles. "*Romance* and the Maiden Archetype." *Conradiana*, 6 (1974), 183-188.

NOEL COWARD

Pomp and Circumstance, 1960

Levin, Milton. *Noel Coward*. 1968. Pp. 129-131.

CHARLOTTE DACRE

Zofloya, 1806

Breitinger, Eckhard. *Der Tod im englischen Roman*. 1971. Pp. 38-40.

MARY DAVYS

The Lady's Tale, 1714

Doody, Margaret Anne. *A Natural Passion*. 1974. Pp. 132-137.

DANIEL DEFOE

Captain Singleton, 1720

Brooks, Douglas. *Number and Pattern*. 1973. Pp. 26-30.
Conti, Paola Colaiacoma. *"Captain Singleton* fra *Robinson Crusoe* e *Moll Flanders."* *English Miscellany*, 20 (1969), 141-161.
Hahn, H. G. "An Approach to Character Development in Defoe's Narrative Prose." *Philological Quarterly*, 51 (1972), 848-851.
Richetti, John J. *Popular Fiction*. 1969. Pp. 84-91.
Shinagel, Michael. *Daniel Defoe*. 1968. Pp. 134-137.
Sutherland, James. *Daniel Defoe*. 1971. Pp. 144-150.
Walton, James. "The Romance of Gentility: Defoe's Heroes and Heroines." *Literary Monographs*, 4 (1971), 95-98.

Colonel Jacque, 1722

Brooks, Douglas. *Number and Pattern*. 1973. Pp. 30-37.
Hahn, H. G. "An Approach to Character Development in Defoe's Narrative Prose." *Philological Quarterly*, 51 (1972), 854-858.
Shinagel, Michael. *Daniel Defoe*. 1968. Pp. 161-177.
Sutherland, James. *Daniel Defoe*. 1971. Pp. 195-205.
Walton, James. "The Romance of Gentility: Defoe's Heroes and Heroines." *Literary Monographs*, 4 (1971), 98-110.

Jonathan Wild, 1725

Hahn, H. G. "An Approach to Character Development in Defoe's Narrative Prose." *Philological Quarterly*, 51 (1972), 848-851.

Journal of the Plague Year, 1722

Blair, Joel. "Defoe's Art in *A Journal of the Plague Year."* *South Atlantic Quarterly*, 72 (1973), 243-254.
Flanders, W. Austin. "Defoe's *Journal of the Plague Year* and the Modern Urban Experience." *Centennial Review*, 16 (1972), 238-248.
Hahn, H. G. "An Approach to Character Development in Defoe's Narrative Prose." *Philological Quarterly*, 51 (1972), 851-854.
James, E. Anthony. *Daniel Defoe's Many Voices*. 1972. Pp. 135-153, 156-158.
Kay, Donald. "Defoe's Sense of History in *A Journal of the Plague Year."* *Xavier University Studies*, 9 (1970), 1-8.
Klotz, Volker. *Die erzählte Stadt*. 1969. Pp. 48-65.
Sutherland, James. *Daniel Defoe*. 1971. Pp. 163-172.
Vickers, Brian. "Daniel Defoe's *Journal of the Plague Year*: Notes for a Critical Analysis." *Filologia Moderna*, 13 (1973), 161-170.
Zimmerman, Everett. "H. F.'s Meditations: *A Journal of the Plague Year."* *Publications of the Modern Language Association*, 87 (1972), 417-423.

The Memoirs of a Cavalier, 1720

Sutherland, James. *Daniel Defoe*. 1971. Pp. 157-163.

Moll Flanders, 1722

Allende, Nora A. de. "Social Context in *Moll Flanders, Pamela*, and *Tom Jones*." *Revista de Literaturas Modernas*, 8 (1969), 81-126.

Brooks, Douglas. *Number and Pattern*. 1973. Pp. 41-52.

Donovan, Robert Alan. *The Shaping Vision*. 1966. Pp. 21-46.

Hahn, H. G. "An Approach to Character Development in Defoe's Narrative Prose." *Philological Quarterly*, 51 (1972), 854-858.

Hartog, Curt. "Aggression, Femininity, and Irony in *Moll Flanders*." *Literature and Psychology*, 22 (1972), 121-137.

James, E. Anthony. *Daniel Defoe's Many Voices*. 1972. Pp. 201-229.

Karl, Frederick R. "Moll's Many-Colored Coat: Veil and Disguise in the Fiction of Defoe." *Studies in the Novel*, 5 (1973), 89-95.

Lieberman, Marcia R. "Sexism and the Double Standard in Literature," in Susan Koppelman Cornillon, ed., *Images of Women in Fiction*. 1973. Pp. 335-338.

Lombardo, Agostino. *Ritratto di Enobarbo*. 1971. Pp. 68-86.

McMaster, Juliet. "The Equation of Love and Money in *Moll Flanders*." *Studies in the Novel*, 2 (1970), 131-144.

Michie, J. A. "The Unity of *Moll Flanders*," in Christine J. Whitbourn, ed., *Knaves and Swindlers*. 1974. Pp. 75-92.

Nolting-Hauff, Ilse. "Die betrügerische Heirat: Realismus und Pikareske in Defoes *Moll Flanders*." *Poetica*, 3 (1970), 412-420.

Olshin, Toby A. "'Thoughtful of the Main Chance': Defoe and the Cycle of Anxiety." *Hartford Studies in Literature*, 6 (1974), 119-121.

Rader, Ralph W. "Defoe, Richardson, Joyce, and the Concept of Form in the Novel," in *Autobiography, Biography, and the Novel*. 1973. Pp. 39-47.

Rogal, Samuel J. "The Profit and Loss of Moll Flanders." *Studies in the Novel*, 5 (1973), 98-103.

Shinagel, Michael. *Daniel Defoe*. 1968. Pp. 142-160.

Smith, LeRoy W. "Daniel Defoe: Incipient Pornographer." *Literature and Psychology*, 22 (1972), 165-177.

Sutherland, James. *Daniel Defoe*. 1971. Pp. 175-194.

Toth, Erwin. "Die Funktion des Dialogs bei Daniel Defoe." *Germanisch-Romanische Monatsschrift*, 22 (1972), 243-247.

Walton, James. "The Romance of Gentility: Defoe's Heroes and Heroines." *Literary Monographs*, 4 (1971), 110-122.

Weisgerber, Jean. "Aspects de l'espace romanesque: *Moll Flanders*." *Revue des Langues Vivantes*, 40 (1974), 503-510.

Winsor, Kathleen, Louis Kronenberger, and Lyman Bryson. "*Moll Flanders*," in George D. Crothers, ed., *Invitation to Learning*. 1966. Pp. 4-14.

Wolff, Erwin. *Der englische Roman*. 1968. Pp. 36-38.

Robinson Crusoe, 1719

Böker, Uwe. "Sir Walter Ralegh, Daniel Defoe und die Namengebung in Aphra Behns *Oroonoko*." *Anglia*, 90 (1972), 98-102.

Brooks, Douglas. *Number and Pattern*. 1973. Pp. 18-26.

Echeruo, M. J. C. "The 'Savage Hero' in English Literature of the Enlightenment." *English Studies in Africa*, 15 (1972), 5-7, 8-11.

Egan, James. "Crusoe's Monarchy and the Puritan Concept of the Self." *Studies in English Literature, 1500-1900*, 13 (1973), 451-460.

Göller, Karl Heinz. *"Romance" und "novel."* 1972. Pp. 144-149.

Hahn, H. G. "An Approach to Character Development in Defoe's Narrative Prose." *Philological Quarterly*, 51 (1972), 854-858.

Hardy, Barbara. *The Appropriate Form*. 1964. Pp. 54-61.

James, E. Anthony. *Daniel Defoe's Many Voices*. 1972. Pp. 165-199.

James, E. Anthony. "Defoe's Narrative Artistry: Naming and Describing in *Robinson Crusoe*." *Costerus*, 5 (1972), 52-66.

Johnson, Abby Arthur. "Old Bones Uncovered: A Reconsideration of *Robinson Crusoe*." *CLA Journal*, 17 (1973), 271-278.

Kahler, Erich. *The Inward Turn of Narrative*. 1973. Pp. 89-96.

Knowles, A. S., Jr. "Defoe, Swift, and Fielding: Notes on the Retirement Theme," in Larry S. Champion, ed., *Quick Springs of Sense*. 1974. Pp. 121-123.

Nordon, Pierre. *"Robinson Crusoe*: Unité et contradictions." *Archives des Lettres Modernes*, 80 (1967), 3-39.

Novak, Maximillian E. "Imaginary Islands and Real Beasts: The Imaginative Genesis of *Robinson Crusoe*." *Tennessee Studies in Literature*, 19 (1974), 57-78.

Otten, Kurt. *Der englische Roman*. 1971. Pp. 52-56.

Peck, Daniel H. *"Robinson Crusoe*: The Moral Geography of Limitation." *Journal of Narrative Technique*, 3 (1973), 20-31.

Rasmussen, Kirk G. *"Robinson Crusoe*: A Motif of Initiation." *Proceedings of the Utah Academy of Sciences, Arts, and Letters*, 47 (1970), 19-24.

Rexroth, Kenneth. *The Elastic Retort*. 1973. Pp. 59-63.

Rogers, Pat. "Crusoe's Home." *Essays in Criticism*, 24 (1974), 375-390.

Rovetto, Matteo. "Influence ou coincidence entre *Robinson Crusoe* de Defoe et *L'Ile des esclaves* de Marivaux." *Belfagor*, 30 (1975), 217-221.

Siegel, Sally Dewald. "Everymen's Defoe: Paradox as Unity in *Robinson Crusoe*." *Thoth*, 14 (1973-1974), 51-56.

Sutherland, James. *Daniel Defoe*. 1971. Pp. 123-143.

Thornburg, Thomas R. *"Robinson Crusoe*." *Ball State University Forum*, 15:3 (1974), 11-18.

Weimann, Robert. "Defoe: *Robinson Crusoe*," in Franz K. Stanzel, ed., *Der englische Roman*. 1969. Vol. I, 108-143.

Wolff, Erwin. *Der englische Roman*. 1968. Pp. 29-36.

Zweig, Paul. *The Adventurer*. 1974. Pp. 113-133.

Roxana, 1724

Brooks, Douglas. *Number and Pattern*. 1973. Pp. 53-60.

Hahn, H. G. "An Approach to Character Development in Defoe's Narrative Prose." *Philological Quarterly*, 51 (1972), 854-858.

Higdon, David Leon. "The Critical Fortunes and Misfortunes of Defoe's *Roxana*." *Bucknell Review*, 20 (1972), 67-82.

James, E. Anthony. *Daniel Defoe's Many Voices*. 1972. Pp. 161-163, 231-253.

Jenkins, Ralph E. "The Structure of *Roxana*." *Studies in the Novel*, 2 (1970), 145-158.

Kestner, Joseph A., III. "Defoe and Madame de LaFayette: *Roxana* and *La Princesse de Monpensier*." *Papers on Language and Literature*, 8 (1972), 297-301.

Kropf, C. R. "Theme and Structure in Defoe's *Roxana*." *Studies in English Literature, 1500-1900*, 12 (1972), 467-480.

Olshin, Toby A. " 'Thoughtful of the Main Chance': Defoe and the Cycle of Anxiety." *Hartford Studies in Literature*, 6 (1974), 121-122.

Shinagel, Michael. *Daniel Defoe*. 1968. Pp. 178-197.

Smith, LeRoy W. "Daniel Defoe: Incipient Pornographer." *Literature and Psychology*, 22 (1972), 165-177.

Sutherland, James. *Daniel Defoe*. 1971. Pp. 205-216.

Toth, Erwin. "Die Funktion des Dialogs bei Daniel Defoe." *Germanisch-Romanische Monatsschrift*, 22 (1972), 247-255.

Walton, James. "The Romance of Gentility: Defoe's Heroes and Heroines." *Literary Monographs*, 4 (1971), 122-135.

WALTER DE LA MARE

At First Sight, 1928

McCrosson, Doris Ross. *Walter de la Mare*. 1966. Pp. 137-140.

Henry Brocken, 1904

McCrosson, Doris Ross. *Walter de la Mare*. 1966. Pp. 84-94.

Memoirs of a Midget, 1921

McCrosson, Doris Ross. *Walter de la Mare*. 1966. Pp. 122-136.

Wagenknecht, Edward. "Walter de la Mare." *Etudes Anglaises*, 26 (1973), 292-295.

The Return, 1910

McCrosson, Doris Ross. *Walter de la Mare*. 1966. Pp. 102-121.

The Three Mulla-Mulgars, 1910

McCrosson, Doris Ross. *Walter de la Mare*. 1966. Pp. 95-101.

THOMAS DELONEY

Jack of Newbury, 1597

Davis, Walter R. *Idea and Act*. 1969. Pp. 238-252.
Dorinsville, Max. "Design in Deloney's *Jack of Newbury*." *Publications of the Modern Language Association*, 88 (1973), 233-239.

Thomas of Reading, 1597

Davis, Walter. *Idea and Act*. 1969. Pp. 270-280.

WILLIAM FREND DE MORGAN

Alice-For-Short, 1907

Kermode, Frank. "The English Novel, circa 1907," in Reuben A. Brower, ed., *Twentieth-Century Literature in Retrospect*. 1971. Pp. 50-52.

CHARLES DICKENS

Barnaby Rudge, 1841

Brown, Arthur Washburn. *Sexual Analysis of Dickens' Props*. 1971. Pp. 58-67, 75-80.
Dabney, Ross H. *Love and Property*. 1967. Pp. 22-30.
Davis, Earle. *The Flint and the Flame*. 1963. Pp. 140-143.
Gold, Joseph. *Charles Dickens*. 1972. Pp. 116-129.
Hollingsworth, Keith. *The Newgate Novel*. 1963. Pp. 177-182.
Hornback, Bert G. *"Noah's Arkitecture."* 1972. Pp. 35-41.
Kincaid, James R. *Dickens and the Rhetoric of Laughter*. 1971. Pp. 105-131.
Klotz, Volker. *Die erzählte Stadt*. 1969. Pp. 147-163.
Lary, N. M. *Dostoevsky and Dickens*. 1973. Pp. 126-134.
Lucas, John. *The Melancholy Man*. 1970. Pp. 92-112.
Manning, Sylvia Bank. *Dickens as Satirist*. 1971. Pp. 63-69.
Robinson, Roger. "The Influence of Fielding on *Barnaby Rudge*." *AUMLA*, No. 40 (1973), 183-197.

Bleak House, 1853

Barnard, Robert. *Imagery and Theme*. 1974. Pp. 62-76.
Bičanič, Sonia. "Cats, Birds and Freedom." *Studia Romanica et Anglica Zagrabiensia*, 29-32 (1970-1971), 515-522.
Bizam, Lenke. *Kritikai allegoriak Dickensröl es Kafkarol*. 1970. Pp. 260-275.
Blount, Trevor. "Dickens and Mr. Krook's Spontaneous Combustion." *Dickens Studies Annual*, 1 (1970), 183-211.
Brook, G. L. *The Language of Dickens*. 1970. Pp. 16-17, 39-41.

Butt, J., and I. F. Clarke. *The Victorians and Social Protest.* 1973. Pp. 88-92.

Carey, John. *The Violent Effigy.* 1973. Pp. 86-93, 120-123.

Conrad, Peter. *The Victorian Treasure-House.* 1973. Pp. 65-105.

Dabney, Ross H. *Love and Property.* 1967. Pp. 79-92.

Daleski, Herman M. *Dickens and the Art of Analogy.* 1970. Pp. 156-190.

Davis, Earle. *The Flint and the Flame.* 1963. Pp. 197-214.

Donovan, Robert Alan. *The Shaping Vision.* 1966. Pp. 206-237.

Ericksen, Donald H. "Harold Skimpole: Dickens and the Early 'Art for Art's Sake' Movement." *Journal of English and Germanic Philology,* 72 (1973), 48-59.

Farrow, Anthony. "The Cosmic Point of View in *Bleak House.*" *Cithara,* 13:2 (1974), 34-45.

Fleissner, R. F. "Charles Dickens and His China: The Architecture of *Bleak House.*" *Tamkang Review,* 3 (October 1972), 159-170.

Gold, Joseph. *Charles Dickens.* 1972. Pp. 185-195.

Goldberg, Michael. *Carlyle and Dickens.* 1972. Pp. 59-77.

Gose, Elliott B., Jr. *Imagination Indulged.* 1972. Pp. 73-97.

Grillo, Virgil. *Charles Dickens' "Sketches by Boz."* 1974. Pp. 213-217.

Grundy, Dominick E. "Growing Up Dickensian." *Literature and Psychology,* 22 (1972), 100-105.

Guerard, Albert J. "The Illuminating Distortion." *Novel,* 5 (1972), 112-115.

Hornback, Bert G. "*Noah's Arkitecture.*" 1972. Pp. 83-99.

Leavis, F. R., and Q. D. Leavis. *Dickens.* 1970. Pp. 118-186.

Lucas, John "Dickens and Arnold." *Renaissance and Modern Studies,* 16 (1972), 102-111.

Lucas, John. *The Melancholy Man.* 1970. Pp. 202-243.

Manning, Sylvia Bank. *Dickens as Satirist.* 1971. Pp. 101-131.

Melada, Ivan. *The Captain of Industry.* 1970. Pp. 157-160.

Middlebro', Tom. "Esther Summerson: A Plea for Justice." *Queen's Quarterly,* 77 (1970), 252-259.

Moers, Ellen. "*Bleak House:* The Agitating Women." *Dickensian,* 69 (1973), 13-24.

Ousby, Ian. "The Broken Glass: Vision and Comprehension in *Bleak House.*" *Nineteenth-Century Fiction,* 29 (1975), 381-392.

Quirk, Eugene F. "Tulkinghorn's Buried Life: A Study of Character in *Bleak House.*" *Journal of English and Germanic Philology,* 72 (1973), 526-535.

Sadoff, Dianne F. "Change and Changelessness in *Bleak House.*" *Victorian Newsletter,* No. 46 (1974), 5-10.

Sampson, Edward. "The Problem of Communication in *Bleak House,*" in Bradford B. Broughton, ed., *Twenty-Seven to One.* 1970. Pp. 121-123.

Smith, Mary Daehler. " 'All Her Perfections Tarnished': The Thematic Function of Esther Summerson." *Victorian Newsletter,* No. 38 (1970), 10-14.

Steele, Peter. "Dickens and the Grotesque." *Quadrant*, 17 (1973), 15-23.

Steig, Michael, and F. A. C. Wilson. "Hortense Versus Bucket: The Ambiguity of Order in *Bleak House*." *Modern Language Quarterly*, 33 (1972), 289-298.

Stoehr, Taylor. *Dickens*. 1965. Pp. 137-170.

Stoll, John E. "Psychological Dissociation in the Victorian Novel." *Literature and Psychology*, 20 (1970), 69-70.

Swinden, Patrick. *Unofficial Selves*. 1973. Pp. 27-47.

Thompson, Leslie M. "*Bleak House*: Dickens's Criticism of the 'Gospel of Work.'" *Re: Arts and Letters*, 1 (1968), 36-42.

Tomlinson, T. B. "Dickens and Individualism: *Dombey and Son, Bleak House*." *Critical Review* (Melbourne), No. 15 (1972), 68-81.

Wallins, Roger P. "Dickens and Decomposition." *Dickens Studies Newsletter*, 5 (1974), 68-70.

Wilson, John R. "Dickens and Christian Mystery." *South Atlantic Quarterly*, 73 (1974), 532-534.

Zwerdling, Alex. "Esther Summerson Rehabilitated." *Publications of the Modern Language Association*, 88 (1973), 429-439.

The Chimes, 1844

Cazamian, Louis. *The Social Novel in England*. 1973. Pp. 126-137.

Goldberg, Michael. *Carlyle and Dickens*. 1972. Pp. 34-38, 41-44.

Slater, Michael. "Carlyle and Jerrold into Dickens: A Study of *The Chimes*," in Ada Nisbet and Blake Nevius, eds., *Dickens Centennial Essays*. 1971. Pp. 184-204.

Tarr, Rodger L. "Dickens' Debt to Carlyle's 'Justice Metaphor' in *The Chimes*." *Nineteenth-Century Fiction*, 27 (1972), 208-215.

A Christmas Carol, 1843

Butt, John. *Pope, Dickens and Others*. 1969. Pp. 130-139.

Donovan, Frank. *Dickens and Youth*. 1968. Pp. 223-226.

Gilbert, Elliot L. "The Ceremony of Innocence: Charles Dickens' *A Christmas Carol*." *Publications of the Modern Language Association*, 90 (1975), 22-31.

Gold, Joseph. *Charles Dickens*. 1972. Pp. 147-154.

Goldberg, Michael. *Carlyle and Dickens*. 1972. Pp. 32-34, 39-41.

Lucas, John. *The Melancholy Man*. 1970. Pp. 137-141.

Patten, Robert L. "Dickens Time and Again." *Dickens Studies Annual*, 2 (1972), 163-196.

David Copperfield, 1850

Brook, G. L. *The Language of Dickens*. 1970. Pp. 118-122.

Brown, Arthur Washburn. *Sexual Analysis of Dickens' Props*. 1971. Pp. 147-152.

Brown, Janet H. "The Narrator's Role in *David Copperfield*." *Dickens Studies Annual*, 2 (1972), 197-207.

Buckley, Jerome Hamilton. *Season of Youth*. 1974. Pp. 30-44.
Butt, J., and I. F. Clarke. *The Victorians and Social Protest*. 1973. Pp. 85-88.
Carey, John. *The Violent Effigy*. 1973. Pp. 126-130, 131-139, 169-172.
Dabney, Ross H. *Love and Property*. 1967. Pp. 66-79.
Davis, Earle. *The Flint and the Flame*. 1963. Pp. 157-182.
Donovan, Frank. *Dickens and Youth*. 1968. Pp. 24-60.
Ganz, Margaret. "The Vulnerable Ego: Dickens' Humor in Decline." *Dickens Studies Annual*, 1 (1970), 32-34.
Gold, Joseph. *Charles Dickens*. 1972. Pp. 175-184.
Grundy, Dominick E. "Growing Up Dickensian." *Literature and Psychology*, 22 (1972), 100-105.
Hornback, Bert G. *"Noah's Arkitecture."* 1972. Pp. 63-82.
Hughes, Felicity. "Narrative Complexity in *David Copperfield*." *ELH*, 41 (1974), 89-105.
Hurley, Edward. "Dickens' Portrait of the Artist." *Victorian Newsletter*, No. 38 (1970), 1-5.
Kettle, Arnold. "Einführung in die englische Romanliteratur," in Viktor Zmegač, ed., *Marxistische Literaturkritik*. 1970. Pp. 222-227.
Kincaid, James R. *Dickens and the Rhetoric of Laughter*. 1971. Pp. 162-191.
Lary, N. M. *Dostoevsky and Dickens*. 1973. Pp. 119-123, 150-153.
Leavis, F. R., and Q. D. Leavis. *Dickens*. 1970. Pp. 34-117.
Lucas, John. *The Melancholy Man*. 1970. Pp. 166-201.
Manning, Sylvia Bank. *Dickens as Satirist*. 1971. Pp. 96-98.
Oppel, Horst. "Dickens: *David Copperfield*," in Franz K. Stanzel, ed., *Der englische Roman*. 1969. Vol. II, 112-157.
Oppel, Horst. "Die Vergegenwärtigung des Erzählten in *David Copperfield*," in Heinz Reinhold, ed., *Charles Dickens*. 1969. Pp. 37-58.
Reed, John R. "Confinement and Character in Dickens' Novels." *Dickens Studies Annual*, 1 (1970), 51-54.
Rogers, Robert. *A Psychoanalytic Study*. 1970. P. 115.
Robison, Roselee. "Time, Death and the River in Dickens' Novels." *English Studies*, 53 (1972), 436-454.
Worth, George J. "The Control of Emotional Response in *David Copperfield*," in George Goodin, ed., *The English Novel*. 1972. Pp. 97-108.

Dombey and Son, 1848

Adamowski, Thomas H. "Dombey and Son and Sutpen and Son." *Studies in the Novel*, 4 (1972), 378-384.
Barnard, Robert. *Imagery and Theme*. 1974. Pp. 49-61.
Dabney, Ross H. *Love and Property*. 1967. Pp. 50-65.
Daleski, Herman M. *Dickens and the Art of Analogy*. 1970. Pp. 116-155.
Davis, Earle. *The Flint and the Flame*. 1963. Pp. 150-156.

Donoghue, Denis. "The English Dickens and *Dombey and Son*," in Ada Nisbet and Blake Nevius, ed., *Dickens Centennial Essays*. 1971. Pp. 1-21.

Donovan, Frank. *Dickens and Youth*. 1968. Pp. 115-125.

Gold, Joseph. *Charles Dickens*. 1972. Pp. 155-174.

Goldberg, Michael. *Carlyle and Dickens*. 1972. Pp. 45-58.

Grillo, Virgil. *Charles Dickens' "Sketches by Boz."* 1974. Pp. 207-211.

Halperin, John. *Egoism and Self-Discovery*. 1974. Pp. 81-103.

Hardy, Barbara. "Dickens and the Passions," in Ada Nisbet and Blake Nevius, ed., *Dickens Centennial Essays*. 1971. Pp. 75-78.

Hornback, Bert G. *"Noah's Arkitecture."* 1972. Pp. 52-62.

Lary, N. M. *Dostoevsky and Dickens*. 1973. Pp. 56-66.

Leavis, F. R., and Q. D. Leavis. *Dickens*. 1970. Pp. 1-30.

Lucas, John. *The Melancholy Man*. 1970. Pp. 141-165.

Manning, Sylvia Bank. *Dickens as Satirist*. 1971. Pp. 87-95.

Meckier, Jerome. "Dickens and *King Lear*: A Myth for Victorian England." *South Atlantic Quarterly*, 71 (1972), 75-90.

Milner, Ian. "The Dickens Drama: Mr. Dombey," in Ada Nisbet and Blake Nevius, eds., *Dickens Centennial Essays*. 1971. Pp. 155-165.

Milner, Ian. "Dickens's Style: A Textual Parallel in *Dombey and Son* and *Daniel Deronda*." *Philologica Pragensia*, 17 (1974), 209-210.

Pickering, Samuel F., Jr. *"Dombey and Son* and Dickens's Unitarian Period." *Georgia Review*, 26 (1972), 442-454.

Robison, Roselee. "Time, Death and the River in Dickens' Novels." *English Studies*, 53 (1972), 436-454.

Sobel, Margaret. "Balzac's *Le Père Goriot* and Dickens's *Dombey and Son*: A Comparison." *Rice University Studies*, 59 (Summer 1973), 71-81.

Steig, Michael. "Iconography of Sexual Conflict in *Dombey and Son*." *Dickens Studies Annual*, 1 (1970), 161-167.

Talon, Henri. *"Dombey and Son*: A Closer Look at the Text." *Dickens Studies Annual*, 1 (1970), 147-160.

Tomlinson, T. B. "Dickens and Individualism: *Dombey and Son, Bleak House."* *Critical Review* (Melbourne), No. 15 (1972), 65-68.

Watson, Thomas L. "The Ethics of Feasting: Dickens' Dramatic Use of *Agape*," in Thomas Austin Kirby and William John Olive, eds., *Essays in Honor of Esmond Linworth Marilla*. 1970. Pp. 248-250.

Williams, Ioan. *The Realist Novel*. 1974. Pp. 145-148.

Great Expectations, 1861

Axton, William F. *"Great Expectations* Yet Again." *Dickens Studies Annual*, 2 (1972), 278-293.

Barnard, Robert. "Imagery and Theme in *Great Expectations*." *Dickens Studies Annual*, 1 (1970), 238-251.

Barnard, Robert. *Imagery and Theme*. 1974. Pp. 106-119.

Brown, Arthur Washburn. *Sexual Analysis of Dickens' Props*. 1971. Pp. 144-146.

Buckley, Jerome Hamilton. *Season of Youth*. 1974. Pp. 43-62.
Butt, J., and I. F. Clarke. *The Victorians and Social Protest*. 1973. Pp. 95-99.
Carey, John. *The Violent Effigy*. 1973. Pp. 45-48, 51-53, 131-134.
Carolan, Katherine. "Dickens' Last Christmases." *Dalhousie Review*, 52 (1972), 373-383.
Colwell, C. Carter. *The Tradition of British Literature*. 1971. Pp. 311-318.
Crawford, John W. "The Garden Imagery in *Great Expectations*." *Research Studies*, 39 (1971), 63-67.
Dabney, Ross H. *Love and Property*. 1967. Pp. 125-148.
Daleski, Herman M. *Dickens and the Art of Analogy*. 1970. Pp. 237-269.
Davis, Earle. *The Flint and the Flame*. 1963. Pp. 254-263.
Donovan, Frank. *Dickens and Youth*. 1968. Pp. 185-196.
Emmett, V. J., Jr. "The Endings of *Great Expectations*." *North Dakota Quarterly*, 41 (Autumn 1973), 5-11.
Ericksen, Donald H. "Demonic Imagery and the Quest for Identity in Dickens' *Great Expectations*." *Illinois Quarterly*, 33 (1970), 4-11.
Flynn, James. "Miss Havisham." *Recovering Literature*, 1 (Fall 1972), 40-49.
French, A. L. "Beating and Cringing: *Great Expectations*." *Essays in Criticism*, 24 (1974), 147-168.
Gold, Joseph. *Charles Dickens*. 1972. Pp. 241-254.
Grundy, Dominick E. "Growing Up Dickensian." *Literature and Psychology*, 22 (1972), 100-105.
Halperin, John. *Egoism and Self-Discovery*. 1974. Pp. 109-123.
d'Hangest, G. "Dickens et les personnages de *Great Expectations*." *Etudes Anglaises*, 24 (1971), 126-146.
Hardy, Barbara. "Dickens and the Passions," in Ada Nisbet and Blake Nevius, eds., *Dickens Centennial Essays*. 1971. Pp. 81-84.
Hornback, Bert G. *"Noah's Arkitecture."* 1972. Pp. 125-137.
Inglis, Fred. *An Essential Discipline*. 1968. Pp. 225-232.
Killy, Walther. *Wirklichkeit und Kunstcharakter*. 1963. Pp. 104-124.
Leavis, F. R., and Q. D. Leavis. *Dickens*. 1970. Pp. 277-313.
Lelchuk, Alan. "Self, Family, and Society in *Great Expectations*." *Sewanee Review*, 78 (1970), 407-426.
von Lempruch, Nils-Göran. "Some Grotesque Characters in Dickens's *Great Expectations*." *Moderna Sprak*, 67 (1973), 328-332.
Lucas, John. *The Melancholy Man*. 1970. Pp. 287-314.
McWilliams, John P., Jr. *"Great Expectations:* The Beacon, the Gibbet, and the Ship." *Dickens Studies Annual*, 2 (1972), 255-266.
Manning, Sylvia Bank. *Dickens as Satirist*. 1971. Pp. 192-198.
Millhauser, Milton. "Great Expectations: The Three Endings." *Dickens Studies Annual*, 2 (1972), 267-277.
Mills, Nicolaus. *American and English Fiction*. 1973. Pp. 93-109.

Robison, Roselee. "Time, Death and the River in Dickens' Novels." *English Studies*, 53 (1972), 436-454.

Rosenberg, Edgar. "A Preface to *Great Expectations*: The Pale Usher Dusts His Lexicons." *Dickens Studies Annual*, 2 (1972), 294-335.

Rosenberg, Edgar. "Small Talk in Hammersmith: Chapter 23 of *Great Expectations.*" *Dickensian*, 69 (1973), 90-101.

Shores, Lucille P. "The Character of Estella in *Great Expectations.*" *Massachusetts Studies in English*, 3 (1972), 91-99.

Silver, Alain. "The Untranquil Light: David Lean's *Great Expectations.*" *Literature/Film Quarterly*, 2 (1974), 140-152.

Smith, John T. "The Two Endings of *Great Expectations*: A Re-evaluation." *Thoth*, 12 (Fall 1971), 11-17.

Sossaman, Stephen. "Language and Communication in *Great Expectations.*" *Dickens Studies Newsletter*, 5 (1974), 66-68.

Stoehr, Taylor. *Dickens.* 1965. Pp. 101-137.

Talon, Henri, "Space, Time, and Memory in *Great Expectations.*" *Dickens Studies Annual*, 3 (1974), 122-133.

Tate, Eleanor. "Kafka's *The Castle*: Another Dickens Novel?" *Southern Review* (Adelaide), 7 (1974), 157-168.

Thomsen, Christian W. "Das Groteske in Charles Dickens' *Great Expectations.*" *Anglia*, 92 (1974), 113-142.

Watkins, G. M. "The Two Endings of *Great Expectations.*" *Anglo-Welsh Review*, 21 (1972), 139-144.

Watson, Thomas L. "The Ethics of Feasting: Dickens' Dramatic Use of *Agape*," in Thomas Austin Kirby and William John Olive, eds., *Essays in Honor of Esmond Linworth Marilla.* 1970. Pp. 250-252.

Weinstein, Arnold L. *Vision and Response.* 1974. Pp. 36-49.

Williams, Ioan. *The Realist Novel.* 1974. Pp. 148-155.

Wilson, John R. "Dickens and Christian Mystery." *South Atlantic Quarterly*, 73 (1974), 534-536.

Winner, Anthony. "Character and Knowledge in Dickens: The Enigma of Jaggers." *Dickens Studies Annual*, 3 (1974), 100-121.

Wolfe, Peter. "The Fictional Crux and the Double Structure of *Great Expectations.*" *South Atlantic Quarterly*, 73 (1974), 335-347.

Zambrano, A. L. "*Great Expectations*: Dickens and David Lean." *Literature/Film Quarterly*, 2 (1974), 154-161.

Zambrano, Ana Laura. "*Great Expectations*: Dickens' Style in Terms of Film." *Hartford Studies in Literature*, 4 (1972), 104-113.

Hard Times, 1854

Barnard, Robert. *Imagery and Theme.* 1974. Pp. 77-90.

Benn, J. Miriam. "A Landscape with Figures: Characterization and Expression in *Hard Times.*" *Dickens Studies Annual*, 1 (1970), 168-182.

Brook, G. L. *The Language of Dickens.* 1970. Pp. 87-88, 125-130.

Cazamian, Louis. *The Social Novel in England.* 1973. Pp. 162-173.

Clayborough, Arthur. *The Grotesque in English Literature.* 1965. Pp. 226-236.

Craig, David. *The Real Foundations*. 1973. Pp. 109-131.
Davis, Earle. *The Flint and the Flame*. 1963. Pp. 214-224.
Dibon, Anne-Marie. "Form and Value in the French and English 19th-Century Novel." *Modern Language Notes*, 87 (1972), 910-911.
Donovan, Frank. *Dickens and Youth*. 1968. Pp. 152-159.
Gold, Joseph. *Charles Dickens*. 1972. Pp. 196-207.
Goldberg, Michael. *Carlyle and Dickens*. 1972. Pp. 78-99.
Goldknopf, David. *The Life of the Novel*. 1972. Pp. 143-158.
Grillo, Virgil. *Charles Dickens' "Sketches by Boz."* 1974. Pp. 211-213.
Heck, Edwin J. "*Hard Times*: The Handwriting on the Factory Wall." *English Journal*, 61 (1972), 23-27.
Hornback, Bert G. *"Noah's Arkitecture."* 1972. Pp. 111-117.
Klotz, Volker. *Die erzählte Stadt*. 1969. Pp. 163-166.
Kotzin, Michael C. *Dickens and the Fairy Tale*. 1972. Pp. 42-44.
Leavis, F. R., and Q. D. Leavis. *Dickens*. 1970. Pp. 187-212.
Leimberg, Ingeborg. "*Hard Times*: Zeitbezug und überzeitliche Bedeutung—Zeitkritische Fakten im fiktionalen Zusammenhang." *Germanisch-Romanische Monatsschrift*, 21 (1971), 269-296.
Lougy, Robert E. "Dickens' *Hard Times*: The Romance as Radical Literature." *Dickens Studies Annual*, 2 (1972), 237-254.
Manning, Sylvia Bank. *Dickens as Satirist*. 1971. Pp. 132-154.
Meckier, Jerome. "Dickens and the Dystopian Novel: From *Hard Times* to *Lady Chatterley*," in R. G. Collins, ed., *The Novel*. 1972. Pp. 51-58.
Meckier, Jerome. "Dickens and *King Lear*: A Myth for Victorian England." *South Atlantic Quarterly*, 71 (1972), 75-90.
Melada, Ivan. *The Captain of Industry*. 1970. Pp. 110-115.
Palmer, William J. "*Hard Times*: A Dickens Fable of Personal Salvation." *Dalhousie Review*, 52 (1972), 67-77.
Sadrin, Anny. "A Plea for Gradgrind." *Yearbook of English Studies*, 3 (1973), 196-205.
Sloane, David E. E. "Phrenology in *Hard Times*." *Dickens Studies Newsletter*, 5 (1974), 9-11.
Smith, Anne. "*Hard Times* and *The Times* Newspaper." *Dickensian*, 69 (1973), 153-162.
Smith, David. "*Mary Barton* and *Hard Times*: Their Social Insights." *Mosaic*, 5 (Winter 1971-1972), 104-112.
Stoehr, Taylor. *Dickens*. 1965. Pp. 171-175.
Sullivan, Mary Rose. "Black and White Characters in *Hard Times*." *Victorian Newsletter*, No. 38 (1970), 5-10.
Tick, Stanley. "*Hard Times*, Page One: An Analysis." *Victorian Newsletter*, No. 46 (1974), 20-22.
Vooys, Sijna de. *The Psychological Element*. 1966. Pp. 43-50.
Watson, Thomas L. "The Ethics of Feasting: Dickens' Dramatic Use of *Agape*," in Thomas Austin Kirby and William John Olive, eds., *Essays in Honor of Esmond Linworth Marilla*. 1970. Pp. 246-248.
Winters, Warrington. "Dickens' *Hard Times*: The Lost Childhood." *Dickens Studies Annual*, 2 (1972), 217-236.

The Haunted Man, 1847

Butt, John. *Pope, Dickens and Others.* 1969. Pp. 143-148.
Donovan, Frank. *Dickens and Youth.* 1968. Pp. 217-223.

Little Dorrit, 1857

Barnard, Robert. *Imagery and Theme.* 1974. Pp. 91-105.
Beaty, Jerome. "The 'Soothing Songs' of *Little Dorrit*: New Light
    on Dickens's Darkness," in Clyde de L. Ryals, ed., *Nineteenth-
    Century Literary Perspectives.* 1974. Pp. 219-236.
Bizam, Lenke. *Kritikai allegoriak Dickensröl es Kafkarol.* 1970.
    Pp. 92-101.
Brook, G. L. *The Language of Dickens.* 1970. Pp. 66-69.
Burgan, William. "Little Dorrit in Italy." *Nineteenth-Century Fic-
    tion,* 29 (1975), 398-411.
Burgan, William. "People in the Setting of *Little Dorrit*." *Texas
    Studies in Literature and Language,* 15 (1973), 111-128.
Carey, John. *The Violent Effigy.* 1973. Pp. 76-79, 113-117.
Dabney, Ross H. *Love and Property.* 1967. Pp. 93-124.
Daleski, Herman M. *Dickens and the Art of Analogy.* 1970. Pp.
    191-236.
Davis, Earle. *The Flint and the Flame.* 1963. Pp. 224-235.
Donovan, Frank. *Dickens and Youth.* 1968. Pp. 103-109.
Easson, Angus. "Marshalsea Prisoners: Mr. Dorrit and Mr. Hemens."
    Dickens Studies Annual, 3 (1974), 77-86.
Feltes, N. N. "Community and the Limits of Liability in Two Mid-
    Victorian Novels." *Victorian Studies,* 17 (1974), 362-367.
Fleishman, Avrom. "Master and Servant in *Little Dorrit*." *Studies
    in English Literature, 1500-1900,* 14 (1974), 575-586.
Gold, Joseph. *Charles Dickens.* 1972. Pp. 208-230.
Grove, T. N. "The Psychological Prison of Arthur Clennam in Dick-
    ens's *Little Dorrit*." *Modern Language Review,* 68 (1973), 750-755.
Hardy, Barbara. "Dickens and the Passions," in Ada Nisbet and Blake
    Nevius, eds., *Dickens Centennial Essays.* 1971. Pp. 79-81.
Hewitt, Douglas. *The Approach to Fiction.* 1972. Pp. 85-102, 113-
    123, 130-132.
Hollington, Mike. "Time in *Little Dorrit*," in George Goodin, ed.,
    The English Novel. 1972. Pp. 109-125.
Hornback, Bert G. *"Noah's Arkitecture."* 1972. Pp. 99-110.
Kincaid, James R. *Dickens and the Rhetoric of Laughter.* 1971.
    Pp. 192-222.
Lary, N. M. *Dostoevsky and Dickens.* 1973. Pp. 85-104, 150-153.
Leavis, F. R., and Q. D. Leavis. *Dickens.* 1970. Pp. 213-276.
Lucas, John. *The Melancholy Man.* 1970. Pp. 244-286.
Manning, Sylvia Bank. *Dickens as Satirist.* 1971. Pp. 155-180.
Myers, William. "The Radicalism of *Little Dorrit*," in John Lucas,
    ed., *Literature and Politics.* 1971. Pp. 77-104.

Reed, John R. "Confinement and Character in Dickens' Novels." *Dickens Studies Annual*, 1 (1970), 45-48.

Roopnaraine, R. Rupert. "Time and the Circle in *Little Dorrit*." *Dickens Studies Annual*, 3 (1974), 54-76.

Stoehr, Taylor. *Dickens*. 1965. Pp. 175-195.

Tick, Stanley. "The Sad Case of Mr. Meagles." *Dickens Studies Annual*, 3 (1974), 87-99.

Martin Chuzzlewit, 1844

Barnard, Robert. *Imagery and Theme*. 1974. Pp. 37-48.

Beasley, Jerry C. "The Role of Tom Pinch in *Martin Chuzzlewit*." *Ariel*, 5:2 (1974), 77-89.

Brook, G. L. *The Language of Dickens*. 1970. Pp. 131-137.

Brown, Arthur Washburn. *Sexual Analysis of Dickens' Props*. 1971. Pp. 110-119, 122-127.

Burke, Alan R. "The House of Chuzzlewit and the Architectural City." *Dickens Studies Annual*, 3 (1974), 14-40.

Dabney, Ross H. *Love and Property*. 1967. Pp. 35-50.

Daleski, Herman M. *Dickens and the Art of Analogy*. 1970. Pp. 79-115.

Ganz, Margaret. "The Vulnerable Ego: Dickens' Humor in Decline." *Dickens Studies Annual*, 1 (1970), 30-32, 36-37.

Gold, Joseph. *Charles Dickens*. 1972. Pp. 130-146.

Gold, Joseph. "'Living in a Wale': *Martin Chuzzlewit*." *Dickens Studies Annual*, 2 (1972), 150-162.

Grillo, Virgil. *Charles Dickens' "Sketches by Boz*." 1974. Pp. 188-206.

Hannaford, Richard. "Irony and Sentimentality: Conflicting Modes in *Martin Chuzzlewit*." *Victorian Newsletter*, No. 46 (1974), 26-28.

Hornback, Bert G. *"Noah's Arkitecture."* 1972. Pp. 41-52.

Kincaid, James R. *Dickens and the Rhetoric of Laughter*. 1971. Pp. 132-161.

Lary, N. M. *Dostoevsky and Dickens*. 1973. Pp. 4-8, 36-40.

Lucas, John. *The Melancholy Man*. 1970. Pp. 113-137.

Manning, Sylvia Bank. *Dickens as Satirist*. 1971. Pp. 71-86.

Woodring, Carl. "Change in *Chuzzlewit*," in Clyde de L. Ryals, ed., *Nineteenth-Century Literary Perspectives*. 1974. Pp. 211-218.

The Mystery of Edwin Drood, 1870

Barnard, Robert. *Imagery and Theme*. 1974. Pp. 134-144.

Brown, Arthur Washburn. *Sexual Analysis of Dickens' Props*. 1971. Pp. 92-96, 168-171.

Carolan, Katherine. "Dickens' Last Christmases." *Dalhousie Review*, 52 (1972), 373-383.

Davis, Earle. *The Flint and the Flame*. 1963. Pp. 283-303.

Fisher, B. F., IV, and J. Turow. "Dickens and Fire Imagery." *Revue des Langues Vivantes*, 40 (1974), 367-370.

Gottschalk, Paul. "Time in *Edwin Drood*." *Dickens Studies Annual*, 1 (1970), 265-272.

Robison, Roselee. "Time, Death and the River in Dickens' Novels." *English Studies*, 53 (1972), 436-454.

Wing, George. "*Edwin Drood* and *Desperate Remedies*: Prototypes of Detective Fiction in 1870." *Studies in English Literature, 1500-1900*, 13 (1973), 677-680, 684-686.

Nicholas Nickleby, 1839

Barnard, Robert. *Imagery and Theme*. 1974. Pp. 25-36.

Dabney, Ross H. *Love and Property*. 1967. Pp. 14-20.

Donovan, Frank. *Dickens and Youth*. 1968. Pp. 110-115, 137-148.

Foltinek, Herbert. *Vorstufen zum viktorianischen Realismus*. 1968. Pp. 157-160.

Gold, Joseph. *Charles Dickens*. 1972. Pp. 66-92.

Grillo, Virgil. *Charles Dickens' "Sketches by Boz."* 1974. Pp. 129-167.

Hannaford, Richard. "Fairy-Tale Fantasy in *Nicholas Nickleby*." *Criticism*, 16 (1974), 247-259.

Hornback, Bert G. *"Noah's Arkitecture."* 1972. Pp. 21-29.

Lary, N. M. *Dostoevsky and Dickens*. 1973. Pp. 24-34.

Lucas, John. *The Melancholy Man*. 1970. Pp. 55-73.

Manning, Sylvia Bank. *Dickens as Satirist*. 1971. Pp. 54-57.

Meckier, Jerome. "The Faint Image of Eden: The Many Worlds of *Nicholas Nickleby*." *Dickens Studies Annual*, 1 (1970), 129-146.

Melada, Ivan. *The Captain of Industry*. 1970. Pp. 103-110.

Noffsinger, John W. "The Complexity of Ralph Nickleby." *Dickens Studies Newsletter*, 5 (1974), 112-114.

The Old Curiosity Shop, 1841

Brown, Arthur Washburn. *Sexual Analysis of Dickens' Props*. 1971. Pp. 26-38.

Dabney, Ross H. *Love and Property*. 1967. Pp. 20-22.

Donovan, Frank. *Dickens and Youth*. 1968. Pp. 88-103, 160-162, 167-176.

Engel, Monroe. "'A Kind of Allegory': *The Old Curiosity Shop*," in Morton W. Bloomfield, ed., *The Interpretation of Narrative*. 1970. Pp. 138-147.

Fisher, B. F., IV, and J. Turow. "Dickens and Fire Imagery." *Revue des Langues Vivantes*, 40 (1974), 360-364.

Gold, Joseph. *Charles Dickens*. 1972. Pp. 93-115.

Grillo, Virgil. *Charles Dickens' "Sketches by Boz."* 1974. Pp. 169-188.

Hornback, Bert G. *"Noah's Arkitecture."* 1972. Pp. 29-34.

Kincaid, James R. *Dickens and the Rhetoric of Laughter*. 1971. Pp. 76-104.

Lucas, John. *The Melancholy Man*. 1970. Pp. 73-92.

Manning, Sylvia Bank. *Dickens as Satirist*. 1971. Pp. 57-63.

Meckier, Jerome. "Dickens and *King Lear*: A Myth for Victorian England." *South Atlantic Quarterly*, 71 (1972), 75-90.

Pickering, Samuel F., Jr. "*The Old Curiosity Shop*: A Religious

Tract?" *Illinois Quarterly*, 36 (1973), 5-20.

Pratt, Branwen. "Sympathy for the Devil: A Dissenting View of Quilp." *Hartford Studies in Literature*, 6 (1974), 129-146.

Rogers, Philip. "The Dynamics of Time in *The Old Curiosity Shop*." *Nineteenth-Century Fiction*, 28 (1973), 127-144.

Oliver Twist, 1838

Cazamian, Louis. *The Social Novel in England*. 1973. Pp. 141-143.

Dabney, Ross H. *Love and Property*. 1967. Pp. 11-14.

Daleski, Herman M. *Dickens and the Art of Analogy*. 1970. Pp. 49-78.

Davis, Earle. *The Flint and the Flame*. 1963. Pp. 134-137.

Donovan, Frank. *Dickens and Youth*. 1968. Pp. 61-87.

Elmalih. N. "Valeurs et récit: *Oliver Twist*," in *Récit et roman*. 1972. Pp. 53-61.

Ferns, John. "*Oliver Twist*: Destruction of Love." *Queen's Quarterly*, 79 (1972), 87-92.

Foltinek, Herbert. *Vorstufen zum viktorianischen Realismus*. 1968. Pp. 132-136.

Gold, Joseph. *Charles Dickens*. 1972. Pp. 25-65.

Hollingsworth, Keith. *The Newgate Novel*. 1963. Pp. 111-131.

Hornback, Bert G. "*Noah's Arkitecture*." 1972. Pp. 14-21.

Johnson, Edgar, George Shuster, and Lyman Bryson. "*Oliver Twist*," in George D. Crothers, ed., *Invitation to Learning*. 1966. Pp. 99-107.

Kincaid, James R. *Dickens and the Rhetoric of Laughter*. 1971. Pp. 41-75.

Kotzin, Michael C. *Dickens and the Fairy Tale*. 1972. Pp. 49-51.

Lucas, John. *The Melancholy Man*. 1970. Pp. 21-54.

Manning, Sylvia Bank. *Dickens as Satirist*. 1971. Pp. 51-54.

Miller, J. Hillis. "The Fiction of Realism: *Sketches by Boz, Oliver Twist*, and Cruikshank's Illustrations," in Ada Nisbet and Blake Nevius, eds., *Dickens Centennial Essays*. 1971. Pp. 112-153.

Miller, J. Hillis. "*Sketches by Boz, Oliver Twist*, and Cruikshank's Illustrations," in *Charles Dickens and George Cruikshank*. 1971. Pp. 28-69.

Otten, Kurt. *Der englische Roman*. 1971. Pp. 126-132.

Slater, Michael. "On Reading *Oliver Twist*." *Dickensian*, 70 (1974), 75-81.

Steig, Michael. "Cruikshank's Peacock Feathers in *Oliver Twist*." *Ariel*, 4:2 (1973), 49-53.

Westburg, Barry. " 'His Allegorical Way of Expressing It': Civil War and Psychic Conflict in *Oliver Twist* and *A Child's History*." *Studies in the Novel*, 6 (1974), 27-37.

Wilson, John R. "Dickens and Christian Mystery." *South Atlantic Quarterly*, 73 (1974), 528-532.

Zambrano, Ana Laura. "Dickens and the Rise of Dramatic Realism: The Problem of Social Reform." *Silliman Journal*, 21 (1974), 69-74.

Our Mutual Friend, 1865

Altick, Richard D. "Education, Print, and Paper in *Our Mutual Friend*," in Clyde de L. Ryals, ed., *Nineteenth-Century Literary Perspectives*. 1974. Pp. 237-254.

Arnoldi, Richard. "Parallels Between *Our Mutual Friend* and the Alice Books." *Children's Literature: The Great Excluded*, 1 (1972), 54-57.

Barnard, Robert. *Imagery and Theme*. 1974. Pp. 120-133.

Borinski, Ludwig. "Dickens' Spätstil," in Heinz Reinhold, ed., *Charles Dickens*. 1969. Pp. 145-159.

Brook, G. L. *The Language of Dickens*. 1970. Pp. 38-40, 171-172.

Brown, Arthur Washburn. *Sexual Analysis of Dickens' Props*. 1971. Pp. 45-48, 133-138, 157-162, 164-168, 204-214.

Butt, J., and I. F. Clarke. *The Victorians and Social Protest*. 1973. Pp. 99-101.

Carey, John. *The Violent Effigy*. 1973. Pp. 108-111.

Conrad, Peter. *The Victorian Treasure-House*. 1973. Pp. 70-77.

Dabney, Ross H. *Love and Property*. 1967. Pp. 149-176.

Daleski, Herman M. *Dickens and the Art of Analogy*. 1970. Pp. 270-336.

Davis, Earle. *The Flint and the Flame*. 1963. Pp. 264-282.

Donovan, Frank. *Dickens and Youth*. 1968. Pp. 176-180.

Fisher, B. F., IV, and J. Turow. "Dickens and Fire Imagery." *Revue des Langues Vivantes*, 40 (1974), 365-367.

Friedman, Stanley. "The Motif of Reading in *Our Mutual Friend*." *Nineteenth-Century Fiction*, 28 (1973), 38-61.

Gold, Joseph. *Charles Dickens*. 1972. Pp. 255-274.

Hornback, Bert G. "*Noah's Arkitecture*." 1972. Pp. 137-155.

Kennedy, G. W. "Naming and Language in *Our Mutual Friend*." *Nineteenth-Century Fiction*, 28 (1973), 165-178.

Kincaid, James R. *Dickens and the Rhetoric of Laughter*. 1971. Pp. 223-252.

Lucas, John. *The Melancholy Man*. 1970. Pp. 315-345.

Manning, Sylvia Bank. *Dickens as Satirist*. 1971. Pp. 199-227.

Marlow, James E. "The Solecism in *Our Mutual Friend*." *Dickens Studies Newsletter*, 5 (1974), 7-9.

Palmer, William J. "The Movement of History in *Our Mutual Friend*." *Publications of the Modern Language Association*, 89 (1974), 487-495.

Patterson, Annabel M. "*Our Mutual Friend*: Dickens as the Compleat Angler." *Dickens Studies Annual*, 1 (1970), 252-264.

Robison, Roselee. "Time, Death and the River in Dickens' Novels." *English Studies*, 53 (1972), 436-454.

Robson, John M. "*Our Mutual Friend*: A Rhetorical Approach to the First Number." *Dickens Studies Annual*, 3 (1974), 198-213.

Stewart, Garrett. "The 'Golden Bower' of *Our Mutual Friend*." *ELH*, 40 (1973), 105-130.

Stoehr, Taylor. *Dickens*. 1965. Pp. 203-225.
Sucksmith, Harvey Peter. "The Dust-Heaps in *Our Mutual Friend*." *Essays in Criticism*, 23 (1973), 206-212.
Wilson, John R. "Dickens and Christian Mystery." *South Atlantic Quarterly*, 73 (1974), 536-538.

The Pickwick Papers, 1837

Dabney, Ross H. *Love and Property*. 1967. Pp. 7-11.
Daleski, Herman M. *Dickens and the Art of Analogy*. 1970. Pp. 17-48.
Davis, Earle. *The Flint and the Flame*. 1963. Pp. 28-36.
Fadiman, Clifton, Arthur Mizener, and Lyman Bryson. "*The Pickwick Papers*," in George D. Crothers, ed., *Invitation to Learning*. 1966. Pp. 90-98.
Gold, Joseph. *Charles Dickens*. 1972. Pp. 12-24.
Grillo, Virgil. *Charles Dickens' "Sketches by Boz."* 1974. Pp. 124-127.
Herbert, Christopher. "Converging Worlds in *Pickwick Papers*." *Nineteenth-Century Fiction*, 27 (1972), 1-20.
Hornback, Bert G. "*Noah's Arkitecture*." 1972. Pp. 9-14.
Kestner, Joseph. "Elements of Epic in *The Pickwick Papers*." *University of Dayton Review*, 9 (Summer 1972), 15-24.
Kincaid, James R. *Dickens and the Rhetoric of Laughter*. 1971. Pp. 20-40.
Lary, N. M. *Dostoevsky and Dickens*. 1973. Pp. 66-79.
Lucas, John. *The Melancholy Man*. 1970. Pp. 1-20.
Manheim, Leonard. "Dickens' Fools and Madmen." *Dickens Studies Annual*, 2 (1972), 74-77.
Manning, Sylvia Bank. *Dickens as Satirist*. 1971. Pp. 41-51.
Marcus, Steven. "Language into Structure: Pickwick Revisited." *Daedalus*, 101 (1972), 183-202.
Reed, John R. "Confinement and Character in Dickens' Novels." *Dickens Studies Annual*, 1 (1970), 41-43.
Reinhold, Heinz. "Dickens' früheste Darstellungen geisteskranker Zustände," in Heinz Reinhold, ed., *Charles Dickens*. 1969. Pp. 84-90.
Reinhold, Heinz. "*The Stroller's Tale* in Charles Dickens' *The Pickwick Papers*," in Heinz Reinhold, ed., *Charles Dickens*. 1969. Pp. 17-36.
Rexroth, Kenneth. *The Elastic Retort*. 1973. Pp. 98-102.
Rogers, Philip. "Mr. Pickwick's Innocence." *Nineteenth-Century Fiction*, 27 (1972), 21-37.
Wagner, Horst. "Zur Frage der Erzähleinschübe in *Don Quijote* und in den *Pickwick Papers*." *Arcadia*, 9 (1974), 3-19.
Watson, Thomas L. "The Ethics of Feasting: Dickens' Dramatic Use of *Agape*," in Thomas Austin Kirby and William John Olive, eds., *Essays in Honor of Esmond Linworth Marilla*. 1970. Pp. 244-246.
Williams, Gwenllian L. "Sam Weller." *Trivium*, No. 1 (1966), 88-101.
Zambrano, Ana Laura. "Dickens and Charles Mathews." *Moderna Sprak*, 66 (1972), 235-242.

A Tale of Two Cities, 1859

Davis, Earle. *The Flint and the Flame*. 1963. Pp. 238-254.
Gold, Joseph. *Charles Dickens*. 1972. Pp. 231-240.
Goldberg, Michael. *Carlyle and Dickens*. 1972. Pp. 100-128.
Halperin, John. *Egoism and Self-Discovery*. 1974. Pp. 103-109.
Hornback, Bert G. *"Noah's Arkitecture."* 1972. Pp. 118-124.
Lindsay, Jack. "A Tale of Two Cities." *Life and Letters*, 62 (1949), 191-204.
Manheim, Leonard. "A Tale of Two Characters: A Study in Multiple Projection." *Dickens Studies Annual*, 1 (1970), 229-237.
Manning, Sylvia Bank. *Dickens as Satirist*. 1971. Pp. 183-192.
Monod, Sylvère. "Dickens's Attitudes in *A Tale of Two Cities*," in Ada Nisbet and Blake Nevius, eds., *Dickens Centennial Essays*. 1971. Pp. 166-183.
Rance, Nicholas. *The Historical Novel*. 1975. Pp. 83-101.
Reinhold, Heinz. "Charles Dickens' Roman *A Tale of Two Cities* und das Publikum," in Heinz Reinhold, ed., *Charles Dickens*. 1969. Pp. 59-80.
Stoehr, Taylor. *Dickens*. 1965. Pp. 195-203.
Zambrano, Ana Laura. "The Styles of Dickens and Griffith: *A Tale of Two Cities* and *Orphans of the Storm*." *Language and Style*, 7 (1974), 53-60.

BENJAMIN DISRAELI

Alroy, 1832

Levine, Richard A. *Benjamin Disraeli*. 1968. Pp. 51-57.

Coningsby, 1844

Cazamian, Louis. *The Social Novel in England*. 1973. Pp. 183-191.
Frietzsche, Arthur H. "Action Is Not For Me: Disraeli's Sidonia and the Dream of Power." *Proceedings of the Utah Academy of Sciences, Arts, and Letters*, 37 (1959-1960), 45-49.
Levine, Richard A. *Benjamin Disraeli*. 1968. Pp. 61-86, 101-106.
Melada, Ivan. *The Captain of Industry*. 1970. Pp. 121-126.
Schwarz, Daniel R. "Progressive Dubiety: The Discontinuity of Disraeli's Political Trilogy." *Victorian Newsletter*, No. 47 (Spring 1975), 12-19.

Contarini Fleming, 1832

Levine, Richard A. *Benjamin Disraeli*. 1968. Pp. 43-51.

Endymion, 1880

Levine, Richard A. *Benjamin Disraeli*. 1968. Pp. 144-154.

Henrietta Temple, 1837

> Levine, Richard A. *Benjamin Disraeli*. 1968. Pp. 57-60.

Lothair, 1870

> Levine, Richard A. *Benjamin Disraeli*. 1968. Pp. 136-144.

Sybil, 1845

> Cazamian, Louis. *The Social Novel in England*. 1973. Pp. 191-207.
> Fido, Martin. "The Treatment of Rural Distress in Disraeli's *Sybil*." *Yearbook of English Studies*, 5 (1975), 153-163.
> Franke, Wolfgang. "Disraeli und Augustin Thierry: Zur Geschichte der Idee der 'Zwei Nationen.'" *Anglia*, 90 (1972), 105-117.
> Levine, Richard A. *Benjamin Disraeli*. 1968. Pp. 61-86, 107-114.
> Melada, Ivan. *The Captain of Industry*. 1970. Pp. 126-134.
> Schwarz, Daniel R. "Art and Argument in Disraeli's *Sybil*." *Journal of Narrative Technique*, 4 (1974), 19-31.
> Schwarz, Daniel R. "Progressive Dubiety: The Discontinuity of Disraeli's Political Trilogy. *Victorian Newsletter*, No. 47 (Spring 1975), 12-19.
> Tomlinson, T. B. "Love and Politics in the Early-Victorian Novel." *Critical Review* (Melbourne), No. 17 (1974), 133-134.

Tancred, 1847

> Cazamian, Louis. *The Social Novel in England*. 1973. Pp. 207-210.
> Harris, Wendell V. "Fiction and Metaphysics in the Nineteenth Century," in R. G. Collins, ed., *The Novel*. 1972. Pp. 66-67.
> Levine, Richard A. *Benjamin Disraeli*. 1968. Pp. 114-134.
> Schwarz, Daniel R. "Progressive Dubiety: The Discontinuity of Disraeli's Political Trilogy." *Victorian Newsletter*, No. 47 (Spring 1975), 12-19.

Venetia, 1837

> Duerksen, Roland A. *Shelleyan Ideas in Victorian Literature*. 1966. Pp. 71-90.
> Levine, Richard A. *Benjamin Disraeli*. 1968. Pp. 57-60.

Vivian Grey, 1826-1827

> Levine, Richard A. *Benjamin Disraeli*. 1968. Pp. 30-37.

The Young Duke, 1831

> Levine, Richard A. *Benjamin Disraeli*. 1968. Pp. 37-43.

NORMAN DOUGLAS

In the Beginning, 1927

Lindeman, Ralph D. *Norman Douglas*. 1965. Pp. 149-158.

South Wind, 1917

Greenlees, Ian. *Norman Douglas*. 1957. Pp. 22-30.
Lindeman, Ralph D. *Norman Douglas*. 1965. Pp. 122-141.
Matthews, Jack. "On Norman Douglas's *South Wind*," in David
Madden, ed., *Rediscoveries*. 1971. Pp. 191-196.

They Went, 1920

Lindeman, Ralph D. *Norman Douglas*. 1965. Pp. 141-149.

ARTHUR CONAN DOYLE

The Sign of the Four, 1890

Galichet, François. " 'Epistémologie' de Sherlock Holmes." *Critique*
(Paris), No. 273 (1970), 115-123.

A Study in Scarlet, 1887

Galichet, François. "'Epistémologie' de Sherlock Holmes. *Critique*
(Paris), No. 273 (1970), 115-123.
Gerber, Richard. "Namen als Symbol: Über Sherlock Holmes und das
Wesen des Kriminalromans." *Neue Rundschau*, 83 (1972), 504-509.

MARGARET DRABBLE

The Garrick Year, 1964

Beards, Virginia K. "Margaret Drabble: Novels of a Cautious Feminist." *Critique* (Atlanta), 15:1 (1973), 38-39, 41-42.
Bonfond, François. "Margaret Drabble: How to Express Subjective
Truth Through Fiction?" *Revue des Langues Vivantes*, 40 (1974),
46-48.

Jerusalem the Golden, 1967

Apter, T. E. "Margaret Drabble: The Glamour of Seriousness."
Human World, No. 12 (1973), 20-21.
Bonfond, François. "Margaret Drabble: How to Express Subjective
Truth Through Fiction?" *Revue des Langues Vivantes*, 40 (1974),
51-55.
Rose, Ellen Cronan. "Margaret Drabble: Surviving the Future."
Critique (Atlanta), 15:1 (1973), 7-9.

The Millstone, 1965

Bonfond, François. "Margaret Drabble: How to Express Subjective

Truth Through Fiction?" *Revue des Langues Vivantes*, 40 (1974), 48-51.

Hardin, Nancy S. "Drabble's *The Millstone*: A Fable for Our Times." *Critique* (Atlanta), 15:1 (1973), 22-34.

Wikborg, Eleanor. "A Comparison of Margaret Drabble's *The Millstone* with Its *Vecko-Revyn* Adaptation, 'Barnet Du Gav Mig.'" *Moderna Sprak*, 65 (1971), 305-311.

The Needle's Eye, 1972

Apter, T. E. "Margaret Drabble: The Glamour of Seriousness." *Human World*, No. 12 (1973), 24-28.

Mannheimer, Monica Lauritzen. "The Individual and Society in Contemporary British Fiction." *Moderna Sprak*, 68 (1974), 320-322.

Rose, Ellen Cronan. "Margaret Drabble: Surviving the Future." *Critique* (Atlanta), 15:1 (1973), 13-20.

A Summer Bird-Cage, 1963

Beards, Virginia K. "Margaret Drabble: Novels of a Cautious Feminist." *Critique* (Atlanta), 15:1 (1973), 36-38.

Bonfond, François. "Margaret Drabble: How to Express Subjective Truth Through Fiction?" *Revue des Langues Vivantes*, 40 (1974), 42-45.

The Waterfall, 1969

Apter, T. E. "Margaret Drabble: The Glamour of Seriousness." *Human World*, No. 12 (1973), 22-24.

Beards, Virginia K. "Margaret Drabble: Novels of a Cautious Feminist." *Critique* (Atlanta), 15:1 (1973), 39-40, 43-46.

Rose, Ellen Cronan. "Margaret Drabble: Surviving the Future." *Critique* (Atlanta), 15:1 (1973), 9-11, 13.

GEORGE DU MAURIER

The Martian, 1897

Ormond, Leonée. *George Du Maurier*. 1969. Pp. 483-491.

Peter Ibbetson, 1892

Ormond, Leonée. *George Du Maurier*. 1969. Pp. 416-430.

Trilby, 1894

Ormond, Léonée, *George Du Maurier*. 1969. Pp. 441-479.

LAWRENCE DURRELL

The Alexandria Quartet, 1961

Beja, Morris. *Epiphany in the Modern Novel*. 1971. Pp. 216-220.

Chapman, R. T. "Dead, or Just Pretending? Reality in *The Alexandria Quartet.*" *Centennial Review*, 16 (1972), 408-418.

Creed, Walter G. "Pieces of the Puzzle: The Multiple-Narrative Structure of *The Alexandria Quartet.*" *Mosaic*, 6 (Winter 1973), 19-35.

Dawson, Carl. "From Einstein to Keats: A New Look at the *Alexandria Quartet.*" *Far-Western Forum*, 1 (1974), 109-128.

Drescher, Horst W. "Raumzeit: Zur Struktur von Lawrence Durrells *Alexandria Quartet.*" *Die Neueren Sprachen*, 70 (1971), 309-318.

Frazer, George S. *Lawrence Durrell.* 1973 . Pp. 114-148.

Friedman, Alan Warren. *Lawrence Durrell.* 1970. Pp. 166-188.

Gossman, Ann. "Love's Alchemy in the *Alexandria Quartet.*" *Critique* (Atlanta), 13:2 (1971), 83-96.

Gottwald, Johannes. "Der Künstlerroman Darleys: Kontinuität in Lawrence Durrells *Alexandria Quartet.*" *Die Neueren Sprachen*, 70 (1971), 319-325.

Isernhagen, Hartwig. "Die Hähne Attikas: Lawrence Durrell und Wolfgang Hildesheimer." *Arcadia*, 8 (1973), 47-54.

Lebas, Gérard. "The Fabric of Durrell's *Alexandria Quartet.*" *Caliban*, 8 (1971), 139-150.

Lebas, Gérard. "The Mechanisms of Space-Time in *The Alexandria Quartet.*" *Caliban*, 7 (1970), 79-97.

Maclay, Joanna Hawkins. "The Interpreter and Modern Fiction: Problems of Point of View and Structural Tensiveness," in Esther M. Doyle and Virginia Hastings Floyd, eds., *Studies in Interpretation.* 1972. Pp. 158-169.

Morris, Robert K. *Continuance and Change.* 1972. Pp. 51-70.

Neuhaus, Volker. *Typen multiperspektivischen Erzählens.* 1971. Pp. 150-159.

Pelletier, Jacques. "*Le Quatuor d'Alexandrie* de Durrell: Roman de la Relativité." *Etudes Littéraires*, 3 (1970), 47-64.

Rubrecht, Werner Hermann. *Durrells "Alexandria Quartet."* 1972. Pp. 81-184.

Sertoli, Giuseppe. "Lawrence Durrell e il *Quartetto di Alessandria.*" *English Miscellany*, 18 (1967), 207-256.

Truchlar, Leo. "Versuch über Lawrence Durrell." *Die Neueren Sprachen*, 70 (1971), 297-308.

Walcutt, Charles Child. *Man's Changing Mask.* 1966. Pp. 296-297.

Wedin, Warren. "The Artist as Narrator in *The Alexandria Quartet.*" *Twentieth-Century Literature*, 18 (1972), 175-180.

Weigel, John A. *Lawrence Durrell.* 1965. Pp. 54-112.

Balthazar, 1958

Friedman, Alan Warren. *Lawrence Durrell.* 1970. Pp. 87-110.

Lebas, Gérard. "The Fabric of Durrell's *Alexandria Quartet.*" *Caliban*, 8 (1971), 141-142.

Rubrecht, Werner Hermann. *Durrells "Alexandria Quartet."* 1972.
Pp. 94-97.

The Black Book, 1938

Frazer, George S. *Lawrence Durrell.* 1973. Pp. 46-68.
Friedman, Alan Warren. *Lawrence Durrell.* 1970. Pp. 4-5.
Weigel, John A. *Lawrence Durrell.* 1965. Pp. 43-48.

Cefalû, 1947

Weigel, John A. *Lawrence Durrell.* 1965. Pp. 48-54.

Clea, 1960

Friedman, Alan Warren. *Lawrence Durrell.* 1970. Pp. 136-165.
Inglis, Fred. *An Essential Discipline.* 1968. Pp. 197-199.
Lebas, Gérard. "The Fabric of Durrell's *Alexandria Quartet.*" *Caliban*, 8 (1971), 146-149.
Rubrecht, Werner Hermann. *Durrells "Alexandria Quartet."* 1972.
Pp. 98-100.

Justine, 1957

Friedman, Alan Warren. *Lawrence Durrell.* 1970. Pp. 62-86.
Lebas, Gérard. "The Fabric of Durrell's *Alexandria Quartet.*" *Caliban,* 8 (1971), 140-141.
Rubrecht, Werner Hermann. *Durrells "Alexandria Quartet."* 1972.
Pp. 85-94.

Mountolive, 1958

Friedman, Alan Warren. *Lawrence Durrell.* 1970. Pp. 111-135.
Lebas, Gérard. "The Fabric of Durrell's *Alexandria Quartet.*" *Caliban*, 8 (1971), 142-144.
Rubrecht, Werner Hermann. *Durrells "Alexandria Quartet."* 1972.
Pp. 119-135.

Nunquam, 1970

Fabre-Luce, Anne. "Le dernier Durrell." *Quinzaine Littéraire*, No. 109 (1971), 8-9.
Frazer, George S. *Lawrence Durrell.* 1973. Pp. 149-163.

Panic Spring, 1937

Weigel, John A. *Lawrence Durrell.* 1965. Pp. 41-43.

Tunc, 1968

Frazer, George S. *Lawrence Durrell.* 1973. Pp. 149-163.

MARIA EDGEWORTH

The Absentee, 1812

> Butler, Marilyn. *Maria Edgeworth.* 1972. Pp. 374-378.
> Harden, O. Elizabeth McWhorter. *Maria Edgeworth's Art.* 1971.
> Pp. 159-180.
> Newcomer, James. *Maria Edgeworth.* 1967. Pp. 130-137.

Belinda, 1801

> Butler, Marilyn. *Maria Edgeworth.* 1972. Pp. 307-315.
> Colby, Vineta. *Yesterday's Woman.* 1974. Pp. 129-131.
> Harden, O. Elizabeth McWhorter. *Maria Edgeworth's Art.* 1971.
> Pp. 76-107.
> Newcomer, James. *Maria Edgeworth.* 1967. Pp. 137-142.

Castle Rackrent, 1800

> Butler, Marilyn. *Maria Edgeworth.* 1972. Pp. 352-360.
> Edwards, Duane. "The Narrator of *Castle Rackrent.*" *South Atlantic Quarterly*, 71 (1972), 124-129.
> Harden, O. Elizabeth McWhorter. *Maria Edgeworth's Art.* 1971.
> Pp. 43-71.
> Newcomer, James. *Maria Edgeworth.* 1967. Pp. 144-167.

Ennui, 1809

> Butler, Marilyn. *Maria Edgeworth.* 1972. Pp. 365-374.
> Harden, O. Elizabeth McWhorter. *Maria Edgeworth's Art.* 1971.
> Pp. 146-155.

Harrington, 1817

> Colby, Vineta. *Yesterday's Woman.* 1974. Pp. 135-137.
> Harden, O. Elizabeth McWhorter. *Maria Edgeworth's Art.* 1971.
> Pp. 198-203.

Helen, 1834

> Butler, Marilyn. *Maria Edgeworth.* 1972. Pp. 468-480.
> Bulter, Marilyn. "The Uniqueness of Cynthia Kirkpatrick: Elizabeth Gaskell's *Wives and Daughters* and Maria Edgeworth's *Helen.*" *Review of English Studies*, 23 (1972), 278-290.
> Harden, O. Elizabeth McWhorter. *Maria Edgeworth's Art.* 1971.
> Pp. 213-224.
> Newcomer, James. *Maria Edgeworth.* 1967. Pp. 137-142.

Lenora, 1806

> Harden, O. Elizabeth McWhorter. *Maria Edgeworth's Art.* 1971.
> Pp. 140-146.
> Rafroidi, Patrick. *L'Irlande et le romantisme.* 1972. Pp. 26-29.

The Modern Griselda, 1805

Butler, Marilyn. *Maria Edgeworth*. 1972. Pp. 320-322.

Ormond, 1817

Butler, Marilyn. *Maria Edgeworth*. 1972. Pp. 380-389.
Gerber, Richard. "Namen als Symbol: Über Sherlock Holmes und das Wesen des Kriminalromans." *Neue Rundschau*, 83 (1972), 509-512.
Harden, O. Elizabeth McWhorter. *Maria Edgeworth's Art*. 1971. Pp. 203-213.
Newcomer, James. *Maria Edgeworth*. 1967. Pp. 112-128.

Patronage, 1814

Harden, O. Elizabeth McWhorter. *Maria Edgeworth's Art*. 1971. Pp. 187-198.
Newcomer, James. *Maria Edgeworth*. 1967. Pp. 80-111.

Vivian, 1812

Harden, O. Elizabeth McWhorter. *Maria Edgeworth's Art*. 1971. Pp. 155-159.

GEORGE ELIOT

Adam Bede, 1859

Adam, Ian. *George Eliot*. 1969. Pp. 10-12, 34-37, 57-63, 85-88.
Buckler, William E. "Memory, Morality, and the Tragic Vision in the Early Novels of George Eliot," in George Goodin, ed., *The Enlish Novel*. 1972. Pp. 146-150.
Edwards, Michael. "A Reading of *Adam Bede*." *Critical Quarterly*, 14 (1972), 205-218.
Griffith, Philip Mahone. "Symbols of the Arm and Handclasp in George Eliot's *Adam Bede*." *South Central Bulletin*, 33 (1973), 200-202.
Halperin, John. *Egoism and Self-Discovery*. 1974. Pp. 126-143.
Hardwick, Elizabeth. *Seduction and Betrayal*. 1970. Pp. 186-190.
Hardy, Barbara. *Rituals and Feeling*. 1973. Pp. 6-8, 10.
Harvey, W. J. *The Art of George Eliot*. 1969. Pp. 43-45, 69-72, 74-82, 84-88, 115-122, 138-143, 156-159, 164-173, 179-184, 226-234, 245-248.
Herbert, Christopher. "Preachers and the Schemes of Nature in *Adam Bede*." *Nineteenth-Century Fiction*, 29 (1975), 412-427.
Higdon, David Leon. "The Iconographic Backgrounds of *Adam Bede*, Chapter 15." *Nineteenth-Century Fiction*, 27 (1972), 155-170.
Higdon, David Leon. "*Sortes Biblicae* in *Adam Bede*." *Papers on Language and Literature*, 9 (1973), 396-405.
Katona, Anna. *A Valóságábrázolás problémái George Eliot regényeiben*. 1969. Pp. 81-87.

Knoepflmacher, U. C. *George Eliot's Early Novels.* 1968. Pp. 89-127.
Lerner, Laurence. *The Truthtellers.* 1967. Pp. 33-40, 89-92, 141-143.
Logu, Pietro de. *La Narrativa di George Eliot.* 1969. Pp. 73-100.
Martin, Bruce K. "Rescue and Marriage in *Adam Bede.*" *Studies in English Literature, 1500-1900,* 12 (1972), 745-763.
Mews, Hazel. *Frail Vessels.* 1969. Pp. 100-104.
Mills, Nicolaus. *American and English Fiction.* 1973. Pp. 52-73.
Moers, Ellen. "Woman's Lit: Profession and Tradition." *Columbia Forum,* 1 (1972), 30-33.
Moynahan, Julian. "Pastoralism as Culture and Counter-Culture in English Fiction, 1800-1928." *Novel,* 6 (1972), 29-30.
Savoia, Dianella. "Le Immagini dell'acqua nel linguaggio di George Eliot." *Aevum,* 47 (1973), 351-356.
Shaw, Patricia. "Humour in the Novels of George Eliot." *Filologia Moderna,* 13 (1973), 320-322, 334-335.
Smalley, Barbara. *George Eliot and Flaubert.* 1974. Pp. 195-198.
Squires, Michael. "*Adam Bede* and the *Locus Amoenus.*" *Studies in English Literature, 1500-1900,* 13 (1973), 670-676.
Stoll, John E. "Psychological Dissociation in the Victorian Novel." *Literature and Psychology,* 20 (1970), 67-69.
Supp, Dorothee. *Tragik bei George Eliot.* 1969. Pp. 29-37, 74-86.
Villgradter, Rudolf. *Die Darstellung des Bösen.* 1970. Pp. 79-101.
Wiesenfarth, Joseph. "*Adam Bede* and Myth." *Papers on Language and Literature,* 8 (1972), 39-52.

Daniel Deronda, 1876

Adam, Ian. *George Eliot.* 1969. Pp. 28-33, 52-56, 77-84, 104-111.
Baker, William. "George Eliot's Readings in Nineteenth-Century Jewish Historians: A Note on the Background of *Daniel Deronda.*" *Victorian Studies,* 15 (1972), 463-473.
Baker, William. "The Kabbalah, Mordecai, and George Eliot's Religion of Humanity." *Yearbook of English Studies,* 3 (1973), 216-221.
Bareiss, Dieter. *Die Vierpersonenkonstellation im Roman.* 1969. Pp. 51-72.
Bedient, Calvin. *Architects of the Self.* 1972. Pp. 57-68.
Beer, Patricia. *Reader, I Married Him.* 1974. Pp. 182-213.
Cirillo, Albert R. "Salvation in *Daniel Deronda*: The Fortunate Overthrow of Gwendolen Harleth." *Literary Monographs,* 1 (1967), 203-243.
Euwema, Ben. "Denial and Affirmation in Victorian Thought." *Journal of General Education,* 21 (1969), 211-213.
Fisch, Harold. *The Dual Image.* 1971. Pp. 66-72.
Fricke, Douglas C. "Art and Artists in *Daniel Deronda.*" *Studies in the Novel,* 5 (1973), 220-228.
Gottfried, Leon. "Structure and Genre in *Daniel Deronda,*" in George Goodin, ed., *The English Novel.* 1972. Pp. 164-175.
Halperin, John. *Egoism and Self-Discovery.* 1974. Pp. 162-192.

Halperin, John. *The Language of Meditation*. 1973. Pp. 68-87.
Hardy, Barbara. *Rituals and Feeling*. 1973. Pp. 5-6.
Harvey, W. J. *The Art of George Eliot*. 1969. Pp. 20-22, 206-211, 218-220, 237-240.
Jackson, Arlene M. "*Daniel Deronda* and the Victorian Search for Identity." *Studies in the Humanities*, 3 (1972), 25-30.
Katona, Anna. *A Valóságábrázolás problémái George Eliot regényeiben*. 1969. Pp. 108-121.
Kroeber, Karl. *Styles in Fictional Structures*. 1971. Pp. 99-109.
Lebowitz, Naomi. *Humanism and the Absurd*. 1971. Pp. 45-65.
Lerner, Laurence. *The Truthtellers*. 1967. Pp. 52-63, 74-76, 128-130.
Logu, Pietro de. *La Narrativa di George Eliot*. 1969. Pp. 231-259.
Mews, Hazel. *Frail Vessels*. 1969. Pp. 119-125, 158-159.
Moynahan, Julian. "Pastoralism as Culture and Counter-Culture in English Fiction, 1800-1928." *Novel*, 6 (1972), 30-31.
Myers, William. "George Eliot: Politics and Personality," in John Lucas, ed., *Literature and Politics*. 1971. Pp. 110-128.
Newton, K. M. "George Eliot, George Henry Lewes, and Darwinism." *Durham University Journal*, 66 (1974), 291-293.
Smalley, Barbara. *George Eliot and Flaubert*. 1974. Pp. 198-216.
Supp, Dorothee. *Tragik bei George Eliot*. 1969. Pp. 54-73.
Swann, Brian. "George Eliot's Ecumenical Jew, or, The Novel as Outdoor Temple." *Novel*, 8 (1974), 39-50.
Swann, Brian. "George Eliot and the Play: Symbol and Metaphor of the Drama in *Daniel Deronda*." *Dalhousie Review*, 52 (1972), 191-202.
Wiesenfarth, Joseph. "The Medea in *Daniel Deronda*." *Die Neueren Sprachen*, 72 (1973), 103-108.
Wing, George. "The Motto to Chapter XXI of *Daniel Deronda*: A Key to All George Eliot's Mythologies?" *Dalhousie Review*, 54 (1974), 16-20, 27-32.

Felix Holt, 1866

Bedient, Calvin. *Architects of the Self*. 1972. Pp. 70-79.
Harvey, W. J. *The Art of George Eliot*. 1969. Pp. 25-27, 132-135, 215-219.
Horowitz, Lenore Wisney. "George Eliot's Vision of Society in *Felix Holt the Radical*." *Texas Studies in Literature and Language*, 17 (1975), 175-191.
Kroeber, Karl. *Styles in Fictional Structures*. 1971. Pp. 135-139.
Lerner, Laurence. *The Truthtellers*. 1967. Pp. 47-52, 139-141, 237-241.
Logu, Pietro de. *La Narrativa di George Eliot*. 1969. Pp. 173-197.
Mews, Hazel. *Frail Vessels*. 1969. Pp. 113-116, 151-153.
Myers, William. "George Eliot: Politics and Personality," in John Lucas, ed., *Literature and Politics*. 1971. Pp. 108-125.
Newton, K. M. "George Eliot, George Henry Lewes, and Darwinism." *Durham University Journal*, 66 (1974), 284-286, 289-290.

Rance, Nicholas. *The Historical Novel.* 1975. Pp. 120-136.

Smalley, Barbara. *George Eliot and Flaubert.* 1974. Pp. 190-193.

Supp, Dorothee. *Tragik bei George Eliot.* 1969. Pp. 50-54.

Tomlinson, T. B. "Love and Politics in the Early-Victorian Novel." *Critical Review* (Melbourne), No. 17 (1974), 134-138.

Vooys, Sijna de. *The Psychological Element.* 1966. Pp. 64-70.

Middlemarch, 1872

Adam, Ian. *George Eliot.* 1969. Pp. 21-28, 45-52, 71-77, 97-104.

Bedient, Calvin. *Architects of the Self.* 1972. Pp. 83-97.

Beer, Patricia. *Reader, I Married Him.* 1974. Pp. 175-213.

Bersani, Leo. "Le Réalisme et la peur du désir." *Poétique,* 22 (1975), 184-187.

Cline, C. L. "Qualifications of the Medical Practitioners of *Middlemarch,*" in Clyde de L. Ryals, ed., *Nineteenth-Century Literary Perspectives.* 1974. Pp. 271-281.

Coles, Robert. *Irony in the Mind's Life.* 1974. Pp. 154-204.

Coles, Robert. "Irony in the Mind's Life: Maturity—George Eliot's *Middlemarch.*" *Virginia Quarterly Review,* 49 (1973), 526-552.

Dibon, Anne-Marie. "Form and Value in the French and English 19th-Century Novel." *Modern Language Notes,* 87 (1972), 911-912.

Duerksen, Roland A. *Shelleyan Ideas in Victorian Literature.* 1966. Pp. 141-149.

Dumitriu, G. "*Middlemarch* si geneza Isabelei Archer." *Analele Universitatii Bucuresti: Literatura Universala si Comparata,* 18:2 (1969), 77-84.

Edwards, Lee R. "Women, Energy, and *Middlemarch.*" *Massachusetts Review,* 13 (1972), 223-238.

Erzgräber, Willi. "Eliot: *Middlemarch,*" in Franz K. Stanzel, ed., *Der englische Roman.* 1969. Vol. II, 174-214.

Fernando, Lloyd. "Special Pleading and Art in *Middlemarch*: The Relations Between the Sexes." *Modern Language Review,* 67 (1972), 44-49.

Fujita, Seiji. *Structure and Motif in "Middlemarch."* 1969. Pp. 7-14, 32-191.

Garrett, Peter K. *Scene and Symbol.* 1969. Pp. 20-37, 58-66.

Haight, Gordon S. "Poor Mr. Casaubon," in Clyde de L. Ryals, ed., *Nineteenth-Century Literary Perspectives.* 1974. Pp. 255-270.

Halperin, John. *Egoism and Self-Discovery.* 1974. Pp. 143-162.

Halperin, John. *The Language of Meditation.* 1973. Pp. 54-68.

Hardy, Barbara. *The Appropriate Form.* 1964. Pp. 105-131.

Hardy, Barbara. *Rituals and Feeling.* 1973. Pp. 11-12.

Harvey, W. J. *The Art of George Eliot.* 1969. Pp. 42-47, 56-62, 74-78, 88-90, 128-130, 142-148, 153-155, 159-164, 174-176, 191-203, 213-215, 241-245.

Heilbrun, Carolyn G. *Towards a Recognition of Androgyny.* 1973. Pp. 83-85.

Hewitt, Douglas. *The Approach to Fiction.* 1972. Pp. 49-55.
Hollahan, Eugene. "The Concept of 'Crisis' in *Middlemarch.*" *Nineteenth-Century Fiction,* 28 (1974), 450-457.
Hornback, Bert G. "The Moral Imagination of George Eliot." *Papers on Language and Literature,* 8 (1972), 380-394.
Inglis, Fred. *An Essential Discipline.* 1968. Pp. 233-240.
Jackson, Arlene M. "Dorothea Brooke of Middle March: Idealism and Victorian Reality." *Cithara,* 12 (1973), 91-102.
Jones, Peter. *Philosophy and the Novel.* 1975. Pp. 9-50.
Katona, Anna. *A Valóságábrázolás problémái George Eliot regényeiben.* 1969. Pp. 92-108.
Kroeber, Karl. *Styles in Fictional Structures.* 1971. Pp. 94-99, 151-180.
Lerner, Laurence. *The Truthtellers.* 1967. Pp. 92-93, 127-128, 130-132, 249-269.
Logu, Pietro de. *La Narrativa di George Eliot.* 1969. Pp. 199-230.
Mews, Hazel. *Frail Vessels.* 1969. Pp. 116-119, 153-158.
Myers, William. "George Eliot: Politics and Personality," in John Lucas, ed., *Literature and Politics.* 1971. Pp. 108-124.
Miller, J. Hillis. "Narrative and History." *ELH,* 41 (1974), 462-471.
Newton, K. M. "The Role of the Narrator in George Eliot's Novels." *Journal of Narrative Technique,* 3 (1973), 101-106.
Savoia, Dianella. "Le Immagini dell'acqua nel linguaggio di George Eliot." *Aevum,* 47 (1973), 356-360.
Scott, James. F. "George Eliot, Positivism, and the Social Vision of *Middlemarch.*" *Victorian Studies,* 16 (1972), 59-76.
Shaw, Patricia. "Humour in the Novels of George Eliot." *Filologia Moderna,* 13 (1973), 309-314, 328-335.
Smalley, Barbara. *George Eliot and Flaubert.* 1974. Pp. 125-186.
Supp, Dorothee. *Tragik bei George Eliot.* 1969. Pp. 87-97.
Swann, Brian. "*Middlemarch* and Myth." *Nineteenth-Century Fiction,* 28 (1973), 210-214.
Swann, Brian. "*Middlemarch:* Realism and Symbolic Form." *ELH,* 39 (1972), 279-308.
Witemeyer, Hugh. "George Eliot, Naumann, and the Nazarenes." *Victorian Studies,* 18 (1974), 145-158.

The Mill on the Floss, 1860

Adam, Ian. *George Eliot.* 1969. Pp. 12-18, 37-41, 63-68, 88-94.
Beer, Patricia. *Reader, I Married Him.* 1974. Pp. 179-205.
Buckler, William E. "Memory, Morality, and the Tragic Vision in the Early Novels of George Eliot," in George Goodin, ed., *The English Novel.* 1972. Pp. 149-159.
Buckley, Jerome Hamilton. *Season of Youth.* 1974. Pp. 95-115.
Cohen, Walter, Judith Evelyn, and Lyman Bryson. "*The Mill on the Floss,*" in George D. Crothers, ed., *Invitation to Learning.* 1966. Pp. 145-152.

Ermarth, Elizabeth. "Maggie Tulliver's Long Suicide." *Studies in English Literature, 1500-1900*, 14 (1974), 587-601.

Feltes, N. N. "Community and the Limits of Liability in Two Mid-Victorian Novels." *Victorian Studies*, 17 (1974), 355-360.

Garrett, Peter K. *Scene and Symbol*. 1969. Pp. 42-45.

Hagan, John. "A Reinterpretation of *The Mill on the Floss*." *Publications of the Modern Language Association*, 87 (1972), 53-63.

Hardy, Barbara. *Rituals and Feeling*. 1973. Pp. 8-9.

Higdon, David Leon. "Failure of Design in *The Mill on the Floss*." *Journal of Narrative Technique*, 3 (1973), 183-192.

Harvey, W. J. *The Art of George Eliot*. 1969. Pp. 75-78, 123-126, 137-139, 186-191, 223-225, 234-237.

Katona, Anna. *A Valóságábrázolás problémái George Eliot regényeiben*. 1969. Pp. 87-92.

Knoepflmacher, U. C. *George Eliot's Early Novels*. 1968. Pp. 162-220.

Lerner, Laurence. *The Truthtellers*. 1967. Pp. 126-127, 228-229, 236-237, 269-278.

Logu, Pietro de. *La Narrativa di George Eliot*. 1969. Pp. 101-126.

Mews, Hazel. *Frail Vessels*. 1969. Pp. 104-110.

Milner, Ian. "The Quest for Community in *The Mill on the Floss*." *Prague Studies in English*, 12 (1967), 77-91.

Moynahan, Julian. "Pastoralism as Culture and Counter-Culture in English Fiction, 1800-1928." *Novel*, 6 (1972), 30.

Paris, Bernard J. *A Psychological Approach*. 1974. Pp. 165-189.

Shaw, Patricia. "Humour in the Novels of George Eliot." *Filologia Moderna*, 13 (1973), 314-321.

Stanculescu, Liana. "Mit si leitmotiv la George Eliot: *The Mill on the Floss*." *Analele Universitatii Bucuresti: Literatura Universala si Comparata*, 18:1 (1969), 107-117.

Sullivan, William J. "Music and Musical Allusion in *The Mill on the Floss*." *Criticism*, 16 (1974), 232-246.

Supp, Dorothee. *Tragik bei George Eliot*. 1969. Pp. 115-131.

Williams, Ioan. *The Realist Novel*. 1974. Pp. 178-182.

Romola, 1863

Conrad, Peter. *The Victorian Treasure-House*. 1973. Pp. 124-127.

Harvey, W. J. *The Art of George Eliot*. 1969. Pp. 112-114, 182-184, 214-216, 236-237.

Lerner, Laurence. *The Truthtellers*. 1967. Pp. 243-249.

Logu, Pietro de. *La Narrativa di George Eliot*. 1969. Pp. 151-172.

Mews, Hazel. *Frail Vessels*. 1969. Pp. 111-113, 150-151.

Myers, William. "George Eliot: Politics and Personality," in John Lucas, ed., *Literature and Politics*. 1971. Pp. 108-122.

Rance, Nicholas. *The Historical Novel*. 1975. Pp. 104-120.

Santangelo, Gennaro A. "Villari's *Life and Times of Savonarola*: A Source for George Eliot's *Romola*." *Anglia*, 90 (1972), 118-131.

Sullivan, Walter J. "Piero di Cosimo and the Higher Primitivism in

Romola." *Nineteenth-Century Fiction*, 26 (1972), 390-405.
Supp, Dorothee. *Tragik bei George Eliot.* 1969. Pp. 38-48, 98-113.

Scenes of Clerical Life, 1858

Colby, Vineta. *Yesterday's Woman.* 1974. Pp. 203-209.
Harvey, W. J. *The Art of George Eliot.* 1969. Pp. 109-112, 201-203, 247-248.
Lerner, Laurence. *The Truthtellers.* 1967. Pp. 28-33.
Shaw, Patricia. "Humour in the Novels of George Eliot." *Filologia Moderna*, 13 (1973), 321-327, 330-332.
Villgradter, Rudolf. *Die Darstellung des Bösen.* 1970. Pp. 47-75.

Silas Marner, 1861

Adam, Ian. *George Eliot.* 1969. Pp. 18-21, 94-97.
Buckler, William E. "Memory, Morality, and the Tragic Vision in the Early Novels of George Eliot," in George Goodin, ed., *The English Novel.* 1972. Pp. 159-163.
Carroll, David R. "*Silas Marner:* Reversing the Oracles of Religion." *Literary Monographs*, 1 (1967), 167-200.
Higdon, David Leon. "Sortilege in George Eliot's *Silas Marner.*" *Papers on Language and Literature*, 10 (1974), 51-57.
Knoepflmacher, U. C. *George Eliot's Early Novels.* 1968. Pp. 221-259.
Logu, Pietro de. *La Narrativa di George Eliot.* 1969. Pp. 127-150.
Martin, Bruce K. "Similarity within Dissimilarity: The Dual Structure of *Silas Marner.*" *Texas Studies in Literature and Language*, 14 (1972), 479-489.
Quick, Jonathan R. "*Silas Marner* as Romance: The Example of Hawthorne." *Nineteenth-Century Fiction*, 29 (1974), 287-298.

GABRIEL FIELDING

The Birthday King, 1962

Borrello, Alfred. *Gabriel Fielding.* 1974. Pp. 101-116.

Brotherly Love, 1954

Borrello, Alfred. *Gabriel Fielding.* 1974. Pp. 37-51, 64-73.

Eight Days, 1958

Borrello, Alfred. *Gabriel Fielding.* 1974. Pp. 76-87.

Gentlemen in Their Season, 1966

Borrello, Alfred. *Gabriel Fielding.* 1974. Pp. 119-134.

In the Time of Greenbloom, 1956

Borrello, Alfred. *Gabriel Fielding.* 1974. Pp. 53-73.

Through Streets Broad and Narrow, 1960

    Borrello, Alfred. *Gabriel Fielding*. 1974. Pp. 90-97.

HENRY FIELDING

Amelia, 1752

    Alter, Robert. *Fielding*. 1968. Pp. 141-177.

    Amory, Hugh. "Magistrate or Censor? The Problem of Authority in Fielding's Later Writings." *Studies in English Literature, 1500-1900*, 12 (1972), 513-518.

    Battestin, Martin C. "The Problem of *Amelia*: Hume, Barrow, and the Conversion of Captain Booth." *ELH*, 41 (1974), 613-648.

    Bloch, Tuvia. "*Amelia* and Booth's Doctrine of the Passions." *Studies in English Literature, 1500-1900*, 13 (1973), 461-473.

    Braudy, Leo. *Narrative Form*. 1970. Pp. 180-211.

    Brooks, Douglas. *Number and Pattern*. 1973. Pp. 111-116.

    Folkenflik, Robert. "Purpose and Narration in Fielding's *Amelia*." *Novel*, 7 (1974), 168-174.

    Hassall, Anthony J. "Fielding's *Amelia*: Dramatic and Authorial Narration." *Novel*, 5 (1972), 225-233.

    Hunter, J. Paul. "The Lesson of *Amelia*," in Larry S. Champion, ed., *Quick Springs of Sense*. 1974. Pp. 157-180.

    Irwin, Michael. *Henry Fielding*. 1967. Pp. 113-134.

    Kropf, C. R. "Educational Theory and Human Nature in Fielding's Works." *Publications of the Modern Language Association*, 89 (1974), 118-119.

    Longmire, Samuel E. "*Amelia* as a Comic Action." *Tennessee Studies in Literature*, 17 (1972), 67-79.

    Maresca, Thomas E. *Epic to Novel*. 1974. Pp. 216-231.

    Rawson, C. J. *Henry Fielding*. 1972. Pp. 67-98.

    Shesgreen, Sean. *Literary Portraits*. 1972. Pp. 154-176.

    Warner, John M. "The Interpolated Narratives in the Fiction of Fielding and Smollett: An Epistemological View." *Studies in the Novel*, 5 (1973), 280-281.

    Williams, Muriel Brittain. *Marriage*. 1973. Pp. 95-120.

Jonathan Wild, 1743

    Braudy, Leo. *Narrative Form*. 1970. Pp. 121-143.

    Pastalosky, Rosa. *Henry Fielding*. 1970. Pp. 102-110.

    Rawson, C. J. "Fielding's 'Good' Merchant: The Problem of Heartfree in *Jonathan Wild* (with Comments on Other 'Good' Characters in Fielding)." *Modern Philology*, 69 (1972), 292-313.

    Rawson, C. J. *Henry Fielding*. 1972. Pp. 101-259.

    Rawson, C. J. "The Hero as Clown: Jonathan Wild, Felix Krull and Others," in R. F. Brissenden, ed., *Studies in the Eighteenth Century*. 1973. Pp. 17-32.

Shesgreen, Sean. *Literary Portraits.* 1972. Pp. 45-71.
Williams, Muriel Brittain. *Marriage.* 1973. Pp. 62-69.

Joseph Andrews, 1742

Alter, Robert. *Fielding.* 1968. Pp. 79-84, 104-107, 123-129, 133-136, 193-195.
Braudy, Leo. *Narrative Form.* 1970. Pp. 95-121.
Brooks, Douglas. *Number and Pattern.* 1973. Pp. 65-85.
Donovan, Robert Alan. *The Shaping Vision.* 1966. Pp. 68-88.
Göller, Karl Heinz. *"Romance" und "novel."* 1972. Pp. 85-89.
Greiner, Walter F. *Studien zur Entstehung der englischen Romantheorie.* 1969. Pp. 109-114.
Irwin, Michael. *Henry Fielding.* 1967. Pp. 65-83.
Iser, Wolfgang. *The Implied Reader.* 1974. Pp. 32-46.
Iser, Wolfgang. "Die Leserolle in Fieldings *Joseph Andrews* und *Tom Jones,*" in Wolfgang Iser, ed., *Henry Fielding.* 1972. Pp. 285-306.
Knowles, A. S., Jr. "Defoe, Swift, and Fielding: Notes on the Retirement Theme," in Larry S. Champion, ed., *Quick Springs of Sense.* 1974. Pp. 126-129.
Kropf, C. R. "Educational Theory and Human Nature in Fielding's Works." *Publications of the Modern Language Association,* 89 (1974), 114-116.
Lemon, Lee T. "The Hostile Universe: A Developing Pattern in Nineteenth-Century Fiction," in George Goodin, ed., *The English Novel.* 1972. Pp. 8-10.
Levine, George R. *Henry Fielding.* 1967. Pp. 91-125.
McDowell, Alfred. "Fielding's Rendering of Speech in *Joseph Andrews* and *Tom Jones.*" *Language and Style,* 6 (1973), 83-94.
Maresca, Thomas E. *Epic to Novel.* 1974. Pp. 184-203.
Pastalosky, Rosa. *Henry Fielding.* 1970. Pp. 43-45, 52-67, 95-99.
Rawson, C. J. "Language, Dialogue, and Point of View in Fielding: Some Considerations," in Larry S. Champion, ed., *Quick Springs of Sense.* 1974. Pp. 142-145.
Rawson, C. J. "Some Considerations on Authorial Intrusion and Dialogue in Fielding's Novels and Plays." *Durham University Journal,* 64 (1971), 32-44.
Rolle, Dietrich. *Fielding und Sterne.* 1963. Pp. 65-72, 82-87.
Shesgreen, Sean. *Literary Portraits.* 1972. Pp. 72-105.
Sokolyansky, Mark G. "Poetics of Fielding's Comic Epics." *Zeitschrift für Anglistik und Amerikanistik,* 22 (1974), 251-258.
Warner, John M. "The Interpolated Narratives in the Fiction of Fielding and Smollett: An Epistemological View." *Studies in the Novel,* 5 (1973), 272-276.
Wiesenfarth, Joseph. " 'High' People and 'Low' in *Joseph Andrews*: A Study of Structure and Style." *CLA Journal,* 16 (1973), 357-365.
Williams, Muriel Brittain. *Marriage.* 1973. Pp. 50-62.
Wolff, Erwin. *Der englische Roman.* 1968. Pp. 53-57.

Shamela, 1741

> Oliver, Theo. *"Pamela* and *Shamela:* A Reassessment." *English Studies in Africa*, 17 (1974), 59-70.
> Rawson, C. J. "Some Considerations on Authorial Intrusion and Dialogue in Fielding's Novels and Plays." *Durham University Journal*, 64 (1971), 32-44.
> Williams, Muriel Brittain. *Marriage*. 1973. Pp. 48-50.

Tom Jones, 1749

> Allende, Nora A. de. "Social Context in *Moll Flanders, Pamela*, and *Tom Jones.*" *Revista de Literaturas Modernas*, 8 (1969), 81-126.
> Alter, Robert. *Fielding*. 1968. Pp. 15-25, 41-58, 66-72, 84-96, 110-124, 130-133, 136-139.
> Anderson, Howard. "Answers to the Author of *Clarissa*: Theme and Narrative Technique in *Tom Jones* and *Tristram Shandy.*" *Philological Quarterly*, 51 (1972), 859-873.
> Battestin, Martin C. *The Providence of Wit*. 1974. Pp. 141-192.
> Braudy, Leo. *Narrative Form*. 1970. Pp. 144-180.
> Brooks, Douglas. *Number and Pattern*. 1973. Pp. 92-111.
> Cleary, Thomas. "Jacobitism in *Tom Jones:* The Basis for an Hypothesis." *Philological Quarterly*, 52 (1973), 239-251.
> Conti, Paola Colaiacoma. "Natura e civiltà in Henry Fielding." *English Miscellany*, 19 (1968), 109-132.
> DeBlois, Peter. "Ulysses at Upton: A Consideration of the Comic Effect of Fielding's Mock-Heroic Style in *Tom Jones.*" *Thoth*, 11 (Spring/Summer 1971), 3-8.
> Dolbier, Maurice, George D. Crothers, and Glenway Wescott. *"Tom Jones,"* in George D. Crothers, ed., *Invitation to Learning*. 1966. Pp. 37-43.
> Folkenflik, Robert. "Tom Jones, the Gypsies, and the Masquerade." *University of Toronto Quarterly*, 44 (1975), 224-237.
> Goldknopf, David. *The Life of the Novel*. 1972. Pp. 125-142.
> Greene, J. Lee. "Fielding's Gypsy Episode and Sancho Panza's Governorship." *South Atlantic Bulletin*, 39 (1974), 117-121.
> Guthrie, William B. "The Comic Celebrant of Life in *Tom Jones.*" *Tennessee Studies in Literature*, 19 (1974), 91-105.
> Hatfield, Glenn W. *Henry Fielding*. 1968. Pp. 179-196.
> Irwin, Michael. *Henry Fielding*. 1967. Pp. 84-112.
> Iser, Wolfgang. *The Implied Reader*. 1974. Pp. 46-56.
> Iser, Wolfgang. "Die Leserolle in Fieldings *Joseph Andrews* und *Tom Jones,"* in Wolfgang Iser, ed., *Henry Fielding*. 1972. Pp. 306-318.
> Kaplan, F. "Fielding's Novel about Novels: The 'Prefaces' and the 'Plot' of *Tom Jones.*" *Studies in English Literature, 1500-1900*, 13 (1973), 535-549.
> Kearney, Anthony. "Tom Jones and the Forty-Five." *Ariel*, 4:2 (1973), 68-78.

Knight, Charles A. "Multiple Structures and the Unity of *Tom Jones*." *Criticism*, 14 (1972), 227-242.

Knowles, A. S., Jr. "Defoe, Swift, and Fielding: Notes on the Retirement Theme," in Larry S. Champion, ed., *Quick Springs of Sense*. 1974. Pp. 129-136.

Kropf, C. R. "Educational Theory and Human Nature in Fielding's Works." *Publications of the Modern Language Association*, 89 (1974), 116-118.

Laimbach, Burkhard, and Karl-H. Löschen. *Fieldings "Tom Jones."* 1974. Pp. 23-49, 55-57.

Laurenson, Diana T., and Alan Swingewood. *The Sociology of Literature*. 1971. Pp. 175-206.

Longmire, Samuel E. "Allworthy and Barrow: The Standards for Good Judgment." *Texas Studies in Literature and Language*, 13 (1972), 629-639.

Longmire, Samuel E. "Partridge's Ghost Story." *Studies in Short Fiction*, 11 (1974), 423-426.

McDowell, Alfred. "Fielding's Rendering of Speech in *Joseph Andrews* and *Tom Jones*." *Language and Style*, 6 (1973), 83-94.

McKenzie, Alan T. "The Process of Discovery in *Tom Jones*." *Dalhousie Review*, 54 (1974-1975), 720-740.

Maresca, Thomas E. *Epic to Novel*. 1974. Pp. 203-216.

Miller, Norbert. *Der empfindsame Erzähler*. 1968. Pp. 104-111.

Otten, Kurt. *Der englische Roman*. 1971. Pp. 75-80.

Pastalosky, Rosa. *Henry Fielding*. 1970. Pp. 43-45, 67-93, 99-102.

Paulson, Ronald. "The Pilgrimage and the Family: Structure in the Novels of Fielding and Smollett," in G. S. Rousseau and P.-G. Boucé, eds., *Tobias Smollett*. 1971. Pp. 57-78.

Rawson, C. J. "Some Considerations on Authorial Intrusion and Dialogue in Fielding's Novels and Plays. *Durham University Journal*, 64 (1971), 32-44.

Robinson, Roger. "Henry Fielding and the English Rococo," in R. F. Brissenden, ed., *Studies in the Eighteenth Century*. 1973. Pp. 93-111.

Rolle, Dietrich. *Fielding und Sterne*. 1963. Pp. 26-31, 41-44, 48-55, 68-72, 82-87, 92-99, 105-114, 121-125, 144-147.

Ruthven, K. K. "Fielding, Square, and the Fitness of Things." *Eighteenth-Century Studies*, 5 (1971-1972), 243-255.

Schonhorn, Manuel. "Heroic Allusion in *Tom Jones*: Hamlet and the Temptation of Jesus." *Studies in the Novel*, 6 (1974), 218-227.

Shesgreen, Sean. *Literary Portraits*. 1972. Pp. 106-153.

Shesgreen, Sean. "The Moral Function of Thwackum, Square, and Allworthy." *Studies in the Novel*, 2 (1970), 159-167.

Sokolyansky, Mark G. "Poetics of Fielding's Comic Epics." *Zeitschrift für Anglistik und Amerikanistik*, 22 (1974), 255-264.

Stanzel, Franz. *Narrative Situations*. 1971. Pp. 38-58.

Vopat, James B. "Narrative Technique in *Tom Jones*: The Balance of Art and Nature." *Journal of Narrative Technique*, 4 (1974), 144-154.

Wess, Robert V. "The Probable and the Marvelous in *Tom Jones.*" *Modern Philology*, 68 (1970), 32-45.
Williams, Muriel Brittain. *Marriage.* 1973. Pp. 71-94.
Wolff, Erwin. "Fielding: *Tom Jones,*" in Franz K. Stanzel, ed., *Der englische Roman.* 1969. Vol. I, 198-231.
Wolff, Erwin. *Der englische Roman.* 1968. Pp. 67-78.

SARAH FIELDING

David Simple, 1744-1753

Russell, H. K. "Unity in Eighteenth-Century Episodic Novels," in Larry S. Champion, ed., *Quick Springs of Sense.* 1974. Pp. 183-194.

RONALD FIRBANK

The Artificial Princess, 1934

Brophy, Brigid. *Prancing Novelist.* 1973. Pp. 420-431.
Merritt, James Douglas. *Ronald Firbank.* 1969. Pp. 38-46.

Caprice, 1917

Brophy, Brigid. *Prancing Novelist.* 1973. Pp. 471-476.
Kiechler, John Anthony. *The Butterfly's Freckled Wings.* 1969. Pp. 45-48.
Merritt, James Douglas. *Ronald Firbank.* 1969. Pp. 63-67.

Concerning the Eccentricities of Cardinal Pirelli, 1926

Benkovitz, Miriam J. *Ronald Firbank.* 1970. Pp. 276-284.
Brophy, Brigid. *Prancing Novelist.* 1973. Pp. 558-568.
Kiechler, John Anthony. *The Butterfly's Freckled Wings.* 1969. Pp. 28-31, 55-57.
Merritt, James Douglas. *Ronald Firbank.* 1969. Pp. 98-113.

The Flower Beneath the Foot, 1923

Brophy, Brigid. *Prancing Novelist.* 1973. Pp. 509-551.
Kiechler, John Anthony. *The Butterfly's Freckled Wings.* 1969. Pp. 51-54.
Merritt, James Douglas. *Ronald Firbank.* 1969. Pp. 80-92.

Inclinations, 1916

Benkovitz, Miriam J. *Ronald Firbank.* 1970. Pp. 153-157.
Brophy, Brigid. *Prancing Novelist.* 1973. Pp. 463-471.
Merritt, James Douglas. *Ronald Firbank.* 1969. Pp. 33-38.

Odette d'Antrevernes, 1905

Brophy, Brigid. *Prancing Novelist.* 1973. Pp. 414-422.

Santal, 1921

>   Brophy, Brigid. *Prancing Novelist*. 1973. Pp. 501-509.
>   Kiechler, John Anthony. *The Butterfly's Freckled Wings*. 1969.
>   Pp. 19-24.
>   Merritt, James Douglas. *Ronald Firbank*. 1969. Pp. 74-77.

Sorrow in Sunlight, 1925

>   Brophy, Brigid. *Prancing Novelist*. 1973. Pp. 551-558.
>   Kiechler, John Anthony. *The Butterfly's Freckled Wings*. 1969.
>   Pp. 24-28, 54-55.
>   Merritt, James Douglas. *Ronald Firbank*. 1969. Pp. 92-98.

A Study in Temperament, 1905

>   Merritt, James Douglas. *Ronald Firbank*. 1969. Pp. 124-127.

Vainglory, 1915

>   Brophy, Brigid. *Prancing Novelist*. 1973. Pp. 432-466.
>   Davis, Robert Murray. "The Ego Triumphant in Firbank's *Vain-glory*." *Papers on Language and Literature*, 9 (1973), 281-296.
>   Kiechler, John Anthony. *The Butterfly's Freckled Wings*. 1969.
>   Pp. 43-45, 85-98.
>   Merritt, James Douglas. *Ronald Firbank*. 1969. Pp. 53-62.

Valmouth, 1919

>   Brophy, Brigid. *Prancing Novelist*. 1973. Pp. 476-485.
>   Kiechler, John Anthony. *The Butterfly's Freckled Wings*. 1969.
>   Pp. 12-15, 67-74.
>   Merritt, James Douglas. *Ronald Firbank*. 1969. Pp. 67-74.

FORD MADOX FORD

The Benefactor, 1905

>   Hoffmann, Charles G. *Ford Madox Ford*. 1963. Pp. 33-36.
>   Mizener, Arthur. *The Saddest Story*. 1971. Pp. 466-468.
>   Ohmann, Carol. *Ford Madox Ford*. 1964. Pp. 41-45.

A Call, 1910

>   Cassell, Richard A. *Ford Madox Ford*. 1961. Pp. 109-113.
>   Hoffmann, Charles G. *Ford Madox Ford*. 1967. Pp. 53-57.
>   Mizener, Arthur. *The Saddest Story*. 1971. Pp. 478-482.
>   Ohmann, Carol. *Ford Madox Ford*. 1964. Pp. 49-62.

An English Girl, 1907

>   Hoffmann, Charles G. *Ford Madox Ford*. 1967. Pp. 43-46.
>   Ohmann, Carol. *Ford Madox Ford*. 1964. Pp. 45-49.

The *Fifth Queen* Trilogy, 1962

> Mizener, Arthur. *The Saddest Story.* 1971. Pp. 469-477.

The *Fifth Queen*, 1906

> Hoffmann, Charles G. *Ford Madox Ford.* 1967. Pp. 36-43.
> Ohmann, Carol. *Ford Madox Ford.* 1964. Pp. 23-31.

The *Fifth Queen Crowned*, 1908

> Cassell, Richard A. *Ford Madox Ford.* 1961. Pp. 130-134.
> Hoffmann, Charles G. *Ford Madox Ford.* 1967. Pp. 36-43.
> Ohmann, Carol. *Ford Madox Ford.* 1964. Pp. 23-31.

The *Good Soldier*, 1915

> Andreach, Robert J. *The Slain and Resurrected God.* 1970. Pp. 128-148.
> Cassell, Richard A. *Ford Madox Ford.* 1961. Pp. 148-201.
> Cohen, Mary. "*The Good Soldier:* Outworn Codes." *Studies in the Novel,* 5 (1973), 284-297.
> Gill, Richard. *Happy Rural Seat.* 1972. Pp. 126-129.
> Gordon, Ambrose, Jr. *The Invisible Tent.* 1964. Pp. 51-65.
> Hoffmann, Charles G. *Ford Madox Ford.* 1967. Pp. 75-91.
> Lentz, Vern B. "Ford's Good Narrator." *Studies in the Novel,* 5 (1973), 483-489.
> Lid, R. W. *Ford Madox Ford.* 1964. Pp. 29-85.
> MacShane, Frank. *The Life and Work of Ford Madox Ford.* 1965. Pp. 110-120.
> Mizener, Arthur. *The Saddest Story.* 1971. Pp. 258-277.
> Ohmann, Carol. *Ford Madox Ford.* 1964. Pp. 71-111.
> Siemens, Reynold. "The Juxtaposition of Composed Renderings in Ford's *The Good Soldier.*" *Humanities Association Bulletin,* 23:3 (1972), 44-49.
> Smith, Grover. *Ford Madox Ford.* 1972. Pp. 26-35.
> Swinden, Patrick. *Unofficial Selves.* 1973. Pp. 127-133.
> Weinstein, Arnold L. *Vision and Response.* 1974. Pp. 57-69.
> Wiley, P. L. "Two Tales of Passion." *Conradiana,* 6 (1974), 193-195.

The *"Half-Moon,"* 1909

> Gordon, Ambrose, Jr. *The Invisible Tent.* 1964. Pp. 69-70.
> Hoffmann, Charles G. *Ford Madox Ford.* 1967. Pp. 48-51.
> Mizener, Arthur. *The Saddest Story.* 1971. Pp. 477-478.
> Ohmann, Carol. *Ford Madox Ford.* 1964. Pp. 31-35.

Henry for Hugh, 1934

> Cassell, Richard A. *Ford Madox Ford.* 1961. Pp. 273-277.
> Hoffmann, Charles G. *Ford Madox Ford.* 1967. Pp. 135-138.
> Mizener, Arthur. *The Saddest Story.* 1971. Pp. 519-522.

Ladies Whose Bright Eyes, 1911

> Cassell, Richard A. *Ford Madox Ford*. 1961. Pp. 90-106.
> Gordon, Ambrose, Jr. *The Invisible Tent*. 1964. Pp. 70-71.
> Hoffmann, Charles G. *Ford Madox Ford*. 1967. Pp. 60-63.
> Mizener, Arthur. *The Saddest Story*. 1971. Pp. 482-484.

Last Post, 1928

> Andreach, Robert J. *The Slain and Resurrected God*. 1970. Pp. 198-207.
> Gordon, Ambrose, Jr. *The Invisible Tent*. 1964. Pp. 132-143.

A Little Less Than Gods, 1928

> Hoffmann, Charles G. *Ford Madox Ford*. 1967. Pp. 132-133.
> Mizener, Arthur. *The Saddest Story*. 1971. Pp. 515-517.

A Man Could Stand Up—, 1926

> Andreach, Robert J. *The Slain and Resurrected God*. 1970. Pp. 181-198.
> Gordon, Ambrose, Jr. *The Invisible Tent*. 1964. Pp. 118-131.

The Marsden Case, 1923

> Gordon, Ambrose, Jr. *The Invisible Tent*. 1964. Pp. 22-29.
> Hoffmann, Charles G. *Ford Madox Ford*. 1967. Pp. 93-94.
> Mizener, Arthur. *The Saddest Story*. 1971. Pp. 489-494.

Mr. Apollo, 1908

> Hoffmann, Charles G. *Ford Madox Ford*. 1967. Pp. 46-48.

Mr. Fleight, 1913

> Hoffmann, Charles G. *Ford Madox Ford*. 1967. Pp. 68-71.

The New Humpty-Dumpty, 1912

> Hoffmann, Charles G. *Ford Madox Ford*. 1967. Pp. 65-68.

No Enemy, 1929

> Gordon, Ambrose, Jr. *The Invisible Tent*. 1964. Pp. 29-37.
> Mizener, Arthur. *The Saddest Story*. 1971. Pp. 487-489.

No More Parades, 1925

> Andreach, Robert J. *The Slain and Resurrected God*. 1970. Pp. 170-181.
> Gordon, Ambrose, Jr. *The Invisible Tent*. 1964. Pp. 4-5, 100-118.

The Panel, 1912

> Hoffmann, Charles G. *Ford Madox Ford*. 1967. Pp. 64-65.

Parade's End, 1950

Andreach, Robert J. *The Slain and Resurrected God*. 1970. Pp. 148-207:

Cassell, Richard A. *Ford Madox Ford*. 1961. Pp. 202-268.

Chapple, J. A. V. *Documentary and Imaginative Literature*. 1970. Pp. 328-331.

Core, George. "Ordered Life and the Abysses of Chaos: *Parade's End*." *Southern Review* (Baton Rouge), 8 (1972), 520-532.

Gill, Richard. *Happy Rural Seat*. 1972. Pp. 129-132.

Gordon, Ambrose, Jr. *The Invisible Tent*. 1964. Pp. 4-9, 72-85, 114-115.

Hays, Peter L. *The Limping Hero*. 1971. Pp. 148-155.

Heldman, James M. "The Last Victorian Novel: Technique and Theme in *Parade's End*." *Twentieth-Century Literature*, 18 (1972), 271-284.

Henighan, T. J. "Tietjens Transformed: A Reading of *Parade's End*." *English Literature in Transition*, 15 (1972), 144-157.

Hoffmann, Charles G. *Ford Madox Ford*. 1967. Pp. 95-130.

Lid, R. W. *Ford Madox Ford*. 1964. Pp. 137-185.

MacShane, Frank. *The Life and Work of Ford Madox Ford*. 1965. Pp. 175-190.

Mizener, Arthur. *The Saddest Story*. 1971. Pp. 494-515.

Mosher, Harold F., Jr. "La Voie oblique dans *L' Education sentimentale* et *Parade's End* (Ford Madox Ford)." *Littératures*, 17 (1970), 15-31.

Ohmann, Carol. *Ford Madox Ford*. 1964. Pp. 112-166.

Rexroth, Kenneth. *The Elastic Retort*. 1973. Pp. 124-127.

Smith, Grover, *Ford Madox Ford*. 1972. Pp. 37-39.

The Portrait, 1910

Hoffmann, Charles G. *Ford Madox Ford*. 1967. Pp. 51-52.

Privy Seal, 1907

Hoffmann, Charles G. *Ford Madox Ford*. 1967. Pp. 36-43.

Ohmann, Carol. *Ford Madox Ford*. 1964. Pp. 23-31.

The Rash Act, 1933

Cassell, Richard A. *Ford Madox Ford*. 1961. Pp. 273-277.

Hoffmann, Charles G. *Ford Madox Ford*. 1967. Pp. 135-138.

Mizener, Arthur. *The Saddest Story*. 1971. Pp. 519-522.

The Shifting of the Fire, 1892

Hoffmann, Charles G. *Ford Madox Ford*. 1967. Pp. 22-24.

Ohmann, Carol. *Ford Madox Ford*. 1964. Pp. 10-13.

The Simple Life Limited, 1911

Hoffmann, Charles G. *Ford Madox Ford*. 1967. Pp. 58-60.

Some Do Not, 1924

 Andreach, Robert J. *The Slain and Resurrected God.* 1970. Pp.
  148-170.
 Gordon, Ambrose, Jr. *The Invisible Tent.* 1964. Pp. 92-100, 109-110.

Vive le Roy, 1937

 Hoffmann, Charles G. *Ford Madox Ford.* 1967. Pp. 138-139.
 Mizener, Arthur. *The Saddest Story.* 1971. Pp. 522-523.

When the Wicked Man, 1932

 Cassell, Richard A. *Ford Madox Ford.* 1961. Pp. 270-273.
 Hoffmann, Charles G. *Ford Madox Ford.* 1967. Pp. 133-135.
 Mizener, Arthur. *The Saddest Story.* 1971. Pp. 517-519.

The Young Lovell, 1913

 Andreach, Robert J. *The Slain and Resurrected God.* 1970. Pp.
  120-128.
 Hoffmann, Charles G. *Ford Madox Ford.* 1967. Pp. 71-73.
 Mizener, Arthur. *The Saddest Story.* 1971. Pp. 485-486.
 Ohmann, Carol. *Ford Madox Ford.* 1964. Pp. 35-38.

EMANUEL FORDE

Ornatus and Artesia, 1595?

 Bonheim, Helmut. "Emanuel Forde: *Ornatus and Artesia.*" *Anglia*,
  90 (1972), 50-59.
 Loiseau, Jean. "Le Récit dans le roman d'Emmanuel Ford: *Ornatus
  and Artesia*," in *Récit et roman*. 1972. Pp. 16-21.

E. M. FORSTER

Howards End, 1910

 Armstrong, Paul B. "E. M. Forster's *Howards End*: The Existential
  Crisis of the Liberal Imagination." *Mosaic*, 8 (Fall 1974), 183-199.
 Bedient, Calvin. *Architects of the Self.* 1972. Pp. 217-233.
 Beer, J. B. *The Achievement of E. M. Forster.* 1962. Pp. 101-130.
 Bradbury, Malcolm. *Possibilities.* 1973. Pp. 98-109.
 Brander, Laurence. *E. M. Forster.* 1968. Pp. 126-162.
 Chapple, J. A. V. *Documentary and Imaginative Literature.* 1970.
  Pp. 333-336.
 Crews, Frederick C. *E. M. Forster.* 1962. Pp. 105-123.
 Finklestein, Bonnie B. *Forster's Women.* 1975. Pp. 89-116.
 Gill, Richard. *Happy Rural Seat.* 1972. Pp. 108-114.
 Gransden, K. W. *E. M. Forster.* 1970. Pp. 54-80.
 Hanquart, Evelyne. "Humanisme féministe ou humanisme au féminin?

—Une lecture de l'oeuvre romanesque de Virginia Woolf et E. M.
Forster." *Etudes Anglaises*, 26 (1973), 286-289.

Heine, Elizabeth. "The Significance of Structure in the Novels of
E. M. Forster and Virginia Woolf." *English Literature in Transition*, 16 (1973), 289-306.

Kelvin, Norman. *E. M. Forster*. 1967. Pp. 103-125.

McDowell, Frederick P. W. *E. M. Forster*. 1969. Pp. 81-98.

McGurk, E. Barry. "Gentlefolk in Philistia: The Influence of Matthew
Arnold on E. M. Forster's *Howards End*." *English Literature in Transition*, 15 (1972), 213-219.

Müllenbrock, Heinz-Joachim. "Modes of Opening in the Works of
E. M. Forster: A Contribution to the Poetics of His Novels."
Modern Philology, 70 (1973), 221-225.

Mulvey, Thomas. "A Paraphrase of Nietszche in Forster's *Howards
End*." *Notes and Queries*, 19 (1972), 52.

Shahane, V. A. *E. M. Forster*. 1962. Pp. 84-94.

Stone, Wilfred. *The Cave and the Mountain*. 1966. Pp. 235-275.

Stone, Wilfred. "Forster on Love and Money," in Oliver Stallybrass,
ed., *Aspects of E. M. Forster*. 1969. Pp. 108-120.

Talon, Henri A. "E. M. Forster: Récit et mythe personnel dans les
premiers romans (1905-1910)." *Archives des Lettres Modernes*,
88 (1968), 24-25, 41-42.

Thomson, George H. *The Fiction of E. M. Forster*. 1967. Pp. 161-199.

Trilling, Lionel. *E. M. Forster*. 1964. Pp. 113-135.

Truitt, Willis H. "Thematic and Symbolic Ideology in the Works of
E. M. Forster." *Journal of Aesthetics and Art Criticism*, 30 (1971),
104-105.

Turk, Jo M. "The Evolution of E. M. Forster's Narrator." *Studies
in the Novel*, 5 (1973), 430-432.

Zeh, Dieter. *Studien zur Erzählkunst*. 1970. Pp. 295-307.

The Longest Journey, 1907

Beer, J. B. *The Achievement of E. M. Forster*. 1962. Pp. 77-100.

Brander, Laurence. *E. M. Forster*. 1968. Pp. 109-125.

Crews, Frederick C. *E. M. Forster*. 1962. Pp. 50-70.

Finkelstein, Bonnie B. *Forster's Women*. 1975. Pp. 35-63.

Gransden, K. W. *E. M. Forster*. 1970. Pp. 38-53.

Hays, Peter L. *The Limping Hero*. 1971. Pp. 141-143.

Heine, Elizabeth. "Rickie Elliot and the Cow: The Cambridge Apostles
and *The Longest Journey*." *English Literature in Transition*, 15
(1972), 116-134.

Heine, Elizabeth. "The Significance of Structure in the Novels of E.
M. Forster and Virginia Woolf." *English Literature in Transition*,
16 (1973), 289-306.

Kelvin, Norman. *E. M. Forster*. 1967. Pp. 58-83.

McDowell, Frederick P. W. *E. M. Forster*. 1969. Pp. 65-80.

Müllenbrock. Heinz-Joachim. "Modes of Opening in the Works of

E. M. Forster: A Contribution to the Poetics of His Novels."
Modern Philology, 70 (1973), 216-221.

Shahane, V. A. *E. M. Forster*. 1962. Pp. 66-75.

Stone, Wilfred. *The Cave and the Mountain*. 1966. Pp. 184-215.

Talon, Henri A. "E. M. Forster: Récit et mythe personnel dans les premiers romans (1905-1910)." *Archives des Lettres Modernes*, 88 (1968), 12-16.

Thomson, George H. *The Fiction of E. M. Forster*. 1967. Pp. 125-159.

Trilling, Lionel. *E. M. Forster*. 1964. Pp. 76-96.

Truitt, Willis H. "Thematic and Symbolic Ideology in the Works of E. M. Forster." *Journal of Aesthetics and Art Criticism*, 30 (1971), 103-104.

Zeh, Dieter. *Studien zur Erzählkunst*. 1970. Pp. 258-271.

Maurice, 1971

Bolling, Douglass. "The Distanced Heart: Artistry in E. M. Forster's *Maurice*." *Modern Fiction Studies*, 20 (1974), 157-167.

Finkelstein, Bonnie B. *Forster's Women*. 1975. Pp. 137-172.

Heine, Elizabeth. "The Significance of Structure in the Novels of E. M. Forster and Virginia Woolf." *English Literature in Transition*, 16 (1973), 289-306.

Hotchkiss, Joyce. "Romance and Reality: The Dualistic Style of E. M. Forster's *Maurice*." *Journal of Narrative Technique*, 4 (1974), 163-175.

Rising, C. "E. M. Forster's *Maurice*: A Summing Up." *Texas Quarterly*, 17 (1974), 84-96.

Salter, Donald. "That Is My Ticket: The Homosexual Writings of E. M. Forster." *London Magazine*, 14:6 (1975), 5-33.

A Passage to India, 1924

Barrett, William. *Time of Need*. 1972. Pp. 300-308.

Bedient, Calvin. *Architects of the Self*. 1972. Pp. 250-265.

Beer, J. B. *The Achievement of E. M. Forster*. 1962. Pp. 131-165.

Bradbury, Malcolm. *Possibilities*. 1973. Pp. 110-120.

Bradbury, Malcolm. "Two Passages to India: Forster as Victorian and Modern," in Oliver Stallybrass, ed., *Aspects of E. M. Forster*. 1969. Pp. 131-154.

Brander, Laurence. *E. M. Forster*. 1968. Pp. 163-201.

Brower, Reuben A. "The Twilight of the Double Vision: Symbol and Irony in *A Passage to India*," in Malcolm Bradbury, ed., *E. M. Forster*. 1970. Pp. 114-131.

Chapple, J. A. V. *Documentary and Imaginative Literature*. 1970. Pp. 213-219.

Crews, Frederick C. *E. M. Forster*. 1962. Pp. 142-163.

Emmett, V. J., Jr. "Verbal Truth and Truth of Mood in E. M. Forster's *A Passage to India*." *English Literature in Transition*, 15 (1972), 199-212.

Finkelstein, Bonnie B. *Forster's Women*. 1975. Pp. 117-136.

Fleishman, Avrom. "Being and Nothing in *A Passage to India*." *Criticism*, 15 (1973), 109-125.

Fraser, G. S. "The English Novel," in C. B. Cox and A. E. Dyson, eds., *The Twentieth-Century Mind*. 1972. Vol. II, 395-399.

Friend, Robert. "The Quest for Rondure: A Comparison of Two Passages to India." *Hebrew University Studies in Literature*, 1 (1973), 76-85.

Goonetilleke, D. C. R. A. "Colonial Neuroses: Kipling and Forster." *Ariel*, 5:4 (1974), 62-68.

Gransden, K. W. *E. M. Forster*. 1970. Pp. 81-107.

Hardy, Barbara. *The Appropriate Form*. 1964. Pp. 76-80.

Heine, Elizabeth. "The Significance of Structure in the Novels of E. M. Forster and Virginia Woolf." *English Literature in Transition*, 16 (1973), 289-306.

Kelvin, Norman. *E. M. Forster*. 1967. Pp. 126-142.

Kennard, Jean E. "*A Passage to India* and Dickinson's Saint at Benares." *Studies in the Novel*, 5 (1973), 417-427.

Lebowitz, Naomi. *Humanism and the Absurd*. 1971. Pp. 67-83.

Levine, June Perry. *Creation and Criticism*. 1971. Pp. 165-190.

Lewis, Robin Jared. "Orwell's *Burmese Days* and Forster's *A Passage to India*: Two Novels of Human Relations in the British Empire." *Massachusetts Studies in English*, 4 (1974), 24-32.

McDonald, Walter M. "The Unity of *A Passage to India*." *CEA Critic*, 36 (1973), 38-42.

McDowell, Frederick P. W. *E. M. Forster*. 1969. Pp. 99-124.

Müllenbrock, Heinz-Joachim. "Die Kunst der Eröffnung im Werk E. M. Forsters: Ein Beitrag zur Poetik seiner Romane." *Germanisch-Romanische Monatsschrift*, 21 (1971), 197-203.

Müllenbrock, Heinz-Joachim. "Modes of Opening in the Works of E. M. Forster: A Contribution to the Poetics of His Novels." *Modern Philology*, 70 (1973), 225-229.

Parry, Benita. *Delusions and Discoveries*. 1972. Pp. 260-320.

Pradhan, S. V. "A 'Song' of Love: Forster's *A Passage to India*." *Centennial Review*, 17 (1973), 297-320.

Shahane, V. A. *E. M. Forster*. 1962. Pp. 95-119.

Shahane, V. A. "A Note on the *Marabar Caves* in E. M. Forster's *A Passage to India*." *Osmania Journal of English Studies*, 2 (1962), 67-75.

Stone, Wilfred. *The Cave and the Mountain*. 1966. Pp. 298-346.

Thomson, George H. *The Fiction of E. M. Forster*. 1967. Pp. 201-250.

Trilling, Lionel. *E. M. Forster*. 1964. Pp. 136-161.

Truitt, Willis H. "Thematic and Symbolic Ideology in the Works of E. M. Forster." *Journal of Aesthetics and Art Criticism*, 30 (1971), 105-107.

Turk, Jo M. "The Evolution of E. M. Forster's Narrator." *Studies in the Novel*, 5 (1973), 432-439.

Viswanathan, K. *India in English Fiction.* 1971. Pp. 91-120.
Wilde, Alan. "Depths and Surfaces: Dimensions of Forsterian Irony."
English Literature in Transition, 16 (1973), 257-274.
Zeh, Dieter. *Studien zur Erzählkunst.* 1970. Pp. 308-339.

A Room with a View, 1908

Beer, J. B. *The Achievement of E. M. Forster.* 1962. Pp. 53-66.
Brander, Laurence. *E. M. Forster.* 1968. Pp. 101-108.
Crews, Frederick C. *E. M. Forster.* 1962. Pp. 81-91.
Finkelstein, Bonnie B. *Forster's Women.* 1975. Pp. 65-88.
Finkelstein, Bonnie Blumenthal. "Forster's Women: *A Room with a View.*" *English Literature in Transition,* 16 (1973), 275-287.
Gransden, K. W. *E. M. Forster.* 1970. Pp. 30-37.
Heine, Elizabeth. "The Significance of Structure in the Novels of E. M. Forster and Virginia Woolf." *English Literature in Transition,* 16 (1973), 289-306.
Kelvin, Norman. *E. M. Forster.* 1967. Pp. 84-102.
McDowell, Frederick P. W. *E. M. Forster.* 1969. Pp. 50-58.
Meyers, Jeffrey. "The Paintings in Forster's Italian Novels." *London Magazine,* 13:6 (1974), 55-62.
Müllenbrock, Heinz-Joachim. "Die Kunst der Eröffnung im Werk E. M. Forsters: Ein Beitrag zur Poetik seiner Romane." *Germanisch-Romanische Monatsschrift,* 21 (1971), 192-197.
Shahane, V. A. *E. M. Forster.* 1962. Pp. 76-83.
Stone, Wilfred. *The Cave and the Mountain.* 1966. Pp. 216-234.
Talon, Henri A. "E. M. Forster: Récit et mythe personnel dans les premiers romans (1905-1910)." *Archives des Lettres Modernes,* 88 (1968), 17-20.
Thomson, George H. *The Fiction of E. M. Forster.* 1967. Pp. 100-113.
Trilling, Lionel. *E. M. Forster.* 1964. Pp. 97-112.
Turk, Jo M. "The Evolution of E. M. Forster's Narrator." *Studies in the Novel,* 5 (1973), 429-430.
Zeh, Dieter. *Studien zur Erzählkunst.* 1970. Pp. 272-295.

Where Angels Fear to Tread, 1905

Beer, J. B. *The Achievement of E. M. Forster.* 1962. Pp. 66-76.
Brander, Laurence. *E. M. Forster.* 1968. Pp. 90-100.
Crews, Frederick C. *E. M. Forster.* 1962. Pp. 71-81.
Finkelstein, Bonnie B. *Forster's Women.* 1975. Pp. 1-33.
Gransden, K. W. *E. M. Forster.* 1970. Pp. 16-20, 22-30.
Heine, Elizabeth. "The Significance of Structure in the Novels of E. M. Forster and Virginia Woolf." *English Literature in Transition,* 16 (1973), 289-306.
Kelvin, Norman. *E. M. Forster.* 1967. Pp. 41-57.
McDowell, Frederick P. W. *E. M. Forster.* 1969. Pp. 42-49.
Meyers, Jeffrey. "The Paintings in Forster's Italian Novels." *London Magazine,* 13:6 (1974), 48-55.

Müllenbrock, Heinz-Joachim. "Die Kunst der Eröffnung im Werk E. M. Forsters: Ein Beitrag zur Poetik seiner Romane." *Germanisch-Romanische Monatsschrift*, 21 (1971), 186-192.

Shahane, V. A. *E. M. Forster*. 1962. Pp. 56-65.

Stone, Wilfred. *The Cave and the Mountain*. 1966. Pp. 162-183.

Talon, Henri A. "E. M. Forster: Récit et mythe personnel dans les premiers romans (1905-1910)." *Archives des Lettres Modernes*, 88 (1968), 9-11.

Thomson, George H. *The Fiction of E. M. Forster*. 1967. Pp. 113-119.

Trilling, Lionel. *E. M. Forster*. 1964. Pp. 57-75.

Wilde, Alan. "Depths and Surfaces: Dimensions of Forsterian Irony." *English Literature in Transition*, 16 (1973), 257-274.

Zeh, Dieter. *Studien zur Erzählkunst*. 1970. Pp. 249-258.

JOHN FOWLES

The Collector, 1963

Binns, Ronald. "John Fowles: Radical Romancer." *Critical Quarterly*, 15 (1973), 319-325.

Laughlin, Rosemary M. "Faces of Power in the Novels of John Fowles." *Critique* (Atlanta), 13:3 (1971), 72-75.

Rackham, Jeff. "John Fowles: The Existential Labyrinth." *Critique* (Atlanta), 13:3 (1971), 90-94.

The French Lieutenant's Woman, 1969

Binns, Ronald. "John Fowles: Radical Romancer." *Critical Quarterly*, 15 (1973), 331-333.

Brontlinger, Patrick, Ian Adam, and Sheldon Rothblatt. "*The French Lieutenant's Woman*: A Discussion." *Victorian Studies*, 15 (1972), 339-356.

DeVitis, A. A., and William J. Palmer. "*A Pair of Blue Eyes* Flash at *The French Lieutenant's Woman*." *Contemporary Literature*, 15 (1974), 90-101.

Evarts, Prescott, Jr. "Fowles' *The French Lieutenant's Woman* as Tragedy." *Critique* (Atlanta), 13:3 (1971), 57-69.

Kaplan, Fred. "Victorian Modernists: Fowles and Nabokov." *Journal of Narrative Technique*, 3 (1973), 109-115.

Laughlin, Rosemary M. "Faces of Power in the Novels of John Fowles." *Critique* (Atlanta), 13:3 (1971), 84-88.

Mellors, John. "Collectors and Creators: The Novels of John Fowles." *London Magazine*, 14:6 (1975), 67-69.

Rackham, Jeff. "John Fowles: The Existential Labyrinth." *Critique* (Atlanta), 13:3 (1971), 98-103.

Rankin, Elizabeth D. "Cryptic Coloration in *The French Lieutenant's Woman*." *Journal of Narrative Technique*, 3 (1973), 193-207.

Rose, Gilbert J. "*The French Lieutenant's Woman:* The Unconscious

Significance of a Novel to Its Author." *American Imago*, 29 (1972), 165-176.

The Magus, 1966

Berets, Ralph. "*The Magus*: A Study in the Creation of a Personal Myth." *Twentieth-Century Literature*, 19 (1973), 89-98.

Binns, Ronald. "John Fowles: Radical Romancer." *Critical Quarterly*, 15 (1973), 326-331.

Bradbury, Malcolm. "John Fowles's *The Magus*," in Brom Weber, ed., *Sense and Sensibility*. 1970. Pp. 26-38.

Bradbury, Malcolm. *Possibilities*. 1973. Pp. 264-271.

Laughlin, Rosemary M. "Faces of Power in the Novels of John Fowles." *Critique* (Atlanta), 13:3 (1971), 75-84.

Presley, Delma E. "The Quest of the Bourgeois Hero: An Approach to Fowles' *The Magus*." *Journal of Popular Culture*, 6 (1972), 394-398.

Rackham, Jeff. "John Fowles: The Existential Labyrinth." *Critique* (Atlanta), 13:3 (1971), 94-98.

Roll-Hansen, Diderik. "John Fowles og den engelske roman i dag." *Edda*, 1974, 314-317.

GEORGE M. FRASER

Flash for Freedom, 1971

Voorhees, Richard J. "Flashman and Richard Hannay." *Dalhousie Review*, 53 (1973), 113-120.

Flashman, 1969

Voorhees, Richard J. "Flashman and Richard Hannay." *Dalhousie Review*, 53 (1973), 113-120.

Royal Flash, 1970

Voorhees, Richard J. "Flashman and Richard Hannay." *Dalhousie Review*, 53 (1973), 113-120.

JAMES ANTHONY FROUDE

The Nemesis of Faith, 1848

McCraw, Harry Wells. "Two Novelists of Despair: James Anthony Froude and William Hale White." *Southern Quarterly*, 13 (1974), 21-51.

JOHN GALSWORTHY

The Burning Spear, 1919

> Frechet, Alec. "Le Secret de Galsworthy." *Etudes Anglaises*, 24 (1971), 152-161.

The Country House, 1907

> Gill, Richard. *Happy Rural Seat*. 1972. Pp. 117-119.
> Kermode, Frank. "The English Novel, circa 1907," in Reuben A. Brower, ed., *Twentieth-Century Literature in Retrospect*. 1971. Pp. 56-60.

The Forsyte Saga, 1922

> Cohen, Walter, Jan Struther, and Lyman Bryson. "*The Forsyte Saga*," in George D. Crothers, ed., *Invitation to Learning*. 1966. Pp. 181-189.
> Gill, Richard. *Happy Rural Seat*. 1972. Pp. 120-124.
> Wootton, Carol. "The Lure of the Basilisk: Chopin's Music in the Writings of Thomas Mann, John Galsworthy and Hermann Hesse." *Arcadia*, 9 (1974), 23-30.

Fraternity, 1909

> Bellamy, William. *The Novels of Wells, Bennett, and Galsworthy*. 1971. Pp. 183-204.

Jocelyn, 1898

> Bellamy, William. *The Novels of Wells, Bennett, and Galsworthy*. 1971. Pp. 88-102.

The Man of Property, 1906

> Bellamy, William. *The Novels of Wells, Bennett, and Galsworthy*. 1971. Pp. 165-180.
> Hart, John E. "Ritual and Spectacle in *The Man of Property*." *Research Studies*, 40 (1972), 34-43.

JOHN GALT

Annals of the Parrish, 1821

> Gibault, Henri. "A propos de deux rééditions de John Galt." *Etudes Anglaises*, 24 (1971), 162-165.

The Entail, 1823

> Gibault, Henri. "A propos de deux rééditions de John Galt." *Etudes Anglaises*, 24 (1971), 162-165.

GEORGE GASCOIGNE

The Adventures of Master F. J., 1573

> Ardolino, Frank. "The Fictionalization of Master F. J.: An Analysis of Gascoigne's *The Pleasant Fable.*" *Essays in Literature* (Denver), 1:2 (1973), 1-16.
> Davis, Walter R. *Idea and Act.* 1969. Pp. 97-109.
> Philmus, M. R. Rohr. "Gascoigne's Fable of the Artist *As* a Young Man." *Journal of English and Germanic Philology*, 73 (1974), 13-31.
> Voytovich, Edward R. "The Poems of 'Master F. J.': A Narrator's Windfall." *Thoth*, 13 (1973), 17-25.

ELIZABETH GASKELL

Cousin Phillis, 1865

> Sharps, John Geoffrey. *Mrs. Gaskell's Observation and Invention.* 1970. Pp. 427-440.

Cranford, 1853

> Beer, Patricia. *Reader, I Married Him.* 1974. Pp. 155-159.
> McVeagh, John. *Elizabeth Gaskell*, 1970. Pp. 55-57.
> Pollard, Arthur. *Mrs. Gaskell.* 1966. Pp. 62-85.
> Sharps, John Geoffrey. *Mrs. Gaskell's Observation and Invention.* 1970. Pp. 125-135.

A Dark Night's Work, 1863

> Sharps, John Geoffrey. *Mrs. Gaskell's Observation and Invention.* 1970. Pp. 353-371.

Mary Barton, 1848

> Beer, Patricia. *Reader, I Married Him.* 1974. Pp. 134-142, 149-150.
> Cazamian, Louis. *The Social Novel in England.* 1973. Pp. 214-226.
> Craik, W. A. *Elizabeth Gaskell.* 1975. Pp. 1-46.
> McVeagh, John. *Elizabeth Gaskell.* 1970. Pp. 51-54, 61-65, 76-77, 79-82.
> Mews, Hazel. *Frail Vessels.* 1969. Pp. 82-84.
> Melada, Ivan. *The Captain of Industry.* 1970. Pp. 73-86.
> Pollard, Arthur. *Mrs. Gaskell.* 1966. Pp. 32-61.
> Sharps, John Geoffrey. *Mrs. Gaskell's Observation and Invention.* 1970. Pp. 51-79.
> Smith, David. "*Mary Barton* and *Hard Times*: Their Social Insights." *Mosaic*, 5 (Winter 1971-1972), 98-104.
> Tomlinson, T. B. "Love and Politics in the Early-Victorian Novel." *Critical Review* (Melbourne), No. 17 (1974), 128-132.
> Vooys, Sijna de. *The Psychological Element.* 1966. Pp. 50-52.

My Lady Ludlow, 1859

Mews, Hazel. *Frail Vessels*. 1969. Pp. 92-94.
Sharps, John Geoffrey. *Mrs. Gaskell's Observation and Invention*.
   1970. Pp. 275-293.

North and South, 1855

Cazamian, Louis. *The Social Novel in England*. 1973. Pp. 226-231.
Craik, W. A. *Elizabeth Gaskell*. 1975. Pp. 89-139.
Furbank, P. N. "Mendacity in Mrs. Gaskell." *Encounter*, 40:6 (1973),
   51-55.
McVeagh, John. *Elizabeth Gaskell*. 1970. Pp. 65-67, 82-85.
Melada, Ivan. *The Captain of Industry*. 1970. Pp. 147-152.
Mews, Hazel. *Frail Vessels*. 1969. Pp. 88-92.
Pollard, Arthur. *Mrs. Gaskell*. 1966. Pp. 108-138.
Sharps, John Geoffrey. *Mrs. Gaskell's Observation and Invention*.
   1970. Pp. 205-240.
Tomlinson, T. B. "Love and Politics in the Early-Victorian Novel."
   Critical Review (Melbourne), No. 17 (1974), 129-132.
Vooys, Sijna de. *The Psychological Element*. 1966. Pp. 52-55.

Ruth, 1853

Beer, Patricia. *Reader, I Married Him*. 1974. Pp. 144-147, 150-153.
Craik, W. A. *Elizabeth Gaskell*. 1975. Pp. 47-88.
McVeagh, John. *Elizabeth Gaskell*. 1970. Pp. 89-90.
Mews, Hazel. *Frail Vessels*. 1969. Pp. 85-88, 186-188.
Pollard, Arthur. *Mrs. Gaskell*. 1966. Pp. 86-107.
Sharps, John Geoffrey. *Mrs. Gaskell's Observation and Invention*.
   1970. Pp. 147-167.

Sylvia's Lovers, 1863

Craik, W. A. *Elizabeth Gaskell*. 1975. Pp. 140-199.
McVeagh, John. *Elizabeth Gaskell*. 1970. Pp. 54-56, 69-71, 77-79.
Pollard, Arthur. *Mrs. Gaskell*. 1966. Pp. 194-223.
Rance, Nicholas. *The Historical Novel*. 1975. Pp. 137-154.
Sharps, John Geoffrey. *Mrs. Gaskell's Observation and Invention*.
   1970. Pp. 373-421.

Wives and Daughters, 1866

Beer, Patricia. *Reader, I Married Him*. 1974. Pp. 160-174.
Butler, Marilyn. "The Uniqueness of Cynthia Kirkpatrick: Elizabeth
   Gaskell's *Wives and Daughters* and Maria Edgeworth's *Helen*."
   Review of English Studies, 23 (1972), 278-290.
Craik, W. A. *Elizabeth Gaskell*. 1975. Pp. 200-268.
McVeagh, John. *Elizabeth Gaskell*. 1970. Pp. 57-59, 67-69, 85-88.
Mews, Hazel. *Frail Vessels*. 1969. Pp. 94-97, 143-144.
Pollard, Arthur. *Mrs. Gaskell*. 1966. Pp. 224-247.

Sharps, John Geoffrey. *Mrs. Gaskell's Observation and Invention.*
1970. Pp. 469-525.

Spacks, Patricia Meyer. "Taking Care: Some Women Novelists."
Novel, 6 (1972), 36-41.

Swinden, Patrick. *Unofficial Selves.* 1973. Pp. 50-53.

GEORGE GISSING

Born in Exile, 1892

Hude, E. Christine. "Feminine Portraiture in *Born in Exile*." *Gissing
Newsletter,* 8:4 (1972), 1-17.

Korg, Jacob. *George Gissing.* 1963. Pp. 168-170, 174-178.

The Crown of Life, 1899

Korg, Jacob. *George Gissing.* 1963. Pp. 230-232.

Demos, 1886

Francis, C. J. *"Demos."* *Gissing Newsletter,* 10:2 (1974), 1-13.

Irwin, Michael. "Cross Purposes in Gissing." *Gissing Newsletter,*
9:1 (1973), 8-12.

Keating, P. J. *The Working Classes.* 1971. Pp. 69-72, 77-79.

Korg, Jacob. *George Gissing.* 1963. Pp. 83-97.

Lucas, John. "Conservatism and Revolution in the 1880's," in John
Lucas, ed., *Literature and Politics.* 1971. Pp. 188-217.

Vooys, Sijna de. *The Psychological Element.* 1966. Pp. 78-87.

Denzil Quarrier, 1892

Korg, Jacob. *George Gissing.* 1963. Pp. 179-181.

Kurman, Stanly P. "The Hero as Politician." *Gissing Newsletter,*
9:2 (1973), 4-6.

The Emancipated, 1890

Korg, Jacob. *George Gissing.* 1963. Pp. 136-140.

Eve's Ransom, 1895

Korg, Jacob. *George Gissing.* 1963. Pp. 198-199.

In the Year of Jubilee, 1894

Korg, Jacob. *George Gissing.* 1963. Pp. 194-197.

Robey, Cora. *"In the Year of Jubilee*: A Satire on Late Victorian
Culture." *Tennessee Studies in Literature,* 17 (1972), 121-127.

Isabel Clarendon, 1886

Korg, Jacob. *George Gissing.* 1963. Pp. 77-80.

A Life's Morning, 1888

Korg, Jacob. *George Gissing.* 1963. Pp. 80-83.

Kurman, Stanly P. *"The Hero as Politican." Gissing Newsletter,*
9:2 (1973), 2-4.

The Nether World, 1889

Chapple, J. A. V. *Documentary and Imaginative Literature.* 1970.
Pp. 96-99.
Keating, P. J. *The Working Classes.* 1971. Pp. 83-92.
Korg, Jacob. *George Gissing.* 1963. Pp. 111-116.
Vooys, Sijna de. *The Psychological Element.* 1966. Pp. 95-101.

New Grub Street, 1891

Collie, Michael. "Gissing's Revision of *New Grub Street." Yearbook
of English Studies,* 4 (1974), 212-224.
Howe, Irving. *A World More Attractive.* 1963. Pp. 183-191.
Irwin, Michael. "Cross Purposes in Gissing." *Gissing Newsletter,*
9:1 (1973), 10-14.
Korg, Jacob. *George Gissing.* 1963. Pp. 154-167.
Lacheze, Henri. "An Introduction to George Gissing's *New Grub
Street." Diliman Review,* 22:2 (1974), 140-161.
Vooys, Sijna de. *The Psychological Element.* 1966. Pp. 101-110.

The Odd Women, 1893

Korg, Jacob. *George Gissing.* 1963. Pp. 188-190.
Maglin, Nan Bauer. "Fictional Feminists in *The Bostonians* and *The
Odd Women,"* in Susan Koppelman Cornillon, ed., *Images of
Women in Fiction.* 1973. Pp. 225-234.

Our Friend the Charlatan, 1901

Korg, Jacob. *George Gissing.* 1963. Pp. 236-239.
Kurman, Stanly P. "The Hero as Politician." *Gissing Newsletter,*
9:2 (1973), 6-9.

The Private Papers of Henry Ryecroft, 1903

Korg, Jacob. *George Gissing.* 1963. Pp. 240-245.

Thyrza, 1887

Blench, J. W. "George Gissing's *Thyrza." Durham University Jour-
nal,* 64 (1972), 85-114.
Keating, P. J. *The Working Classes.* 1971. Pp. 61-63, 68-69, 79-83.
Korg, Jacob. *George Gissing.* 1963. Pp. 99-107.
Vooys, Sijna de. *The Psychological Element.* 1966. Pp. 87-95.

The Unclassed, 1884

Francis, C. J. *"The Unclassed." Gissing Newsletter,* 10:1 (1974), 1-11.
Keating, P. J. *The Working Classes.* 1971. Pp. 76-77.
Korg, Jacob. *George Gissing.* 1963. Pp. 62-69.

Veranilda, 1904

Korg, Jacob. *George Gissing*. 1963. Pp. 255-257.

The Whirlpool, 1897

Fernando, Lloyd. "Gissing's Studies in 'Vulgarism': Aspects of His Anti-feminism." *Southern Review* (Adelaide), 4 (1970), 47-50.
Korg, Jacob. *George Gissing*. 1963. Pp. 207-210.
Partridge, Colin. "The Humane Centre: George Gissing's *The Whirlpool*." *Gissing Newsletter*, 9:3 (1973), 1-10.

Workers in the Dawn, 1880

Ballard, Michel. "Love and Culture in *Workers in the Dawn*." *Gissing Newsletter*, 10:4 (1974), 1-14.
Keating, P. J. *The Working Classes*. 1971. Pp. 55-56, 58-60, 63-67, 73-76.
Korg, Jacob. *George Gissing*. 1963. Pp. 33-41.

ELINOR SUTHERLAND GLYN

Three Weeks, 1907

Kermode, Frank. "The English Novel, circa 1907," in Reuben A. Brower, ed., *Twentieth-Century Literature in Retrospect*. 1971. Pp. 47-48.

MARGARET RUMER GODDEN

The Battle of the Villa Fiorita, 1963

Simpson, Hassell A. *Rumer Godden*. 1973. Pp. 53-54, 88-89.

Black Narcissus, 1939

Simpson, Hassell A. *Rumer Godden*. 1973. Pp. 38-42.

Breakfast with the Nikolides, 1942

Simpson, Hassell A. *Rumer Godden*. 1973. Pp. 46-47, 87-88.

A Breath of Air, 1950

Simpson, Hassell A. *Rumer Godden*. 1973. Pp. 99-101.

China Court, 1961

Simpson, Hassell A. *Rumer Godden*. 1973. Pp. 68-74.

Chinese Puzzle, 1936

Simpson, Hassell A. *Rumer Godden*. 1973. Pp. 32-35.

An Episode of Sparrows, 1956

Simpson, Hassell A. *Rumer Godden*. 1973. Pp. 83-86.

A Fugue in Time, 1945

Simpson, Hassell A. *Rumer Godden*. 1973. Pp. 61-68.

The Greengage Summer, 1958

Simpson, Hassell A. *Rumer Godden*. 1973. Pp. 52-53, 86-87.

Gypsy, Gypsy, 1940

Simpson, Hassell A. *Rumer Godden*. 1973. Pp. 44-46.

In This House of Brede, 1969

Simpson, Hassell A. *Rumer Godden*. 1973. Pp. 110-115.

Kingfishers Catch Fire, 1953

Simpson, Hassell A. *Rumer Godden*. 1973. Pp. 47-50.

The Lady and the Unicorn, 1937

Simpson, Hassell A. *Rumer Godden*. 1973. Pp. 35-37.

The River, 1946

Simpson, Hassell A. *Rumer Godden*. 1973. Pp. 74-79.

FRANCIS GODWIN

The Man in the Moone, 1638

Cuadrado, Beatriz G. P. de. "*The Man in the Moon*, de Francis Godwin." *Revista de Literaturas Modernas*, 7 (1968), 75-86.

WILLIAM GODWIN

Caleb Williams, 1794

Breitinger, Eckhard. *Der Tod im englischen Roman*. 1971. Pp. 136-144, 146-153.

Cobb, Joann P. "Godwin's Novels and *Political Justice*." *Enlightenment Essays*, 4 (1973), 18-19.

Kiely, Robert. *The Romantic Novel in England*. 1972. Pp. 81-97.

Myers, Mitzi. "Godwin's Changing Conception of *Caleb Williams*." *Studies in English Literature, 1500-1900*, 12 (1972), 591-628.

Ousby, Ian. "'My Servant Caleb': Godwin's *Caleb Williams* and the Political Trials of the 1790s." *University of Toronto Quarterly*, 44 (1974), 47-55.

Pollin, Burton R. "The Significance of Names in the Fiction of William Godwin." *Revue des Langues Vivantes*, 37 (1971), 390-391.

Smith, Elton Edward, and Esther Greenwell Smith. *William Godwin*. 1965. Pp. 85-90.

Stamper, Rexford. "*Caleb Williams*: The Bondage of Truth." *Southern Quarterly*, 12 (1973), 39-50.

Vooys, Sijna de. *The Psychological Element*. 1966. Pp. 27-37.

Woodcock, George. "Things As They Might Be: Things As They Are —Notes on the Novels of William Godwin." *Dalhousie Review*, 54 (1974-1975), 686-689.

Cloudesley, 1830

Cobb, Joann P. "Godwin's Novels and *Political Justice*." *Enlightenment Essays*, 4 (1973), 24-26.

Pollin, Burton R. "The Significance of Names in the Fiction of William Godwin." *Revue des Langues Vivantes*, 37 (1971), 395-397.

Smith, Elton Edward, and Esther Greenwell Smith. *William Godwin*. 1965. Pp. 106-109.

Deloraine, 1833

Cobb, Joann P. "Godwin's Novels and *Political Justice*." *Enlightenment Essays*, 4 (1973), 26-28.

Pollin, Burton R. "The Significance of Names in the Fiction of William Godwin." *Revue des Langues Vivantes*, 37 (1971), 397-399.

Smith, Elton Edward, and Esther Greenwell Smith. *William Godwin*. 1965. Pp. 109-111.

Fleetwood, 1805

Cobb, Joann P. "Godwin's Novels and *Political Justice*." *Enlightenment Essays*, 4 (1973), 21-23.

Smith, Elton Edward, and Esther Greenwell Smith. *William Godwin*. 1965. Pp. 96-102.

Mandeville, 1817

Cobb, Joann P. "Godwin's Novels and *Political Justice*." *Enlightenment Essays*, 4 (1973), 23-24.

Pollin, Burton R. "The Significance of Names in the Fiction of William Godwin." *Revue des Langues Vivantes*, 37 (1971), 394-395.

Smith, Elton Edward, and Esther Greenwell Smith. *William Godwin*. 1965. Pp. 102-106.

Woodcock, George. "Things As They Might Be: Things As They Are —Notes on the Novels of William Godwin." *Dalhousie Review*, 54 (1974-1975), 693-694.

St. Leon, 1799

Cobb, Joann P. "Godwin's Novels and *Political Justice*." *Enlightenment Essays*, 4 (1973), 19-21.

Pollin, Burton R. "The Significance of Names in the Fiction of William Godwin." *Revue des Langues Vivantes*, 37 (1971), 391-393.

Smith, Elton Edward, and Esther Greenwell Smith. *William Godwin*. 1965. Pp. 90-96.

Woodcock, George. "Things As They Might Be: Things As They Are
—Notes on the Novels of William Godwin." *Dalhousie Review*,
54 (1974-1975), 690-692.

WILLIAM GOLDING

Free Fall, 1959

Biles, Jack I. *Talk*. 1970. Pp. 78-87.
Buckley, Jerome Hamilton. *Season of Youth*. 1974. Pp. 269-280.
Byczkowska, Ewa. "William Golding's Novels and the Anglo-American Tradition of Allegory in Fiction." *Anglica Wratislaviensia*,
2 (1972), 63-74.
Delbaere-Garant, Jeanne. "From the Cellar to the Rock: A Recurrent Pattern in William Golding's Novels." *Modern Fiction Studies*,
17 (1971-1972), 507-510.
Mužina, Matej. "William Golding: The World of Perception and the
World of Cognition." *Studia Romanica et Anglica Zagrabiensia*,
27-28 (1969), 117-123.
Stinson, John J. "Trying to Exorcise the Beast: The Grotesque in
the Fiction of William Golding." *Cithara*, 11:1 (1971), 7-8, 14-19.

The Inheritors, 1955

Biles, Jack I. *Talk,* 1970. Pp. 105-108.
Byczkowska, Ewa. "William Golding's Novels and the Anglo-Ameri-
can Tradition of Allegory in Fiction." *Anglica Wratislaviensia*,
2 (1972), 63-74.
Delbaere-Garant, Jeanne. "From the Cellar to the Rock: A Recurrent
Pattern in William Golding's Novels." *Modern Fiction Studies*,
17 (1971-1972), 504-505.
Halliday, M. A. K. "Linguistic Function and Literary Style: An
Inquiry into the Language of William Golding's *The Inheritors*,"
in Seymour Chatman, ed., *Literary Style*. 1971. Pp. 348-362.
Mužina, Matej. "William Golding: The World of Perception and the
World of Cognition." *Studia Romanica et Anglica Zagrabiensia*,
27-28 (1969), 107-116.
Schrey, Helmut. *Didaktik des zeitgenössischen englischen Romans*.
1970. Pp. 71-73.
Ryan, J. S. "The Two Pincher Martins: From Survival Adventure to
Golding's Myth of Dying." *English Studies*, 55 (1974), 141-143.

Lord of the Flies, 1954

Byczkowska, Ewa. "William Golding's Novels and the Anglo-American Tradition of Allegory in Fiction." *Anglica Wratislaviensia*,
2 (1972), 63-74.
Capey, A. C. " 'Will' and 'Idea' in *Lord of the Flies*." *Use of English*,
24 (1972), 99-107.

Delbaere-Garant, Jeanne. "From the Cellar to the Rock: A Recurrent Pattern in William Golding's Novels." *Modern Fiction Studies*, 17 (1971-1972), 503-504.

Fleck, A. D. "The Golding Bough: Aspects of Myth and Ritual in *The Lord of the Flies*," in B. S. Benedikz, ed., *On the Novel*. 1971. Pp. 189-204.

Freese, Peter. "Verweisende Zeichen in William Goldings *Lord of the Flies*." *Die Neueren Sprachen*, 71 (1972), 162-172.

Kahrmann, Bernd. *Die idyllische Szene*. 1969. Pp. 80-84.

Morgan, George. "Le Symbolisme du paysage dans *Lord of the Flies*." *Annales de la Faculté des Lettres et Sciences Humaines de Nice*, 18 (1972), 77-96.

Mužina, Matej. "William Golding: Novels of Extreme Situations." *Studia Romanica et Anglica Zagrabiensia*, 27-28 (1969), 50-66.

Raphaël, André. "La Pesanteur et la grâce dans *Lord of the Flies*: Notes pour une interprétation weilienne de l'oeuvre de Golding." *Langues Modernes*, 66 (1972), 450-468.

Ruotolo, Lucio P. *Six Existential Heroes*. 1973. Pp. 101-118.

Ryan, J. S. "The Two Pincher Martins: From Survival Adventure to Golding's Myth of Dying." *English Studies*, 55 (1974), 140-141.

Schrey, Helmut. *Didaktik des zeitgenössischen englischen Romans*. 1970. Pp. 65-71.

Smith, Eric. *Some Versions of the Fall*. 1973. Pp. 163-202.

Stern, J. P. *On Realism*. 1973. Pp. 20-27.

Stinson, John J. "Trying to Exorcise the Beast: The Grotesque in the Fiction of William Golding." *Cithara*, 11:1 (1971), 6-7, 8, 13.

Pincher Martin, 1956

Biles, Jack I. *Talk*. 1970. Pp. 69-77.

Byczkowska, Ewa. "William Golding's Novels and the Anglo-American Tradition of Allegory in Fiction." *Anglica Wratislaviensia*, 2 (1972), 63-74.

Delbaere-Garant, Jeanne. "From the Cellar to the Rock: A Recurrent Pattern in William Golding's Novels." *Modern Fiction Studies*, 17 (1971-1972), 506-507.

Mužina, Matej. "William Golding: The World of Perception and the World of Cognition." *Studia Romanica et Anglica Zagrabiensia*, 27-28 (1969), 123-127.

Ryan, J. S. "The Two Pincher Martins: From Survival Adventure to Golding's Myth of Dying." *English Studies*, 55 (1974), 143-151.

Schrey, Helmut. *Didaktik des zeitgenössischen englischen Romans*. 1970. Pp. 73-76.

Stinson, John J. "Trying to Exorcise the Beast: The Grotesque in the Fiction of William Golding." *Cithara*, 11:1 (1971), 11-12.

The Spire, 1964

Biles, Jack I. *Talk*. 1970. Pp. 96-100.

Byczkowska, Ewa. "William Golding's Novels and the Anglo-American can Tradition of Allegory in Fiction." *Anglica Wratislaviensia*, 2 (1972), 63-74.

Delbaere-Garant, Jeanne. "From the Cellar to the Rock: A Recurrent Pattern in William Golding's Novels." *Modern Fiction Studies*, 17 (1971-1972), 510-511.

Kahrmann, Bernd. *Die idyllische Szene*. 1969. Pp. 109-113.

Sternlicht, Sanford. "Two Views of the Builder in Graham Greene's *A Burnt-Out Case* and William Golding's *The Spire.*" *Studies in the Humanities*, 2 (1970-1971), 17-19.

Stinson, John J. "Trying to Exorcise the Beast: The Grotesque in the Fiction of William Golding." *Cithara*, 11:1 (1971), 19-25.

OLIVER GOLDSMITH

The Vicar of Wakefield, 1766

Bäckman, Sven. *This Singular Tale*. 1971. Pp. 40-120, 137-210, 223-254.

Battestin, Martin C. *The Providence of Wit*. 1974. Pp. 193-214.

Bozzoli, Adriano. "Manzoni e Goldsmith." *Aevum*, 45 (1971), 46-56.

Brissenden, R. F. *Virtue in Distress*. 1974. Pp. 245-250.

Burton, Dolores M. "Intonation Patterns of Sermons in Seven Novels." *Language and Style*, 3 (1970), 210-212, 217-218.

Chute, B. J., W. G. Rogers, and George D. Crothers. "*The Vicar of Wakefield*," in George D. Crothers, ed., *Invitation to Learning*. 1966. Pp. 62-69.

Grudis, Paul J. "The Narrator and the Vicar of Wakefield." *Essays in Literature* (Denver), 1:1 (1973), 51-66.

Helgerson, Richard. "The Two Worlds of Oliver Goldsmith." *Studies in English Literature, 1500-1900*, 13 (1973), 529-534.

Hopkins, Robert H. *The True Genius of Oliver Goldsmith*. 1969. Pp. 166-230.

Hunting, Robert. "The Poems in *The Vicar of Wakefield*." *Criticism*, 15 (1973), 234-241.

Kirk, Clara M. *Oliver Goldsmith*. 1967. Pp. 84-117.

Otten, Kurt. *Der englische Roman*. 1971. Pp. 89-92.

Passon, Richard H. "Goldsmith and His Vicar: Another Look." *Modern Language Studies*, 3 (1973), 59-69.

Quintana, Ricardo. "Oliver Goldsmith, Ironist to the Georgians," in W. H. Bond, ed., *Eighteenth-Century Studies*. 1970. Pp. 305-309.

Wolff, Erwin. *Der englische Roman*. 1968. Pp. 135-139.

CATHERINE GORE

Cecil, 1841

Colby, Vineta. *Yesterday's Woman*. 1974. Pp. 59-70.

Mrs. Armytage, 1836

> Colby, Vineta. *Yesterday's Woman*. 1974. Pp. 79-81.

The Two Aristocracies, 1857

> Melada, Ivan. *The Captain of Industry*. 1970. Pp. 154-157.

ELIZABETH GOUDGE

The Bird in the Tree, 1940

> Marsden, Madonna. "Gentle Truths for Gentle Readers: The Fiction of Elizabeth Goudge," in Susan Koppelman Cornillon, ed., *Images of Women in Fiction*. 1973. Pp. 72-74.

The Heart of the Family, 1953

> Marsden, Madonna. "Gentle Truths for Gentle Readers: The Fiction of Elizabeth Goudge," in Susan Koppelman Cornillon, ed., *Images of Women in Fiction*. 1973. Pp. 72-76.

Pilgrim's Inn, 1948

> Marsden, Madonna. "Gentle Truths for Gentle Readers: The Fiction of Elizabeth Goudge," in Susan Koppelman Cornillon, ed., *Images of Women in Fiction*. 1973. Pp. 72-75.

RICHARD GRAVES

The Spiritual Quixote, 1773

> Lyons, N. J. L. "Another Key to *The Spiritual Quixote*." *Notes and Queries*, 20 (1973), 20-22.
> Lyons, Nicholas. "Satiric Technique in *The Spiritual Quixote*: Some Comments." *Durham University Journal*, 66 (1974), 266-277.
> Rymer, Michael. "Satiric Technique in *The Spiritual Quixote*." *Durham University Journal*, 65 (1972), 54-64.

HENRY GREEN

Back, 1946

> Russell, John. *Henry Green*. 1960. Pp. 141-178.
> Ryf, Robert S. *Henry Green*. 1967. Pp. 29-33.
> Weatherhead, A. Kingsley. *A Reading of Henry Green*. 1961. Pp. 93-105.

Blindness, 1926

> Russell, John. *Henry Green*. 1960. Pp. 50-73.
> Ryf, Robert S. *Henry Green*. 1967. Pp. 4-10.
> Weatherhead, A. Kingsley. *A Reading of Henry Green*. 1961. Pp. 7-20.

Caught, 1943

> Russell, John. *Henry Green*. 1960. Pp. 141-178.
> Ryf, Robert S. *Henry Green*. 1967. Pp. 22-26.
> Weatherhead, A. Kingsley. *A Reading of Henry Green*. 1961. Pp. 55-72.

Concluding, 1948

> Russell, John. *Henry Green*. 1960. Pp. 179-201.
> Ryf, Robert S. *Henry Green*. 1967. Pp. 33-36.
> Weatherhead, A. Kingsley. *A Reading of Henry Green*. 1961. Pp. 106-122.

Doting, 1952

> Russell, John. *Henry Green*. 1960. Pp. 202-225.
> Ryf, Robert S. *Henry Green*. 1967. Pp. 39-42.
> Weatherhead, A. Kingsley. *A Reading of Henry Green*. 1961. Pp. 135-143.

Living, 1929

> Bassoff, Bruce. "Prose Consciousness in the Novels of Henry Green." *Language and Style*, 5 (1972), 276-280.
> Russell, John. *Henry Green*. 1960. Pp. 74-113.
> Ryf, Robert S. *Henry Green*. 1967. Pp. 10-15.
> Weatherhead, A. Kingsley. *A Reading of Henry Green*. 1961. Pp. 21-39.

Loving, 1945

> Gill, Richard. *Happy Rural Seat*. 1972. Pp. 191-193.
> Russell, John. *Henry Green*. 1960. Pp. 114-140.
> Ryf, Robert S. *Henry Green*. 1967. Pp. 26-29.
> Weatherhead, A. Kingsley. *A Reading of Henry Green*. 1961. Pp. 73-92.

Nothing, 1950

> Russell, John. *Henry Green*. 1960. Pp. 202-225.
> Ryf, Robert S. *Henry Green*. 1967. Pp. 37-39.
> Weatherhead, A. Kingsley. *A Reading of Henry Green*. 1961. Pp. 123-135.

Party Going, 1939

> Bassoff, Bruce. "Prose Consciousness in the Novels of Henry Green." *Language and Style*, 5 (1972), 280-285.
> Hart, Clive. "The Structure and Technique of *Party Going*." *Yearbook of English Studies*, 1 (1971), 185-199.
> Russell, John. *Henry Green*. 1960. Pp. 74-113.
> Ryf, Robert S. *Henry Green*. 1967. Pp. 15-20.

Weatherhead, A. Kingsley. *A Reading of Henry Green.* 1961. Pp. 40-54.

GRAHAM GREENE

Brighton Rock, 1938

Boardman, Gwenn R. *Graham Greene.* 1971. Pp. 41-50.
Fricker, Robert. "Graham Greene," in Otto Mann, ed., *Christliche Dichter.* 1968. Pp. 255-257.
Kellogg, Gene. *The Vital Tradition.* 1970. Pp. 117-122.
Kulkarni, H. B. "Redemptive Sin in Graham Greene." *Proceedings of the Utah Academy of Sciences, Arts, and Letters,* 49:2 (1972), 36-50.
Lenfest, David S. "*Brighton Rock/Young Scarface.*" *Literature/Film Quarterly,* 2 (1974), 373-378.
Lodge, David. *Graham Greene.* 1966. Pp. 20-24.
Lodge, David. *The Novelist at the Crossroads.* 1971. Pp. 99-101.
Pérez Minik, Domingo. *Introducción a la novela inglesa actual.* 1968. Pp. 135-138.
Pryce-Jones, David. *Graham Greene.* 1963. Pp. 29-38.
Ruotolo, Lucio P. *Six Existential Heroes.* 1973. Pp. 39-53.
Sonnenfeld, Albert. "Children's Faces: Graham Greene," in Melvin J. Friedman, ed., *The Vision Obscured.* 1970. Pp. 115-120.

A Burnt-Out Case, 1961

Boardman, Gwenn R. *Graham Greene.* 1971. Pp. 137-158.
Lodge, David. *Graham Greene.* 1966. Pp. 39-42.
Lodge, David. *The Novelist at the Crossroads.* 1971. Pp. 113-116.
Milner, Ian. "Values and Irony in Graham Greene." *Prague Studies in English,* 14 (1971), 65-67.
Pryce-Jones, David. *Graham Greene.* 1963. Pp. 94-97.
Shor, Ira Neil. "Greene's Later Humanism: *A Burnt-Out Case.*" *Literary Review,* 16 (1973), 397-411.
Sternlicht, Sanford. "Two Views of the Builder in Graham Greene's *A Burnt-Out Case* and William Golding's *The Spire.*" *Studies in the Humanities,* 2 (1970-1971), 17-19.
Stratford, Philip. *Faith and Fiction.* 1964. Pp. 1-30.
Van Kaam, Adrian, and Kathleen Healy. *The Demon and the Dove.* 1967. Pp. 259-285.

The Comedians, 1966

Boardman, Gwenn R. *Graham Greene.* 1971. Pp. 170-173.
Fricker, Robert. "Graham Greene," in Otto Mann, ed., *Christliche Dichter.* 1968. Pp. 264-266.
Lodge, David. *Graham Greene.* 1966. Pp. 42-45.
Routh, Michael. "Greene's Parody of Farce and Comedy in *The Comedians.*" *Renascence,* 26 (1974), 139-151.

The Confidential Agent, 1939

Lodge, David. *Graham Greene.* 1966. Pp. 16-18.
Pérez Minik, Domingo. *Introducción a la novela inglesa actual.* 1968. Pp. 129-135.
Wolfe, Peter. *Graham Greene.* 1972. Pp. 80-100.

The End of the Affair, 1951

Boardman, Gwenn R. *Graham Greene.* 1971. Pp. 90-96.
Braybrooke, Neville. "Graham Greene y el 'Hombre Desdoblado': Un Estudio de *The End of the Affair* (1951)." *Arbor,* 78 (1971), 361-370.
Fricker, Robert. "Graham Greene," in Otto Mann, ed., *Christliche Dichter.* 1968. Pp. 260-263.
Lodge, David. *Graham Greene.* 1966. Pp. 31-35.
Lodge, David. *The Novelist at the Crossroads.* 1971. Pp. 108-111.
Mass, Roslyn. "The Presentation of the Character of Sarah Miles in the Film Version of *The End of the Affair.*" *Literature/Film Quarterly,* 2 (1974), 347-351.
Pryce-Jones, David. *Graham Greene.* 1963. Pp. 82-88.
Woodward, Anthony. "Graham Greene: The War Against Boredom," in Gildas Roberts, ed., *Seven Studies in English.* 1971. Pp. 97-100.

England Made Me, 1935

Keyser, Les. "*England Made Me.*" *Literature/Film Quarterly,* 2 (1974), 364-372.
Lodge, David. *Graham Greene.* 1966. Pp. 18-19.
Pryce-Jones, David. *Graham Greene.* 1963. Pp. 22-28.
Stratford, Philip. *Faith and Fiction.* 1964. Pp. 132-137.

A Gun for Sale, 1936

Boardman, Gwenn R. *Graham Greene.* 1971. Pp. 36-41.
Lodge, David. *Graham Greene.* 1966. Pp. 14-16.
Lodge, David. *The Novelist at the Crossroads.* 1971. Pp. 95-96, 100.
Stratford, Philip. *Faith and Fiction.* 1964. Pp. 188-192.
Wolfe, Peter. *Graham Greene.* 1972. Pp. 51-79.

The Heart of the Matter, 1948

Blondel Jacques. "*The Heart of the Matter*: Roman catholique." *Langues Modernes,* 65 (1971), 56-60.
Blondel, Jacques. "*The Heart of the Matter*: Le Cas de Scobie." *Langues Modernes,* 65 (1971), 51-55.
Boardman, Gwenn R. *Graham Greene.* 1971. Pp. 83-90.
Cassis, A. F. "The Dream as Literary Device in Graham Greene's Novels." *Literature and Psychology,* 24 (1974), 102-104.
Hynes, Joseph. "The 'Facts' at *The Heart of the Matter.*" *Texas Studies in Literature and Language,* 13 (1972), 711-726.

Inglis, Fred. *An Essential Discipline*. 1968. Pp. 192-194.
Kellogg, Gene. *The Vital Tradition*. 1970. Pp. 127-133.
Kulkarni, H. B. "Redemptive Sin in Graham Greene." *Proceedings of the Utah Academy of Sciences, Arts, and Letters*, 49:2 (1972), 36-50.
Lodge, David. *Graham Greene*. 1966. Pp. 27-31.
McGugan, Ruth E. "*The Heart of the Matter*." *Literature/Film Quarterly*, 2 (1974), 359-363.
Pryce-Jones, David. *Graham Greene*. 1963. Pp. 78-82.
Sonnenfeld, Albert. "Children's Faces: Graham Greene," in Melvin J. Friedman, ed., *The Vision Obscured*. 1970. Pp. 120-127.
Stratford, Philip. *Faith and Fiction*. 1964. Pp. 234-237.
Walker, Ronald C. "Seriation as Stylistic Norm in Graham Greene's *The Heart of the Matter*." *Language and Style*, 6 (1973), 161-174.
Woodward, Anthony. "Graham Greene: The War Against Boredom," in Gildas Roberts, ed., *Seven Studies in English*. 1971. Pp. 84-97.

The Honorary Consul, 1973

Boisdeffre, Pierre de. "Chronique du Mois: La Revue littéraire." *Nouvelle Revue des Deux Mondes*, December 1973, pp. 671-677.
Kerchove, Arnold de. "Arthur Lambert de Fonseca, Suzanne Prou et Graham Greene." *Revue Générale*, 9 (1973), 84-86.

It's a Battlefield, 1934

Pryce-Jones, David. *Graham Greene*. 1963. Pp. 20-22.
Stratford, Philip. *Faith and Fiction*. 1964. Pp. 120-122.

Loser Takes All, 1955

Wolfe, Peter. *Graham Greene*. 1972. Pp. 133-145.

The Man Within, 1929

Lodge, David. *Graham Greene*. 1966. Pp. 11-12.
Pryce-Jones, David. *Graham Greene*. 1963. Pp. 15-16.
Stratford, Philip. *Faith and Fiction*. 1964. Pp. 91-98.

The Ministry of Fear, 1943

Boardman, Gwenn R. *Graham Greene*. 1971. Pp. 78-83.
Lodge, David. *The Novelist at the Crossroads*. 1971. Pp. 105-108.
Stratford, Philip. *Faith and Fiction*. 1964. Pp. 106-109.
Welsh, James M., and Gerald R. Barrett. "Graham Greene's *Ministry of Fear*: The Transformation of an Entertainment." *Literature/Film Quarterly*, 2 (1974), 310-323.
Wolfe, Peter. *Graham Greene*. 1972. Pp. 101-121.

The Name of Action, 1930

Stratford, Philip. *Faith and Fiction*. 1964. Pp. 98-102.

Our Man in Havana, 1958

> Bedard, B. J. "Reunion in Havana." *Literature/Film Quarterly*, 2 (1974), 352-358.
> Boardman, Gwenn R. *Graham Greene*. 1971. Pp. 123-126.
> Stratford, Philip. *Faith and Fiction*. 1964. Pp. 318-325.
> Wolfe, Peter. *Graham Greene*. 1972. Pp. 146-165.

The Power and the Glory, 1940

> Boardman, Gwenn R. *Graham Greene*. 1971. Pp. 62-75.
> Brock, D. Heyward, and James M. Welsh. "Graham Greene and the Structure of Salvation." *Renascence*, 27 (1974), 31-39.
> Cassis, A. F. "The Dream as Literary Device in Graham Greene's Novels." *Literature and Psychology*, 24 (1974), 101-102.
> Dubu, Jean. *La Poétique de Graham Greene*. 1972. Pp. 13-143.
> Fricker, Robert. "Graham Greene," in Otto Mann, ed., *Christliche Dichter*. 1968. Pp. 257-259.
> Kellogg, Gene. *The Vital Tradition*. 1970. Pp. 122-127.
> Kulkarni, H. B. "Redemptive Sin in Graham Greene." *Proceedings of the Utah Academy of Sciences, Arts, and Letters*, 49:2 (1972), 36-50.
> Lodge, David. *Graham Greene*. 1966. Pp. 24-27.
> Lodge, David. *The Novelist at the Crossroads*. 1971. Pp. 102-104.
> Milner, Ian. "Values and Irony in Graham Greene." *Prague Studies in English*, 14 (1971), 67-72.
> Pryce-Jones, David. *Graham Greene*. 1963. Pp. 47-58.

The Quiet American, 1955

> Boardman, Gwenn R. *Graham Greene*. 1971. Pp. 106-117.
> Lodge, David. *Graham Greene*. 1966. Pp. 35-37.
> Lodge, David. *The Novelist at the Crossroads*. 1971. Pp. 111-112.
> Pryce-Jones, David. *Graham Greene*. 1963. Pp. 90-93.
> Stratford, Philip. *Faith and Fiction*. 1964. Pp. 308-316.
> Zimmermann, Peter. "Graham Greenes Auseinandersetzung mit der imperialistischen Vietnamaggression in dem Roman *The Quiet American*." *Zeitschrift für Anglistik und Amerikanistik*, 21 (1973), 34-49.

Rumour at Nightfall, 1931

> Stratford, Philip. *Faith and Fiction*. 1964. Pp. 103-106, 171-173.

Stamboul Train, 1932

> Lodge, David. *Graham Greene*. 1966. Pp. 12-14.
> Pryce-Jones, David. *Graham Greene*. 1963. Pp. 17-20.
> Stratford, Philip. *Faith and Fiction*. 1964. Pp. 111-116.
> Wolfe, Peter. *Graham Greene*. 1972. Pp. 29-50.

The Third Man, 1950

> Gomez, Joseph A. "*The Third Man*: Capturing the Visual Essence of

Literary Conception." *Literature/Film Quarterly*, 2(1974), 332-339.

Van Wert, William F. "Narrative Structure in *The Third Man*." *Literature/Film Quarterly*, 2 (1974), 241-246.

Wolfe, Peter. *Graham Greene*. 1972. Pp. 122-132.

Travels with My Aunt, 1969

Avvisati, Marilena. "Graham Greene contra se." *Revista di Letteratura Moderne e Comparate*, 26 (1973), 222-230.

Boardman, Gwenn R. *Graham Greene*. 1971. Pp. 173-177.

Fagin, Steven. "Narrative Design in *Travels with My Aunt*." *Literature/Film Quarterly*, 2 (1974), 379-383.

ROBERT GREENE

Ciceronis Amor: Tullies Love, 1589

Larson, Charles H. "Robert Greene's *Ciceronis Amor*: Fictional Biography in the Romance Genre." *Studies in the Novel*, 6 (1974), 256-267.

Menaphon, 1589

Davis, Walter R. *Idea and Act*. 1969. Pp. 171-178.

Pandosto, 1588

Lindheim, Nancy R. "Lyly's Golden Legacy: *Rosalynde* and *Pandosto*." *Studies in English Literature, 1500-1900*, 15 (1975), 13-19.

HENRY RIDER HAGGARD

She, 1887

Hinz, Evelyn J. "Rider Haggard's *She*: An Archetypal 'History of Adventure.'" *Studies in the Novel*, 4 (1972), 416-431.

Moss, John G. "Three Motifs in Haggard's *She*." *English Literature in Transition*, 16 (1973), 27-34.

THOMAS HARDY

Desperate Remedies, 1871

Carpenter, Richard. *Thomas Hardy*. 1964. Pp. 39-42.

Gittings, Robert. *Young Thomas Hardy*. 1975. Pp. 139-143.

Page, Norman. "Visual Techniques in Hardy's *Desperate Remedies*." *Ariel*, 4:1 (1973), 65-71.

Springer, Marline. "Invention and Traditions: Allusions in *Desperate Remedies*." *Colby Library Quarterly*, Series 10 (December 1974), 475-485.

Wing, George. "*Edwin Drood* and *Desperate Remedies*: Prototypes of

Detective Fiction in 1870." *Studies in English Literature, 1500-1900,* 13 (1973), 680-684.

Far From the Madding Crowd, 1874

Carpenter, Richard. *Thomas Hardy.* 1964. Pp. 81-91.
Halperin, John. *Egoism and Self-Discovery.* 1974. Pp. 217-228.
May, Charles E. "*Far From the Madding Crowd* and *The Woodlanders*: Hardy's Grotesque Pastorals." *English Literature in Transition,* 17 (1974), 150-152.
Meisel, Perry. *Thomas Hardy.* 1972. Pp. 43-52.
Otten, Kurt. *Der englische Roman.* 1971. Pp. 162-165.
Schwarz, Daniel R. "The Narrator as Character in Hardy's Major Fiction." *Modern Fiction Studies,* 18 (1972), 157-159.
Southerington, F. R. *Hardy's Vision of Man.* 1971. Pp. 60-75.
Stewart, J. I. M. *Thomas Hardy.* 1971. Pp. 74-90.
Sullivan, Tom R. "The Temporal Leitmotif in *Far From the Madding Crowd.*" *Colby Library Quarterly,* Series 10 (March 1974), 296-303.
Vigar, Penelope. *The Novels of Thomas Hardy.* 1974. Pp. 101-124.
Williams, Merryn. *Thomas Hardy.* 1972. Pp. 130-135.

The Hand of Ethelberta, 1876

Carpenter, Richard. *Thomas Hardy.* 1964. Pp. 54-57.
Southerington, F. R. *Hardy's Vision of Man.* 1971. Pp. 76-80.
Wing, George. " 'Forbear, Hostler, Forbear!': Social Satire in *The Hand of Ethelberta.*" *Studies in the Novel,* 4 (1972), 568-579.

Jude the Obscure, 1895

Baker, Christopher P. "The 'Grand Delusion' of Jude Fawley." *Colby Library Quarterly,* Series 10 (September 1974), 432-441.
Buckley, Jerome Hamilton. *Season of Youth.* 1974. Pp. 162-185.
Burns, Wayne. "Flesh and Spirit in *Jude the Obscure.*" *Recovering Literature,* 1 (Winter 1972), 5-21.
Burstein, Janet. "The Journey Beyond Myth in *Jude the Obscure.*" *Texas Studies in Literature and Language,* 15 (1973), 499-515.
Carpenter, Richard. *Thomas Hardy.* 1964. Pp. 138-152.
Cassis, A. F. "Idea and Execution in *Jude the Obscure.*" *Colby Library Quarterly,* Series 9 (June 1972), 501-509.
Clipper, Lawrence J. "Saturn in Wessex: The Role of Little Father Time." *Ball State University Forum,* 14 (Winter 1973), 36-42.
Duerksen, Roland A. *Shelleyan Ideas in Victorian Literature.* 1966. Pp. 161-163.
Fass, Barbara. "Hardy and St. Paul: Patterns of Conflict in *Jude the Obscure.*" *Colby Library Quarterly,* Series 10 (March 1974), 274-286.
Giordano, Frank R., Jr. "*Jude the Obscure* and the *Bildungsroman.*" *Studies in the Novel,* 4 (1972), 580-591.

Goetsch, Paul. *Die Romankonzeption in England*. 1967. Pp. 114-118.
Hellstrom, Ward. "Hardy's Scholar-Gipsy," in George Goodin, ed., *The English Novel*. 1972. Pp. 196-213.
Horne, Lewis B. " 'The Art of Renunciation' in Hardy's Novels." *Studies in the Novel*, 4 (1972), 563-566.
Horne, Lewis B. "Hardy's Little Father Time." *South Atlantic Quarterly*, 73 (1974), 213-223.
Hyman, Virginia Riley. "The Ethical Dimension in Hardy's Novels." *Essays in Literature* (Macomb, Illinois), 1:2 (1974), 186-189.
Lemon, Lee T. "The Hostile Universe: A Developing Pattern in Nineteenth-Century Fiction," in George Goodin, ed., *The English Novel*. 1972. Pp. 11-13.
Meisel, Perry. *Thomas Hardy*. 1972. Pp. 136-158.
Mills, Nicolaus. *American and English Fiction*. 1973. Pp. 74-91.
Rachman, Shalom. "Character and Theme in Hardy's *Jude the Obscure*." *English*, 22 (1973), 45-53.
Schwarz, Daniel R. "The Narrator as Character in Hardy's Major Fiction." *Modern Fiction Studies*, 18 (1972), 169-171.
Southerington, F. R. *Hardy's Vision of Man*. 1971. Pp. 136-147.
Starzyk, Lawrence J. "The Coming Universal Wish Not To Live in Hardy's 'Modern' Novels." *Nineteenth-Century Fiction*, 26 (1972), 419-435.
Stewart, J. I. M. *Thomas Hardy*. 1971. Pp. 184-203.
Stoll, John E. "Psychological Dissociation in the Victorian Novel." *Literature and Psychology*, 20 (1970), 71-73.
Sutherland, John. "A Note on the Teasing Narrator in *Jude the Obscure*." *English Literature in Transition*, 17 (1974), 159-162.
Swigg, Richard. *Lawrence, Hardy, and American Literature*. 1972. Pp. 24-31.
Vigar, Penelope. *The Novels of Thomas Hardy*. 1974. Pp. 189-212.
Williams, Merryn. *Thomas Hardy*. 1972. Pp. 180-190.

A Laodicean, 1881

Carpenter, Richard. *Thomas Hardy*. 1964. Pp. 62-63.
Jarrett, David W. "Hawthorne and Hardy as Modern Romancers." *Nineteenth-Century Fiction*, 28 (1974), 460-471.

The Mayor of Casterbridge, 1886

Carpenter, Richard. *Thomas Hardy*. 1964. Pp. 102-114.
Edwards, Duane D. "*The Mayor of Casterbridge* as Aeschylean Tragedy." *Studies in the Novel*, 4 (1972), 608-618.
Egan, Joseph J. "The Bull and the Songbird: A Portrait of Hardy's Mayor." *North Dakota Quarterly*, 41 (Autumn 1973), 55-58.
Goetsch, Paul. *Die Romankonzeption in England*. 1967. Pp. 105-110.
Halperin, John. *Egoism and Self-Discovery*. 1974. Pp. 228-234.
Kazin, Alfred, David Hardman, and George D. Crothers. "*The Mayor*

of Casterbridge," in George D. Crothers, ed., *Invitation to Learning*. 1966. Pp. 172-179.

Meisel, Perry. *Thomas Hardy*. 1972. Pp. 90-108.

Page, Norman. "Hardy's Pictorial Art in *The Mayor of Casterbridge*." *Etudes Anglaises*, 25 (1972), 486-492.

Schwarz, Daniel R. "The Narrator as Character in Hardy's Major Fiction." *Modern Fiction Studies*, 18 (1972), 162-164.

Southerington, F. R. *Hardy's Vision of Man*. 1971. Pp. 96-105.

Starzyk, Lawrence J. "Hardy's *Mayor*: The Antitraditional Basis of Tragedy." *Studies in the Novel*, 4 (1972), 592-607.

Stewart, J. I. M. *Thomas Hardy*. 1971. Pp. 108-126.

Toliver, Harold E. *Pastoral Forms and Attitudes*. 1971. Pp. 291-298.

Vigar, Penelope. *The Novels of Thomas Hardy*. 1974. Pp. 146-168.

Williams, Merryn. *Thomas Hardy*. 1972. Pp. 146-156.

A Pair of Blue Eyes, 1873

Amos, Arthur K. "Accident and Fate: The Possibility for Action in *A Pair of Blue Eyes*." *English Literature in Transition*, 15 (1972), 158-167.

Carpenter, Richard. *Thomas Hardy*. 1964. Pp. 48-54.

Meisel, Perry. *Thomas Hardy*. 1972. Pp. 52-66.

Southerington, F. R. *Hardy's Vision of Man*. 1971. Pp. 50-59.

Stewart, J. I. M. *Thomas Hardy*. 1971. Pp. 63-73.

The Return of the Native, 1878

Björk, Lennart A. " 'Visible Essences' as Thematic Structure in Hardy's *The Return of the Native*." *English Studies*, 53 (1972), 52-63.

Brinkley, Richard. *Thomas Hardy as a Regional Novelist*. 1968. Pp. 159-168.

Carpenter, Richard. *Thomas Hardy*. 1964. Pp. 91-102.

Fricker, Robert. "Hardy: *The Return of the Native*," in Franz K. Stanzel, ed., *Der englische Roman*. 1969. Pp. 215-250.

Goetsch, Paul. *Die Romankonzeption in England*. 1967. Pp. 103-105.

Gose, Elliott B., Jr. *Imagination Indulged*. 1972. Pp. 99-125.

Martin, Bruce K. "Whatever Happened to Eustacia Vye?" *Studies in the Novel*, 4 (1972), 619-627.

Meisel, Perry. *Thomas Hardy*. 1972. Pp. 68-89.

Mickelson, Anne Z. "The Family Trap in *The Return of the Native*." *Colby Library Quarterly*, Series 10 (December 1974), 463-475.

Schwarz, Daniel R. "The Narrator as Character in Hardy's Major Fiction." *Modern Fiction Studies*, 18 (1972), 160-162.

Southerington, F. R. *Hardy's Vision of Man*. 1971. Pp. 80-95.

Starzyk, Lawrence J. "The Coming Universal Wish Not To Live in Hardy's 'Modern' Novels." *Nineteenth-Century Fiction*, 26 (1972), 419-435.

Stewart, J. I. M. *Thomas Hardy*. 1971. Pp. 91-107.

Swigg, Richard. *Lawrence, Hardy, and American Literature.* 1972.
Pp. 4-13.
Toliver, Harold E. *Pastoral Forms and Attitudes.* 1971. Pp. 276-278.
Vigar, Penelope. *The Novels of Thomas Hardy.* 1974. Pp. 125-145.
Walcutt, Charles Child. *Man's Changing Mask.* 1966. Pp. 159-174.
Williams, Merryn. *Thomas Hardy.* 1972. Pp. 136-145.
Zellefrow, Ken. "*The Return of the Native*: Hardy's Map and Eu-
stacia's Suicide." *Nineteenth-Century Fiction*, 28 (1973), 214-220.

Tess of the d'Urbervilles, 1891

Burns, Wayne. "The Panzaic Principle in Hardy's *Tess of the d'Urber-
villes.*" *Recovering Literature*, 1 (Spring 1972), 26-41.
Carpenter, Richard. *Thomas Hardy.* 1964. Pp. 124-138.
Chapple, J. A. V. *Documentary and Imaginative Literature.* 1970.
Pp. 46-52.
Edwards, Duane. "*Tess of the d'Urbervilles* and *Hippolytus.*" *Mid-
west Quarterly*, 15 (1974), 392-405.
Feibleman, James, Alice Leone Moats, and Lyman Bryson. "*Tess of
the d'Urbervilles,*" in George D. Crothers, ed., *Invitation to Learn-
ing.* 1966. Pp. 164-172.
Goetsch, Paul. *Die Romankonzeption in England.* 1967. Pp. 111-114.
Guthke, Karl S. *Die Mythologie der entgötterten Welt.* 1971. Pp. 285-
289.
Halperin, John. *Egoism and Self-Discovery.* 1974. Pp. 234-245.
Hardwick, Elizabeth. *Seduction and Betrayal.* 1970. Pp. 202-206.
Kozicki, Henry. "Myths of Redemption in Hardy's *Tess of the d'Urber-
villes.*" *Papers on Language and Literature*, 10 (1974), 150-158.
Lerner, Laurence. *The Truthtellers.* 1967. Pp. 113-120.
Meisel, Perry. *Thomas Hardy.* 1972. Pp. 118-135.
Morton, Peter R. "*Tess of the d'Urbervilles:* A Neo-Darwinian Read-
ing." *Southern Review* (Adelaide), 7 (1974), 43-49.
Moynahan, Julian. "Pastoralism as Culture and Counter-Culture in
English Fiction, 1800-1928." *Novel*, 6 (1972), 31-33.
O'Neill, T. "Cassola e Hardy: Lettura di *Un Cuore Arido.*" *Revista di
Letterature Moderne e Comparate*, 25 (1972), 145-152.
Otten, Kurt. *Der englische Roman.* 1971. Pp. 166-170.
Schwarz, Daniel R. "The Narrator as Character in Hardy's Major Fic-
tion." *Modern Fiction Studies*, 18 (1972), 167-168.
Southerington, F. R. *Hardy's Vision of Man.* 1971. Pp. 123-135.
Starzyk, Lawrence J. "The Coming Universal Wish Not To Live in
Hardy's 'Modern' Novels." *Nineteenth-Century Fiction*, 26 (1972),
419-435.
Stewart, J. I. M. *Thomas Hardy.* 1971. Pp. 165-183.
Swigg, Richard. *Lawrence, Hardy, and American Literature.* 1972.
Pp. 13-24.
Toliver, Harold E. *Pastoral Forms and Attitudes.* 1971. Pp. 278-279,
285-291.

Tomlinson, T. B. "Hardy's Universe: *Tess of the d'Urbervilles.*" *Critical Review* (Melbourne), No. 16 (1973), 18-38.

Vigar, Penelope. *The Novels of Thomas Hardy.* 1974. Pp. 169-188.

Wagner, Geoffrey. *Five for Freedom.* 1972. Pp. 183-211.

Williams, Merryn. *Thomas Hardy.* 1972. Pp. 90-99, 169-179.

Wright, Terence. "Rhetorical and Lyrical Imagery in *Tess of the d'Urbervilles.*" *Durham University Journal,* 65 (1973), 79-85.

The Trumpet-Major, 1880

Carpenter, Richard. *Thomas Hardy.* 1964. Pp. 57-62.

Vigar, Penelope. *The Novels of Thomas Hardy.* 1974. Pp. 94-100.

White, R. J. *Thomas Hardy and History.* 1974. Pp. 60-67.

Two on a Tower, 1882

Carpenter, Richard. *Thomas Hardy.* 1964. Pp. 63-67.

Southerington, F. R. *Hardy's Vision of Man.* 1971. Pp. 112-118.

Under the Greenwood Tree, 1872

Carpenter, Richard. *Thomas Hardy.* 1964. Pp. 43-48.

Draffan, Robert A. "Hardy's *Under the Greenwood Tree.*" *English,* 22 (1973), 55-60.

Kossick, S. G. *"Under the Greenwood Tree." Essays in Literature* (Denver), 1:1 (1973), 30-34.

Meisel, Perry. *Thomas Hardy.* 1972. Pp. 33-42.

Schwarz, Daniel R. "The Narrator as Character in Hardy's Major Fiction." *Modern Fiction Studies,* 18 (1972), 159-160.

Southerington, F. R. *Hardy's Vision of Man.* 1971. Pp. 44-50.

Stewart, J. I. M. *Thomas Hardy.* 1971. Pp. 57-62.

Vigar, Penelope. *The Novels of Thomas Hardy.* 1974. Pp. 85-94.

Williams, Merryn. *Thomas Hardy.* 1972. Pp. 123-129.

The Well-Beloved, 1892

Carpenter, Richard. *Thomas Hardy.* 1964. Pp. 67-68.

Stewart, J. I. M. *Thomas Hardy.* 1971. Pp. 158-161.

The Woodlanders, 1887

Carpenter, Richard. *Thomas Hardy.* 1964. Pp. 114-124.

May, Charles E. *"Far From the Madding Crowd* and *The Woodlanders*: Hardy's Grotesque Pastorals." *English Literature in Transition,* 17 (1974), 152-155.

Meisel, Perry. *Thomas Hardy.* 1972. Pp. 109-117.

Saunders, Mary M. "The Significance of the Man-Trap in *The Woodlanders." Modern Fiction Studies,* 20 (1974-1975), 529-531.

Schwarz, Daniel R. "The Narrator as Character in Hardy's Major Fiction." *Modern Fiction Studies,* 18 (1972), 165-167.

Schweik, Robert G. "The Ethical Structure of Hardy's *The Wood-landers.*" *Archiv für das Studium der Neueren Sprachen und Literaturen*, 126 (1974), 31-44.

Southerington, F. R. *Hardy's Vision of Man.* 1971. Pp. 119-123.

Stewart, J. I. M. *Thomas Hardy.* 1971. Pp. 127-146.

Toliver, Harold E. *Pastoral Forms and Attitudes.* 1971. Pp. 279-285.

Williams, Merryn. *Thomas Hardy.* 1972. Pp. 157-168.

L. P. HARTLEY

Facial Justice, 1960

Sorensen, Knud. "Language and Society in L. P. Hartley's *Facial Justice.*" *Orbis Litterarum*, 26 (1971), 69-78.

ELIZA HAYWOOD

Betsy Thoughtless, 1751

Doody, Margaret Anne. *A Natural Passion.* 1974. Pp. 307-309, 317.

Idalia, 1723

Doody, Margaret Anne. *A Natural Passion.* 1974. Pp. 146-149.

Love in Excess, 1719

Richetti, John J. *Popular Fiction.* 1969. Pp. 183-207.

Memoirs of Utopia, 1725

Richetti, John J. *Popular Fiction.* 1969. Pp. 153-167.

RICHARD HEAD

The English Rogue, 1665

Mosely, C. W. R. D. "Richard Head's *The English Rogue*: A Modern Mandeville?" *Yearbook of English Studies*, 1 (1971), 102-107.

BARRY HINES

A Kestrel for a Knave, 1968

Gray, Nigel. *The Silent Majority.* 1973. Pp. 25-45.

JOHN OLIVER HOBBES

Robert Orange, 1900

Colby, Vineta. *The Singular Anomaly.* 1970. Pp. 202-210.

The School for Saints, 1897

  Colby, Vineta. *The Singular Anomaly*. 1970. Pp. 202-210.

H. S. HOFF

Scenes from Provincial Life, 1950

  Bradbury, Malcolm. *Possibilities*. 1973. Pp. 192-200.

JAMES HOGG

The Private Memoirs and Confessions of a Justified Sinner, 1824

  Kiely, Robert. *The Romantic Novel in England*. 1972. Pp. 208-232.
  Rogers, Robert. *A Psychoanalytic Study*. 1970. Pp. 32-34.

THOMAS HOLCROFT

The Adventures of Hugh Trevor, 1797

  Baine, Rodney M. *Thomas Holcroft*. 1965. Pp. 73-95.

Alwyn, 1780

  Baine, Rodney M. *Thomas Holcroft*. 1965. Pp. 13-19.

Anna St. Ives, 1792

  Baine, Rodney M. *Thomas Holcroft*. 1965. Pp. 20-72.
  Rice, Leonard W. "Thomas Holcroft's *Anna St. Ives*." *Proceedings of the Utah Academy of Sciences, Arts, and Letters*, 31 (1953-1954), 24-27.
  Vooys, Sijna de. *The Psychological Element*. 1966. Pp. 13-17.

Manthorn, the Enthusiast, 1779

  Baine, Rodney M. *Thomas Holcroft*. 1965. Pp. 6-13.

Memoirs of Bryan Perdue, 1805

  Baine, Rodney M. *Thomas Holcroft*. 1965. Pp. 96-107.

INEZ HOLDEN

Born Old; Died Young, 1932

  Powell, Anthony. "Inez Holden: A Memoir." *London Magazine*, 14:4 (1974), 90-91.

WILLIAM HENRY HUDSON

A Crystal Age, 1887

  Frederick, John T. *William Henry Hudson*. 1972. Pp. 40-45.

Fan, 1892

Frederick, John T. *William Henry Hudson.* 1972. Pp. 45-47.

Green Mansions, 1904

Frederick, John T. *William Henry Hudson.* 1972. Pp. 51-59.

The Purple Land, 1885

Frederick, John T. *William Henry Hudson.* 1972. Pp. 38-40.

RICHARD HUGHES

The Fox in the Attic, 1961

Swinden, Patrick. *Unofficial Selves.* 1973. Pp. 190-202.
Thomas, Peter. *Richard Hughes.* 1973. Pp. 74-83.

A High Wind in Jamaica, 1929

Poole, Richard. "Irony in *A High Wind in Jamaica.*" *Anglo-Welsh Review*, 23:51 (1974), 41-57.
Swinden, Patrick. *Unofficial Selves.* 1973. Pp. 182-187.
Thomas, Peter. *Richard Hughes.* 1973. Pp. 48-59.

The Human Predicament, 1961-

Pérez Minik, Domingo. *Introducción a la novela inglesa actual.* 1968. Pp. 151-157.

In Hazard, 1938

Thomas, Peter. *Richard Hughes.* 1973. Pp. 63-70.

The Wooden Shepherdess, 1973

Thomas, Peter. *Richard Hughes.* 1973. Pp. 84-93.

ALDOUS HUXLEY

After Many a Summer Dies the Swan, 1939

Bedford, Sybille. *Aldous Huxley.* 1973-1974. Vol. I, 377-381.
Brander, Laurence. *Aldous Huxley.* 1970. Pp. 80-85.
Fietz, Lothar. *Menschenbild und Romanstruktur.* 1969. Pp. 117-139.
Firchow, Peter E. *Aldous Huxley.* 1972. Pp. 157-164.
May, Keith. *Aldous Huxley.* 1972. Pp. 141-157.
Meckier, Jerome. "Quarles Among the Monkeys: Huxley's Zoological Novels." *Modern Language Review*, 68 (1973), 279-280.
Woodcock, George. *Dawn and the Darkest Hour.* 1972. Pp. 219-224.

Antic Hay, 1923

Bedford, Sybille. *Aldous Huxley.* 1973-1974. Vol. I, 142-145.
Brander, Laurence. *Aldous Huxley.* 1970. Pp. 24-26.
Firchow, Peter E. *Aldous Huxley.* 1972. Pp. 64-76.

May, Keith. *Aldous Huxley*. 1972. Pp. 41-60.
Woodcock, George. *Dawn and the Darkest Hour*. 1972. Pp. 96-108.

Ape and Essence, 1949

Bedford, Sybille. *Aldous Huxley*. 1973-1974. Vol. II, 91-95.
Brander, Laurence. *Aldous Huxley*. 1970. Pp. 92-95.
Firchow, Peter E. *Aldous Huxley*. 1972. Pp. 133-137.
May, Keith. *Aldous Huxley*. 1972. Pp. 177-191.
Meckier, Jerome. "Quarles Among the Monkeys: Huxley's Zoological Novels." *Modern Language Review*, 68 (1973), 280-281.
Woodcock, George. *Dawn and the Darkest Hour*. 1972. Pp. 253-258.

Brave New World, 1932

Bedford, Sybille. *Aldous Huxley*. 1973-1974. Vol. I, 244-246.
Bonicelli, Elena. "Libertà dell'utopia, utopia della libertà in Aldous Huxley." *Revista di Letterature Moderne e Comparate*, 26 (1973), 307-314.
Brander, Laurence. *Aldous Huxley*. 1970. Pp. 61-71.
Elliott, Robert C. *The Shape of Utopia*. 1970. Pp. 95-97.
Firchow, Peter E. *Aldous Huxley*. 1972. Pp. 118-133, 138-139, 178-182.
Hienger, Jörg. *Literarische Zukunftsphantastik*. 1971. Pp. 85-89.
May, Keith. *Aldous Huxley*. 1972. Pp. 98-117.
Millichap, Joseph A. "Huxley's *Brave New World*, Chapter V." *Explicator*, 32 (1973), Item 1.
Seeber, Hans Ulrich. *Wandlungen der Form*. 1970. Pp. 145-158.
Westlake, J. H. J. "Aldous Huxley's *Brave New World* and George Orwell's *Nineteen Eighty-Four*: A Comparative Study." *Die Neueren Sprachen*, 71 (1972), 94-102.
Woodcock, George. *Dawn and the Darkest Hour*. 1972. Pp. 173-181.

Crome Yellow, 1921

Firchow, Peter E. *Aldous Huxley*. 1972. Pp. 48-64, 80-82, 122-123.
Gill, Richard. *Happy Rural Seat*. 1972. Pp. 140-143.
Kolek, Leszek. "English Novel of Ideas: An Attempt at a Preliminary Definition and Description of the Genre." *Zagadnienia Rodzajow Literackich*, 17 (1974), 24-30.
Laurent, Camille. "Thèmes et structures de *Crome Yellow*." *Annales de la Faculté des Lettres et Sciences Humaines de Nice*, 18 (1972), 47-57.
May, Keith. *Aldous Huxley*. 1972. Pp. 23-40.
Montgomery, Marion. "Lord Russell and Madame Sesostris." *Georgia Review*, 28 (1974), 269-282.
Woodcock, George. *Dawn and the Darkest Hour*. 1972. Pp. 77-86.

Eyeless in Gaza, 1936

Bedford, Sybille. *Aldous Huxley*. 1973-1974. Vol. I, 315-324.
Brander, Laurence. *Aldous Huxley*. 1970. Pp. 72-79.

Fietz, Lothar. *Menschenbild und Romanstruktur.* 1969. Pp. 75-115.
Firchow, Peter E. *Aldous Huxley.* 1972. Pp. 145-157.
May, Keith. *Aldous Huxley.* 1972. Pp. 118-138.
Vitoux, Pierre. "Structure and Meaning in Aldous Huxley's *Eyeless in Gaza.*" *Yearbook of English Studies,* 2 (1972), 212-224.
Walcutt, Charles Child. *Man's Changing Mask.* 1966. P. 298.
Woodcock, George. *Dawn and the Darkest Hour.* 1972. Pp. 195-206.

The Genius and the Goddess, 1955

Brander, Laurence. *Aldous Huxley.* 1970. Pp. 96-100.
Firchow, Peter E. *Aldous Huxley.* 1972. Pp. 171-177.
May, Keith. *Aldous Huxley.* 1972. Pp. 192-205.
Woodcock, George. *Dawn and the Darkest Hour.* 1972. Pp. 278-280.

Island, 1962

Bedford, Sybille. *Aldous Huxley.* 1973-1974. Vol. II, 322-331.
Brander, Laurence. *Aldous Huxley.* 1970. Pp. 101-110.
Elliott, Robert C. *The Shape of Utopia.* 1970. Pp. 137-144.
Fietz, Lothar. *Menschenbild und Romanstruktur.* 1969. Pp. 172-187.
Firchow, Peter E. *Aldous Huxley.* 1972. Pp. 177-189.
May, Keith. *Aldous Huxley.* 1972. Pp. 206-223.
Meckier, Jerome. "Cancer in Utopia: Positive and Negative Elements in Huxley's *Island.*" *Dalhousie Review,* 54 (1974-1975), 619-633.
Woodcock, George. *Dawn and the Darkest Hour.* 1972. Pp. 280-285.

Point Counter Point, 1928

Baker, Robert S. "Spandrell's 'Lydian Heaven': Moral Masochism and the Centrality of Spandrell in Huxley's *Point Counter Point.*" *Criticism,* 16 (1974), 120-135.
Bedford, Sybille. *Aldous Huxley.* 1973-1974. Vol. I, 196-208.
Brander, Laurence. *Aldous Huxley.* 1970. Pp. 33-41.
Fietz, Lothar. *Menschenbild und Romanstruktur.* 1969. Pp. 39-73.
Firchow, Peter E. *Aldous Huxley.* 1972. Pp. 93-117, 138-139, 154-155.
Glicksberg, Charles I. *Modern Literary Perspectivism.* 1970. Pp. 25-27.
Kolek, Leszek. "Music in Literature: Presentation of Huxley's Experiment in 'Musicalization of Fiction.'" *Zagadnienia Rodzajow Literackich,* 14 (1972), 113-122.
May, Keith. *Aldous Huxley.* 1972. Pp. 79-97.
Meckier, Jerome. "Quarles Among the Monkeys: Huxley's Zoological Novels." *Modern Language Review,* 68 (1973), 271-279.
Mužina, Matej. "Reverberations of Jung's 'Psychological Types' in the Novels of Aldous Huxley." *Studia Romanica et Anglica Zagrabiensia,* 33-36 (1972-1973), 313-334.
Vitoux, Pierre. "Aldous Huxley and D. H. Lawrence: An Attempt at Intellectual Sympathy." *Modern Language Review,* 69 (1974), 501-522.

Woodcock, George. *Dawn and the Darkest Hour*. 1972. Pp. 150-160.

Those Barren Leaves, 1925

Bedford, Sybille. *Aldous Huxley*. 1973-1974. Vol. I, 152-158.
Bienvenu, M. "Le Voyage dans l'oeuvre d'Aldous Huxley." *Etudes Anglaises*, 24 (1971), 30-35.
Brander, Laurence. *Aldous Huxley*. 1970. Pp. 27-32.
Firchow, Peter E. *Aldous Huxley*. 1972. Pp. 80-92.
May, Keith. *Aldous Huxley*. 1972. Pp. 61-78.
Woodcock, George. *Dawn and the Darkest Hour*. 1972. Pp. 120-129.

Time Must Have a Stop, 1944

Brander, Laurence. *Aldous Huxley*. 1970. Pp. 86-91.
Fietz, Lothar. *Menschenbild und Romanstruktur*. 1969. Pp. 140-164.
Firchow, Peter E. *Aldous Huxley*. 1972. Pp. 164-170.
May, Keith. *Aldous Huxley*. 1972. Pp. 158-176.
Woodcock, George. *Dawn and the Darkest Hour*. 1972. Pp. 228-236.

CHRISTOPHER ISHERWOOD

All the Conspirators, 1928

Heilbrun, Carolyn G. *Christopher Isherwood*. 1970. Pp. 33-35.

Down There on a Visit, 1962

Hamard, J. "Christopher Isherwood et l'Allemagne: Un Itinéraire spirituel." *Revue de Littérature Comparée*, 45 (1971), 531-537.
Heilbrun, Carolyn G. *Christopher Isherwood*. 1970. Pp. 29-33.

A Meeting by the River, 1967

Dewsnap, Terence. "Isherwood Couchant." *Critique* (Atlanta), 13:1 (1971), 41-46.
Heilbrun, Carolyn G. *Christopher Isherwood*. 1970. Pp. 44-46.

The Memorial, 1932

Heilbrun, Carolyn G. *Christopher Isherwood*. 1970. Pp. 35-36.

Mr. Norris Changes Trains, 1935

Hamard, J. "Christopher Isherwood et l'Allemagne: Un Itinéraire spirituel." *Revue de Littérature Comparée*, 45 (1971), 520-524.

Prater Violet, 1946

Hamard, J. "Christopher Isherwood et l'Allemagne: Un Itinéraire spirituel." *Revue de Littérature Comparée*, 45 (1971), 524-526.

A Single Man, 1964

Dewsnap, Terence. "Isherwood Couchant." *Critique* (Atlanta), 13:1 (1971), 34-41.

Heilbrun, Carolyn G. *Christopher Isherwood*. 1970. Pp. 42-44.
Nagarajan, S. "Christopher Isherwood and the Vedantic Novel: A Study of *A Single Man*." *Ariel*, 3:4 (1972), 63-71.

The World in the Evening, 1954

Hamard J. "Christopher Isherwood et l'Allemagne: Un Itinéraire spirituel." *Revue de Littérature Comparée*, 45 (1971), 526-530.
Heilbrun, Carolyn G. *Christopher Isherwood*. 1970. Pp. 37-42.

RICHARD JEFFERIES

After London, 1885

Meier, Paul. *La Pensée utopique*. 1972. Pp. 107-114.

Hodge and His Masters, 1880

Chapple, J. A. V. *Documentary and Imaginative Literature*. 1970. Pp. 37-43.

JEROME K. JEROME

All Roads Lead to Calvary, 1919

Faurot, Ruth Marie. *Jerome K. Jerome*. 1974. Pp. 162-170.

Anthony John, 1923

Faurot, Ruth Marie. *Jerome K. Jerome*. 1974. Pp. 170-176.

Paul Kelver, 1902

Faurot, Ruth Marie. *Jerome K. Jerome*. 1974. Pp. 135-154.

They and I, 1909

Faurot, Ruth Marie. *Jerome K. Jerome*. 1974. Pp. 160-162.

Tommy and Co., 1904

Faurot, Ruth Marie. *Jerome K. Jerome*. 1974. Pp. 154-159.

DOUGLAS WILLIAM JERROLD

A Man Made of Money, 1849

Kelly, Richard M. *Douglas Jerrold*. 1972. Pp. 137-140.

St. Giles and St. James, 1851

Kelly, Richard M. *Douglas Jerrold*. 1972. Pp. 133-137.

The Story of a Feather, 1844

Kelly, Richard M. *Douglas Jerrold*. 1972. Pp. 128-133.

GERALDINE JEWSBURY

The Half-Sisters, 1848

Melada, Ivan. *The Captain of Industry.* 1970. Pp. 134-139.

Marian Withers, 1851

Melada, Ivan. *The Captain of Industry.* 1970. Pp. 40-48.

B. S. JOHNSON

Albert Angelo, 1964

Lodge, David. *The Novelist at the Crossroads.* 1971. Pp. 12-13.

SAMUEL JOHNSON

Rasselas, 1759

Altieri, Charles. "Organic and Humanist Models in Some English Bildungsroman." *Journal of General Education*, 23 (1971), 227-230.

Bate, W. Jackson. "Johnson and Satire Manqué," in W. H. Bond, ed., *Eighteenth-Century Studies*. 1970. Pp. 156-159.

Brinton, George. "*Rasselas* and the Problem of Evil." *Papers on Language and Literature*, 8 (1972), 92-96.

Butterick, George F. "The Comedy of Johnson's *Rasselas.*" *Studies in the Humanities*, 2 (1970-1971), 25-31.

Byrd, Max. *Visits to Bedlam.* 1974. Pp. 94-102.

Curley, Thomas M. "The Spiritual Journey Moralized in *Rasselas.*" *Anglia*, 91 (1973), 35-55.

Eberwein, Robert. "The Astronomer in Johnson's *Rasselas.*" *Michigan Academician*, 5 (Summer 1972), 9-15.

Einbond, Bernard L. *Samuel Johnson's Allegory.* 1971. Pp. 83-96.

Fussell, Paul. *Samuel Johnson.* 1971. Pp. 216-245.

Golden, Morris. *The Self Observed.* 1972. Pp. 96-99.

Greene, Donald J. *Samuel Johnson.* 1970. Pp. 133-139.

Hewitt, Douglas. *The Approach to Fiction.* 1972. Pp. 165-167.

Lascelles, Mary. *Notions and Facts.* 1972. Pp. 102-129.

Lombardo, Agostino. *Ritratto di Enobarbo.* 1971. Pp. 87-106.

McIntosh, Carey. *The Choice of Life.* 1973. Pp. 163-212.

Margolis, John. "Pekuah and the Theme of Imprisonment in Johnson's *Rasselas.*" *English Studies*, 53 (1972), 339-343.

Nicholls, Peter. "Science Fiction and the Mainstream: Part 2—The Great Tradition of Proto-Science Fiction." *Foundation*, No. 5 (1974), 30-33.

Omasreiter, Ria. *Naturwissenschaft und Literaturkritik.* 1971. Pp. 105-110.

Pagliaro, Harold E. "Structural Patterns of Control in *Rasselas*," in John H. Middendorf, ed., *English Writers*. 1971. Pp. 208-229.

Rose, Steven. "The Fear of Utopia." *Essays in Criticism*, 24 (1974), 56-58.

Scouten, Arthur. "Dr. Johnson and Imlac." *Eighteenth-Century Studies*, 6 (1973), 506-508.

Southall, Raymond. *Literature and the Rise of Capitalism*. 1973. Pp. 155-162.

White, Ian. "On *Rasselas*." *Cambridge Quarterly*, 6 (1972), 6-31.

Wolff, Erwin. *Der englische Roman*. 1968. Pp. 131-134.

Wiltshire, John. "Dr. Johnson's Seriousness." *Critical Review*, 10 (1967), 63-73.

DAVID JONES

In Parenthesis, 1937

Blamires, David. *David Jones*. 1971. Pp. 74-112.

Chapple, J. A. V. *Documentary and Imaginative Literature*. 1970. Pp. 313-319.

Murray, Atholl C. C. "In Perspective: A Study of David Jones's *In Parenthesis*." *Critical Quarterly*, 16 (1974), 254-263.

JAMES JOYCE

Finnegans Wake, 1939

Adams, Robert M. *Proteus, His Lies, His Truth*. 1973. Pp. 147-150.

Arnold, Armin. *James Joyce*. 1969. Pp. 82-113.

Atherton, J. S. "Islam and the *Qur-an* in James Joyce's *Finnegans Wake*." *Litera*, 1 (1954), 68-71.

Atherton, James S. "Shaun A," in Michael H. Begnal and Fritz Senn, eds., *A Conceptual Guide*. 1974. Pp. 149-170.

Atherton, James S. "Sport and Games in *Finnegans Wake*," in Jack P. Dalton and Clive Hart, eds., *Twelve and a Tilly*. 1965. Pp. 52-63.

Barrett, William. *Time of Need*. 1972. Pp. 339-350.

Beechhold, Henry F. "Joyce's Otherworld." *Éire-Ireland*, 7:1 (1972), 103-115.

Begnal, Michael H. "James Joyce and the Mythologizing of History," in Stanley Weintraub and Philip Young, eds., *Directions in Literary Criticism*. 1973. Pp. 217-218.

Begnal, Michael H. "Love That Dares to Speak Its Name," in Michael H. Begnal and Fritz Senn, eds., *A Conceptual Guide*. 1974. Pp. 139-148.

Begnal, Michael H. "Who Speaks When I Dream? Who Dreams When I Speak?: A Narrational Approach to *Finnegans Wake*," in Ronald Bates and Harry J. Pollock, eds., *Litters from Aloft*. 1971. Pp. 74-89.

Begnal, Michael H., and Grace Eckley. *Narrator and Character in "Finnegans Wake"*. 1975. Pp. 19-120, 129-235.

Benstock, Bernard. "Concerning Lost Historeve," in Michael H.

Begnal and Fritz Senn, eds., *A Conceptual Guide.* 1974. Pp. 33-55.

Benstock, Bernard. *Joyce-Again's Wake.* 1965. Pp. 3-264, 267-296.

Boldereff, Frances M. *Hermes to His Son Thoth.* 1968. Pp. 39-230.

Bonheim, Helmut. *Joyce's Benefictions.* 1964. Pp. 46-129.

Boyle, Robert, S. J. "The Artist as Balzacian Wilde Ass," in Michael H. Begnal and Fritz Senn, eds., *A Conceptual Guide.* 1974. Pp. 71-81.

Boyle, Robert, S. J. "Miracle in Black Ink: A Glance at Joyce's Use of His Eucharistic Image." *James Joyce Quarterly,* 10 (1972), 53-59.

Buckalew, Ronald E. "Night Lessons on Language," in Michael H. Begnal and Fritz Senn, eds., *A Conceptual Guide.* 1974. Pp. 93-115.

Budgen, Frank. "Resurrection," in Jack P. Dalton and Clive Hart, eds.,*Twelve and a Tilly.* 1965. Pp. 11-15.

Burgess, Anthony. *Joysprick.* 1973. Pp. 130-178.

Christiani, Dounia Bunis. "The Polyglot Poetry of *Finnegans Wake,*" in Wolodymyr T. Zyla, ed., *James Joyce.* 1969. Pp. 23-38.

Christiani, Dounia Bunis. *Scandinavian Elements.* 1965. Pp. 89-231.

Cross, Richard K. *Flaubert and Joyce.* 1971. Pp. 186-192.

Culler, Jonathan. *Structuralist Poetics.* 1975. Pp. 106-107.

Dalton, Jack P. "Advertisement for the Restoration," in Jack P. Dalton and Clive Hart, eds., *Twelve and a Tilly.* 1965. Pp. 119-133.

Dohmen, William F. " 'Chilly Spaces': Wyndham Lewis as Ondt." *James Joyce Quarterly,* 11 (1974), 368-386.

Durant, Will, and Ariel Durant. *Interpretations of Life.* 1970. Pp. 85-88.

Duytschaever, Joris. *James Joyce.* 1970. Pp. 53-56.

Eckley, Grace. "Eggoarchicism and the Bird Lore of *Finnegans Wake.*" *Literary Monographs,* 5 (1973), 141-184.

Eckley, Grace. "Looking Forward to a Brightening Day," in Michael H. Begnal and Fritz Senn, eds., *A Conceptual Guide.* 1974. Pp. 211-233.

Eckley, Grace. " 'Petween Peas Like Ourselves': The Folklore of the Prankquean." *James Joyce Quarterly,* 9 (1971), 177-188.

Eckley, Grace. "Shem Is a Sham but Shaun Is a Ham, or Samuraising the Twins in *Finnegans Wake.*" *Modern Fiction Studies,* 20 (1974-1975), 469-481.

Egri, Peter. *Avantgardism and Modernity.* 1972. Pp. 19-72.

Egri, Peter. *James Joyce és Thomas Mann.* 1967. Pp. 183-204.

Epstein, E. L. "The Turning Point," in Michael H. Begnal and Fritz Senn, eds., *A Conceptual Guide.* 1974. Pp. 56-69.

Fáj, Attila. "Alcune fonti importanti, finora ignorate, del *Finnegans Wake.*" *Rivista di Letterature Moderne e Comparate,* 24 (1971), 223-234.

Fáj, Attila. "Some Important, Hitherto Unnoticed, Sources of *Finnegans Wake.*" *Neuphilologische Mitteilungen,* 75 (1974), 650-662.

Fáj, Attila. "Some Important, Hitherto Unnoticed, Sources of *Finnegans Wake.*" *Wake Newslitter,* 10 (1973), 3-12.

Garzilli, Enrico. *Circles Without Center*. 1972. Pp. 65-74.

Gleckner, Robert F. "Byron in *Finnegans Wake*," in Jack P. Dalton and Clive Hart, eds., *Twelve and a Tilly*. 1965. Pp. 40-49.

Glasheen, Adaline. *A Second Census of "Finnegans Wake*." 1963. Pp. xxiii-lxvi, 1-285.

Gross, John. *James Joyce*. 1970. Pp. 75-89.

Hart, Clive. *Structure and Motif in "Finnegans Wake*." 1962. Pp. 13-208.

Hassan, Ihab. *Paracriticisms*. 1975. Pp. 77-94.

Hayman, David. "Farcical Themes and Forms in *Finnegans Wake*." *James Joyce Quarterly*, 11 (1974), 323-342.

Hayman, David. "'Scribbledehobbles' and How They Grew: A Turning Point in the Development of a Chapter," in Jack P. Dalton and Clive Hart, eds., *Twelve and a Tilly*, 1965. Pp. 107-117.

Heath, Stephen. "Ambiviolences: Notes pour la lecture de Joyce." *Tel Quel*, No. 50 (1972), 22-43, and No. 51 (1972), 64-76.

Heath, Stephen. "Trames de lecture: A propos de la dernière section de *Finnegans Wake*." *Tel Quel*, No. 54 (1973), 4-15.

Hodgart, M. J. C. "Music and the Mime of Mick, Nick, and the Maggies," in Michael H. Begnal and Fritz Senn, eds., *A Conceptual Guide*. 1974. Pp. 83-92.

Hoffman, Frederick J. "'The Seim Anew': Flux and Family in *Finnegans Wake*," in Jack P. Dalton and Clive Hart, eds., *Twelve and a Tilly*. 1965. Pp. 16-25.

Jacquet, Claude. *Joyce et Rabelais*. 1972. Pp. 13-38.

Kain, Richard M. "'Nothing Odd Will Do Long': Some Thoughts on *Finnegans Wake* Twenty-Five Years Later," in Jack P. Dalton and Clive Hart, eds., *Twelve and a Tilly*. 1965. Pp. 91-98.

Knuth, Leo. "Shem's Riddle of the Universe." *Wake Newslitter*, 9 (1972), 79-89.

Koch, Ronald J. "Giordano Bruno and *Finnegans Wake*: A New Look at Shaun's Objection to the 'Nolanus Theory.'" *James Joyce Quarterly*, 9 (1971), 237-249.

Kopper, Edward A., Jr. "'. . . But Where He Is Eaten': Earwicker's Tavern Feast," in Michael H. Begnal and Fritz Senn, eds., *A Conceptual Guide*. 1974. Pp. 116-137.

Kreutzer, Eberhard. *Sprache und Spiel*. 1969. Pp. 137-139.

Levin, Harry. *James Joyce*. 1960. Pp. 139-205.

Lyons, J. B. *James Joyce and Medicine*. 1973. Pp. 174-184.

McHugh, Roland. "Recipis for the Price of the Coffin," in Michael H. Begnal and Fritz Senn, eds., *A Conceptual Guide*. 1974. Pp. 18-31.

McLuhan, Eric. "The Rhetorical Structure of *Finnegans Wake*." *James Joyce Quarterly*, 11 (1974), 394-404.

Mercier, Vivian. "James Joyce and the Macaronic Tradition," in Jack P. Dalton and Clive Hart, eds., *Twelve and a Tilly*. 1965. Pp. 26-34.

Mink, Louis O. "Reading *Finnegans Wake*." *Southern Humanities*

Review, 9 (1975), 1-16.

Morse, J. Mitchell. "On Teaching *Finnegans Wake*," in Jack P. Dalton and Clive Hart, eds., *Twelve and a Tilly*, 1965. Pp. 65-71.

Morse, J. Mitchell. "The Solence of That Stilling." *Wake Newslitter*, 9 (1972), 107-109.

Morse, J. Mitchell. "Where Terms Begin," in Michael H. Begnal and Fritz Senn, eds., *A Conceptual Guide*. 1974. Pp. 1-17.

Murillo, L. A. *The Cyclical Night*. 1968. Pp. 61-115.

Norris, Margot C. "The Consequences of Deconstruction: A Technical Perspective of Joyce's *Finnegans Wake*." *ELH*, 41 (1974), 130-148.

Norris, Margot C. "The Function of Mythic Repetition in *Finnegans Wake*." *James Joyce Quarterly*, 11 (1974), 343-354.

Norris, Margot C. "The Language of Dream in *Finnegans Wake*." *Literature and Psychology*, 24 (1974), 4-10.

O'Brian, Darcy. "Joyce, Dogs, Eros, Metamorphosis, Revolution, and the Unity of Creation." *New Blackfriars*, 53 (1972), 466-470.

O'Brien, Flann. "Soûlographie dans le tunnel: A propos de James Joyce." *Lettres Nouvelles*, March 1973, 50-51.

Paci, Francesca Romana. *Vita e opere*. 1968. Pp. 278-292.

Praz, Mario. "Notes on James Joyce." *Mosaic*, 6 (Fall 1972), 87-91.

Pütz, Manfred. "The Identity of the Reader in *Finnegans Wake*." *James Joyce Quarterly*, 11 (1974), 387-393.

Rabate, Jean-Michel. "La 'Missa parodia' de *Finnegans Wake*." *Poétique*, No. 17 (1974), 75-95.

Scarry, John. "'Joan Mockcomic' and 'Jean Souslevin' in Joyce's *Finnegans Wake*." *Etudes Anglaises*, 27 (1974), 180-184.

Senn, Fritz. "Insects Appalling," in Jack P. Dalton and Clive Hart, eds., *Twelve and a Tilly*. 1965. Pp. 36-39.

Sidnell, M. J. "A Daintical Pair of Accomplasses: Joyce and Yeats," in Ronald Bates and Harry J. Pollock, eds., *Litters from Aloft*. 1971. Pp. 50-73.

Solomon, Margaret C. "The Porters: A Square Performance of Three Tiers in the Round," in Michael H. Begnal and Fritz Senn, eds., *A Conceptual Guide*. 1974. Pp. 201-209.

Staples, Hugh B. "Growing Up Absurd in Dublin," in Michael H. Begnal and Fritz Senn, eds., *A Conceptual Guide*. 1974. Pp. 173-197.

Swinson, Ward. "Riddles in *Finnegans Wake*." *Twentieth-Century Literature*, 19 (1973), 165-180.

Tindall, William York. *A Reader's Guide to "Finnegans Wake."* 1969.

Vickery, John B. *The Literary Impact of "The Golden Bough."* 1973. Pp. 408-423.

Vickery, John B. "*Finnegans Wake* and Sexual Metamorphosis." *Contemporary Literature*, 13 (1972), 213-242.

Von Phul, Ruth. "*Chamber Music* at the *Wake*." *James Joyce Quarterly*, 11 (1974), 355-367.

Von Phul, Ruth. "Circling the Square: A Study of Structure," in

Marvin Magalaner, ed., *A James Joyce Miscellany*. 1962. Pp. 239-277.

Worthington, Mabel P. "The Moon and Sidhe: Songs of Isabel," in Fritz Senn, ed., *New Light on Joyce*. 1972. Pp. 167-179.

A Portrait of the Artist as a Young Man, 1917

Aubert, Jacques. *Introduction à l'esthétique de James Joyce*. 1973. Pp. 150-158.

Beja, Morris. *Epiphany in the Modern Novel*. 1971. Pp. 89-93.

Benstock, Bernard. "James Joyce and the Women of the Western World," in Ronald Bates and Harry J. Pollock, eds., *Litters from Aloft*. 1971. Pp. 99-108.

Brandabur, Edward. *A Scrupulous Meanness*. 1971. Pp. 159-165.

Brown, Homer Obed. *James Joyce's Early Fiction*. 1972. Pp. 108-131.

Brown, Malcolm. *The Politics of Irish Literature*. 1972. Pp. 385-387.

Buckley, Jerome Hamilton. *Season of Youth*. 1974. Pp. 225-247.

Burgess, Anthony. *Joysprick*. 1973. Pp. 62-67.

Burton, Dolores M. "Intonation Patterns of Sermons in Seven Novels." *Language and Style*, 3 (1970), 213-214, 217-218.

Carr, Duane R. "Stephen's Retreat to the Word: A Post-Victorian Fallacy." *Western Humanities Review*, 28 (1974), 381-384.

Chapple, J. A. V. *Documentary and Imaginative Literature*. 1970. Pp. 360-365.

Cross, Richard K. *Flaubert and Joyce*. 1971. Pp. 35-38, 44-52, 58-67.

Duytschaever, Joris. *James Joyce*. 1970. Pp. 20-36.

Epstein, Edmund L. *The Ordeal of Stephen Dedalus*. 1971. Pp. 26-173.

Farkas, Paul D. "The Irony of the Artist as a Young Man: A Study in the Structure of Joyce's *Portrait*." *Thoth*, 11 (Spring-Summer 1971), 22-32.

Fortuna, Diane. "The Labyrinth as Controlling Image in Joyce's *A Portrait of the Artist as a Young Man*." *Bulletin of the New York Public Library*, 76 (1972), 120-180.

Füger, Wilhelm. "Joyces *Portrait* und Nietzsche." *Arcadia*, 7 (1972), 234-259.

Füger, Wilhelm. "Türsymbolik in Joyces *Portrait*." *Germanisch-Romanische Monatsschrift*, 22 (1972), 40-57.

Füger, Wilhelm. "Stephen in Wonderland? A Note on the Beginning of Joyce's *Portrait*." *Archiv für das Studium der Neueren Sprachen und Literaturen*, 126 (1974), 72-75.

Gabler, Hans W. " 'Pull Out His Eyes, Apologise.' " *James Joyce Quarterly*, 11 (1974), 167-168.

Garrett, Peter K. *Scene and Symbol*. 1969. Pp. 237-245.

Goldberg, S. L. *The Classical Temper*. 1961. Pp. 41-65.

Goodheart, Eugene. *The Cult of the Ego*. 1968. Pp. 186-191.

Gordon, William A. "Submission and Autonomy: Identity Patterns in Joyce's *Portrait*." *Psychoanalytic Review*, 61 (1974-1975), 535-555.

Gross, John. *James Joyce.* 1970. Pp. 37-41.

Halper, Nathan. *The Early James Joyce.* 1973. Pp. 34-46.

Hart, Clive. *James Joyce's "Ulysses."* 1968. Pp. 28-36.

Heston, Lilla A. "The Interpreter and the Structure of the Novel," in Esther M. Doyle and Virginia Hastings Floyd, eds., *Studies in Interpretation.* 1972. Pp. 146-152.

Hoffman, Frederick J. *The Imagination's New Beginning.* 1967. Pp. 22-33, 36-40.

Johnson, Robert G. "The Daedalus Myth in Joyce's *A Portrait of the Artist as a Young Man." Studies in the Humanities,* 3 (1973), 17-19.

Levin, Harry. *James Joyce.* 1960. Pp. 41-62.

Mueller, William R. *Celebration of Life.* 1972. Pp. 9-29.

Murillo, L. A. *The Cyclical Night.* 1968. Pp. 24-32.

Praz, Mario. "Notes on James Joyce." *Mosaic,* 6 (Fall 1972), 87-91.

Rader, Ralph W. "Defoe, Richardson, Joyce, and the Concept of Form in the Novel," in *Autobiography, Biography, and the Novel.* 1973. Pp. 52-60.

Reid, John. "Joyce, Alas." *Antigonish Review,* No. 16 (1974), 90-97.

Robinson, K. E. "The Stream of Consciousness Technique and the Structure of Joyce's *Portrait." James Joyce Quarterly,* 9 (1971), 63-84.

Rubin, Louis D., Jr. *The Teller in the Tale.* 1967. Pp. 143-148, 150-165.

Scotto, Robert M. "'Visions' and 'Epiphanies': Fictional Technique in Pater's *Marius* and Joyce's *Portrait." James Joyce Quarterly,* 11 (1973), 45-50.

Smith, John B. "Image and Imagery in Joyce's *Portrait*: A Computer-Assisted Analysis," in Stanley Weintraub and Philip Young, eds., *Directions in Literary Criticism.* 1973. Pp. 220-227.

Staley, Harry C. "The Spheretual Exercises of Dedalus and Bloom." *James Joyce Quarterly,* 10 (1973), 209-212.

Vickery, John B. *The Literary Impact of "The Golden Bough."* 1973. Pp. 333-345.

Stephen Hero, 1944

Aubert, Jacques. *Introduction à l'esthétique de James Joyce.* 1973. Pp. 166-171.

Brown, Homer Obed. *James Joyce's Early Fiction.* 1972. Pp. 62-84.

Garrett, Peter K. *Scene and Symbol.* 1969. Pp. 218-228.

Jones, David E. "The Essence of Beauty in James Joyce's Aesthetics." *James Joyce Quarterly,* 10 (1973), 291-311.

Murillo, L. A. *The Cyclical Night.* 1968. Pp. 5-13.

Ulysses, 1922

Adams, R. M. "Hades," in Clive Hart and David Hayman, eds., *James Joyce's "Ulysses."* 1974. Pp. 91-114.

Adams, Robert M. *Proteus, His Lies, His Truth.* 1973. Pp. 136-143.

Adams, Robert Martin. *Surface and Symbol.* 1962. Pp. 3-256.

Allott, Miriam. "James Joyce: The Hedgehog and the Fox," in B. S. Benedikz, ed., *On the Novel.* 1971. Pp. 169-176.

Altieri, Charles. "Organic and Humanistic Models in Some English Bildungsroman." *Journal of General Education*, 23 (1971), 231-233.

Anderson, Chester G. "Leopold Bloom as Dr. Sigmund Freud." *Mosaic*, 6 (Fall 1972), 23-43.

Arnold, Armin. *James Joyce.* 1969. Pp. 52-79.

Atherton, J. S. "The Oxen of the Sun," in Clive Hart and David Hayman, eds., *James Joyce's "Ulysses."* 1974. Pp. 313-339.

Aubert, Jacques. *Introduction à l'esthétique de James Joyce.* 1973. Pp. 137-142.

Barrett, William. *Time of Need.* 1972. Pp. 313-321, 324-331.

Beausang, Michael. "Seeds for the Planting of Bloom." *Mosaic*, 6 (Fall 1972), 11-22.

Beebe, Maurice. "Ulysses and the Age of Modernism." *James Joyce Quarterly*, 10 (1972), 172-188.

Begnal, Michael H. "James Joyce and the Mythologizing of History," in Stanley Weintraub and Philip Young, eds., *Directions in Literary Criticism.* 1973. Pp. 212-217.

Begnal, Michael H. "The Mystery Man of *Ulysses." Journal of Modern Literature*, 2 (1972), 565-568.

Beja, Morris. *Epiphany in the Modern Novel.* 1971. Pp. 103-111.

Benjamin, Judy-Lynn. "A Symphony for Calliope," in Judy-Lynn Benjamin, ed., *The Celtic Bull.* 1966. Pp. 62-68.

Benjamin, Judy-Lynn. "'The Wandering Rocks': The Heart of *Ulysses*," in Judy-Lynn Benjamin, ed., *The Celtic Bull.* 1966. Pp. 54-61.

Benstock, Bernard. "Telemachus," in Clive Hart and David Hayman, eds., *James Joyce's "Ulysses."* 1974. Pp. 1-16.

Benstock, Bernard. "*Ulysses* Without Dublin." *James Joyce Quarterly*, 10 (1972), 90-117.

Biro, Diana. "Leopold in Noman's Land: The 5:00 Chapter of *Ulysses." Thoth*, 11 (Spring-Summer 1971), 9-21.

Blamires, Harry. *The Bloomsday Book.* 1966. Pp. 1-263.

Blot, Jean. "James Joyce: Portrait de l'artiste comme correspondent." *Nouvelle Revue Française*, No. 253 (1974), 90-95.

Bonheim, Helmut. *Joyce's Benefictions.* 1964. Pp. 17-45.

Bowen, Zack. "The Bronzegold Sirensong: A Musical Analysis of the Sirens Episode in Joyce's *Ulysses." Literary Monographs*, 1 (1967), 247-298.

Bowen, Zack. "Libretto for Bloomusalem in Song: The Music of Joyce's *Ulysses*," in Fritz Senn, ed., *New Light on Joyce.* 1972. Pp. 149-166.

Boyle, Robert, S. J. "Miracle in Black Ink: A Glance at Joyce's Use of His Eucharistic Image." *James Joyce Quarterly*, 10 (1972), 47-56.

Boyle, Robert, S. J. "Penelope," in Clive Hart and David Hayman, eds., *James Joyce's "Ulysses."* 1974. Pp. 407-433.

Brandabur, Edward. *A Scrupulous Meanness.* 1971. Pp. 165-173.

Broch, Hermann. "James Joyce und die Gegenwart," in Hartmut Stein-ecke, ed., *Theorie und Technik.* 1972. Pp. 49-55.

Brown, Malcolm. *The Politics of Irish Literature.* 1972. Pp. 224-226, 387-389.

Bruns, Gerald L. "Eumaeus," in Clive Hart and David Hayman, eds., *James Joyce's "Ulysses."* 1974. Pp. 363-383.

Burgess, Anthony. *Joysprick.* 1973. Pp. 21-45, 163-178.

Cambon, Glauco. *La Lotta con Proteo.* 1963. Pp. 17-38.

Card, James Van Dyck. " 'Contradicting': The Word for Joyce's 'Penel-ope.' " *James Joyce Quarterly*, 11 (1973), 17-26.

Cole, David W. "Fugal Structure in the Sirens Episode of *Ulysses.*" *Modern Fiction Studies*, 19 (1973), 221-226.

Cope, Jackson I. "Sirens," in Clive Hart and David Hayman, eds., *James Joyce "Ulysses."* 1974. Pp. 217-242.

Cross, Richard K. *Flaubert and Joyce.* 1971. Pp. 72-79, 83-88, 95-99, 110-121, 157-163, 187-192.

Curtius, E. R. *Essays on European Literature.* 1973. Pp. 327-354.

Dahl, Liisa. "A Comment on Similarities Between Edouard Dujar-din's *Monologue Intérieur* and James Joyce's Interior Monologue." *Neuphilologische Mitteilungen*, 73 (1972), 47-54.

Dahl, Liisa. *Linguistic Features.* 1970. Pp. 21-41.

Durant, Will, and Ariel Durant. *Interpretations of Life.* 1970. Pp. 81-85.

Duytschaever, Joris. *James Joyce.* 1970. Pp. 36-53.

Eckley, Grace. "Ohio's Irish Militia and Joyce's *Ulysses.*" *Éire-Ireland*, 9:4 (1974), 102-116.

Egri, Peter. *Avantgardism and Modernity.* 1972. Pp. 19-65.

Egri, Peter. *James Joyce és Thomas Mann.* 1967. Pp. 126-181.

Ellmann, Richard. *Ulysses on the Liffey.* 1972. Pp. 1-185.

Epstein, E. L. "Nestor," in Clive Hart and David Hayman, eds., *James Joyce's "Ulysses."* 1974. Pp. 17-28.

Finholt, Richard D. "Method in the Cyclops Episode: Joyce on the Nature of Epic Heroes in the Modern World." *University of Dayton Review*, 9 (Summer 1972), 3-13.

Fiol, J. M., and J. C. Santoyo. "Joyce, Ulysses y España." *Papeles de son Armadans*, 67 (1972), 121-140.

Fisch, Harold. *The Dual Image.* 1971. Pp. 83-86.

Fitzpatrick, William P. "The Myth of Creation: Joyce, Jung, and *Ulysses.*" *James Joyce Quarterly*, 11 (1974), 123-144.

Fraser, G. S. "The English Novel," in C. B. Cox and A. E. Dyson, eds., *The Twentieth-Century Mind.* 1972. Vol. II, 378-384.

Friedman, Melvin J. "Lestrygonians," in Clive Hart and David Hay-man, eds., *James Joyce's "Ulysses."* 1974. Pp. 131-146.

Garrett, Peter K. *Scene and Symbol.* 1969. Pp. 245-271.

Gifford, Don, with Robert J. Seidman. *Notes for Joyce.* 1974. Pp.

6-517.

Glasheen, Adaline. "Calypso," in Clive Hart and David Hayman, eds., *James Joyce's "Ulysses."* 1974. Pp. 51-70.

Goldberg, S. L. *The Classical Temper.* 1961. Pp. 66-315.

Goodheart, Eugene. *The Cult of the Ego.* 1968. Pp. 191-197.

Gross, John. *James Joyce.* 1970. Pp. 43-75.

Hall, Vernon, and Gene Arnold Rister. "Joyce's *Ulysses* and Homer's *Odyssey." Complit-Litcomp,* 1 (1973), 12-58.

Hardy, Anne. "A Fugal Analysis of the Siren Episode in Joyce's *Ulysses." Massachusetts Studies in English,* 2 (1970), 59-67.

Hart, Clive. *James Joyce's "Ulysses."* 1968. Pp. 37-77, 81-89, 91-98.

Hart, Clive. "Wandering Rocks," in Clive Hart and David Hayman, eds., *James Joyce's "Ulysses."* 1974. Pp. 181-216.

Hartley, Sandra. "Bloom's Dilemma: Odysseus versus the Cyclops," in Judy-Lynn Benjamin, ed., *The Celtic Bull.* 1966. Pp. 70-73.

Hayman, David. "Clowns et farce chez Joyce." *Poétique,* No. 6 (1971), 173-199.

Hayman, David. "Cyclops," in Clive Hart and David Hayman, eds., *James Joyce's "Ulysses."* 1974. Pp. 243-275.

Hayman, David. *Ulysses.* 1970. Pp. 15-102.

Henke, Suzette. "James Joyce and Philip James Bailey's *Festus." James Joyce Quarterly,* 9 (1972), 445-451.

Herring, Phillip F. "Experimentation with a Landscape: Pornotopography in *Ulysses*—The Phallocy of Imitative Form." *Modern Fiction Studies,* 20 (1974), 375-378.

Herring, Phillip F. "Lotuseaters," in Clive Hart and David Hayman, eds., *James Joyce's "Ulysses."* 1974. Pp. 71-89.

Hodgart, M. J. C. "Aeolus," in Clive Hart and David Hayman, eds., *James Joyce's "Ulysses."* 1974. Pp. 115-130.

Hodgart, Matthew. *Satire.* 1969. Pp. 232-237.

Hoffman, Frederick J. *The Imagination's New Beginning.* 1967. Pp. 39-43.

Horia, Vintila. "James Joyce y el sentido de la autoridad." *Arbor,* 90 (1975), 201-213.

Iser, Wolfgang. "Der Archetyp als Leerform: Erzählschablonen und Kommunikation in Joyces *Ulysses,"* in Manfred Fuhrmann, ed., *Terror und Spiel.* 1971. Pp. 369-408.

Iser, Wolfgang. *The Implied Reader.* 1974. Pp. 179-233.

Johnson, E. Bond, III. "Parody and Myth: Flaubert, Joyce, Nabokov." *Far-Western Forum,* 1 (1974), 158-164.

Kain, Richard M. "The Significance of Stephen's Meeting Bloom: A Survey of Interpretations." *James Joyce Quarterly,* 10 (1972), 147-160.

Kain, Richard M. "Treasures and Trifles in *Ulysses,"* in Ronald Bates and Harry J. Pollock, eds., *Litters from Aloft.* 1971. Pp. 1-13.

Kellogg, Robert. "Scylla and Charybdis," in Clive Hart and David Hayman, eds., *James Joyce's "Ulysses."* 1974. Pp. 147-179.

Kenner, Hugh. "Circe," in Clive Hart and David Hayman, eds., *James Joyce's "Ulysses."* 1974. Pp. 341-362.

Kenner, Hugh. "Molly's Masterstroke." *James Joyce Quarterly*, 10 (1972), 19-28.

Kimball, Jean. "The Hypostasis in *Ulysses.*" *James Joyce Quarterly*, 10 (1973), 422-438.

Knuth, Leo. "A Bathymetric Reading of Joyce's *Ulysses*, Chapter X." *James Joyce Quarterly*, 9 (1972), 405-422.

Knuth, Leo. "Joyce's Verbal Acupuncture." *James Joyce Quarterly*, 10 (1972), 61-71.

Kolbe, Joanne. "Parallel/Parallax," in Judy-Lynn Benjamin, ed., *The Celtic Bull.* 1966. Pp. 83-94.

Kolbe, Joanne. "A Protean Mollylogue," in Judy-Lynn Benjamin, ed., *The Celtic Bull.* 1966. Pp. 96-100.

Kopper, Edward A., Jr. "*Ulysses* and James Joyce's Use of Comedy." *Mosaic*, 6 (Fall 1972), 45-55.

Kreutzer, Eberhard. *Sprache und Spiel.* 1969. Pp. 8-101, 127-137, 140-143.

Lagercrantz, Olof. *Att finnas till.* 1970. Pp. 25-139.

Lane, Mervin. "A Synecdochic Reading of 'Wandering Rocks' in *Ulysses.*" *Western Humanities Review*, 28 (1974), 125-140.

Leithauser, Gladys G., and Paul Sporn. "Hypsopadia: Linguistic Guidepost to the Themes of the 'Circe' Episode in *Ulysses.*" *Journal of Modern Literature*, 4 (1974), 109-114.

Levenston, E. A. "Narrative Technique in *Ulysses*: A Stylistic Comparison of 'Telemachus' and 'Eumaeus.'" *Language and Style*, 5 (1972), 260-275.

Levin, Harry. "Due saggi su James Joyce." *Inventario*, 17 (1962), 1-14.

Levin, Harry. *James Joyce.* 1960. Pp. 65-135.

Levitt, Morton P. "The Family of Bloom," in Fritz Senn, ed., *New Light on Joyce.* 1972. Pp. 141-148.

Levitt, Morton P. "A Hero for Our Time: Leopold Bloom and the Myth of Ulysses." *James Joyce Quarterly*, 10 (1972), 132-145.

Litz, A. Walton. "Ithaca," in Clive Hart and David Hayman, eds., *James Joyce's "Ulysses."* 1974. Pp. 385-405.

Lord, George de F. "The Heroes of *Ulysses* and Their Homeric Prototypes." *Yale Review*, 62 (1972), 43-58.

McCarthy, Patrick A. "The Riddle in Joyce's *Ulysses.*" *Texas Studies in Literature and Language*, 17 (1975), 195-205.

Maddox, James H., Jr. "'Eumaeus' and the Theme of Return in *Ulysses.*" *Texas Studies in Literature and Language*, 16 (1974), 211-220.

Magalaner, Marvin. "The Humanization of Stephen Dedalus." *Mosaic*, 6 (Fall 1972), 63-67.

Marre, K. E. "Experimentation with a Symbol from Mythology: The Courses of the Comets in the 'Ithaca' Chapter of *Ulysses.*" *Modern Fiction Studies*, 20 (1974), 385-390.

Mason, Michael. *James Joyce: "Ulysses."* 1972.

Medioli, Joann. "Sabellian Shakespeare: Bull, Ba'al, or Bard?", in Judy-Lynn Benjamin, ed., *The Celtic Bull.* 1966. Pp. 45-52.

Melchiori, Giorgio. "Joyce, Eliot and the Nightmare of History." *Revue des Langues Vivantes*, 40 (1974), 582-598.

Meskin, Carol. "The Paralleled Virgin and the Unparalleled Mother," in Judy-Lynn Benjamin, ed., *The Celtic Bull.* 1966. Pp. 74-76.

Mitchell, Breon. "Hans Henny Jahnn and James Joyce: The Birth of the Inner Monologue in the German Novel." *Arcadia*, 6 (1971), 49-51.

Morse, J. Mitchell. "Proteus," in Clive Hart and David Hayman, eds., *James Joyce's "Ulysses."* 1974. Pp. 29-49.

Mundigo, Axel. "Bloom's Litany: Sacred and Profane," in Judy-Lynn Benjamin, ed., *The Celtic Bull.* 1966. Pp. 39-44.

Mundigo, Axel. "Decussated Keys in Dublin," in Judy-Lynn Benjamin, ed., *The Celtic Bull.* 1966. Pp. 32-37.

Murillo, L. A. *The Cyclical Night.* 1968. Pp. 35-58.

Nichols, Maryann. "An Epochal Palimpsest," in Judy-Lynn Benjamin, ed., *The Celtic Bull.* 1966. Pp. 1-20.

Noon, William T., S. J. "Song the Syrens Sang." *Mosaic*, 6 (Fall 1972), 77-83.

O'Brien, Flann. "Soûlographie dans le tunnel: A propos de James Joyce." *Lettres Nouvelles*, March 1973. Pp. 49-50.

Paci, Francesca Romana. *Vita e opere.* 1968. Pp. 265-274.

Palomo, Dolores. "Alpha and Omega: Of Chaucer and Joyce." *Mosaic*, 8 (Winter 1975), 19-31.

Parr, Mary. *James Joyce.* 1961.

Pearce, Richard. "Experimentation with the Grotesque: Comic Collisions in the Grotesque World of *Ulysses*." *Modern Fiction Studies*, 20 (1974), 378-384.

Paterakis, Deborah T. "Keylessness, Sex and the Promised Land: Associated Themes in *Ulysses*." *Eire-Ireland*, 8:1 (1973), 97-108.

Paterakis, Deborah T. "Mananaan MacLir in *Ulysses*." *Eire-Ireland*, 7:3 (1972), 29-35.

Petta, Rochelle. "From Corpus to Corpse: 'Lotus Eaters' to 'Hades,'" in Judy-Lynn Benjamin, ed., *The Celtic Bull.* 1966. Pp. 24-31.

Pinsker, Sanford. "*Ulysses* and the Post-Modern Temper." *Midwest Quarterly*, 15 (1974), 406-416.

Pomerance, Victory. "The Frowning Face of Bethel." *James Joyce Quarterly*, 10 (1973), 342-344.

Price, Rosemary. "Nighttown: Lethartic Cathargy," in Judy-Lynn Benjamin, ed., *The Celtic Bull.* 1966. Pp. 77-82.

Praz, Mario. "Notes on James Joyce." *Mosaic*, 6 (Fall 1972), 91-98.

Prescott, Joseph. "The Characterization of Molly Bloom," in Marvin Magalaner, ed., *A James Joyce Miscellany.* 1962. Pp. 79-126.

Rader, Ralph W. "Defoe, Richardson, Joyce, and the Concept of Form in the Novel," in *Autobiography, Biography, and the Novel.* 1973.

Pp. 60-65.

Rauter, Herbert. "Joyce: *Ulysses*," in Franz K. Stanzel, ed., *Der englische Roman*. 1969. Vol. II, 317-355.

Read, Forrest. "Pound, Joyce and Flaubert: Nachfahren des Odysseus." *Akzente*, 17 (1970), 260-278.

Reilly, Kevin P. "Ethic and Ritual in *Ulysses*." *Essays in Literature* (Denver), 2:3 (1974), 59-74.

Robaud, Enzo. "Nota su Joyce." *Ausonia*, 26:5-6 (1971), 58-60.

Rogers, W. G., William Y. Tindall, and Lyman Bryson. "Ulysses," in George D. Crothers, ed., *Invitation to Learning*. 1966. Pp. 199-207.

Rubin, Louis D., Jr. "Don Quixote and Selected Progeny: Or, the Journey-man as Outsider." *Southern Review*, 10 (1974), 47-52.

Rubin, Louis D., Jr. *The Teller in the Tale*. 1967. Pp. 141-150, 160-177.

Schneider, Ulrich. *Die Funktion der Zitate*. 1970. Pp. 14-152.

Scholes, Robert. "*Ulysses*: A Structuralist Perspective." *James Joyce Quarterly*, 10 (1972), 161-171.

Schutte, William M. "Leopold Bloom: A Touch of the Artist." *James Joyce Quarterly*, 10 (1972), 118-131.

Senn, Fritz. "Book of Many Turns." *James Joyce Quarterly*, 10 (1972), 29-46.

Senn, Fritz. "Nausicaa," in Clive Hart and David Hayman, eds., *James Joyce's "Ulysses."* 1974. Pp. 277-311.

Shechner, Mark. "The Song of the Wandering Aengus: James Joyce and His Mother." *James Joyce Quarterly*, 10 (1972), 83-88.

Smith, Don Noel. "Musical Form and Principles in the Scheme of *Ulysses*." *Twentieth-Century Literature*, 18 (1972), 79-92.

Smoot, Jean Johannessen. "Variations in Water Imagery in James Joyce and Bossuet." *Romance Notes*, 9 (1968), 252-257.

Solomon, Albert J. "A Moore in *Ulysses*." *James Joyce Quarterly*, 10 (1973), 215-227.

Staley, Harry C. "The Spheretual Exercises of Dedalus and Bloom." *James Joyce Quarterly*, 10 (1973), 212-214.

Stanzel, Franz. *Narrative Situations*. 1971. Pp. 121-144.

Steinberg, Erwin R. *The Stream of Consciousness and Beyond in "Ulysses."* 1973.

Sultan, Stanley. *The Argument of "Ulysses."* 1964.

Tindall, William York. "Mosaic Bloom." *Mosaic*, 6 (Fall 1972), 3-9.

Tolomeo, Diane. "The Final Octagon of *Ulysses*." *James Joyce Quarterly*, 10 (1973), 439-454.

Tomasi, Barbara R. "The Fraternal Theme in Joyce's *Ulysses*." *American Imago*, 30 (1973), 177-191.

Varela Jácome, Benito. *Renovación de la novela*. 1967. Pp. 152-168.

Vickery, John B. *The Literary Impact of "The Golden Bough."* 1973. Pp. 346-407.

Walcott, William. "Notes by a Jungian Analyst on the Dreams in *Ulysses*." *James Joyce Quarterly*, 9 (1971), 37-48.

Weinstein, Arnold L. *Vision and Response*. 1974. Pp. 169-190.

Weiss, Wolfgang. "Joyces Pastiche des *Carmen Arvale*." *Anglia*, 91 (1973), 487-492.

White, John J. "Myths and Patterns in the Modern Novel," in R. G. Collins. ed., *The Novel*. 1972. Pp. 91-94, 96-97.

White, Patrick. "The Key in *Ulysses*." *James Joyce Quarterly*, 9 (1971), 10-25.

White, Patrick. "Vico's Institution of Burial in *Ulysses*." *Ball State University Forum*, 14 (Autumn 1973), 59-68.

Wlassics, Tibor. "Nota su Dante nell'*Ulisse*." *Rivista de Litterature Moderne e Comparate*, 24 (1971), 151-154.

Zéraffa, Michel. *Personne et personnage*. 1969. Pp. 140-147.

Zhantieva, B. G. "Joyce's *Ulysses*," in Gaylord C. LeRoy and Ursula Beitz, eds., *Preserve and Create*. 1973. Pp. 138-171.

JAMES PHILLIPS KAY-SHUTTLEWORTH

Ribblesdale, 1874

Melada, Ivan. *The Captain of Industry*. 1970. Pp. 26-33.

Scarsdale, 1860

Melada, Ivan. *The Captain of Industry*. 1970. Pp. 17-24.

BENEDICT KIELY

Call for a Miracle, 1950

Eckley, Grace. *Benedict Kiely*. 1972. Pp. 75-85.

The Captain with the Whiskers, 1960

Eckley, Grace. *Benedict Kiely*. 1972. Pp. 124-140.

The Cards of the Gambler, 1953

Eckley, Grace. *Benedict Kiely*. 1972. Pp. 96-111.

Dogs Enjoy the Morning, 1968

Eckley, Grace. *Benedict Kiely*. 1972. Pp. 141-156.

Honey Seems Bitter, 1954

Eckley, Grace. *Benedict Kiely*. 1972. Pp. 86-95.

In a Harbour Green, 1949

Eckley, Grace. *Benedict Kiely*. 1972. Pp. 62-74.

Land Without Stars, 1946

Eckley, Grace. *Benedict Kiely*. 1972. Pp. 54-61.

There Was an Ancient House, 1955

   Eckley, Grace. *Benedict Kiely*. 1972. Pp. 112-123.

CHARLES KINGSLEY

Alton Locke, 1850

   Cazamian, Louis. *The Social Novel in England*. 1973. Pp. 268-288.
   Colloms, Brenda. *Charles Kingsley*. 1975. Pp. 127-135.
   Duerksen, Roland A. *Shelleyan Ideas in Victorian Literature*. 1966.
      Pp. 100-104, 112-114.
   Vooys, Sijna de. *The Psychological Element*. 1966. Pp. 56-64.

Hypatia, 1853

   Colloms, Brenda. *Charles Kingsley*. 1975. Pp. 150-156.
   Downes, David A. *The Temper of Victorian Belief*. 1972. Pp. 58-81.

Two Years Ago, 1857

   Duerksen, Roland A. *Shelleyan Ideas in Victorian Literature*. 1966.
      Pp. 102-108.

Westward Ho!, 1855

   Colloms, Brenda. *Charles Kingsley*. 1975. Pp. 194-203.

Yeast, 1848

   Cazamian, Louis. *The Social Novel in England*. 1973. Pp. 254-266.
   Colloms, Brenda. *Charles Kingsley*. 1975. Pp. 102-110.
   Duerksen, Roland A. *Shelleyan Ideas in Victorian Literature*. 1966.
      Pp. 98-100, 105-106, 108-112.

HENRY KINGSLEY

Geoffrey Hamlyn, 1859

   Scheuerle, William H. *The Neglected Brother*. 1971. Pp. 27-52.

The Hillyars and the Burtons, 1865

   Scheuerle, William H. *The Neglected Brother*. 1971. Pp. 100-105.

Mademoiselle Mathilde, 1868

   Scheuerle, William H. *The Neglected Brother*. 1971. Pp. 112-120.

Oakshott Castle, 1873

   Scheuerle, William H. *The Neglected Brother*. 1971. Pp. 146-155.

Ravenshoe, 1862

   Scheuerle, William H. *The Neglected Brother*. 1971. Pp. 60-85.

Silcote of Silcotes, 1867

   Scheuerle, William H. *The Neglected Brother*. 1971. Pp. 105-111.

RUDYARD KIPLING

Captains Courageous, 1897

   Shahane, Vasant A. *Rudyard Kipling*. 1973. Pp. 70-74.
   Stewart, J. I. M. *Rudyard Kipling*. 1966. Pp. 114-117.

Kim, 1901

   Chapple, J. A. V. *Documentary and Imaginative Literature*. 1970.
      Pp. 176-184.
   Parry, Benita. *Delusions and Discoveries*. 1972. Pp. 242-255.
   Rao, K. Bhaskara. *Rudyard Kipling's India*. 1967. Pp. 123-159.
   Shahane, Vasant A. *Rudyard Kipling*. 1973. Pp. 41-69.
   Stewart, J. I. M. *Rudyard Kipling*. 1966. Pp. 144-146.
   Sühnel, Rudolf. "Kontemplation und Aktion: Orient und Okzident im
      Werk von Rudyard Kipling." *Sitzungsberichte der Heidelberger
      Akademie der Wissenschaften*, 3 (1972), 8-18.
   Tompkins, J. M. S. *The Art of Rudyard Kipling*. 1959. Pp. 21-32.
   Viswanathan, K. *India in English Fiction*. 1971. Pp. 50-90.

The Light That Failed, 1890

   Shahane, Vasant A. *Rudyard Kipling*. 1973. Pp. 74-81.
   Stewart, J. I. M. *Rudyard Kipling*. 1966. Pp. 88-95.
   Tompkins, J. M. S. *The Art of Rudyard Kipling*. 1959. Pp. 8-16,
      18-21.

The Naulahka, 1892

   Parry, Benita. *Delusions and Discoveries*. 1972. Pp. 225-228.
   Rao, K. Bhaskara. *Rudyard Kipling's India*. 1967. Pp. 102-122.

FRANCIS KING

A Domestic Animal, 1970

   Dick, Kay. *Friends and Friendship*. 1974. Pp. 131-132.

D. H. LAWRENCE

Aaron's Rod, 1922

   Daleski, Herman M. *The Forked Flame*. 1965. Pp. 188-213.
   Delavenay, Emile. *D. H. Lawrence*. 1972. Pp. 446-449.
   Kermode, Frank. *D. H. Lawrence*. 1973. Pp. 81-86.
   Lerner, Laurence. *The Truthtellers*. 1967. Pp. 226-227.
   Miles, Kathleen M. *The Hellish Meaning*. 1969. Pp. 13-14.

Moynahan, Julian. *The Deed of Life.* 1963. Pp. 95-101.
Nahal, Chaman. *D. H. Lawrence.* 1970. Pp. 173-179.
Pritchard, R. E. *D. H. Lawrence.* 1971. Pp. 136-140.
Sagar, Keith. *The Art of D. H. Lawrence.* 1966. Pp. 102-114.
Slade, Tony. *D. H. Lawrence.* 1969. Pp. 80-82.
Wagner, Jeanie. "A Botanical Note on *Aaron's Rod.*" *D. H. Lawrence Review*, 4 (1971), 287-290.

Kangaroo, 1923

Bedient, Calvin. *Architects of the Self.* 1972. Pp. 165-169.
Hochman, Baruch. *Another Ego.* 1970. Pp. 180-183.
Inniss, Kenneth. *D. H. Lawrence's Bestiary.* 1971. Pp. 154-155, 163-168.
Moynahan, Julian. *The Deed of Life.* 1963. Pp. 101-107.
Pritchard, R. E. *D. H. Lawrence.* 1971. Pp. 150-154.
Sagar, Keith. *The Art of D. H. Lawrence.* 1966. Pp. 131-137.
Samuels, Marilyn Schauer. "Water, Ships, and the Sea: Unifying Symbols in Lawrence's *Kangaroo.*" *University Review*, 37 (1970), 46-57.
Sepčić, Višnja. "The Category of Landscape in D. H. Lawrence's *Kangaroo.*" *Studia Romanica et Anglica Zagrabiensia*, 27-28 (1969), 129-152.
Slade, Tony. *D. H. Lawrence.* 1969. Pp. 82-87.

Lady Chatterley's Lover, 1928

Bedient, Calvin. *Architects of the Self.* 1972. Pp. 172-182.
Black, Michael. "That Which Is Perfectly Ourselves (IV): Connie Chatterley." *Human World*, No. 8 (1972), 45-54.
Clarke, Colin. *River of Dissolution.* 1969. Pp. 131-147.
Daleski, Herman M. *The Forked Flame.* 1965. Pp. 258-311.
Gill, Richard. *Happy Rural Seat.* 1972. Pp. 147-155.
Hardy, Barbara. *The Appropriate Form.* 1964. Pp. 162-172.
Hinz, Evelyn J. "D. H. Lawrence and 'Something Called "Canada." ' " *Dalhousie Review*, 54 (1974), 246-248.
Hochman, Baruch. *Another Ego.* 1970. Pp. 221-228.
Inniss, Kenneth. *D. H. Lawrence's Bestiary.* 1971. Pp. 191-194.
Kermode, Frank. *D. H. Lawrence.* 1973. Pp. 134-143.
Lerner, Laurence. *The Truthtellers.* 1967. Pp. 215-220.
Miles, Kathleen M. *The Hellish Meaning.* 1969. Pp. 26-31, 51-53.
Moynahan, Julian. *The Deed of Life.* 1963. Pp. 140-172.
Negriolli, Claude. *La Symbolique de D.-H. Lawrence.* 1970. Pp. 89-99.
Pritchard, R. E. *D. H. Lawrence.* 1971. Pp. 186-195.
Sagar, Keith. *The Art of D. H. Lawrence.* 1966. Pp. 179-198.
Sanders, Scott. *D. H. Lawrence.* 1973. Pp. 172-205.
Scott, James F. "The Emasculation of *Lady Chatterley's Lover.*" *Literature/Film Quarterly*, 1 (1973), 37-45.
Sepčić, Višnja. "The Dialogue in *Lady Chatterley's Lover.*" *Studia*

Romanica et Anglica Zagrabiensia, 29-32 (1970-1971), 461-480.

Slade, Tony. *D. H. Lawrence.* 1969. Pp. 88-94.

Squires, Michael. "Pastoral Patterns and Pastoral Variants in *Lady Chatterley's Lover.*" *ELH,* 39 (1972), 129-146.

Taube, Myron. "Fanny and the Lady: The Treatment of Sex in *Fanny Hill* and *Lady Chatterley's Lover.*" *Lock Haven Review,* 15 (1974), 37-40.

Widmer, Kingsley. "The Pertinence of Modern Pastoral: The Three Versions of *Lady Chatterley's Lover.*" *Studies in the Novel,* 5 (1973), 298-313.

The Lost Girl, 1920

Moynahan, Julian. *The Deed of Life.* 1963. Pp. 121-140.

Pritchard, R. E. *D. H. Lawrence.* 1971. Pp. 129-132.

Sagar, Keith. *The Art of D. H. Lawrence.* 1966. Pp. 36-38, 114-115.

The Plumed Serpent, 1926

Baldwin, Alice. "The Structure of the Coatl Symbol in *The Plumed Serpent.*" *Style,* 5 (1971), 138-150.

Bedient, Calvin. *Architects of the Self.* 1972. Pp. 147-153.

Brotherston, J. G. "Revolution and the Ancient Literature of Mexico, for D. H. Lawrence and Antonin Artaud." *Twentieth-Century Literature,* 18 (1972), 181-189.

Clarke, Colin. *River of Dissolution.* 1969. Pp. 131-147.

Cowan, James C. *D. H. Lawrence's American Journey.* 1970. Pp. 99-121.

Daleski, Herman M. *The Forked Flame.* 1965. Pp. 213-256.

Fairbanks, N. David. " 'Strength Through Joy' in the Novels of D. H. Lawrence." *Literature and Ideology,* No. 8 (1971), 69-71, 75-78.

Glicksberg, Charles I. *Modern Literary Perspectivism.* 1970. Pp. 144-147.

Hochman, Baruch. *Another Ego.* 1970. Pp. 230-254.

Inniss, Kenneth. *D. H. Lawrence's Bestiary.* 1971. Pp. 176-188.

Kermode, Frank. *D. H. Lawrence.* 1973. Pp. 113-118.

Lerner, Laurence. *The Truthtellers.* 1967. Pp. 172-180.

Meyers, Jeffrey. "D. H. Lawrence and Homosexuality." *London Magazine,* 13:4 (1973), 94-98.

Miles, Kathleen M. *The Hellish Meaning.* 1969. Pp. 22-24, 43-48, 58-59.

Moynahan, Julian. *The Deed of Life.* 1963. Pp. 107-111.

Pritchard, R. E. *D. H. Lawrence.* 1971. Pp. 171-177.

Sagar, Keith. *The Art of D. H. Lawrence.* 1966. Pp. 159-168.

Sanders, Scott. *D. H. Lawrence.* 1973. Pp. 136-171.

Slade, Tony. *D. H. Lawrence.* 1969. Pp. 87-88.

Vickery, John B. "*The Plumed Serpent* and the Reviving God." *Journal of Modern Literature,* 2 (1972), 505-532.

The Rainbow, 1915

Adam, Ian. "Lawrence's Anti-Symbol: The Ending of *The Rainbow."
Journal of Narrative Technique*, 3 (1973), 77-84.

Adamowski, T. H. *"The Rainbow* and 'Otherness.' " *D. H. Lawrence
Review*, 7 (1974), 58-77.

Alinei, Tamara. "Imagery and Meaning in D. H. Lawrence's *The Rainbow." Yearbook of English Studies*, 2 (1972), 205-211.

Bedient, Calvin. *Architects of the Self*. 1972. Pp. 124-135.

Brandabur, A. M. "The Ritual Corn Harvest Scene in *The Rainbow."
D. H. Lawrence Review*, 6 (1973), 284-302.

Brown, Homer O. " 'The Passionate Struggle into Conscious Being':
D. H. Lawrence's *The Rainbow." D. H. Lawrence Review*, 7 (1974),
275-290.

Burns, Robert. "The Novel as a Metaphysical Statement: Lawrence's
The Rainbow." Southern Review (Adelaide), 4 (1970), 139-160.

Butler, Gerald J. "Sexual Experience in D. H. Lawrence's *The Rainbow." Recovering Literature*, 2 (Fall-Winter 1973), 1-92.

Chapple, J. A. V. *Documentary and Imaginative Literature*. 1970.
Pp. 72-80.

Charis, Geraldine Giebel. "Ursula Brangwen: Toward Self and Selflessness." *Thoth*, 12 (Fall 1971), 19-25.

Clarke, Colin. *River of Dissolution*. 1969. Pp. 45-69.

Daleski, Herman M. *The Forked Flame*. 1965. Pp. 74-125.

Delavenay, Emile. *D. H. Lawrence*. 1972. Pp. 344-385.

Elsbree, Langdon. "D. H. Lawrence, *Homo Ludens*, and the Dance."
D. H. Lawrence Review, 1 (1968), 13-20.

Engelberg, Edward. "Escape from the Circles of Experience: D. H.
Lawrence's *The Rainbow* as a Modern *Bildungsroman." Publications of the Modern Language Association*, 78 (1963), 103-113.

Garrett, Peter K. *Scene and Symbol*. 1969. Pp. 189-198.

Goodheart, Eugene. *The Utopian Vision of D. H. Lawrence*. 1963.
Pp. 25-30, 115-125.

Heilbrun, Carolyn G. *Towards a Recognition of Androgyny*. 1973.
Pp. 102-110.

Hill, G. Ordelle, and Potter Woodberg. "Ursula Brangwen of *The
Rainbow*: Christian Saint or Pagan Goddess?" *D. H. Lawrence
Review*, 4 (1971), 274-279.

Hochman, Baruch. *Another Ego*. 1970. Pp. 35-44.

Inglis, Fred. *An Essential Discipline*. 1968. Pp. 240-251.

Inniss, Kenneth. *D. H. Lawrence's Bestiary*. 1971. Pp. 115, 118-136.

Kay, Wallace G. "Lawrence and *The Rainbow*: Apollo and Dionysus
in Conflict." *Southern Quarterly*, 10 (1972), 209-222.

Kermode, Frank. *D. H. Lawrence*. 1973. Pp. 42-49.

Klienbard, David J. "D. H. Lawrence and Ontological Insecurity."
Publications of the Modern Language Association, 89 (1974), 154-
163.

Lerner, Laurence. *The Truthtellers*. 1967. Pp. 79-81, 203-204.

Meyers, Jeffrey. "*The Rainbow* and Fra Angelico." *D. H. Lawrence Review*, 7 (1974), 139-155.

Miko, Stephen J. *Toward "Women in Love."* 1971. Pp. 108-185.

Miles, Kathleen M. *The Hellish Meaning*. 1969. Pp. 14, 34-36, 61.

Moynahan, Julian. *The Deed of Life*. 1963. Pp. 42-72.

Mueller, William R. *Celebration of Life*. 1972. Pp. 150-168.

Nahal, Chaman. *D. H. Lawrence.* 1970. Pp. 137-173.

Negriolli, Claude. *La Symbolique de D.-H. Lawrence.* 1970. Pp. 61-67.

Pritchard, R. E. *D. H. Lawrence*. 1971. Pp. 66-78.

Raddatz, Volker. "Lyrical Elements in D. H. Lawrence's *The Rainbow*." *Revue des Langues Vivantes*, 40 (1974), 235-242.

Sagar, Keith. *The Art of D. H. Lawrence*. 1966. Pp. 41-72.

Sale, Roger. *Modern Heroism*. 1973. Pp. 52-76.

Sanders, Scott. *D. H. Lawrence*. 1973. Pp. 60-93.

Slade, Tony. *D. H. Lawrence*. 1969. Pp. 55-67.

Smith, Frank Glover. *D. H. Lawrence: "The Rainbow."* 1971.

Swigg, Richard. *Lawrence, Hardy, and American Literature*. 1972. Pp. 81-131.

Swinden, Patrick. *Unofficial Selves*. 1973. Pp. 175-178.

Terry, C. J. "Aspects of D. H. Lawrence's Struggle with Christianity." *Dalhousie Review*, 54 (1974), 116-122.

Tysdal, Bjørn. "Kvinnesak og skjønnlitteratur—D. H. Lawrence: *The Rainbow*." *Edda*, 1975, Pp. 29-35.

Sons and Lovers, 1913

Baldanza, Frank. "*Sons and Lovers*: Novel to Film as a Record of Cultural Growth." *Literature/Film Quarterly*, 1 (1973), 64-70.

Beatty, C. J. P. "Konrad Lorenz and D. H. Lawrence." *Notes and Queries*, 19 (1972), 54.

Bedient, Calvin. *Architects of the Self*. 1972. Pp. 117-125.

Buckley, Jerome H. "Autobiography in the English *Bildungsroman*," in Morton W. Bloomfield, ed., *The Interpretation of Narrative*. 1970. Pp. 99-104.

Buckley, Jerome Hamilton. *Season of Youth*. 1974. Pp. 204-224.

Burwell, Rose Marie. "Schopenhauer, Hardy and Lawrence: Toward a New Understanding of *Sons and Lovers*." *Western Humanities Review*, 28 (1974), 105-117.

Daleski, Herman M. *The Forked Flame*. 1965. Pp. 42-73.

Delavenay, Emile. *D. H. Lawrence*. 1972. Pp. 15-29, 48-53, 115-126.

DiMaggio, Richard. "A Note on *Sons and Lovers* and Emerson's 'Experience.'" *D. H. Lawrence Review*, 6 (1973), 214-216.

Elsbree, Langdon. "D. H. Lawrence, *Homo Ludens*, and the Dance." *D. H. Lawrence Review*, 1 (1968), 8-12.

Garrett, Peter K. *Scene and Symbol*. 1969. Pp. 186-189.

Hardy, Barbara. *The Appropriate Form*. 1964. Pp. 135-146.

Hinz, Evelyn J. "*Sons and Lovers*: The Archetypal Dimensions of

Lawrence's Oedipal Tragedy." *D. H. Lawrence Review*, 5 (1972), 26-53.

Hochman, Baruch. *Another Ego*. 1970. Pp. 29-35, 39-40.

Hornick, Edward J., Harry T. Moore, and George D. Crothers. "*Sons and Lovers*," in George D. Crothers, ed., *Invitation to Learning*. 1966. Pp. 191-197.

Kermode, Frank. *D. H. Lawrence*. 1973. Pp. 12-17.

Lerner, Laurence. *The Truthtellers*. 1967. Pp. 211-214.

Miko, Stephen J. *Toward "Women in Love."* 1971. Pp. 59-107.

Moynahan, Julian. *The Deed of Life*. 1963. Pp. 13-31.

Nahal, Chaman. *D. H. Lawrence*. 1970. Pp. 129-137.

Panken, Shirley. "Some Psychodynamics in *Sons and Lovers*: A New Look at the Oedipal Theme." *Psychoanalytic Review*, 61 (1974-1975), 571-589.

Pritchard, R. E. *D. H. Lawrence*. 1971. Pp. 32-44.

Sagar, Keith. *The Art of D. H. Lawrence*. 1966. Pp. 19-35.

Sale, Roger. *Modern Heroism*. 1973. Pp. 22-39.

Sanders, Scott. *D. H. Lawrence*. 1973. Pp. 21-59.

Sepčić, Višnja. "Realism versus Symbolism: The Double Patterning of *Sons and Lovers*." *Studia Romanica et Anglica Zagrabiensia*, 33-36 (1972-1973), 185-208.

Slade, Tony. *D. H. Lawrence*. 1969. Pp. 39-54.

Swigg, Richard. *Lawrence, Hardy, and American Literature*. 1972. Pp. 44-57.

Swinden, Patrick. *Unofficial Selves*. 1973. Pp. 160-168.

Taylor, John A. "The Greatness in *Sons and Lovers*." *Modern Philology*, 71 (1974), 380-387.

The Trespasser, 1912

Delavenay, Emile. *D. H. Lawrence*. 1972. Pp. 98-103.

Hinz, Evelyn J. "*The Trespasser*: Lawrence's Wagnerian Tragedy and Divine Comedy." *D. H. Lawrence Review*, 4 (1971), 122-141.

Miko, Stephen J. *Toward "Women in Love."* 1971. Pp. 35-58.

Millett, Robert. "Great Expectations: D. H. Lawrence's *The Trespasser*," in Bradford B. Broughton, ed., *Twenty-Seven to One*. 1970. Pp. 125-131.

Moynahan, Julian. *The Deed of Life*. 1963. Pp. 5-7.

Pritchard, R. E. *D. H. Lawrence*. 1971. Pp. 27-29.

Slade, Tony. *D. H. Lawrence*. 1969. Pp. 38-39.

Swigg, Richard. *Lawrence, Hardy, and American Literature*. 1972. Pp. 39-43.

The White Peacock, 1911

Daleski, Herman M. *The Forked Flame*. 1965. Pp. 312-315.

Delavenay, Emile. *D. H. Lawrence*. 1972. Pp. 88-97.

Elsbree, Langdon. "D. H. Lawrence, *Homo Ludens*, and the Dance." *D. H. Lawrence Review*, 1 (1968), 5-7.

Gajdusek, Robert E. "A Reading of 'A Poem of Friendship': A Chapter in Lawrence's *The White Peacock*." *D. H. Lawrence Review*, 3 (1970), 47-62.

Hinz, Evelyn J. "D. H. Lawrence and 'Something Called "Canada." ' " *Dalhousie Review*, 54 (1974), 240-245.

Hinz, Evelyn J. "Juno and *The White Peacock*: Lawrence's English Epic." *D. H. Lawrence Review*, 3 (1970), 115-135.

Inniss, Kenneth. *D. H. Lawrence's Bestiary*. 1971. Pp. 108-116.

Miko, Stephen J. *Toward "Women in Love*." 1971. Pp. 5-34.

Miles, Kathleen M. *The Hellish Meaning*. 1969. P. 14.

Moynahan, Julian. *The Deed of Life*. 1963. Pp. 5-12.

Nahal, Chaman. *D. H. Lawrence*. 1970. Pp. 55-76.

Pritchard, R. E. *D. H. Lawrence*. 1971. Pp. 26-27.

Sagar, Keith. *The Art of D. H. Lawrence*. 1966. Pp. 9-13.

Slade, Tony. *D. H. Lawrence*. 1969. Pp. 35-38.

Swigg, Richard. *Lawrence, Hardy, and American Literature*. 1972. Pp. 32-38.

Women in Love, 1920

Bareiss, Dieter. *Die Vierpersonenkonstellation im Roman*. 1969. Pp. 93-118.

Bedient, Calvin. *Architects of the Self*. 1972. Pp. 135-147.

Charis, Geraldine Giebel. "Ursula Brangwen: Toward Self and Selflessness." *Thoth*, 12 (Fall 1971), 25-28.

Clarke, Colin. *River of Dissolution*. 1969. Pp. 70-110.

Craig, David. *The Real Foundations*. 1973. Pp. 143-167.

Daleski, Herman M. *The Forked Flame*. 1965. Pp. 126-187.

Delavenay, Emile. *D. H. Lawrence*. 1972. Pp. 386-428.

Delavenay, Emile. *D. H. Lawrence and Edward Carpenter*. 1971. Pp. 89-97, 100-110, 215-221.

Elsbree, Langdon. "D. H. Lawrence, *Homo Ludens*, and the Dance." *D. H. Lawrence Review*, 1 (1968), 20-26.

Garrett, Peter K. *Scene and Symbol*. 1969. Pp. 198-213.

Gerber, Stephen. "Character, Language, and Experience in 'Water Party.' " *Paunch*, Nos. 36-37 (April 1973), 3-29.

Goodheart, Eugene. *The Cult of the Ego*. 1968. Pp. 165-170.

Hardy, Barbara. *The Appropriate Form*. 1964. Pp. 146-161.

Hochman, Baruch. *Another Ego*. 1970. Pp. 36-44, 101-117, 137-138, 142-146.

Inniss, Kenneth. *D. H. Lawrence's Bestiary*. 1971. Pp. 118-119, 137-158.

Jacobson, Sibyl. "The Paradox of Fulfillment: A Discussion of *Women in Love*." *Journal of Narrative Technique*, 3 (1973), 53-65.

Kay, Wallace G. "*Women in Love* and 'The Man Who Had Died': Resolving Apollo and Dionysus." *Southern Quarterly*, 10 (1972), 325-337.

Kermode, Frank. *D. H. Lawrence*. 1973. Pp. 63-78.

Lerner, Laurence. *The Truthtellers*. 1967. Pp. 195-205.

Miko, Stephen J. *Toward "Women in Love."* 1971. Pp. 215-289.

Miles, Kathleen M. *The Hellish Meaning*. 1969. Pp. 15-22, 36-39, 56-58, 62-66.

Moynahan, Julian. *The Deed of Life*. 1963. Pp. 72-91.

Nahal, Chaman. *D. H. Lawrence*. 1970. Pp. 140-148, 154-156, 168-173.

Negriolli, Claude. *La Symbolique de D.-H. Lawrence*. 1970. Pp. 150-157.

Panichas, George A. *The Reverent Discipline*. 1973. Pp. 205-228.

Pritchard, R. E. *D. H. Lawrence*. 1971. Pp. 85-106.

Rachman, Shalom. "Art and Value in D. H. Lawrence's *Women in Love*." *D. H. Lawrence Review*, 5 (1972), 1-25.

Reddick, Bryan D. "Point of View and Narrative Tone in *Women in Love*: The Portrayal of Interpsychic Space." *D. H. Lawrence Review*, 7 (1974), 156-171.

Remsbury, John. "*Women in Love* as a Novel of Change." *D. H. Lawrence Review*, 6 (1973), 149-172.

Sagar, Keith. *The Art of D. H. Lawrence*. 1966. Pp. 74-98.

Sale, Roger. *Modern Heroism*. 1973. Pp. 79-105.

Sanders, Scott. *D. H. Lawrence*. 1973. Pp. 94-135.

Sharma, Radhe Shyam. "The Symbol as Archetype: A Study of Symbolic Mode in D. H. Lawrence's *Women in Love*." *Osmania Journal of English Studies*, 8 (1971), 31-53.

Slade, Tony. *D. H. Lawrence*. 1969. Pp. 67-78.

Swigg, Richard. *Lawrence, Hardy, and American Literature*. 1972. Pp. 132-186.

Zambrano, Ana Laura. "*Women in Love*: Counterpoint on Film." *Literature/Film Quarterly*, 1 (1973), 46-54.

Zéraffa, Michel. *Personne et personnage*. 1969. Pp. 229-234.

SOPHIA LEE

The Recess, 1785

Lévy, Maurice. *Le Roman "gothique" anglais*. 1968. Pp. 180-191.

JOSEPH SHERIDAN LEFANU

The Cock and Anchor, 1845

Begnal, Michael H. *Joseph Sheridan LeFanu*. 1971. Pp. 19-22.

The Fortunes of Colonel Torlogh O'Brien, 1847

Begnal, Michael H. *Joseph Sheridan LeFanu*. 1971. Pp. 22-25.

Guy Deverell, 1865

Begnal, Michael H. *Joseph Sheridan LeFanu*. 1971. Pp. 60-63.

Haunted Lives, 1868

    Begnal, Michael H. *Joseph Sheridan LeFanu*. 1971. Pp. 65-67.

The House by the Church-Yard, 1863

    Begnal, Michael H. *Joseph Sheridan LeFanu*. 1971. Pp. 47-51.

Uncle Silas, 1864

    Begnal, Michael H. *Joseph Sheridan LeFanu*. 1971. Pp. 55-60.

Willing to Die, 1873

    Begnal, Michael H. *Joseph Sheridan LeFanu*. 1971. Pp. 69-71.

Wylder's Hand, 1864

    Begnal, Michael H. *Joseph Sheridan LeFanu*. 1971. Pp. 51-55.

ROSAMOND LEHMANN

The Ballad and the Source, 1944

    Gindin, James. "Rosamond Lehmann: A Revaluation." *Contemporary Literature*, 15 (1974), 206, 209.
    LeStourgeon, Diana E. *Rosamond Lehmann*. 1965. Pp. 89-107.

Dusty Answer, 1927

    Gindin, James. "Rosamond Lehmann: A Revaluation." *Contemporary Literature*, 15 (1974), 204, 207, 208, 210.
    LeStourgeon, Diana E. *Rosamond Lehmann*. 1965. Pp. 29-42.

The Echoing Grove, 1953

    Coopman, Tony. "Symbolism in Rosamond Lehmann's *The Echoing Grove*." *Revue des Langues Vivantes*, 40 (1974), 116-121.
    Gindin, James. "Rosamond Lehmann: A Revaluation." *Contemporary Literature*, 15 (1974), 204, 207, 208, 210, 211.
    LeStourgeon, Diana E. *Rosamond Lehmann*. 1965. Pp. 108-121.

Invitation to the Waltz, 1932

    Gindin, James. "Rosamond Lehmann: A Revaluation." *Contemporary Literature*, 15 (1974), 204-205, 207, 210.
    LeStourgeon, Diana E. *Rosamond Lehmann*. 1965. Pp. 57-75.

A Note in Music, 1930

    Gindin, James. "Rosamond Lehmann: A Revaluation." *Contemporary Literature*, 15 (1974), 204-205, 206, 209.
    LeStourgeon, Diana E. *Rosamond Lehmann*. 1965. Pp. 43-56.

The Weather in the Streets, 1936

    Gindin, James. "Rosamond Lehmann: A Revaluation." *Contempo-*

rary Literature, 15 (1974), 205-208, 210.

LeStourgeon, Diana E. Rosamond Lehmann. 1965. Pp. 76-88.

DORIS LESSING

Briefing for a Descent into Hell, 1971

Thorpe, Michael. Doris Lessing. 1973. Pp. 30-32.

Children of Violence, 1952-1969

Marchino, Lois A. "The Search for Self in the Novels of Doris Lessing."
Studies in the Novel, 4 (1972), 252-261.

Morris, Robert K. Continuance and Change. 1972. Pp. 1-27.

Thorpe, Michael. Doris Lessing. 1973. Pp. 19-25.

The Four-Gated City, 1969

Karl, Frederick R. "Doris Lessing in the Sixties: The New Anatomy of
Melancholy." Contemporary Literature, 13 (1972), 15-16, 23-33.

Mannheimer, Monica Lauritzen. "The Individual and Society in Contemporary British Fiction." Moderna Sprak, 68 (1974), 322-325.

Sudrann, Jean. "Hearth and Horizon: Changing Concepts of the 'Domestic' Life of the Heroine." Massachusetts Review, 14 (1973),
241-250.

The Golden Notebook, 1962

Bergonzi, Bernard. The Situation of the Novel. 1971. Pp. 200-204.

Brooks, Ellen W. "The Image of Woman in Lessing's The Golden
Notebook." Critique (Atlanta), 15:1 (1973), 101-109.

Craig, Joanne. "The Golden Notebook: The Novelist as Heroine."
University of Windsor Review, 10 (1974), 55-66.

Hynes, Joseph. "The Construction of The Golden Notebook." Iowa
Review, 4:3 (1973), 100-113.

Joyner, Nancy. "The Underside of the Butterfly: Lessing's Debt to
Woolf." Journal of Narrative Technique, 4 (1974), 204-211.

Karl, Frederick R. "Doris Lessing in the Sixties: The New Anatomy
of Melancholy." Contemporary Literature, 13 (1972), 15-23.

Lebowitz, Naomi. Humanism and the Absurd. 1971. Pp. 132-136.

Lessing, Doris. "On The Golden Notebook." Partisan Review, 40
(1973), 14-30.

Libby, Marion Vlastos. "Sex and the New Woman in The Golden Notebook." Iowa Review, 5:4 (1974), 106-120.

Marchino, Lois A. "The Search for Self in the Novels of Doris Lessing."
Studies in the Novel, 4 (1972), 252-261.

Markow, Alice Bradley. "The Pathology of a Feminine Failure in the
Fiction of Doris Lessing." Critique (Atlanta), 16:1 (1974), 91-93, 97.

Mutti, Giuliana. "Female Roles and the Function of Art in The Golden
Notebook." Massachusetts Studies in English, 3 (1972), 78-83.

Porter, Dennis. "Realism and Failure in *The Golden Notebook*."
Modern Language Quarterly, 35 (1974), 56-65.
Thorpe, Michael. *Doris Lessing*. 1973. Pp. 25-29.
Tiger, Virginia. "Advertisements for Herself." *Columbia Forum*, 3:2
(1974), 15-16, 18-19.

The Grass Is Singing, 1950

Thorpe, Michael. *Doris Lessing*. 1973. Pp. 9-11.

The Summer Before the Dark, 1973

Markow, Alice Bradley. "The Pathology of a Feminine Failure in the
Fiction of Doris Lessing." *Critique* (Atlanta), 16:1 (1974), 90-92,
96-99.

ADA LEVERSON

Bird of Paradise, 1914

Burkhart, Charles. *Ada Leverson*. 1973. Pp. 132-139.

The Limit, 1911

Burkhart, Charles. *Ada Leverson*. 1973. Pp. 111-122.

Love at Second Sight, 1916

Burkhart, Charles. *Ada Leverson*. 1973. Pp. 140-148.

Love's Shadow, 1908

Burkhart, Charles. *Ada Leverson*. 1973. Pp. 103-110.

Tenterhooks, 1912

Burkhart, Charles. *Ada Leverson*. 1973. Pp. 123-131.

The Twelfth Hour, 1907

Burkhart, Charles. *Ada Leverson*. 1973. Pp. 92-102.

GEORGE HENRY LEWES

Ranthorpe, 1847

Hirshberg, Edgar W. *George Henry Lewes*. 1970. Pp. 38-40.

Rose, Blanche and Violet, 1848

Hirshberg, Edgar W. *George Henry Lewes*. 1970. Pp. 40-46.

C. S. LEWIS

Out of the Silent Planet, 1938

> Gibbons, Stella. "Imaginative Writing," in Jocelyn Gibb, ed., *Light on C. S. Lewis*. 1965. Pp. 87-92.
>
> Green, Roger Lancelyn, and Walter Hooper. *C. S. Lewis*. 1974. Pp. 162-166.
>
> Hume, Kathryn. "C. S. Lewis' Trilogy: A Cosmic Romance." *Modern Fiction Studies*, 20 (1974-1975), 505-517.
>
> Puttkammer, Annemarie von. "Clive Staples Lewis," in Otto Mann, ed., *Christliche Dichter*. 1968. Pp. 228-229.
>
> Rose, Lois, and Stephen Rose. *The Shattered Ring*. 1970. Pp. 60-61.

Perelandra, 1943

> Gibbons, Stella. "Imaginative Writing," in Jocelyn Gibb, ed., *Light on C. S. Lewis*. 1965. Pp. 87-94.
>
> Green, Roger Lancelyn, and Walter Hooper. *C. S. Lewis*. 1974. Pp. 166-172.
>
> Hannay, Margaret. "The Mythology of Perelandra." *Tolkien Journal/ Mythlore*, No. 12 (1970), 14-16.
>
> Hume, Kathryn. "C. S. Lewis' Trilogy: A Cosmic Romance." *Modern Fiction Studies*, 20 (1974-1975), 505-517.
>
> Kranz, Gisbert. "Mythos und Weltraumfahrt: Zum Werk von C. S. Lewis." *Antaios*, 10 (1969), 570-574.
>
> Puttkammer, Annemarie von. "Clive Staples Lewis," in Otto Mann, ed., *Christliche Dichter*. 1968. Pp. 229-231.
>
> Rose, Lois, and Stephen Rose. *The Shattered Ring*. 1970. Pp. 61-64.
>
> Wright, Marjorie Evelyn. "The Vision of Cosmic Order in the Oxford Mythmakers," in Charles A. Huttar, ed., *Imagination and the Spirit*. 1971. Pp. 261-262, 266-267, 269-270, 273-274.

That Hideous Strength, 1945

> Callahan, Patrick J. "The Two Gardens in C. S. Lewis's *That Hideous Strength*," in Thomas D. Clareson, ed., *SF: The Other Side of Realism*. 1971. Pp. 147-156.
>
> Gibbons, Stella. "Imaginative Writing," in Jocelyn Gibb, ed., *Light on C. S. Lewis*. 1965. Pp. 97-101.
>
> Green, Roger Lancelyn, and Walter Hooper. *C. S. Lewis*. 1974. Pp. 174-180.
>
> Hume, Kathryn. "C. S. Lewis' Trilogy: A Cosmic Romance." *Modern Fiction Studies*, 20 (1974-1975), 505-517.
>
> Puttkammer, Annemarie von. "Clive Staples Lewis," in Otto Mann, ed., *Christliche Dichter*. 1968. Pp. 231-234.
>
> Rose, Lois, and Stephen Rose. *The Shattered Ring*. 1970. Pp. 62-64.

Till We Have Faces, 1956

> Gibbons, Stella. "Imaginative Writing," in Jocelyn Gibb, ed., *Light on C. S. Lewis*. 1965. Pp. 94-97.

MATTHEW GREGORY LEWIS

Feudal Tyrants, 1806

> Lévy, Maurice. *Le Roman "gothique" anglais*. 1968. Pp. 375-380.

The Monk, 1796

> Breitinger, Eckhard. *Der Tod im englischen Roman*. 1971. Pp. 24-28, 176-180.
> Brooks, Peter. "Virtue and Terror: *The Monk*." *ELH*, 40 (1973), 249-263.
> Göller, Karl Heinz. *"Romance" und "novel."* 1972. Pp. 224-231.
> Gose, Elliott B., Jr. *Imagination Indulged*. 1972. Pp. 27-40.
> Kiely, Robert. *The Romantic Novel in England*. 1972. Pp. 98-117.
> Lévy, Maurice. *Le Roman "gothique" anglais*. 1968. Pp. 332-357.
> Poenicke, Klaus. " 'Schönheit im Schosse des Schreckens': Raumgefüge und Menschenbild im englischen Schauerroman." *Archiv für das Studium der Neueren Sprachen und Literaturen*, 207 (1970), 14-19.
> Volker, Klaus. *"Der Mönch." Neue Rundschau*, 82 (1971), 774-779.

WYNDHAM LEWIS

The Apes of God, 1930

> Chapman, Robert T. *Wyndham Lewis*. 1973. Pp. 99-109.
> Pritchard, William H. *Wyndham Lewis*. 1968. Pp. 77-85.

The Childermass, 1928

> Chapman, Robert T. *Wyndham Lewis*. 1973. Pp. 165-176.
> Jameson, Frederic. "Wyndham Lewis as Futurist." *Hudson Review*, 26 (1973), 313-317.
> Pritchard, William H. *Wyndham Lewis*. 1968. Pp. 71-76.

The Human Age, 1955

> Chapman, Robert T. *Wyndham Lewis*. 1973. Pp. 165-182.
> Pritchard, William H. *Wyndham Lewis*. 1968. Pp. 156-165.

Malign Fiesta, 1955

> Chapman, Robert T. *Wyndham Lewis*. 1973. Pp. 180-182.

Monstre Gai, 1955

> Chapman, Robert T. *Wyndham Lewis*. 1973. Pp. 176-180.

The Revenge for Love, 1937

>   Chapman, Robert T. *Wyndham Lewis.* 1973. Pp. 122-131.
>   Pritchard, William H. *Wyndham Lewis.* 1968. Pp. 115-130.

The Roaring Queen, 1936

>   Chapman, Robert T. *Wyndham Lewis.* 1973. Pp. 116-121.

Self Condemned, 1954

>   Chapman, Robert T. *Wyndham Lewis.* 1973. Pp. 153-164.
>   Pritchard, William H. *Wyndham Lewis.* 1968. Pp. 147-156.

Snooty Baronet, 1932

>   Chapman, Robert T. *Wyndham Lewis.* 1973. Pp. 109-116.
>   Materer, Timothy. "Wyndham Lewis: Satirist of the Machine Age."
>   *Satire Newsletter*, 10 (1972), 9-18.
>   Pritchard, William H. *Wyndham Lewis.* 1968. Pp. 108-115.

Tarr, 1918

>   Chapman, Robert T. *Wyndham Lewis.* 1973. Pp. 68-82.
>   Pritchard, William H. *Wyndham Lewis.* 1968. Pp. 28-44.

The Vulgar Streak, 1941

>   Chapman, Robert T. *Wyndham Lewis.* 1973. Pp. 131-139.
>   Pritchard, William H. *Wyndham Lewis.* 1968. Pp. 130-135.

CHARLES LLOYD

Edmund Oliver, 1798

>   Vooys, Sijna de. *The Psychological Element.* 1966. Pp. 23-26.

JOHN GIBSON LOCKHART

Some Passages in the Life of Mr. Adam Blair, 1822

>   Craig, David. *The Real Foundations.* 1973. Pp. 39-51.

THOMAS LODGE

Rosalynde, 1590

>   Davis, Walter R. *Idea and Act.* 1969. Pp. 83-93.
>   Lindheim, Nancy R. "Lyly's Golden Legacy: *Rosalynde* and *Pandosto*." *Studies in English Literature, 1500-1900*, 15 (1975), 4-13.

MALCOLM LOWRY

Dark as the Grave Wherein My Friend Is Laid, 1968

Bareham, Terence. "After the Volcano: An Assessment of Malcolm Lowry's Posthumous Fiction." *Studies in the Novel*, 6 (1974), 349-362.
Costa, Richard Hauer. *Malcolm Lowry*. 1972. Pp. 115-123.
Dodson, Daniel B. *Malcolm Lowry*. 1970. Pp. 43-46.
New, William H. *Malcolm Lowry*. 1971. Pp. 44-51.

Lunar Caustic, 1968

Day, Douglas. *Malcolm Lowry*. 1973. Pp. 197-212.
Dodson, Daniel B. *Malcolm Lowry*. 1970. Pp. 9-10.
New, William H. *Malcolm Lowry*. 1971. Pp. 25-27.

October Ferry to Gabriola, 1970

Bareham, Terence. "After the Volcano: An Assessment of Malcolm Lowry's Posthumous Fiction." *Studies in the Novel*, 6 (1974), 349-362.
Costa, Richard Hauer. *Malcolm Lowry*. 1972. Pp. 146-154.
Day, Douglas. *Malcolm Lowry*. 1973. Pp. 438-443.
Fernandez, Diane. "Malcolm Lowry: *En route vers l'île de Gabriola*." *Nouvelle Revue Française*, No. 239 (1972), 97-99.
Forrester, Viviane. "Toujours la quête éperdue." *Quinzaine Littéraire*, No. 145 (1972), 7-8.
New, William H. "Gabriola: Malcolm Lowry's Floating Island." *Literary Half-Yearly*, 13 (1972), 115-124.
New, William H. *Malcolm Lowry*. 1971. Pp. 42-44.

Ultramarine, 1933

Costa, Richard Hauer. *Malcolm Lowry*. 1972. Pp. 37-40.
Day, Douglas. *Malcolm Lowry*. 1973. Pp. 161-169.
Dodson, Daniel B. *Malcolm Lowry*. 1970. Pp. 6-9.
Kilgallin, Tony. *Lowry*. 1973. Pp. 85-114.
New, William H. *Malcolm Lowry*. 1971. Pp. 20-25.

Under the Volcano, 1947

Bareham, T. "Paradigms of Hell: Symbolic Patterning in *Under the Volcano*," in B. S. Benedikz, ed., *On the Novel*. 1971. Pp. 113-126.
Bradbury, Malcolm. *Possibilities*. 1973. Pp. 187-189.
Costa, Richard Hauer. *Malcolm Lowry*. 1972. Pp. 61-83.
Costa, Richard Hauer. "Pietà, Pelado, and 'the Ratification of Death': The Ten-Year Evolvement of Malcolm Lowry's *Volcano*." *Journal of Modern Literature*, 2 (1971), 3-18.
Cross, Richard K. "*Moby-Dick* and *Under the Volcano*: Poetry from the Abyss." *Modern Fiction Studies*, 20 (1974), 149-156.

Day, Douglas. *Malcolm Lowry*. 1973. Pp. 258-274, 316-350.
Dodson, Daniel B. *Malcolm Lowry*. 1970. Pp. 10-34.
Doyen, Victor. "La Genèse d'*Au-dessous du Volcan.*" *Lettres Nouvelles*, May-June 1974, pp. 87-120.
Epstein, Perle S. *The Private Labyrinth*. 1969. Pp. 3-216.
Kilgallin, Tony. *Lowry*. 1973. Pp. 119-211.
Makowiecki, Stefan. "An Analysis of Humour in the Works of Malcolm Lowry." *Studia Anglica Posnaniensia*, 4 (1972), 195-201.
New, William H. *Malcolm Lowry*. 1971. Pp. 29-41.
Pagnoulle, Christine. "Par-delà les miroirs." *Lettres Nouvelles*, May-June 1974, pp. 170-181.
Raab, Lawrence. "The Two Consuls: *Under the Volcano.*" *Thoth*, 12 (Spring-Summer 1972), 20-29.
Sister Christella Marie, S.B.S. "*Under the Volcano:* A Consideration of the Novel by Malcolm Lowry." *Xavier University Studies*, 4 (1965), 13-27.
Zéraffa, Michel. *Personne et personnage*. 1969. Pp. 343-345.

JOHN LYLY

Euphues, 1578

Davis, Walter R. *Idea and Act*. 1969. Pp. 109-121.

ROSE MACAULAY

Abbots Verney, 1906

Bensen, Alice R. *Rose Macaulay*. 1969. Pp. 21-27.

And No Man's Wit, 1940

Bensen, Alice R. *Rose Macaulay*. 1969. Pp. 133-137.

Crewe Train, 1926

Bensen, Alice R. *Rose Macaulay*. 1969. Pp. 95-101.

Dangerous Ages, 1921

Bensen, Alice R. *Rose Macaulay*. 1969. Pp. 77-80.

The Furnace, 1907

Bensen, Alice R. *Rose Macaulay*. 1969. Pp. 27-29.

Going Abroad, 1934

Bensen, Alice R. *Rose Macaulay*. 1969. Pp. 119-125.

The Lee Shore, 1912

Bensen, Alice R. *Rose Macaulay*. 1969. Pp. 39-45.

The Making of a Bigot, 1914

    Bensen, Alice R. *Rose Macaulay*. 1969. Pp. 46-50.

Orphan Island, 1924

    Bensen, Alice R. *Rose Macaulay*. 1969. Pp. 86-91.

Potterism, 1920

    Bensen, Alice R. *Rose Macaulay*. 1969. Pp. 68-77.

They Were Defeated, 1932

    Bensen, Alice R. *Rose Macaulay*. 1969. Pp. 106-112.

Told by an Idiot, 1923

    Bensen, Alice R. *Rose Macaulay*. 1969. Pp. 81-86.

The Towers of Trebizond, 1956

    Bensen, Alice R. *Rose Macaulay*. 1969. Pp. 154-164.

Views and Vagabonds, 1912

    Bensen, Alice R. *Rose Macaulay*. 1969. Pp. 33-39.

The World My Wilderness, 1950

    Bensen, Alice R. *Rose Macaulay*. 1969. Pp. 146-151.

GEORGE MACDONALD

Alec Forbes of Howglen, 1865

    Reis, Richard H. *George MacDonald*. 1972. Pp. 61-64.

Lilith, 1895

    Reis, Richard H. *George MacDonald*. 1972. Pp. 94-105.

Phantastes, 1858

    Reis, Richard H. *George MacDonald*. 1972. Pp. 87-94.
    Sadler, Glenn Edward. "The Fantastic Imagination in George Mac-Donald," in Charles A. Huttar, ed., *Imagination and the Spirit*. 1971. Pp. 216-222.

ARTHUR MACHEN

The Hill of Dreams, 1907

    Vessey, David. "Arthur Machen's *The Hill of Dreams*: A Novel of the 'Nineties." *Contemporary Review*, 223 (1973), 124-128.

HENRY MACKENZIE

The Man of Feeling, 1771

Brissenden, R. F. *Virtue in Distress*. 1974. Pp. 250-258.
Gassenmeier, Michael. *Der Typus des "man of feeling."* 1972. Pp. 124-152.

ALISTAIR MACLEAN

HMS Ulysses, 1955

Gadney, Reg. "Middle-Class Heroics: The Novels of Alistair MacLean." *London Magazine*, 12:5 (1972-1973), 95-102.

FRANCIS MACMANUS

Watergate, 1942

Kiely, Benedict. "On Francis MacManus's *Watergate*," in David Madden, ed., *Rediscoveries*. 1971. Pp. 271-279.

JANET MCNEILL

A Child in the House, 1955

Foster, John Wilson. "Zoo Stories: The Novels of Janet McNeill." *Eire-Ireland*, 9:1 (1974), 104-114.

The Maiden Dinosaur, 1964

Foster, John Wilson. "Zoo Stories: The Novels of Janet McNeill." *Eire-Ireland*, 9:1 (1974), 104-114.

Talk to Me, 1965

Foster, John Wilson. "Zoo Stories: The Novels of Janet McNeill." *Eire-Ireland*, 9:1 (1974), 104-114.

CHARLES ERIC MAINE

Fire Past the Future, 1959

Blish, James. *More Issues at Hand*. 1970. Pp. 107-110.

WILLIAM HURRELL MALLOCK

The Old Order Changes, 1886

Lucas, John. "Conservatism and Revolution in the 1880's," in John Lucas, ed., *Literature and Politics*. 1971. Pp. 186-217.

THOMAS MALORY

Le Morte Darthur, 1485

Ackerman, Robert W. "'The Tale of Gareth' and the Unity of *Le Morte Darthur*," in James L. Rosier, ed., *Philological Essays*. 1970. Pp. 196-203.

Benson, Larry D. "Sir Thomas Malory's *Le Morte Darthur*," in R. M. Lumiansky and Herschel Baker, eds., *Critical Approaches*. 1968. Pp. 81-123.

Field, P. J. C. *Romance and Chronicle*. 1971. Pp. 36-159.

Göller, Karl Heinz. *"Romance" und "novel."* 1972. Pp. 22-26.

Greaves, Margaret. *The Blazon of Honour*. 1964. Pp. 46-61.

Hartung, Albert E. "Narrative Technique, Characterization, and the Sources in Malory's 'Tale of Sir Lancelot.'" *Studies in Philology*, 70 (1973), 252-268.

Hellenga, Robert. "The Tournaments in Malory's *Morte Darthur*." *Forum for Modern Language Studies*, 10 (1974), 67-78.

Kelly, Robert L. "Arthur, Galahad and the Scriptural Pattern in Malory." *American Benedictine Review*, 23 (1972), 9-23.

Kimball, Arthur Samuel. "Merlin's Miscreation and the Repetition Compulsion in Malory's *Morte Darthur*." *Literature and Psychology*, 25 (1975), 27-32.

Kinghorn, A. M. *The Chorus of History*. 1971. Pp. 141-145, 147-151.

Moorman, Charles. *Kings and Captains*. 1971. Pp. 161-171.

Morris, Celia. "From Malory to Tennyson: Spiritual Triumph to Spiritual Defeat." *Mosaic*, 7 (Spring 1974), 87-95.

Pochoda, Elizabeth T. *Arthurian Propaganda*. 1971. Pp. 61-140.

Snyder, Robert Lance. "Malory and 'Historical' Adaptation." *Essays in Literature* (Macomb, Illinois), 1:2 (1974), 135-148.

Soudek, Ernst. "Chivalry and Sir Thomas Malory's 'Knight of the Cart' Tale." *Rice University Studies*, 58 (Winter 1972), 25-50.

Stroud, Michael. "Malory and the Chivalric Ethos: The Hero of *Arthur and the Emperor Lucius*." *Mediaeval Studies*, 36 (1974), 335-350.

Vinaver, Eugène. *The Rise of Romance*. 1971. Pp. 123-139.

Whitaker, M. A. "Allegorical Imagery in Malory's 'Tale of the Noble King Arthur and the Emperor Lucius.'" *Neuphilologische Mitteilungen*, 74 (1973), 497-509.

MARY DE LA RIVIERE MANLY

The Secret History of Queen Zarah and the Zarazians, 1705

Richetti, John J. *Popular Fiction*. 1969. Pp. 126-132.

Secret Memoirs and Manners of Several Persons of Quality of Both Sexes from the New Atlantis, 1709

Richetti, John J. *Popular Fiction*. 1969. Pp. 132-140, 142-152.

OLIVIA MANNING

The Balkan Trilogy, 1960-1965

Morris, Robert K. *Continuance and Change.* 1972. Pp. 29-49.

FREDERICK MARRYAT

Jacob Faithful, 1834

Foltinek, Herbert. *Vorstufen zum viktorianischen Realismus.* 1968. Pp. 154-157.

The King's Own, 1830

Pickering, Sam, Jr. " 'The Most "Harum-Scarum" Sort of Novel We Have Ever Encountered': Marryat's *The King's Own* and Shandyism." *English Studies in Africa*, 17 (1974), 71-77.

ANNE MARSH-CALDWELL

Emilia Wyndham, 1846

Colby, Vineta. *Yesterday's Woman.* 1974. Pp. 35-37.

HARRIET MARTINEAU

Deerbrook, 1839

Colby, Vineta. *Yesterday's Woman.* 1974. Pp. 241-256.

CHARLES ROBERT MATURIN

The Albigenses, 1824

Kramer, Dale. *Charles Robert Maturin.* 1973. Pp. 127-140.
Lougy, Robert E. *Charles Robert Maturin.* 1975. Pp. 75-84.

Fatal Revenge, 1807

Kramer, Dale. *Charles Robert Maturin.* 1973. Pp. 26-38.
Lévy, Maurice. *Le Roman "gothique" anglais.* 1968. Pp. 534-547.
Lougy, Robert E. *Charles Robert Maturin.* 1975. Pp. 16-23.

Melmoth the Wanderer, 1820

Breitinger, Eckhard. *Der Tod im englischen Roman.* 1971. Pp. 48-52, 123-128.
Kiely, Robert. *The Romantic Novel in England.* 1972. Pp. 189-207.
Kramer, Dale. *Charles Robert Maturin.* 1973. Pp. 94-126.
Lévy, Maurice. *Le Roman "gothique" anglais.* 1968. Pp. 566-588.
Lougy, Robert E. *Charles Robert Maturin.* 1975. Pp. 64-75.

Otten, Kurt. *Der englischen Roman.* 1971. Pp. 108-110.
Rafroidi, Patrick. *L'Irlande et le romantisme.* 1972. Pp. 307-310.

The Milesian Chief, 1812

Kramer, Dale. *Charles Robert Maturin.* 1973. Pp. 44-52.
Lévy, Maurice. *Le Roman "gothique" anglais.* 1968. Pp. 547-553.
Lougy, Robert E. *Charles Robert Maturin.* 1975. Pp. 32-40.

The Wild Irish Boy, 1808

Kramer, Dale. *Charles Robert Maturin.* 1973. Pp. 38-43.
Lougy, Robert E. *Charles Robert Maturin.* 1975. Pp. 23-30.

Women, 1818

Kramer, Dale. *Charles Robert Maturin.* 1973. Pp. 84-93.
Lévy, Maurice. *Le Roman "gothique" anglais.* 1968. Pp. 560-563.
Lougy, Robert E. *Charles Robert Maturin.* 1975. Pp. 51-57.

WILLIAM SOMERSET MAUGHAM

Cakes and Ale, 1930

Calder, Robert Lorin. *W. Somerset Maugham.* 1973. Pp. 172-199.
Cordell, Richard A. *Somerset Maugham.* 1969. Pp. 114-131.
Curtis, Anthony. *The Pattern of Maugham.* 1974. Pp. 139-149.
Naik, M. K. *W. Somerset Maugham.* 1966. Pp. 73-82.

Christmas Holiday, 1939

Naik, M. K. *W. Somerset Maugham.* 1966. Pp. 89-93.

The Explorer, 1908

Calder, Robert Lorin. *W. Somerset Maugham.* 1973. Pp. 69-72.

The Hero, 1901

Calder, Robert Lorin. *W. Somerset Maugham.* 1973. Pp. 56-60.

Liza of Lambeth, 1897

Calder, Robert Lorin. *W. Somerset Maugham.* 1973. Pp. 39-51.
Chapple, J. A. V. *Documentary and Imaginative Literature.* 1970.
    Pp. 132-134.
Cordell, Richard A. *Somerset Maugham.* 1969. Pp. 133-136.
Curtis, Anthony. *The Pattern of Maugham.* 1974. Pp. 17-25.
Keating, P. J. *The Working Classes.* 1971. Pp. 186-191.
Naik, M. K. *W. Somerset Maugham.* 1966. Pp. 30-33.

The Magician, 1908

Calder, Robert Lorin. *W. Somerset Maugham.* 1973. Pp. 72-76.

The Merry-Go-Round, 1904

    Calder, Robert Lorin. *W. Somerset Maugham*. 1973. Pp. 65-68.
    Curtis, Anthony. *The Pattern of Maugham*. 1974. Pp. 42-46.

The Moon and Sixpence, 1919

    Calder, Robert Lorin. *W. Somerset Maugham*. 1973. Pp. 131-151.
    Curtis, Anthony. *The Pattern of Maugham*. 1974. Pp. 100-108.
    Naik, M. K. *W. Somerset Maugham*. 1966. Pp. 57-63.

Mrs. Craddock, 1902

    Calder, Robert Lorin. *W. Somerset Maugham*. 1973. Pp. 60-65.
    Cordell, Richard A. *Somerset Maugham*. 1969. Pp. 137-140.
    Naik, M. K. *W. Somerset Maugham*. 1966. Pp. 33-39.

The Narrow Corner, 1932

    Cordell, Richard A. *Somerset Maugham*. 1969. Pp. 144-148.
    Naik, M. W. *W. Somerset Maugham*. 1966. Pp. 83-90.

Of Human Bondage, 1915

    Buckley, Jerome Hamilton. *Season of Youth*. 1974. Pp. 249-254.
    Calder, Robert Lorin. *W. Somerset Maugham*. 1973. Pp. 78-130.
    Cordell, Richard A. *Somerset Maugham*. 1969. Pp. 86-103.
    Curtis, Anthony. *The Pattern of Maugham*. 1974. Pp. 76-90.
    Naik, M. K. *W. Somerset Maugham*. 1966. Pp. 45-59.
    Walcutt, Charles Child. *Man's Changing Mask*. 1966. Pp. 290-292.

The Painted Veil, 1925

    Calder, Robert Lorin. *W. Somerset Maugham*. 1973. Pp. 153-158.
    Cordell, Richard A. *Somerset Maugham*. 1969. Pp. 140-144.
    Curtis, Anthony. *The Pattern of Maugham*. 1974. Pp. 165-169.
    Naik, M. K. *W. Somerset Maugham*. 1966. Pp. 63-66.

The Razor's Edge, 1944

    Calder, Robert Lorin. *W. Somerset Maugham*. 1973. Pp. 227-253.
    Cordell, Richard A. *Somerset Maugham*. 1969. Pp. 154-158.
    Curtis, Anthony. *The Pattern of Maugham*. 1974. Pp. 222-231.
    Naik, M. K. *W. Somerset Maugham*. 1966. Pp. 93-98.
    Viswanathan, K. *India in English Fiction*. 1971. Pp. 217-242.

Theatre, 1937

    Calder, Robert Lorin. *W. Somerset Maugham*. 1973. Pp. 158-164.

FREDERICK DENISON MAURICE

Eustace Conway, 1834

    Williams, Ioan. *The Realist Novel*. 1974. Pp. 90-93.

GEORGE MEREDITH

The Amazing Marriage, 1895

Hardy, Barbara. *"Lord Ormont and His Aminta* and *The Amazing Marriage,"* in Ian Fletcher, ed., *Meredith Now.* 1971. Pp. 295-312.

Kelvin, Norman. *A Troubled Eden.* 1961. Pp. 188-197.

McCullen, M. L. "Handsome Heroes and Healthy Heroines: Patterns of the Ideal in George Meredith's Later Novels." *Cithara,* 14:1 (1974), 95-106.

Beauchamp's Career, 1875

Howard, David. "George Meredith: 'Delicate' and 'Epical' Fiction," in John Lucas, ed., *Literature and Politics.* 1971. Pp. 160-171.

Kelvin, Norman. *A Troubled Eden.* 1961. Pp. 83-100.

Kettle, Arnold. *"Beauchamp's Career,"* in Ian Fletcher, ed., *Meredith Now.* 1971. Pp. 188-204.

Mannheimer, Monica. *The Generations.* 1972. Pp. 105-119, 147-155.

Williams, Ioan. *The Realist Novel.* 1974. Pp. 196-200.

Diana of the Crossways, 1885

Conrow, Margaret. "Coming to Terms with George Meredith's Fiction," in George Goodin, ed., *The English Novel.* 1972. Pp. 191-193.

Fowler, Lois Josephs. *"Diana of the Crossways:* A Prophecy for Feminism," in Joseph Ann L. Hayes, and Robert J. Gangewere, eds., *In Honor of Austin Wright.* 1972. Pp. 32-36.

Gordon, Jan B. *"Diana of the Crossways:* Internal History and the Brainstuff of Fiction," in Ian Fletcher, ed., *Meredith Now.* 1971. Pp. 246-264.

Kelvin, Norman. *A Troubled Eden.* 1961. Pp. 58-61.

The Egoist, 1879

Baker, Robert S. "Sir Willoughby Patterne's 'Inner Temple': Psychology and 'Sentimentalism' in *The Egoist." Texas Studies in Literature and Language,* 16 (1975), 691-703.

Conrow, Margaret. "Coming to Terms with George Meredith's Fiction," in George Goodin, ed., *The English Novel.* 1972. Pp. 188-191.

Cottereau, Serge. "Répression, censure et justification dans les romans de George Meredith." *Etudes Anglaises,* 27 (1974), 72-83.

Goode, John. *"The Egoist:* Anatomy or Striptease?", in Ian Fletcher, ed., *Meredith Now.* 1971. Pp. 205-230.

Halperin, John. *Egoism and Self-Discovery.* 1974. Pp. 195-202.

Halperin, John. *The Language of Meditation.* 1973. Pp. 98-114.

Jedrzejkiewicz, Maria. "The Exposure of Literary Conventions in *The Egoist* by George Meredith." *Studia Anglica Posnaniensia,* 5 (1973), 185-191.

Kelvin, Norman. *A Troubled Eden.* 1961. Pp. 104-113.

Mannheimer, Monica. *The Generations.* 1972. Pp. 155-164.

Stevenson, Richard C. "Laetitia Dale and the Comic Spirit in *The Egoist.*" *Nineteenth-Century Fiction*, 26 (1972), 406-418.

Evan Harrington, 1861

Kelvin, Norman. *A Troubled Eden*. 1961. Pp. 16-25.
Mannheimer, Monica. *The Generations*. 1972. Pp. 80-90.
Stevenson, Richard C. "Innovations of Comic Method in George Meredith's *Evan Harrington.*" *Texas Studies in Literature and Language*, 15 (1973), 311-323.
Tarratt, Margaret. " 'Snips,' 'Snobs' and the 'True Gentleman' in *Evan Harrington*," in Ian Fletcher, ed., *Meredith Now*. 1971. Pp. 95-113.
Tompkins, J. M. S. "On Re-reading *Evan Harrington*," in Ian Fletcher, ed., *Meredith Now*. 1971. Pp. 114-129.

Harry Richmond, 1871

Buckley, Jerome Hamilton. *Season of Youth*. 1974. Pp. 82-91.
Hardy, Barbara. *The Appropriate Form*. 1964. Pp. 83-104.
Kelvin, Norman. *A Troubled Eden*. 1961. Pp. 56-57, 73-83.
Mannheimer, Monica. *The Generations*. 1972. Pp. 90-105, 143-147.
Tarratt, Margaret. "*The Adventures of Harry Richmond: Bildungsroman* and Historical Novel," in Ian Fletcher, ed., *Meredith Now*. 1971. Pp. 165-187.
Williams, Ioan. *The Realist Novel*. 1974. Pp. 193-196.

Lord Ormont and His Aminta, 1894

Cottereau, Serge. "Répression, censure et justification dans les romans de George Meredith." *Etudes Anglaises*, 27 (1974), 76-82.
Hardy, Barbara. "*Lord Ormont and His Aminta* and *The Amazing Marriage*," in Ian Fletcher, ed., *Meredith Now*. 1971. Pp. 295-312.
Kelvin, Norman. *A Troubled Eden*. 1961. Pp. 112-113, 180-189.

One of Our Conquerors, 1891

Beer, Gillian. "*One of Our Conquerors*: Language and Music," in Ian Fletcher, ed., *Meredith Now*. 1971. Pp. 265-280.
Cottereau, Serge. "Répression, censure et justification dans les romans de George Meredith." *Etudes Anglaises*, 27 (1974), 72-79.
Kelvin, Norman. *A Troubled Eden*. 1961. Pp. 167-180.
Mannheimer, Monica. *The Generations*. 1972. Pp. 165-181.
Richards, Bernard A. "*One of Our Conquerors* and the Country of the Blue," in Ian Fletcher, ed., *Meredith Now*. 1971. Pp. 281-294.

The Ordeal of Richard Feverel, 1859

Baker, Robert S. "*The Ordeal of Richard Feverel*: A Psychological Approach to Structure." *Studies in the Novel*, 6 (1974), 200-217.
Buckley, Jerome Hamilton. *Season of Youth*. 1974. Pp. 68-82.
Fisher, Benjamin Franklin, IV. "Sensation Fiction in a Minor Key: *The Ordeal of Richard Feverel*," in Clyde de L. Ryals, ed., *Nineteenth-Century Literary Perspectives*. 1974. Pp. 283-294.

Halperin, John. *Egoism and Self-Discovery.* 1974. Pp. 202-214.
Holt, Carolyn D. "Sir Austin and His Scrip: A New Approach to *The Ordeal of Richard Feverel.*" *Journal of Narrative Technique*, 4 (1974), 129-143.
Kelvin, Norman. *A Troubled Eden.* 1961. Pp. 5-14.
Korg, Jacob. "Expressive Styles in *The Ordeal of Richard Feverel.*" *Nineteenth-Century Fiction*, 27 (1972), 253-267.
Mannheimer, Monica. *The Generations.* 1972. Pp. 67-80, 128-130.
Mitchell, Juliet. "*The Ordeal of Richard Feverel*: A Sentimental Education," in Ian Fletcher, ed., *Meredith Now.* 1971. Pp. 69-94.
Ogino, Masatoshi. "The Allegorical Pattern in *The Ordeal of Richard Feverel.*" *Studies in English Literature* (Tokyo), English Number (1972), 79-95.
Spånberg, Sven Johan. "The Theme of Sexuality in *The Ordeal of Richard Feverel.*" *Studia Neophilologica*, 46 (1974), 202-224.
Stoll, John E. "Psychological Dissociation in the Victorian Novel." *Literature and Psychology*, 20 (1970), 70-71.
Viebrock, Helmut. "Meredith: *The Ordeal of Richard Feverel*," in Franz K. Stanzel, ed., *Der englische Roman.* 1969. Vol. II, 158-173.
Williams, Ioan. *The Realist Novel.* 1974. Pp. 191-193.

Rhoda Fleming, 1865

Howard, David. "*Rhoda Fleming*: Meredith in the Margin," in Ian Fletcher, ed., *Meredith Now.* 1971. Pp. 130-143.
Mannheimer, Monica. *The Generations.* 1972. Pp. 132-141.

Sandra Belloni, 1886

Howard, David. "George Meredith: 'Delicate' and 'Epical' Fiction," in John Lucas, ed., *Literature and Politics.* 1971. Pp. 131-151.
Mannheimer, Monica. *The Generations.* 1972. Pp. 130-132.
Rance, Nicholas. *The Historical Novel.* 1975. Pp. 155-171.
Williams, Ioan. "Emilia in England and Italy," in Ian Fletcher, ed., *Meredith Now.* 1971. Pp. 144-164.

The Shaving of Shagpat, 1856

Highet, Gilbert. *Explorations.* 1971. Pp. 27-35.

The Tragic Comedians, 1880

Ormond, Leonée. "*The Tragic Comedians*: Meredith's Use of Image Patterns," in Ian Fletcher, ed., *Meredith Now.* 1971. Pp. 231-245.

Vittoria, 1867

Friebe, Freimut. "Politisches Geschehen und erzählerisches Gestalten: Das Risorgimento in englischer und italienischer Sicht bei Meredith und Fogazzaro." *Arcadia*, 6 (1971), 284-296.
Howard, David. "George Meredith: 'Delicate' and 'Epical' Fiction," in John Lucas, ed., *Literature and Politics.* 1971. Pp. 151-159.
Kelvin, Norman. *A Troubled Eden.* 1961. Pp. 40-51.

Rance, Nicholas. *The Historical Novel.* 1975. Pp. 155-171.
Williams, Ioan. "Emilia in England and Italy," in Ian Fletcher, ed., *Meredith Now.* 1971. Pp. 144-164.

HENRY SETON MERRIMAN

Barlasch of the Guard, 1903

Cox, Homer T. *Henry Seton Merriman.* 1967. Pp. 114-120.

Dross, 1899

Cox, Homer T. *Henry Seton Merriman.* 1967. Pp. 94-101.

Flotsam, 1896

Cox, Homer T. *Henry Seton Merriman.* 1967. Pp. 75-79.

From One Generation to Another, 1892

Cox, Homer T. *Henry Seton Merriman.* 1967. Pp. 48-53.

The Grey Lady, 1895

Cox, Homer T. *Henry Seton Merriman.* 1967. Pp. 60-65.

In Kedar's Tents, 1897

Cox, Homer T. *Henry Seton Merriman.* 1967. Pp. 80-86.

The Isle of Unrest, 1900

Cox, Homer T. *Henry Seton Merriman.* 1967. Pp. 102-105.

The Last Hope, 1904

Cox, Homer T. *Henry Seton Merriman.* 1967. Pp. 120-125.

The Phantom Future, 1888

Cox, Homer T. *Henry Seton Merriman.* 1967. Pp. 37-39.

Prisoners and Captives, 1891

Cox, Homer T. *Henry Seton Merriman.* 1967. Pp. 41-43.

Roden's Corner, 1898

Cox, Homer T. *Henry Seton Merriman.* 1967. Pp. 86-94.

The Slave of the Lamp, 1892

Cox, Homer T. *Henry Seton Merriman.* 1967. Pp. 44-48.

The Sowers, 1896

Cox, Homer T. *Henry Seton Merriman.* 1967. Pp. 65-74.

Suspense, 1890

Cox, Homer T. *Henry Seton Merriman.* 1967. Pp. 39-41.

The Velvet Glove, 1901

> Cox, Homer T. *Henry Seton Merriman*. 1967. Pp. 105-109.

The Vultures, 1902

> Cox, Homer T. *Henry Seton Merriman*. 1967. Pp. 109-114.

With Edged Tools, 1894

> Cox, Homer T. *Henry Seton Merriman*. 1967. Pp. 53-59.

Young Mistley, 1888

> Cox, Homer T. *Henry Seton Merriman*. 1967. Pp. 33-37.

A. A. MILNE

Chloe Marr, 1946

> Swann, Thomas Burnett. *A. A. Milne*. 1971. Pp. 113-116.

Four Days' Wonder, 1933

> Swann, Thomas Burnett. *A. A. Milne*. 1971. Pp. 111-113.

The House at Pooh Corner, 1928

> Swann, Thomas Burnett. *A. A. Milne*. 1971. Pp. 93-97.

Mr. Pim Passes By, 1921

> Swann, Thomas Burnett. *A. A. Milne*. 1971. Pp. 100-104.

Once on a Time, 1917

> Swann, Thomas Burnett. *A. A. Milne*. 1971. Pp. 66-73.

The Red House Mystery, 1922

> Swann, Thomas Burnett. *A. A. Milne*. 1971. Pp. 104-108.

Two People, 1931

> Swann, Thomas Burnett. *A. A. Milne*. 1971. Pp. 109-111.

Winnie-the-Pooh, 1926

> Swann, Thomas Burnett. *A. A. Milne*. 1971. Pp. 89-93.

JOHN LESLIE MITCHELL

Gay Hunter, 1934

> Campbell, Ian. "The Science Fiction of John Leslie Mitchell." *Extrapolation*, 16 (1974), 58-59.

Sunset Song, 1932

> Campbell, Ian. "The Science Fiction of John Leslie Mitchell." *Extrapolation*, 16 (1974), 60-62.

Three Go Back, 1932

> Campbell, Ian. "The Science Fiction of John Leslie Mitchell." *Extrapolation*, 16 (1974), 53-58.

JULIAN MITCHELL

The Undiscovered Country, 1968

> Lodge, David. *The Novelist at the Crossroads*. 1971. Pp. 24-32.

MARY RUSSELL MITFORD

Our Village, 1824-1832

> Colby, Vineta. *Yesterday's Woman*. 1974. Pp. 231-235.

NANCY MITFORD

Don't Tell Alfred, 1960

> Walcutt, Charles Child. *Man's Changing Mask*. 1966. Pp. 228-236.

GEORGE MOORE

Aphrodite in Aulis, 1930

> Dobrée, Bonamy. "George Moore's Final Works," in Graham Owens, ed., *George Moore's Mind and Art*. 1970. Pp. 137-141.
> Papajewski, Helmut. "Realistisches und Mythisches in George Moores *Aphrodite in Aulis*," in Gero Bauer, Franz K. Stanzel, and Franz Zaic, eds., *Festschrift Prof. Dr. Herbert Koziol*. 1973. Pp. 223-237.

The Brook Kerith, 1916

> Dobrée, Bonamy. "George Moore's Final Works," in Graham Owens, ed., *George Moore's Mind and Art*. 1970. Pp. 123-132.
> Dunleavy, Janet Egleston. *George Moore*. 1973. Pp. 130-136.

A Drama in Muslin, 1886

> Goetsch, Paul. *Die Romankonzeption in England*. 1967. Pp. 136-139.
> Jeffares, A. Norman. "*A Drama in Muslin*," in Graham Owens, ed., *George Moore's Mind and Art*. 1970. Pp. 1-20.
> Sporn, Paul. "Marriage and Class Conflict: The Subversive Link in George Moore's *A Drama in Muslin*." *Clio*, 3 (1973), 7-20.

Esther Waters, 1894

> Dunleavy, Janet Egleston. *George Moore*. 1973. Pp. 96-110.
> Goetsch, Paul. *Die Romankonzeption in England*. 1967. Pp. 144-148.
> Keating, P. J. *The Working Classes*. 1971. Pp. 133-136.
> Morton, Donald E. "Lyrical Form and the World of *Esther Waters*." *Studies in English Literature, 1500-1900*, 13 (1973), 688-700.

"Hail and Farewell," 1911-1914

> Cary, Meredith. "George Moore's *Roman Expérimental*." *Eire-Ireland*, 9:4 (1974), 142-150.

Héloïse and Abelard, 1921

> Dobrée, Bonamy. "George Moore's Final Works," in Graham Owens, ed., *George Moore's Mind and Art*. 1970. Pp. 132-137.

The Lake, 1905

> Dunleavy, Janet Egleston. *George Moore*. 1973. Pp. 121-126.

Mike Fletcher, 1889

> Dunleavy, Janet Egleston. *George Moore*. 1973. Pp. 90-92.

A Modern Lover, 1883

> Dunleavy, Janet Egleston. *George Moore*. 1973. Pp. 51-62.

A Mummer's Wife, 1885

> Dunleavy, Janet Egleston. *George Moore*. 1973. Pp. 63-85.
> Goetsch, Paul. *Die Romankonzeption in England*. 1967. Pp. 132-136.

WILLIAM MORRIS

A Dream of John Ball, 1888

> Goode, John. "William Morris and the Dream of Revolution," in John Lucas, ed., *Literature and Politics*. 1971. Pp. 247-261.
> Kocmanova, Jessie. "The Aesthetic Purpose of William Morris in the Context of His Late Prose Romances." *Brno Studies in English*, 6 (1966), 93-94.
> Kocmanova, Jessie. "Two Uses of the Dream-Form as a Means of Confronting the Present with the National Past: William Morris and Svatopluk Cech." *Brno Studies in English*, 2 (1960), 116-128, 142-145.
> Meier, Paul. *La Pensée utopique*. 1972. Pp. 381-388.

The House of the Wolfings, 1889

> Goode, John. "William Morris and the Dream of Revolution," in John Lucas, ed., *Literature and Politics*. 1971. Pp. 265-269.

News from Nowhere, 1890

> Chapple, J. A. V. *Documentary and Imaginative Literature*. 1970. Pp. 108-113.
> Furbank, P. N. *Samuel Butler*. 1948. Pp. 85-88.
> Goode, John. "William Morris and the Dream of Revolution," in John Lucas, ed., *Literature and Politics*. 1971. Pp. 273-278.
> Kocmanova, Jessie. "The Aesthetic Purpose of William Morris in the Context of His Late Prose Romances." *Brno Studies in English*, 6 (1966), 94-97.
> Meier, Paul. *La Pensée utopique*. 1972. Pp. 91-107, 419-442, 458-463, 469-474, 486-509, 536-544, 583-589, 593-605, 632-642, 817-834.
> Meier, Paul. "L'Utopie de William Morris: Aboutissement ou étape." *Journal of the William Morris Society*, 1 (Summer 1963), 10-13.
> Middlebro', Tom. "Brief Thoughts on *News from Nowhere.*" *Journal of the William Morris Society*, 2 (Summer 1970), 8-12.
> Parssinen, T. M. "Bellamy, Morris, and the Image of the Industrial City in Victorian Social Criticism." *Midwest Quarterly*, 14 (1973), 257-266.
> Seeber, Hans Ulrich. *Wandlungen der Form*. 1970. Pp. 120-134.

The Water of the Wondrous Isles, 1897

> Kocmanova, Jessie. "The Aesthetic Purpose of William Morris in the Context of His Late Prose Romances." *Brno Studies in English*, 6 (1966), 131-139.

ARTHUR MORRISON

A Child of the Jago, 1896

> Keating, P. J. *The Working Classes*. 1971. Pp. 177-184.
> Vooys, Sijna de. *The Psychological Element*. 1966. Pp. 132-142.

To London Town, 1899

> Keating, P. J. *The Working Classes*. 1971. Pp. 184-185.
> Vooys, Sijna de. *The Psychological Element*. 1966. Pp. 130-132.

PENELOPE MORTIMER

The Pumpkin Eater, 1962

> Kahrmann, Bernd. *Die idyllische Szene*. 1969. Pp. 44-47.

DINAH MARIA MULOCK

John Halifax, Gentleman, 1856

> Melada, Ivan. *The Captain of Industry*. 1970. Pp. 172-177.

H. H. MUNRO

The Unbearable Bassington, 1912

Gillen, Charles H. *H. H. Munro (Saki)*. 1969. Pp. 91-106.

When William Came, 1913

Gillen, Charles H. *H. H. Munro (Saki)*. 1969. Pp. 107-122.

IRIS MURDOCH

An Accidental Man, 1971

Baldanza, Frank. *Iris Murdoch*. 1974. Pp. 164-168.

The Bell, 1958

Baldanza, Frank. *Iris Murdoch*. 1974. Pp. 70-83.
Emerson, Donald. "Violence and Survival in the Novels of Iris Murdoch." *Transactions of the Wisconsin Academy of Sciences, Arts, and Letters*, 57 (1969), 25-26.
Escudié, Danièle. "Un Roman d'Iris Murdoch: *The Bell* (1958)," in *Récit et roman*. 1972. Pp. 86-90.
Gerstenberger, Donna. *Iris Murdoch*. 1975. Pp. 31-33.
Kahrmann, Bernd. *Die idyllische Szene*. 1969. Pp. 33-39.
Majdiak, Daniel. "Romanticism in the Aesthetics of Iris Murdoch." *Texqs Studies in Literature and Language*, 14 (1972), 370-372.

The Black Prince, 1973

Baldanza, Frank. *Iris Murdoch*. 1974. Pp. 168-173.

Bruno's Dream, 1969

Baldanza, Frank. *Iris Murdoch*. 1974. Pp. 148-159.
Baroche, Christiane. "Une merveilleuse horlogère." *Quinzaine Littéraire*, No. 133 (1972), 10-11.
Gerstenberger, Donna. *Iris Murdoch*. 1975. Pp. 45-49.
Martz, Louis L. "Iris Murdoch: The London Novels," in Reuben A. Brower, ed., *Twentieth-Century Literature in Retrospect*. 1971. Pp. 69-71.
Swinden, Patrick. *Unofficial Selves*. 1973. Pp. 1-4.

A Fairly Honourable Defeat, 1970

Baldanza, Frank. *Iris Murdoch*. 1974. Pp. 160-164.
Berthoff, Warner. *Fictions and Events*. 1971. Pp. 153-154.
Hoskins, Robert. "Iris Murdoch's Midsummer Nightmare." *Twentieth-Century Literature*, 18 (1972), 191-198.
Martz, Louis L. "Iris Murdoch: The London Novels," in Reuben A. Brower, ed., *Twentieth-Century Literature in Retrospect*. 1971. Pp. 82-86.

Mirisch, Lionel. "Iris Murdoch: *Une Défaite assez honorable."*
   Nouvelle Revue Française, No. 247 (1973), 106-108.
Riisøen, Helge. "Iris Murdoch og eksistensialismen." *Samtiden*, 82
   (1973), 600-602.
Swinden, Patrick. *Unofficial Selves.* 1973. Pp. 247-256.
Watrin, Jany. "Iris Murdoch's *A Fairly Honourable Defeat."* *Revue
   des Langues Vivantes*, 38 (1972), 48-64.

The Flight from the Enchanter, 1956

Baldanza, Frank. *Iris Murdoch.* 1974. Pp. 43-56.
Gerstenberger, Donna. *Iris Murdoch.* 1975. Pp. 25-29.
Kahrmann, Bernd. *Die idyllische Szene.* 1969. Pp. 47-53.

The Italian Girl, 1964

Baldanza, Frank. *Iris Murdoch.* 1974. Pp. 116-125.
Bronzwaer, W. J. M. *Tense in the Novel.* 1970. Pp. 83-116.
German, Howard. "The Range of Allusions in the Novels of Iris
   Murdoch." *Journal of Modern Literature*, 2 (1971), 69-75.
Kahrmann, Bernd. *Die idyllische Szene.* 1969. Pp. 102-105.

The Nice and the Good, 1968

Baldanza, Frank. *Iris Murdoch.* 1974. Pp. 138-147.
Kahrmann, Bernd. *Die idyllische Szene.* 1969. Pp. 28-32.

The Red and the Green, 1965

Baldanza, Frank. *Iris Murdoch.* 1974. Pp. 126-130.
Berthoff, Warner. *Fictions and Events.* 1971. Pp. 130-143.
German, Howard. "The Range of Allusions in the Novels of Iris
   Murdoch." *Journal of Modern Literature*, 2 (1971), 75-79.
Gerstenberger, Donna. *Iris Murdoch.* 1975. Pp. 51-69.
Kahrmann, Bernd. *Die idyllische Szene.* 1969. Pp. 53-56.

The Sandcastle, 1957

Baldanza, Frank. *Iris Murdoch.* 1974. Pp. 57-69.
Gerstenberger, Donna. *Iris Murdoch.* 1975. Pp. 29-31.
Goshgarian, Gary. "Feminist Values in the Novels of Iris Murdoch."
   Revue des Langues Vivantes, 40 (1974), 522-524.
Kahrmann, Bernd. *Die idyllische Szene.* 1969. Pp. 90-92.

A Severed Head, 1961

Baldanza, Frank. *Iris Murdoch.* 1974. Pp. 84-95.
Baldanza, Frank. "The Manuscript of Iris Murdoch's *A Severed Head."*
   Journal of Modern Literature, 3 (1973), 75-90.
Gerstenberger, Donna. *Iris Murdoch.* 1975. Pp. 33-35.
Goshgarian, Gary. "Feminist Values in the Novels of Iris Murdoch."
   Revue des Langues Vivantes, 40 (1974), 524-526.
Kahrmann, Bernd. *Die idyllische Szene.* 1969. Pp. 119-121.

The Time of the Angels, 1966

Baldanza, Frank. *Iris Murdoch*. 1974. Pp. 130-137.
Berthoff, Warner. *Fictions and Events*. 1971. Pp. 147-152.
Emerson, Donald. "Violence and Survival in the Novels of Iris Murdoch." *Transactions of the Wisconsin Academy of Sciences, Arts, and Letters*, 57 (1969), 28.
German, Howard. "The Range of Allusions in the Novels of Iris Murdoch." *Journal of Modern Literature*, 2 (1971), 79-84.
Majdiak, Daniel. "Romanticism in the Aesthetics of Iris Murdoch." *Texas Studies in Literature and Language*, 14 (1972), 370-372.

Under the Net, 1954

Baldanza, Frank. *Iris Murdoch*. 1974. Pp. 30-42.
Bradbury, Malcolm. *Possibilities*. 1973. Pp. 231-246.
Emerson, Donald. "Violence and Survival in the Novels of Iris Murdoch." *Transactions of the Wisconsin Academy of Sciences, Arts, and Letters*, 57 (1969), 24-25.
Gerstenberger, Donna. *Iris Murdoch*. 1975. Pp. 21-24.
Kahrmann, Bernd. *Die idyllische Szene*. 1969. Pp. 39-44.
Martz, Louis L. "Iris Murdoch: The London Novels," in Reuben A. Brower, ed., *Twentieth-Century Literature in Retrospect*. 1971. Pp. 71-75.
Riisøen, Helge. "Iris Murdoch og eksistensialismen." *Samtiden*, 82 (1973), 597-600.
Schleussner, Bruno. *Der neopikareske Roman*. 1969. Pp. 137-145.
Schrey, Helmut. *Didaktik des zeitgenössichen englischen Romans*. 1970. Pp. 94-98.
Swinden, Patrick. *Unofficial Selves*. 1973. Pp. 237-247.

The Unicorn, 1963

Baldanza, Frank. *Iris Murdoch*. 1974. Pp. 105-116.
Emerson, Donald. "Violence and Survival in the Novels of Iris Murdoch." *Transactions of the Wisconsin Academy of Sciences, Arts, and Letters*, 57 (1969), 26-27.
German, Howard. "The Range of Allusions in the Novels of Iris Murdoch." *Journal of Modern Literature*, 2 (1971), 65-68.
Gerstenberger, Donna. *Iris Murdoch*. 1975. Pp. 40-44.
Goshgarian, Gary. "Feminist Values in the Novels of Iris Murdoch." *Revue des Langues Vivantes*, 40 (1974), 519-527.

An Unofficial Rose, 1962

Baldanza, Frank. *Iris Murdoch*. 1974. Pp. 96-104.
German, Howard. "The Range of Allusions in the Novels of Iris Murdoch." *Journal of Modern Literature*, 2 (1971), 58-64.

LEOPOLD HAMILTON MYERS

The Near and the Far, 1929

> Gupta, B. S. "L. H. Myers's Treatment of Buddhism in *The Near and the Far.*" *Revue des Langues Vivantes*, 37 (1971), 64-74.
> Viswanathan, K. *India in English Fiction*. 1971. Pp. 171-216.

V. S. NAIPAUL

A House for Mr. Biswas, 1961

> Fido, Martin. "Mr. Biswas and Mr. Polly." *Ariel*, 5:4 (1974), 30-37.
> Shenfield, Margaret. "Mr. Biswas and Mr. Polly." *English*, 23 (1974), 95-100.

Mr. Stone and the Knights Companion, 1963

> Boxill, Anthony. "The Concept of Spring in V. S. Naipaul's *Mr. Stone and the Knights Companion.*" *Ariel*, 5:4 (1974), 21-28.

THOMAS NASHE

The Unfortunate Traveller, 1594

> Davis, Walter R. *Idea and Act*. 1969. Pp. 214-237.
> Demadre, A. "Le Récit dans *The Unfortunate Traveller* de Thomas Nashe," in *Récit et roman*. 1972. Pp. 9-15.
> Leggatt, Alexander. "Artistic Coherence in *The Unfortunate Traveller.*" *Studies in English Literature, 1500-1900*, 14 (1974), 31-46.

BILL NAUGHTON

Alfie, 1966

> Gray, Nigel. *The Silent Majority*. 1973. Pp. 164-194.

JOHN HENRY NEWMAN

Callista, 1856

> Downes, David A. *The Temper of Victorian Belief*. 1972. Pp. 112-122.

Loss and Gain, 1848

> Downes, David A. *The Temper of Victorian Belief*. 1972. Pp. 110-112.

NORMAN NICHOLSON

The Fire of the Lord, 1944

> Gardner, Philip. "No Man Is an Island: Norman Nicholson's Novels." *Ariel*, 3:1 (1972), 44-49.

The Green Shore, 1947

> Gardner, Philip. "No Man Is an Island: Norman Nicholson's Novels."
> *Ariel*, 3:1 (1972), 49-53.

FLANN O'BRIEN

At Swim—Two Birds, 1939

> Orvell, Miles. "Entirely Fictitious: The Fictions of Flann O'Brien."
> *Journal of Irish Literature*, 3 (1974), 94-98.

The Dalkey Archive, 1964

> Orvell, Miles. "Entirely Fictitious: The Fictions of Flann O'Brien."
> *Journal of Irish Literature*, 3 (1974), 101-103.

The Hard Life, 1961

> Orvell, Miles. "Entirely Fictitious: The Fictions of Flann O'Brien."
> *Journal of Irish Literature*, 3 (1974), 101-103.

The Third Policeman, 1967

> Orvell, Miles. "Entirely Fictitious: The Fictions of Flann O'Brien."
> *Journal of Irish Literature*, 3 (1974), 94-98.

EIMAR O'DUFFY

Asses in Clover, 1933

> Hogan, Robert. *Eimar O'Duffy*. 1972. Pp. 73-80.

King Goshawk and the Birds, 1926

> Hogan, Robert. *Eimar O'Duffy*. 1972. Pp. 51-57.

The Lion and the Fox, 1922

> Hogan, Robert. *Eimar O'Duffy*. 1972. Pp. 40-46.

Miss Rudd and Some Lovers, 1923

> Hogan, Robert. *Eimar O'Duffy*. 1972. Pp. 46-50.

Printer's Errors, 1922

> Hogan, Robert. *Eimar O'Duffy*. 1972. Pp. 36-40.

The Spacious Adventures of the Man in the Street, 1928

> Hogan, Robert. *Eimar O'Duffy*. 1972. Pp. 57-65.

The Wasted Island, 1919

> Hogan, Robert. *Eimar O'Duffy*. 1972. Pp. 28-36.

SEAN O'FAOLAIN

Bird Alone, 1936

> Doyle, Paul A. *Sean O'Faolain*. 1968. Pp. 39-40, 49-58, 70-71.
> Harmon, Maurice. *Sean O'Faolain*. 1966. Pp. 141-143, 148-153, 156-160, 176-178.

Come Back to Erin, 1940

> Doyle, Paul A. *Sean O'Faolain*. 1968. Pp. 39-40, 58-71.
> Harmon, Maurice. *Sean O'Faolain*. 1966. Pp. 152-154, 160-163.

A Nest of Simple Folk, 1933

> Doyle, Paul A. *Sean O'Faolain*. 1968. Pp. 40-49, 70-71.
> Harmon, Maurice. *Sean O'Faolain*. 1966. Pp. 139-141, 145-148, 181-182.

LIAM O'FLAHERTY

The Assassin, 1928

> O'Brien, H. J. "Liam O'Flaherty's Ego-Anarchist." *University of Dayton Review*, 7 (Spring 1971), 73-75.
> Zneimer, John. *The Literary Vision*. 1970. Pp. 80-83.

The Black Soul, 1924

> Zneimer, John. *The Literary Vision*. 1970. Pp. 65-67.

Famine, 1937

> Zneimer, John. *The Literary Vision*. 1970. Pp. 127-131.

The House of Gold, 1929

> Zneimer, John. *The Literary Vision*. 1970. Pp. 100-107.

The Informer, 1925

> Zneimer, John. *The Literary Vision*. 1970. Pp. 70-72.

Insurrection, 1950

> Zneimer, John. *The Literary Vision*. 1970. Pp. 138-144.

Land, 1946

> Zneimer, John. *The Literary Vision*. 1970. Pp. 132-136.

The Martyr, 1933

> Zneimer, John. *The Literary Vision*. 1970. Pp. 115-122.

Mr. Gilhooley, 1926

> Zneimer, John. *The Literary Vision*. 1970. Pp. 74-79.

The Puritan, 1931

    Zneimer, John. *The Literary Vision*. 1970. Pp. 84-89.

Thy Neighbour's Wife, 1923

    Zneimer, John. *The Literary Vision*. 1970. Pp. 89-93.

MARGARET OLIPHANT

A Beleaguered City, 1880

    Colby, Vineta, and Robert A. Colby. *The Equivocal Virtue*. 1966.
    Pp. 90-95.

Miss Marjoribanks, 1866

    Colby, Vineta, and Robert A. Colby. *The Equivocal Virtue*. 1966.
    Pp. 62-67.

The Perpetual Curate, 1864

    Colby, Vineta, and Robert A. Colby. *The Equivocal Virtue*. 1966.
    Pp. 55-63.

Phoebe, Junior, 1876

    Colby, Vineta, and Robert A. Colby. *The Equivocal Virtue*. 1966.
    Pp. 67-74.

Salem Chapel, 1863

    Colby, Vineta, and Robert A. Colby. *The Equivocal Virtue*. 1966.
    Pp. 49-55.

GEORGE ORWELL

Burmese Days, 1934

    Alldritt, Keith. *The Making of George Orwell*. 1969. Pp. 20-26.
    Calder, Jenni. *Chronicles of Conscience*. 1968. Pp. 82-87.
    Fiderer, Gerald. "Masochism as Literary Strategy: Orwell's Psycho-
      logical Novels." *Literature and Psychology*, 20 (1970), 4-6.
    Kahrmann, Bernd. *Die idyllische Szene*. 1969. Pp. 84-86.
    Kalechofsky, Roberta. *George Orwell*. 1973. Pp. 28-35.
    Knapp, John V. "Dance to a Creepy Minuet: Orwell's *Burmese Days*,
      Precursor of *Animal Farm*." *Modern Fiction Studies*, 21 (1975),
      11-29.
    Kubal, David L. *Outside the Whale*. 1972. Pp. 70-79.
    Lewis, Robin Jared. "Orwell's *Burmese Days* and Forster's *A Passage
      to India:* Two Novels of Human Relations in the British Empire."
      Massachusetts Studies in English, 4 (1974), 13-24.
    Lief, Ruth Ann. *Homage to Oceania*. 1969. Pp. 104-105, 123-124.
    Woodcock, George. *The Crystal Spirit*. 1966. Pp. 84-104.

A Clergyman's Daughter, 1935

Alldritt, Keith. *The Making of George Orwell.* 1969. Pp. 27-31.
Beadle, Gordon B. "George Orwell and the Death of God." *Colorado Quarterly*, 23 (1974), 53-57.
Calder, Jenni. *Chronicles of Conscience.* 1968. Pp. 87-90.
Kahrmann, Bernd. *Die idyllische Szene.* 1969. Pp. 114-116.
Kalechofsky, Roberta. *George Orwell.* 1973. Pp. 44-51.
Kubal, David L. *Outside the Whale.* 1972. Pp. 79-85.
Lief, Ruth Ann. *Homage to Oceania.* 1969. Pp. 79-83, 103-104.
Smyer, Richard I. "Orwell's *A Clergyman's Daughter*: The Flight from History." *Modern Fiction Studies.* 21 (1975), 31-47
Woodcock, George. *The Crystal Spirit.* 1966. Pp. 125-141.

Coming Up for Air, 1939

Alldritt, Keith. *The Making of George Orwell.* 1969. Pp. 37-41.
Calder, Jenni. *Chronicles of Conscience.* 1968. Pp. 163-165.
Fink, Howard. "*Coming Up for Air:* Orwell's Ambiguous Satire on the Wellsian Utopia." *Studies in the Literary Imagination*, 6 (Fall 1973), 51-60.
Kahrmann, Bernd. *Die idyllische Szene.* 1969. Pp. 70-73.
Kalechofsky, Roberta. *George Orwell.* 1973. Pp. 85-97.
Kubal, David L. *Outside the Whale.* 1972. Pp. 115-122.
Lief, Ruth Ann. *Homage to Oceania.* 1969. Pp. 21-22, 67-68, 105-107, 117-118.
Meyers, Jeffrey. "Orwell's Apocalypse: *Coming Up for Air.*" *Modern Fiction Studies*, 21 (1975), 69-80.
Rees, Richard. *George Orwell.* 1961. Pp. 73-78.
Van Dellen, Robert J. "George Orwell's *Coming Up for Air*: The Politics of Powerlessness." *Modern Fiction Studies*, 21 (1975), 57-68.
Woodcock, George. *The Crystal Spirit.* 1966. Pp. 176-187.

Down and Out in Paris and London, 1933

Alldritt, Keith. *The Making of George Orwell.* 1969. Pp. 44-63.
Bonifas, Gilbert. "Notes sur la genèse de *Down and Out in Paris and London.*" *Annales de la Faculté des Lettres et Sciences Humaines de Nice*, 18 (1972), 55-64.
Calder, Jenni. *Chronicles of Conscience.* 1968. Pp. 32-40.
Kubal, David L. *Outside the Whale.* 1972. Pp. 59-69.
Lief, Ruth Ann. *Homage to Oceania.* 1969. Pp. 9-10, 35-39.

Keep the Aspidistra Flying, 1936

Alldritt, Keith. *The Making of George Orwell.* 1969. Pp. 31-36.
Calder, Jenni. *Chronicles of Conscience.* 1968. Pp. 90-98.
Guild, Nicholas. "In Dubious Battle: George Orwell and the Victory of the Money-God." *Modern Fiction Studies*, 21 (1975), 49-56.

Kahrmann, Bernd. *Die idyllische Szene.* 1969. Pp. 87-89.
Kalechofsky, Roberta. *George Orwell.* 1973. Pp. 51-60.
Kubal, David L. *Outside the Whale.* 1972. Pp. 89-104.
Lief, Ruth Ann. *Homage to Oceania.* 1969. Pp. 21-22, 44-47, 64-65, 115-117.
Rees, Richard. *George Orwell.* 1961. Pp. 31-36.
Woodcock, George. *The Crystal Spirit.* 1966. Pp. 140-150.

Nineteen Eighty-Four, 1948

Aldiss, Brian W. *Billion Year Spree.* 1973. Pp. 254-256.
Alldritt, Keith. *The Making of George Orwell.* 1969. Pp. 150-178.
Beadle, Gordon B. "George Orwell and the Death of God." *Colorado Quarterly*, 23 (1974), 59-63.
Beauchamp, Gorman. "Of Man's Last Disobedience: Zamiatin's *We* and Orwell's *1984.*" *Comparative Literature Studies*, 10 (1973), 293-298.
Calder, Jenni. *Chronicles of Conscience.* 1968. Pp. 233-248.
Connors, James. "Zamyatin's *We* and the Genesis of *1984.*" *Modern Fiction Studies*, 21 (1975), 107-124.
Fiderer, Gerald. "Masochism as Literary Strategy: Orwell's Psychological Novels." *Literature and Psychology*, 20 (1970), 7-20.
Fink, Howard. "Newspeak: The Epitome of Parody Techniques in *Nineteen Eighty-Four.*" *Critical Survey*, 5 (1971), 155-163.
Kahrmann, Bernd. *Die idyllische Szene.* 1969. Pp. 94-98.
Kalechofsky, Roberta. *George Orwell.* 1973. Pp. 111-134.
Kubal, David L. *Outside the Whale.* 1972. Pp. 130-141.
Laurenson, Diana T., and Alan Swingewood. *The Sociology of Literature.* 1971. Pp. 264-275.
Lief, Ruth Ann. *Homage to Oceania.* 1969. Pp. 14-15, 39-40, 41-43, 55-58, 69-70, 76-77, 84-88, 93-101, 107-114, 118-121, 137-138.
Meyers, Jeffrey. "The Evolution of *1984.*" *English Miscellany*, 23 (1972), 247-261.
Mueller, William R. *Celebration of Life.* 1972. Pp. 173-187.
New, Melvyn. "Orwell and Antisemitism: Toward *1984.*" *Modern Fiction Studies*, 21 (1975), 100-105.
Philmus, Robert M. "The Language of Utopia." *Studies in the Literary Imagination*, 6 (Fall 1973), 74-78.
Rees, Richard. *George Orwell.* 1961. Pp. 88-108.
Seeber, Hans Ulrich. *Wandlungen der Form.* 1970. Pp. 219-232.
Steinhoff, William. *George Orwell.* 1975. Pp. 148-222.
Westlake, J. H. J. "Aldous Huxley's *Brave New World* and George Orwell's *Nineteen Eighty-Four*: A Comparative Study." *Die Neueren Sprachen*, 71 (1972), 94-102.
Woodcock, George. *The Crystal Spirit.* 1966. Pp. 201-221.

The Road to Wigan Pier, 1937

Alldritt, Keith. *The Making of George Orwell.* 1969. Pp. 63-84.

Calder, Jenni. *Chronicles of Conscience.* 1968. Pp. 41-51.
Kalechofsky, Roberta. *George Orwell.* 1973. Pp. 64-76.
Lief, Ruth Ann. *Homage to Oceania.* 1969. Pp. 49-51.
Rees, Richard. *George Orwell.* 1961. Pp. 44-56.
Woodcock, George. *The Crystal Spirit.* 1966. Pp. 151-165.

WALTER HORATIO PATER

Gaston de Latour, 1896

Monsman, Gerald Cornelius. *Pater's Portraits.* 1967. Pp. 139-161.

Marius the Epicurean, 1885

Bloom, Harold. *The Ringers in the Tower.* 1971. Pp. 186-194.
Buckley, Jerome Hamilton. *Season of Youth.* 1974. Pp. 140-161.
Crinkley, Richmond. *Walter Pater.* 1970. Pp. 133-171.
Dahl, Curtis. "Pater's *Marius* and Historical Novels on Early Christian Times." *Nineteenth-Century Fiction,* 28 (1973), 1-24.
DeLaura, David J. *Hebrew and Hellene.* 1969. Pp. 263-285, 314-328.
Downes, David A. *The Temper of Victorian Belief.* 1972. Pp. 16-47.
Goetsch, Paul. *Die Romankonzeption in England.* 1967. Pp. 195-201.
McCraw, Harry Wells. "Walter Pater's 'Religious Phase': The Riddle of *Marius the Epicurean.*" *Southern Quarterly,* 10 (1972), 254-273.
Monsman, Gerald Cornelius. *Pater's Portraits.* 1967. Pp. 65-97.
Scotto, Robert M. "'Visions' and 'Epiphanies': Fictional Technique in Pater's *Marius* and Joyce's *Portrait.*" *James Joyce Quarterly,* 11 (1973), 41-50.
Uhlig, Claus. "Walter Pater und die Poetik der Reminiszenz: Zur literarischen Methode einer Spätzeit." *Poetica,* 6 (1974), 205-227.

THOMAS LOVE PEACOCK

Crotchet Castle, 1831

Chekalov, Ivan. "The Satire of Thomas Peacock (*Crotchet Castle*)." *Literatura* (Vilnius), 15 (1973), 55-60.
Dawson, Carl. *Thomas Love Peacock.* 1968. Pp. 32-38.
Felton, Felix. *Thomas Love Peacock.* 1972. Pp. 213-228.
Foltinek, Herbert. *Vorstufen zum viktorianischen Realismus.* 1968. Pp. 46-49.
Hewitt, Douglas. *The Approach to Fiction.* 1972. Pp. 147-160.
Hollingsworth, Keith. *The Newgate Novel.* 1963. Pp. 48-50.
Mills, Howard. *Peacock.* 1969. Pp. 208-213.

Gryll Grange, 1860

Dawson, Carl. *Thomas Love Peacock.* 1968. Pp. 82-93.
Felton, Felix. *Thomas Love Peacock.* 1972. Pp. 263-278.
Mills, Howard. *Peacock.* 1969. Pp. 214-218.

Headlong Hall, 1816

> Dawson, Carl. *Thomas Love Peacock*. 1968. Pp. 41-48, 63-69.
> Felton, Felix. *Thomas Love Peacock*. 1972. Pp. 98-110.
> Mills, Howard. *Peacock*. 1969. Pp. 84-96.

Maid Marian, 1822

> Dawson, Carl. *Thomas Love Peacock*. 1968. Pp. 73-82.
> Felton, Felix. *Thomas Love Peacock*. 1972. Pp. 168-191.
> Mills, Howard. *Peacock*. 1969. Pp. 206-208.

Melincourt, 1817

> Dawson, Carl. *Thomas Love Peacock*. 1968. Pp. 96-106.
> Felton, Felix. *Thomas Love Peacock*. 1972. Pp. 120-132.
> Mills, Howard. *Peacock*. 1969. Pp. 97-134.

The Misfortunes of Elphin, 1829

> Dawson, Carl. *Thomas Love Peacock*. 1968. Pp. 24-32.
> Felton, Felix. *Thomas Love Peacock*. 1972. Pp. 192-203.

Nightmare Abbey, 1818

> Dawson, Carl. *Thomas Love Peacock*. 1968. Pp. 52-61.
> Felton, Felix. *Thomas Love Peacock*. 1972. Pp. 143-156.
> Kiely, Robert. *The Romantic Novel in England*. 1972. Pp. 174-188.
> Mills, Howard. *Peacock*. 1969. Pp. 135-164.

JAMES PLUNKETT

Strumpet City, 1969

> Göhler, Dagmar. "James Plunkett: Manche, sagt man, sind verdammt." *Weimarer Beiträge*, 20:6 (1974), 158-166.

ANTHONY POWELL

The Acceptance World, 1955

> Brennan, Neil. *Anthony Powell*. 1974. Pp. 152-162.

Afternoon Men, 1931

> Bergonzi, Bernard. *The Situation of the Novel*. 1971. Pp. 118-120.
> Brennan, Neil. *Anthony Powell*. 1974. Pp. 84-100.
> Morris, Robert K. *The Novels of Anthony Powell*. 1968. Pp. 13-31.

Agents and Patients, 1936

> Brennan, Neil. *Anthony Powell*. 1974. Pp. 114-120.
> Morris, Robert K. *The Novels of Anthony Powell*. 1968. Pp. 69-84.

At Lady Molly's, 1957

> Brennan, Neil. *Anthony Powell*. 1974. Pp. 162-168.

Books Do Furnish a Room, 1971

> Bailey, Paul. "Sniffing the Scandal." *London Magazine*, 11:3 (1971), 147-150.
> Brennan, Neil. *Anthony Powell*. 1974. Pp. 192-198.

A Buyer's Market, 1952

> Brennan, Neil. *Anthony Powell*. 1974. Pp. 147-152.

Casanova's Chinese Restaurant, 1960

> Brennan, Neil. *Anthony Powell*. 1974. Pp. 168-173.

A Dance to the Music of Time, 1951-

> Bergonzi, Bernard. *The Situation of the Novel*. 1971. Pp. 121-133.
> Brooke, Jocelyn. "Anthony Powell." *Unilit*, May 1964, pp. 41-43.
> Gutierrez, Donald. "Power in *A Dance to the Music of Time*." *Connecticut Review*, 6:2 (1973), 50-60.
> Morris, Robert K. *Continuance and Change*. 1972. Pp. 123-155.
> Morris, Robert K. *The Novels of Anthony Powell*. 1968. Pp. 103-246.
> Russell, John. "The War Trilogies of Anthony Powell and Evelyn Waugh." *Modern Age*, 16 (1972), 289-300.
> Walcutt, Charles Child. *Man's Changing Mask*. 1966. Pp. 336-339.
> Woodward, A. G. "The Novels of Anthony Powell." *English Studies in Africa*, 10 (1967), 117-128.

From a View to a Death, 1933

> Brennan, Neil. *Anthony Powell*. 1974. Pp. 104-114.
> Morris, Robert K. *The Novels of Anthony Powell*. 1968. Pp. 49-68.

The Kindly Ones, 1962

> Brennan, Neil. *Anthony Powell*. 1974. Pp. 173-178.

The Military Philosophers, 1968

> Brennan, Neil. *Anthony Powell*. 1974. Pp. 187-191.

A Question of Upbringing, 1951

> Brennan, Neil. *Anthony Powell*. 1974. Pp. 137-146.

The Soldier's Art, 1966

> Brennan, Neil. *Anthony Powell*. 1974. Pp. 182-187.

Temporary Kings, 1973

> Brennan, Neil. *Anthony Powell*. 1974. Pp. 198-203.

The Valley of Bones, 1964

   Brennan, Neil. *Anthony Powell*. 1974. Pp. 178-182.

Venusburg, 1932

   Brennan, Neil. *Anthony Powell*. 1974. Pp. 100-104.
   Morris, Robert K. *The Novels of Anthony Powell*. 1968. Pp. 32-48.

What's Become of Waring, 1939

   Brennan, Neil. *Anthony Powell*. 1974. Pp. 120-123.
   Morris, Robert K. *The Novels of Anthony Powell*. 1968. Pp. 85-100.

JOHN COWPER POWYS

All or Nothing, 1960

   Cavaliero, Glen. *John Cowper Powys*. 1973. Pp. 150-153.

Atlantis, 1954

   Brebner, John A. "The Anarchy of the Imagination," in Belinda Humfrey, ed., *Essays on John Cowper Powys*. 1973. Pp. 278-279.
   Cavaliero, Glen. *John Cowper Powys*. 1973. Pp. 133-140.

The Brazen Head, 1956

   Brebner, John A. "The Anarchy of the Imagination," in Belinda Hum-
   frey, ed., *Essays on John Cowper Powys*. 1972. Pp. 280-283.
   Cavaliero, Glen. *John Cowper Powys*. 1973. Pp. 140-144.
   Collins, H. P. *John Cowper Powys*. 1967. Pp. 147-149.

Ducdame, 1925

   Cavaliero, Glen. *John Cowper Powys*. 1973. Pp. 33-41.
   Cavaliero, Glen. "John Cowper Powys: Landscape and Personality
   in the Early Novels," in Belinda Humfrey, ed., *Essays on John
   Cowper Powys*. 1972. Pp. 90-101.
   Collins, H. P. *John Cowper Powys*. 1967. Pp. 58-64.
   Fernandez, Diane. "Powys et l'eau de l'inconscient maternel." *Nou-
   velle Revue Française*, No. 233 (1972), 37-38.
   Fernandez, Diane. "Whiteness," in Belinda Humfrey, ed., *Essays on
   John Cowper Powys*. 1972. Pp. 110-112.
   Hooker, Jeremy. *John Cowper Powys*. 1973. Pp. 24-29.
   Miguel, Andre. "Une Oeuvre prodigieuse." *Quinzaine Littéraire*,
   No. 173, (1973), 15-17.

A Glastonbury Romance, 1932

   Cavaliero, Glen. *John Cowper Powys*. 1973. Pp. 60-78.
   Collins, H. P. *John Cowper Powys*. 1967. Pp. 78-91.
   Cook, David A. "John Cowper Powys' *A Glastonbury Romance*: A

Modern Mystery Play." *Contemporary Literature*, 13 (1972), 341-360.

Hooker, Jeremy. *John Cowper Powys*. 1973. Pp. 44-52.

Hyman, Timothy. "The Modus Vivendi of John Cowper Powys," in Belinda Humfrey, ed., *Essays on John Cowper Powys*. 1972. Pp. 131-137.

Knight, G. Wilson. "Powys on Death," in Belinda Humfrey, ed., *Essays on John Cowper Powys*. 1972. Pp. 191-197.

The Inmates, 1952

Brebner, John A. "The Anarchy of the Imagination," in Belinda Humfrey, ed., *Essays on John Cowper Powys*. 1972. Pp. 275-278.

Cavaliero, Glen. *John Cowper Powys*. 1973. Pp. 131-133.

Maiden Castle, 1936

Cavaliero, Glen. *John Cowper Powys*. 1973. Pp. 93-102.

Collins, H. P. *John Cowper Powys*. 1967. Pp. 133-138.

Fernandez, Diane. "Powys et l'eau de l'inconscient maternel." *Nouvelle Revue Française*, No. 233 (1972), 35-40.

Hooker, Jeremy. *John Cowper Powys*. 1973. Pp. 62-74.

Miles, Gwyneth F. "The Pattern of Homecoming," in Belinda Humfrey, ed., *Essays on John Cowper Powys*. 1972. Pp. 223-227.

Morwyn, 1937

Cavaliero, Glen. *John Cowper Powys*. 1973. Pp. 103-106.

Owen Glendower, 1940

Cavaliero, Glen. *John Cowper Powys*. 1973. Pp. 107-119.

Collins, H. P. *John Cowper Powys*. 1967. Pp. 138-143.

Hooker, Jeremy. *John Cowper Powys*. 1973. Pp. 74-78.

Mathias, Roland. "The Sacrificial Prince: A Study of *Owen Glendower*," in Belinda Humfrey, ed., *Essays on John Cowper Powys*. 1972. Pp. 234-261.

Miles, Gwyneth F. "The Pattern of Homecoming," in Belinda Humfrey, ed., *Essays on John Cowper Powys*. 1972. Pp. 227-231.

Porius, 1951

Brebner, John A. "The Anarchy of the Imagination," in Belinda Humfrey, ed., *Essays on John Cowper Powys*. 1972. Pp. 264-275.

Cavaliero, Glen. *John Cowper Powys*. 1973. Pp. 119-130, 185-187.

Collins, H. P. *John Cowper Powys*. 1967. Pp. 143-147.

Hooker, Jeremy. *John Cowper Powys*. 1973. Pp. 78-91.

Rodmoor, 1916

Cavaliero, Glen. *John Cowper Powys*. 1973. Pp. 27-33.

Cavaliero, Glen. "John Cowper Powys: Landscape and Personality in the Early Novels," in Belinda Humfrey, ed., *Essays on John Cowper*

Powys. 1972. Pp. 88-90.

Fernandez, Diane. "Powys et l'eau de l'inconscient maternel." *Nouvelle Revue Française*, No. 233 (1972), 36-38.

Fernandez, Diane. "Whiteness," in Belinda Humfrey, ed., *Essays on John Cowper Powys.* 1972. Pp. 109-110.

Hooker, Jeremy. *John Cowper Powys.* 1973. Pp. 22-24.

Weymouth Sands, 1935

Cavaliero, Glen. *John Cowper Powys.* 1973. Pp. 79-93.

Collins, H. P. *John Cowper Powys.* 1967. Pp. 106-115.

Collins, H. P. "The Sands Do Not Run Out," in Belinda Humfrey, ed., *Essays on John Cowper Powys.* 1972. Pp. 207-218.

Hooker, Jeremy. *John Cowper Powys.* 1973. Pp. 53-61.

Hyman, Timothy. "The Modus Vivendi of John Cowper Powys," in Belinda Humfrey, ed., *Essays on John Cowper Powys.* 1972. Pp. 137-141.

Wolf Solent, 1929

Cavaliero, Glen. *John Cowper Powys.* 1973. Pp. 44-60.

Collins, H. P. *John Cowper Powys.* 1967. Pp. 65-77.

Fauconnier, Guillaume. "Powysiana." *Nouvelle Revue Française*, No. 259 (1974), 56-60.

Fernandez, Diane. "Powys et l'eau de l'inconscient maternel." *Nouvelle Revue Française*, No. 233 (1972), 35-44.

Fernandez, Diane. "Whiteness," in Belinda Humfrey, ed., *Essays on John Cowper Powys.* 1972. Pp. 112-113.

Hooker, Jeremy. *John Cowper Powys.* 1973. Pp. 33-43.

Miles, Gwyneth F. "The Pattern of Homecoming," in Belinda Humfrey, ed., *Essays on John Cowper Powys.* 1972. Pp. 221-223.

Wood and Stone, 1915

Cavaliero, Glen. *John Cowper Powys.* 1973. Pp. 21-26.

Cavaliero, Glen. "John Cowper Powys: Landscape and Personality in the Early Novels," in Belinda Humfrey, ed., *Essays on John Cowper Powys.* 1972. Pp. 86-88.

THEODORE FRANCIS POWYS

Mr. Tasker's Gods, 1925

Boulton, J. A. "The Moods of God: An Early Version of *Mr. Tasker's Gods." Notes and Queries*, 19 (1972), 56-59.

J. B. PRIESTLEY

Angel Pavement, 1930

Cooper, Susan. *J. B. Priestley.* 1971. Pp. 65-75.

Benighted, 1927

Cooper, Susan. *J. B. Priestley.* 1971. Pp. 42-50.

Bright Day, 1946

Cooper, Susan. *J. B. Priestley.* 1971. Pp. 19-29.

The Good Companions, 1929

Brown, Ivor. *J. B. Priestley.* 1957. Pp. 15-17.
Cooper, Susan. *J. B. Priestley.* 1971. Pp. 55-65.

ANN RADCLIFFE

The Castles of Athlin and Dunbayne, 1789

Lévy, Maurice. *Le Roman "gothique" anglais.* 1968. Pp. 232-236.
Murray, E. B. *Ann Radcliffe.* 1972. Pp. 61-74.

Gaston de Blondeville, 1826

Lévy, Maurice. *Le Roman "gothique" anglais.* 1968. Pp. 262-266.

The Italian, 1797

Murray E. B. *Ann Radcliffe.* 1972. Pp. 135-158.
Poenicke, Klaus. " 'Schönheit im Schosse des Schreckens': Raumge-
füge und Menschenbild im englischen Schauerroman." *Archiv für
das Studium der Neueren Sprachen und Literaturen*, 207 (1970),
12-14.

The Mysteries of Udolpho, 1794

Breitinger, Eckhard. *Der Tod im englischen Roman.* 1971. Pp. 28-30,
54-61, 80-83, 157-162, 167-173.
Göller, Karl Heinz. *"Romance" und "novel."* 1972. Pp. 219-222.
Kiely, Robert. *The Romantic Novel in England.* 1972. Pp. 65-80.
Korniger, Siegfried. "Radcliffe: *The Mysteries of Udolpho*," in Franz
K. Stanzel, ed., *Der englische Roman.* 1969. Vol. I, 312-337.
Lévy, Maurice. *Le Roman "gothique" anglais.* 1968. Pp. 246-251.
Murray, E. B. *Ann Radcliffe.* 1972. Pp. 112-134.
Poenicke, Klaus. " 'Schönheit im Schosse des Schreckens': Raumge-
füge und Menschenbild im englischen Schauerroman." *Archiv für
das Studium der Neueren Sprachen und Literaturen*, 207 (1970),
8-12.
Smith, Nelson C. "Sense, Sensibility and Ann Radcliffe." *Studies in
English Literature, 1500-1900*, 13 (1973), 577-590.

The Romance of the Forest, 1791

Lévy, Maurice. *Le Roman "gothique" anglais.* 1968. Pp. 240-246.
Murray, E. B. *Ann Radcliffe.* 1972. Pp. 90-111.
Poenicke, Klaus. " 'Schönheit im Schosse des Schreckens': Raumge-

füge und Menschenbild im englischen Schauerroman." *Archiv für das Studium der Neueren Sprachen und Literaturen*, 207 (1970), 8-11.

A Sicilian Romance, 1790

> Lévy, Maurice. *Le Roman "gothique" anglais*. 1968. P. 237.
> Murray, E. B. *Ann Radcliffe*. 1972. Pp. 75-89.

HERBERT READ

The Green Child, 1935

> Harder, Worth T. "Crystal Source: Herbert Read's *The Green Child*." *Sewanee Review*, 81 (1973), 714-738.

PIERS PAUL READ

Upstart, 1973

> Mannheimer, Monica Lauritzen. "The Individual and Society in Contemporary British Fiction." *Moderna Sprak*, 68 (1974), 318-320.

CHARLES READE

The Cloister and the Hearth, 1861

> Burns, Wayne. *Charles Reade*. 1961. Pp. 309-321.

Griffith Gaunt, 1865

> Burns, Wayne. *Charles Reade*. 1961. Pp. 243-267.

It Is Never Too Late to Mend, 1856

> Burns, Wayne. *Charles Reade*. 1961. Pp. 165-171.

CLARA REEVE

The Old English Baron, 1778

> Lévy, Maurice. *Le Roman "gothique" anglais*. 1968. Pp. 173-177.

MARY RENAULT

The Bull from the Sea, 1962

> Dick, Bernard F. *The Hellenism of Mary Renault*. 1972. Pp. 70-85.
> Wolfe, Peter. *Mary Renault*. 1969. Pp. 168-187.

The Charioteer, 1953

> Dick, Bernard F. *The Hellenism of Mary Renault*. 1972. Pp. 30-37.
> Wolfe, Peter. *Mary Renault*. 1969. Pp. 103-121.

Fire from Heaven, 1970

> Dick, Bernard F. *The Hellenism of Mary Renault*. 1972. Pp. 100-118.

The Friendly Young Ladies, 1944

> Dick, Bernard F. *The Hellenism of Mary Renault*. 1972. Pp. 13-22.
> Wolfe, Peter. *Mary Renault*. 1969. Pp. 54-64.

Kind Are Her Answers, 1940

> Dick, Bernard F. *The Hellenism of Mary Renault*. 1972. Pp. 9-12.
> Wolfe, Peter. *Mary Renault*. 1969. Pp. 45-54.

The King Must Die, 1958

> Dick, Bernard F. *The Hellenism of Mary Renault*. 1972. Pp. 57-70.
> Wolfe, Peter. *Mary Renault*. 1969. Pp. 155-168.

The Last of the Wine, 1956

> Dick, Bernard F. *The Hellenism of Mary Renault*. 1972. Pp. 37-53.
> Wolfe, Peter. *Mary Renault*. 1969. Pp. 122-140.

The Mask of Apollo, 1966

> Dick, Bernard F. *The Hellenism of Mary Renault*. 1972. Pp. 86-99.
> Wolfe, Peter. *Mary Renault*. 1969. Pp. 140-146.

North Face, 1948

> Dick, Bernard F. *The Hellenism of Mary Renault*. 1972. Pp. 26-29.
> Wolfe, Peter. *Mary Renault*. 1969. Pp. 85-102.

Purposes of Love, 1939

> Dick, Bernard F. *The Hellenism of Mary Renault*. 1972. Pp. 2-9.
> Wolfe, Peter. *Mary Renault*. 1969. Pp. 34-45.

Return to Night, 1947

> Dick, Bernard F. *The Hellenism of Mary Renault*. 1972. Pp. 22-25.
> Wolfe, Peter. *Mary Renault*. 1969. Pp. 68-85.

JEAN RHYS

After Leaving Mr. Mackenzie, 1931

> Mellown, Elgin W. "Character and Themes in the Novels of Jean
> Rhys." *Contemporary Literature*, 13 (1972), 458-475.

Good Morning, Midnight, 1939

> Mellown, Elgin W. "Character and Themes in the Novels of Jean
> Rhys." *Contemporary Literature*, 13 (1972), 458-475.

Quartet, 1928

> Baroche, Christiane. "L'Univers implacable de Jean Rhys." *Quinzaine Littéraire*, No. 158 (1973), 15-16.
> Mellown, Elgin W. "Character and Themes in the Novels of Jean Rhys." *Contemporary Literature*, 13 (1972), 458-475.

Voyage in the Dark, 1934

> Mellown, Elgin W. "Character and Themes in the Novels of Jean Rhys." *Contemporary Literature*, 13 (1972), 458-475.

Wide Sargasso Sea, 1966

> Fernandez, Diane. "Jean Rhys." *Quinzaine Littéraire*, No. 113 (1971), 12-13.
> Mellown, Elgin W. "Character and Themes in the Novels of Jean Rhys." *Contemporary Literature*, 13 (1972), 462-463, 470-475.

DOROTHY RICHARDSON

Pilgrimage, 1938

> Donovan, Josephine. "Feminist Style Criticism," in Susan Koppelman Cornillon, ed., *Images of Women in Fiction*. 1973. Pp. 349-352.
> Rose, Shirley. "Dorothy Richardson's Focus on Time." *English Literature in Transition*, 17 (1974), 163-172.
> Rose, Shirley. "Dorothy Richardson: The First Hundred Years, A Retrospective View." *Dalhousie Review*, 53 (1973), 92-96.

SAMUEL RICHARDSON

Clarissa, 1748

> Ball, Donald L. *Samuel Richardson's Theory of Fiction*. 1971. Pp. 77-113, 140-146, 152-159, 169-173, 182-187, 197-201, 214-223, 236-239, 244-248, 256-260, 267-271.
> Brissenden, R. F. *Virtue in Distress*. 1974. Pp. 159-186.
> Brophy, Elizabeth Bergen. *Samuel Richardson*. 1974. Pp. 91-107.
> Carroll, John. "Richardson at Work: Revisions, Allusions, and Quotations in *Clarissa*," in R. F. Brissenden, ed., *Studies in the Eighteenth Century*. 1973. Pp. 53-71.
> Cohen, Richard. "The Social-Christian and Christian-Social Doctrines of Samuel Richardson." *Hartford Studies in Literature*, 4 (1972), 136, 139-142.
> Copeland, Edward. "Allegory and Analogy in *Clarissa*: The 'Plan' and the 'No-Plan.'" *ELH*, 39 (1972), 254-265.
> Copeland, Edward. "*Clarissa* and *Fanny Hill*: Sisters in Distress." *Studies in the Novel*, 4 (1972), 343-352.

Detig, Joseph. "Clarissa and Her Modern Critics." *Leyte-Samar Studies*, 4 (1970), 131-136.

Doody, Margaret Anne. *A Natural Passion*. 1974. Pp. 99-127, 151-240.

Eaves, T. C. Duncan, and Ben D. Kimpel. *Samuel Richardson*. 1971. Pp. 238-284.

Frank, Frederick S. "From Boudoir to Castle Crypt: Richardson and the Gothic Novel." *Revue des Langues Vivantes*, 41 (1975), 54-59.

Golden, Morris. *Richardson's Characters*. 1963. Pp. 4-5, 10-11, 14-15, 18-21, 23-25, 31-34, 39-40, 50-54, 63-67, 73-75, 80-84, 89-90, 95-97, 99, 102-103, 111-117, 120-122, 131-133, 137-148, 151-154, 157-158, 161-178.

Goldknopf, David. *The Life of the Novel*. 1972. Pp. 59-78.

Gopnik, Irwin. *A Theory of Style*. 1970. Pp. 64-116.

Greiner, Walter F. *Studien zur Entstehung der englischen Romantheorie*. 1969. Pp. 69-72.

Guilhamet, Leon M. "From *Pamela* to *Grandison*: Richardson's Moral Revolution in the Novel," in Paul J. Korshin, ed., *Studies in Change and Revolution*. 1972. Pp. 198-202.

Hardwick, Elizabeth. *Seduction and Betrayal*. 1970. Pp. 196-202.

Heilbrun, Carolyn G. *Towards a Recognition of Androgyny*. 1973. Pp. 59-62.

Kahler, Erich. *The Inward Turn of Narrative*. 1973. Pp. 150-168.

Kearney, Anthony. "A Recurrent Motif in Richardson's Novels." *Neophilologus*, 55 (1971), 447-450.

Kinkead-Weeks, Mark. *Samuel Richardson*. 1973. Pp. 123-276, 404-411, 433-447.

Konigsberg, Ira. *Samuel Richardson*. 1968. Pp. 28-29, 33-34, 64-65, 74-94.

Levin, Gerald. "Lovelace's Dream." *Literature and Psychology*, 20 (1970), 121-127.

Miller, Norbert. *Der empfindsame Erzähler*. 1968. Pp. 175-186.

Neuhaus, Volker. *Typen multiperspektivischen Erzählens*. 1971. Pp. 43-59.

Otten, Kurt. *Der englische Roman*. 1971. Pp. 66-71.

Palmer, William J. "Two Dramatists: Lovelace and Richardson in *Clarissa*." *Studies in the Novel*, 5 (1973), 7-21.

Sacks, Sheldon. "*Clarissa* and the Tragic Traditions," in Harold E. Pagliaro, ed., *Studies in Eighteenth-Century Culture*. 1972. Pp. 195-221.

Spacks, Patricia Meyer. "Early Fiction and the Frightened Male." *Novel*, 8 (1974), 8-11.

Ulmer, Gregory L. "*Clarissa* and *La Nouvelle Héloïse*." *Comparative Literature*, 24 (1972), 289-309.

Van Marter, Shirley. "Hidden Virtue: An Unsolved Problem in *Clarissa*." *Yearbook of English Studies*, 4 (1974), 140-148.

Viglieno, Laurence. "Richardson et Rousseau devant la loi du père: Tentative de psychocritique comparée." *Annales de la Faculté des Lettres et Sciences Humaines de Nice*, 22 (1974), 167-178.

Wills, Antony A. "The World of Clarissa." *Rendezvous*, 9 (1974-1975), 1-14.

Winner, Anthony. "Richardson's Lovelace: Character and Prediction." *Texas Studies in Literature and Language*, 14 (1972), 53-75.

Wolff, Cynthia Griffin. "The Problem of Eighteenth-Century Secular Heroinism." *Modern Language Studies*, 4 (1974), 35-37.

Wolff, Cynthia Griffin. *Samuel Richardson*. 1972. Pp. 74-173.

Wolpers, Theodor. "Richardson: *Clarissa*," in Franz K. Stanzel, ed., *Der englische Roman*. 1969. Vol. I, 144-197.

Pamela, 1740

Allende, Nora A. de. "Social Context in *Moll Flanders, Pamela*, and *Tom Jones*." *Revista de Literaturas Modernas*, 8 (1969), 81-126.

Allentuck, Marcia Epstein. "Narration and Illustration: The Problem of Richardson's *Pamela.*" *Philological Quarterly*, 51 (1972), 874-886.

Ball, Donald L. *Samuel Richardson's Theory of Fiction*. 1971. Pp. 77-85, 88-93, 149-152, 166-169, 179-182, 194-196, 210-214, 232-236, 241-244, 253-256, 265-267.

Brophy, Elizabeth Bergen. *Samuel Richardson*. 1974. Pp. 53-76.

Cohen, Richard. "The Social-Christian and Christian-Social Doctrines of Samuel Richardson." *Hartford Studies in Literature*, 4 (1972), 136-139.

Donovan, Robert Alan. *The Shaping Vision*. 1966. Pp. 47-67.

Doody, Margaret Anne. *A Natural Passion*. 1974. Pp. 14-98.

Eaves, T. C. Duncan, and Ben D. Kimpel. *Samuel Richardson*. 1971. Pp. 100-118, 149-153.

Folkenflik, Robert. "A Room of Pamela's Own." *ELH*, 39 (1972), 585-596.

Frank, Frederick S. "From Boudoir to Castle Crypt: Richardson and the Gothic Novel." *Revue des Langues Vivantes*, 41 (1975), 51-54.

Guilhamet, Leon M. "From *Pamela* to *Grandison:* Richardson's Moral Revolution in the Novel," in Paul J. Korshin, ed., *Studies in Change and Revolution*. 1972. Pp. 194-198.

Golden, Morris. *Richardson's Characters*. 1963. Pp. 12-14, 17-18, 29-31, 38-39, 47-50, 61-63, 73, 88-89, 98, 135-137, 155-157, 159-161.

Kay, Donald. "Pamela and the Poultry." *Satire Newsletter*, 10 (1972), 25-27.

Kearney, Anthony. "A Recurrent Motif in Richardson's Novels." *Neophilologus*, 55 (1971), 447-450.

Kinkead-Weeks, Mark. *Samuel Richardson*. 1973. Pp. 7-120.

Konigsberg, Ira. *Samuel Richardson*. 1968. Pp. 17-19, 63.

Leed, Jacob. "Richardson's Pamela and Sidney's." *AUMLA*, No. 40 (1973), 240-245.

Miller, Norbert. *Der empfindsame Erzähler*. 1968. Pp. 175-186.

Oliver, Theo. "*Pamela* and *Shamela*: A Reassessment." *English Studies in Africa*, 17 (1974), 59-70.

Otten, Kurt. *Der englische Roman*. 1971. Pp. 63-66.

Rader, Ralph W. "Defoe, Richardson, Joyce, and the Concept of Form in the Novel," in *Autobiography, Biography, and the Novel.* 1973. Pp. 33-38.

Rogers, Agnes, Pierre Szamek, and Lyman Bryson. "*Pamela,*" in George D. Crothers, ed., *Invitation to Learning.* 1966. Pp. 27-35.

Roussel, Roy. "Reflections on the Letter: The Reconciliation of Distance and Presence in *Pamela.*" *ELH,* 41 (1974), 375-399.

Stein, William Bysshe. "*Pamela*: The Narrator as Unself-Conscious Hack." *Bucknell Review,* 20 (Spring 1972), 39-66.

Wilson, Stuart. "Richardson's *Pamela*: An Interpretation." *Publications of the Modern Language Association,* 88 (1973), 79-91.

Wolff, Cynthia Griffin. *Samuel Richardson.* 1972. Pp. 58-73.

Wolff, Erwin. *Der englische Roman.* 1968. Pp. 44-48.

Sir Charles Grandison, 1754

Ball, Donald L. *Samuel Richardson's Theory of Fiction.* 1971. Pp. 78-82, 88-93, 100-103, 146-149, 159-161, 173-178, 187-192, 201-203, 223-227, 239-241, 248-250, 260-264, 271-276.

Brophy, Elizabeth Bergen. *Samuel Richardson.* 1974. Pp. 76-90.

Cohen, Richard. "The Social-Christian and Christian-Social Doctrines of Samuel Richardson." *Hartford Studies in Literature,* 4 (1972), 142-145.

Doody, Margaret Anne. *A Natural Passion.* 1974. Pp. 241-367.

Eaves, T. C. Duncan, and Ben D. Kimpel. *Samuel Richardson.* 1971. Pp. 387-400.

Gassenmeier, Michael. *Der Typus des "man of feeling."* 1972. Pp. 37-57.

Guilhamet, Leon M. "From *Pamela* to *Grandison:* Richardson's Moral Revolution in the Novel," in Paul J. Korshin, ed., *Studies in Change and Revolution.* 1972. Pp. 194-198.

Golden, Morris. *Richardson's Characters.* 1963. Pp. 15-17, 21-22, 25, 34-38, 40-43, 54-58, 67-71, 75-80, 84-88, 90-91, 103-106, 113-114, 117-118, 122-123, 133-135, 148-151, 154-155, 178-181.

Kearney, Anthony. "A Recurrent Motif in Richardson's Novels." *Neophilologus,* 55 (1971), 448-450.

Kinkead-Weeks, Mark. *Samuel Richardson.* 1973. Pp. 279-391, 420-423, 447-451.

Konigsberg, Ira. *Samuel Richardson.* 1968. Pp. 48, 50-52, 65-69.

Levin, Gerald. "Character and Fantasy in Richardson's *Sir Charles Grandison.*" *Connecticut Review,* 7 (1973), 93-99.

Miller, Norbert. *Der empfindsame Erzähler.* 1968. Pp. 175-186.

Wolff, Cynthia Griffin. "The Problem of Eighteenth-Century Secular Heroinism." *Modern Language Studies,* 4 (1974), 37-38.

Wolff, Cynthia Griffin. *Samuel Richardson.* 1972. Pp. 174-229.

FREDERICK ROLFE

Hadrian the Seventh, 1904

  Jones, G. P. "Frederick Rolfe's Papal Dream." *Mosaic*, 7 (Winter
  1974), 109-122.
  Kellogg, Gene. *The Vital Tradition*. 1970. Pp. 93-94.

VICTORIA SACKVILLE-WEST

All Passion Spent, 1931

  Watson, Sara Ruth. *V. Sackville-West*. 1972. Pp. 103-109.

The Challenge, 1923

  Watson, Sara Ruth. *V. Sackville-West*. 1972. Pp. 91-95.

The Dark Island, 1934

  Watson, Sara Ruth. *V. Sackville-West*. 1972. Pp. 97-100.

Devil at Westease, 1947

  Watson, Sara Ruth. *V. Sackville-West*. 1972. Pp. 129-131.

The Dragon in Shallow Waters, 1921

  Watson, Sara Ruth. *V. Sackville-West*. 1972. Pp. 80-84.

The Easter Party, 1953

  Watson, Sara Ruth. *V. Sackville-West*. 1972. Pp. 131-135.

The Edwardians, 1930

  Gill, Richard. *Happy Rural Seat*. 1972. Pp. 143-147.
  Watson, Sara Ruth. *V. Sackville-West*. 1972. Pp. 109-114.

Family History, 1932

  Watson, Sara Ruth. *V. Sackville-West*. 1972. Pp. 114-121.

Grand Canyon, 1942

  Watson, Sara Ruth. *V. Sackville-West*. 1972. Pp. 124-129.

Grey Wethers, 1923

  Watson, Sara Ruth. *V. Sackville-West*. 1972. Pp. 84-88.

Heritage, 1919

  Watson, Sara Ruth. *V. Sackville-West*. 1972. Pp. 75-80.

No Signposts in the Sea, 1961

  Watson, Sara Ruth. *V. Sackville-West*. 1972. Pp. 135-137.

Seducers in Ecuador, 1924

>   Watson, Sara Ruth. *V. Sackville-West*. 1972. Pp. 95-97.

SIEGFRIED SASSOON

Memoirs of a Fox-Hunting Man, 1928

>   Thorpe, Michael. *Siegfried Sassoon*. 1967. Pp. 69-92.

Memoirs of an Infantry Officer, 1930

>   Thorpe, Michael. *Siegfried Sassoon*. 1967. Pp. 93-114.

Sherston's Progress, 1936

>   Thorpe, Michael. *Siegfried Sassoon*. 1967. Pp. 93-114.

DOROTHY L. SAYERS

Murder Must Advertise, 1933

>   Dingeldey, Erika. "Drei 'klassische' Kriminalromane: Didaktische
>   Beispiele für den Unterricht über Trivialliteratur." *Sprache im
>   technischen Zeitalter*, 44 (1972), 320-321.

WALTER SCOTT

The Abbot, 1820

>   Cusac, Marian H. *Narrative Structure*. 1969. Pp. 41-44.
>   Hart, Francis R. *Scott's Novels*. 1966. Pp. 194-196, 210-219.
>   Johnson, Edgar. *Sir Walter Scott*. 1970. Vol. I, 751-755.

Anne of Geierstein, 1829

>   Chandler, Alice. "Chivalry and Romance: Scott's Medieval Novels."
>   *Studies in Romanticism*, 14 (1975), 197.
>   Hart, Francis R. *Scott's Novels*. 1966. Pp. 223-225.
>   Johnson, Edgar. *Sir Walter Scott*. 1970. Vol. II, 1201-1207.

The Antiquary, 1816

>   Elbers, Joan S. "Isolation and Community in *The Antiquary*."
>   *Nineteenth-Century Fiction*, 27 (1973), 405-423.
>   Hart, Francis R. *Scott's Novels*. 1966. Pp. 246-258.
>   Jefferson, D. W. "The Virtuosity of Scott," in A. Norman Jeffares,
>   ed., *Scott's Mind and Art*. 1970. Pp. 64-71.
>   Johnson, Edgar. *Sir Walter Scott*. 1970. Vol. I, 536-543.
>   Mayhead, Robin. "The Problem of Coherence in *The Antiquary*," in
>   Alan Bell, ed., *Scott Bicentenary Essays*. 1973. Pp. 134-146.

The Betrothed, 1825

    Chandler, Alice. "Chivalry and Romance: Scott's Medieval Novels." *Studies in Romanticism,* 14 (1975), 194-195.
    Hart, Francis R. *Scott's Novels.* 1966. Pp. 167-168, 171-174.
    Johnson, Edgar. *Sir Walter Scott.* 1970. Vol. II, 928-933.

The Black Dwarf, 1816

    Hart, Francis R. *Scott's Novels.* 1966. Pp. 308-313, 318-321.
    Johnson, Edgar. *Sir Walter Scott.* 1970. Vol. I, 589-594.

The Bride of Lammermoor, 1819

    Beaty, Frederick L. *Light from Heaven.* 1971. Pp. 104-106.
    Cameron, Donald. "The Web of Destiny: The Structure of *The Bride of Lammermoor,*" in A. Norman Jeffares, ed., *Scott's Mind and Art.* 1970. Pp. 185-205.
    Cusac, Marian H. *Narrative Structure.* 1969. Pp. 49-51.
    Devlin, David. *The Author of Waverley.* 1971. Pp. 99-113.
    Devlin, D. D. "Scott and History," in A. Norman Jeffares, ed., *Scott's Mind and Art.* 1970. Pp. 86-88.
    Hart, Francis R. *Scott's Novels.* 1966. Pp. 236-237, 259-260, 305-310, 313-318, 321-334.
    Johnson, Edgar. "Scott and the Corners of Time." *Virginia Quarterly Review,* 49 (1973), 58.
    Johnson, Edgar. *Sir Walter Scott.* 1970. Vol. I, 662-670.

Castle Dangerous, 1832

    Johnson, Edgar. *Sir Walter Scott.* 1970. Vol. II, 1215-1218.

Count Robert of Paris, 1832

    Hart, Francis R. *Scott's Novels.* 1966. Pp. 168-175.
    Johnson, Edgar. "Scott and the Corners of Time." *Virginia Quarterly Review,* 49 (1973), 60-61.
    Johnson, Edgar. *Sir Walter Scott.* 1970. Vol. II, 1207-1215.

The Fair Maid of Perth, 1828

    Hart, Francis R. *Scott's Novels.* 1966. Pp. 235-245.
    Johnson, Edgar. "Scott and the Corners of Time." *Virginia Quarterly Review,* 49 (1973), 60.
    Johnson, Edgar. *Sir Walter Scott.* 1970. Vol. II, 1072-1078.
    Rubenstein, Jill. "The Defeat and Triumph of Bourgeois Pacifism: Scott's *Fair Maid of Perth* and *The Fortunes of Nigel.*" *Wordsworth Circle,* 2 (1971), 136-141.

The Fortunes of Nigel, 1822

    Cusac, Marian H. *Narrative Structure.* 1969. Pp. 54-57.
    Hart, Francis R. *Scott's Novels.* 1966. Pp. 198-203.

Johnson, Edgar. *Sir Walter Scott.* 1970. Vol. II, 822-828.
Rubenstein, Jill. "The Defeat and Triumph of Bourgeois Pacifism: Scott's *Fair Maid of Perth* and *The Fortunes of Nigel.*" *Wordsworth Circle,* 2 (1971), 136-141.

Guy Mannering, 1815

Hart, Francis R. *Scott's Novels.* 1966. Pp. 259-266, 270-275.
Johnson, Edgar. *Sir Walter Scott.* 1970. Vol. I, 530-536.
Mayhead, Robin. "Scott and the Idea of Justice," in A. Norman Jeffares, ed., *Scott's Mind and Art.* 1970. Pp. 173-180.

The Heart of Mid-Lothian, 1818

Beaty, Frederick L. *Light from Heaven.* 1971. Pp. 102-104.
Clements, Frances M. " 'Queens Love Revenge as well as Their Subjects': Thematic Unity in *The Heart of Mid-Lothian.*" *Studies in Scottish Literature,* 10 (1972), 10-17.
Cockshut, Anthony O. J. *The Achievement of Walter Scott.* 1969. Pp. 171-192.
Craig, David. "Scott's Shortcomings as an Artist," in Alan Bell, ed., *Scott Bicentenary Essays.* 1973. Pp. 103-108.
Cusac, Marian H. *Narrative Structure.* 1969. Pp. 33-36.
Foltinek, Herbert. *Vorstufen zum viktorianischen Realismus.* 1968. Pp. 171-174.
Hart, Francis R. *Scott's Novels.* 1966. Pp. 127-149.
Hyde, William J. "Jeanie Deans and the Queen: Appearance and Reality." *Nineteenth-Century Fiction,* 28 (1973), 86-92.
Johnson, Edgar. "Scott and the Corners of Time." *Virginia Quarterly Review,* 49 (1973), 58.
Johnson, Edgar. *Sir Walter Scott.* 1970. Vol. I, 655-662.
Mayhead, Robin. "Scott and the Idea of Justice," in A. Norman Jeffares, ed., *Scott's Mind and Art.* 1970. Pp. 168-173.
Müllenbrock, Heinz-Joachim. "Scott und der historische Roman: Aspekte der neueren Forschung." *Die Neueren Sprachen,* 71 (1972), 667-669.
Otten, Kurt. *Der englische Roman.* 1971. Pp. 114-117.
Sühnel, Rudolf. "Scott: *The Heart of Mid-Lothian,*" in Franz K. Stanzel, ed., *Der englische Roman.* 1969. Vol. I, 338-373.

Ivanhoe, 1819

Chandler, Alice. "Chivalry and Romance: Scott's Medieval Novels." *Studies in Romanticism,* 14 (1975), 191-194.
Fisch, Harold. *The Dual Image.* 1971. Pp. 59-62.
Hart, Francis R. *Scott's Novels.* 1966. Pp. 155-166, 180-186, 191-192.
Johnson, Edgar. *Sir Walter Scott.* 1970. Vol. I, 736-746.
Tindall, William Y., Perry Miller, and Lyman Bryson. "*Ivanhoe,*" in George D. Crothers, ed., *Invitation to Learning.* 1966. Pp. 81-88.
Tippkötter, Horst. *Walter Scott.* 1971. Pp. 90-112.

Kenilworth, 1821

> Hart, Francis R. *Scott's Novels*. 1966. Pp. 196-198, 203-210.
> Johnson, Edgar. *Sir Walter Scott*. 1970. Vol. I, 755-759.

A Legend of Montrose, 1819

> Devlin, David D. *The Author of Waverley*. 1971. Pp. 81-90.
> Garside, P. D. "*A Legend of Montrose* and the History of War."
> *Yearbook of English Studies*, 4 (1974), 159-171.
> Hart, Francis R. *Scott's Novels*. 1966. Pp. 117-127.
> Johnson, Edgar. *Sir Walter Scott*. 1970. Vol. I, 670-676.

The Monastery, 1820

> Hart, Francis R. *Scott's Novels*. 1966. Pp. 187-194.
> Johnson, Edgar. *Sir Walter Scott*. 1970. Vol. I, 746-751.

Old Mortality, 1816

> Calder, Angus, and Jenni Calder. *Scott*. 1971. Pp. 100-106.
> Cockshut, Anthony O. J. *The Achievement of Walter Scott*. 1969.
> Pp. 129-151.
> Craig, David. "Scott's Shortcomings as an Artist," in Alan Bell, ed.,
> *Scott Bicentenary Essays*. 1973. Pp. 108-112.
> Cusac, Marian H. *Narrative Structure*. 1969. Pp. 47-49.
> Foltinek, Herbert. *Vorstufen zum viktorianischen Realismus*. 1968.
> Pp. 177-179.
> Goodin, George. "Walter Scott and the Tradition of the Political
> Novel," in George Goodin, ed., *The English Novel*. 1972. Pp. 14-24.
> Hart, Francis R. *Scott's Novels*. 1966. Pp. 67-86, 90-92, 316-317.
> Johnson, Edgar. "Scott and the Corners of Time." *Virginia Quarterly
> Review*, 49 (1973), 56-57.
> Johnson, Edgar. *Sir Walter Scott*. 1970. Vol. I, 594-600.
> Tippkötter, Horst. *Walter Scott*. 1971. Pp. 180-221.

Peveril of the Peak, 1822

> Hart, Francis R. *Scott's Novels*. 1966. Pp. 104-117, 129-130.
> Johnson, Edgar. *Sir Walter Scott*. 1970. Vol. II, 828-832.

The Pirate, 1821

> Hart, Francis R. *Scott's Novels*. 1966. Pp. 286-305.
> Johnson, Edgar. *Sir Walter Scott*. 1970. Vol. II, 816-821.

Quentin Durward, 1823

> Chandler, Alice. "Chivalry and Romance: Scott's Medieval Novels."
> *Studies in Romanticism*, 14 (1975), 190-191.
> Cusac, Marian H. *Narrative Structure*. 1969. Pp. 73-76.
> Hart, Francis R. *Scott's Novels*. 1966. Pp. 220-235.
> Johnson, Edgar. "Scott and the Corners of Time." *Virginia Quarterly
> Review*, 49 (1973), 59.

Johnson, Edgar. *Sir Walter Scott.* 1970. Vol. II, 832-836.
Tippkötter, Horst. *Walter Scott.* 1971. Pp. 221-231.

Redgauntlet, 1824

Calder, Angus, and Jenni Calder. *Scott.* 1971. Pp. 141-149.
Cockshut, Anthony O. J. *The Achievement of Walter Scott.* 1969. Pp. 193-213.
Cusac, Marian H. *Narrative Structure.* 1969. Pp. 58-60.
Daiches, David. "Sir Walter Scott and History." *Etudes Anglaises,* 24 (1971), 475-477.
Devlin, David D. *The Author of Waverley.* 1971. Pp. 114-133.
Devlin, David D. "Scott and History," in A. Norman Jeffares, ed., *Scott's Mind and Art.* 1970. Pp. 75-77.
Donovan, Robert Alan. *The Shaping Vision.* 1966. Pp. 177-192.
Hart, Francis R. *Scott's Novels.* 1966. Pp. 48-64.
Jefferson, D. W. "The Virtuosity of Scott," in A. Norman Jeffares, ed., *Scott's Mind and Art.* 1970. Pp. 53-61.
Johnson, Edgar. "Scott and the Corners of Time." *Virginia Quarterly Review,* 49 (1973), 59.
Johnson, Edgar. *Sir Walter Scott.* 1970. Vol. II, 920-928.
Mayhead, Robin. "Scott and the Idea of Justice," in A. Norman Jeffares, ed., *Scott's Mind and Art.* 1970. Pp. 180-184.

Rob Roy, 1817

Cockshut, Anthony O. J. *The Achievement of Walter Scott.* 1969. Pp. 152-170.
Cusac, Marian H. *Narrative Structure.* 1969. Pp. 36-39.
Devlin, David D. *The Author of Waverley.* 1971. Pp. 90-98.
Hart, Francis R. *Scott's Novels.* 1966. Pp. 31-48.
Johnson, Edgar. "Scott and the Corners of Time." *Virginia Quarterly Review,* 49 (1973), 57-58.
Johnson, Edgar. *Sir Walter Scott.* 1970. Vol. I, 600-609.
Mills, Nicolaus. *American and English Fiction.* 1973. Pp. 33-51.
Tippkötter, Horst. *Walter Scott.* 1971. Pp. 61-73.

St. Ronan's Well, 1824

Hart, Francis R. *Scott's Novels.* 1966. Pp. 260-263, 266-270, 275-286.
Johnson, Edgar. *Sir Walter Scott.* 1970. Vol. II, 915-920.
Pittock, Joan. "Scott and the Novel of Manners: The Case of *St. Ronan's Well.*" *Durham University Journal,* 66 (1973), 1-9.

The Surgeon's Daughter, 1827

Hart, Francis R. *Scott's Novels.* 1966. Pp. 286-288.
Viswanathan, K. *India in English Fiction.* 1971. Pp. 18-30.

The Talisman, 1825

Hart, Francis R. *Scott's Novels.* 1966. Pp. 153-154, 168-169, 175-180.

Johnson, Edgar. *Sir Walter Scott.* 1970. Vol. II, 933-938.

The Two Drovers, 1827

Williams, Ioan. *The Realist Novel.* 1974. Pp. 26-30.

Waverley, 1814

Clipper, Lawrence J. "Edward Waverley's Night Journey." *South Atlantic Quarterly*, 73 (1974), 541-553.

Cockshut, Anthony O. J. *The Achievement of Walter Scott.* 1969. Pp. 107-128.

Cusac, Marian H. *Narrative Structure.* 1969. Pp. 27-32.

Daiches, David. "Sir Walter Scott and History." *Etudes Anglaises*, 24 (1971), 467-470.

Devlin, David D. *The Author of Waverley.* 1971. Pp. 56-80.

Devlin, David D. "Scott and History," in A. Norman Jeffares, ed., *Scott's Mind and Art.* 1970. Pp. 78-80, 89-91.

Hahn, H. G. "Historiographic and Literary: The Fusion of Two Eighteenth-Century Modes in Scott's *Waverley.*" *Hartford Studies in Literature*, 6 (1974), 243-267.

Hart, Francis R. *Scott's Novels.* 1966. Pp. 14-31, 42-44, 80-81, 317-318.

Hennelly, Mark M. "*Waverley* and Romanticism." *Nineteenth-Century Fiction*, 28 (1973), 194-209.

Iser, Wolfgang. *The Implied Reader.* 1974. Pp. 81-99.

Jefferson, D. W. "The Virtuosity of Scott," in A. Norman Jeffares, ed., *Scott's Mind and Art.* 1970. Pp. 61-63.

Johnson, Edgar. *Sir Walter Scott.* 1970. Vol. I, 520-530.

Kiely, Robert. *The Romantic Novel in England.* 1972. Pp. 136-154.

Tippkötter, Horst. *Walter Scott.* 1971. Pp. 23-48.

Williams, Ioan. *The Realist Novel.* 1974. Pp. 25-40.

Wolff, Erwin. "Sir Walter Scott und Dr. Dryasdust: Zum Problem der Entstehung des historischen Romans im 19.Jh.," in Wolfgang Iser and Fritz Schalk, eds., *Dargestellte Geschichte.* 1970. Pp. 17-32.

Waverley Novels

Welsh, Alexander. "Contrast of Styles in the Waverley Novels." *Novel*, 6 (1973), 218-228.

Welsh, Alexander. *The Hero of the Waverley Novels.* 1963.

Woodstock, 1826

Hart, Francis R. *Scott's Novels.* 1966. Pp. 86-104.

Johnson, Edgar. "Scott and the Corners of Time." *Virginia Quarterly Review*, 49 (1973), 59.

Johnson, Edgar. *Sir Walter Scott.* 1970. Vol. II, 1055-1064.

GEORGE BERNARD SHAW

Cashel Byron's Profession, 1886

Dietrich, R. F. *Portrait of the Artist as a Young Superman*. 1969. Pp. 131-149.

Hummert, Paul A. *Bernard Shaw's Marxian Romance*. 1973. Pp. 11-12.

Immaturity, 1930

Adams, Elsie B. *Bernard Shaw*. 1971. Pp. 87-94.

Dietrich, R. F. *Portrait of the Artist as a Young Superman*. 1969. Pp. 12-49, 71-88.

Hummert, Paul A. *Bernard Shaw's Marxian Romance*. 1973. Pp. 6-8.

The Irrational Knot, 1905

Adams, Elsie B. *Bernard Shaw*. 1971. Pp. 94-96.

Dietrich, R. F. *Portrait of the Artist as a Young Superman*. 1969. Pp. 89-112.

Hummert, Paul A. *Bernard Shaw's Marxian Romance*. 1973. Pp. 8-10.

Love Among the Artists, 1914

Adams, Elsie B. *Bernard Shaw*. 1971. Pp. 96-100.

Dietrich, R. F. *Portrait of the Artist as a Young Superman*. 1969. Pp. 113-130.

An Unsocial Socialist, 1887

Adams, Elsie B. *Bernard Shaw*. 1971. Pp. 100-105.

Dietrich, R. F. *Portrait of the Artist as a Young Superman*. 1969. Pp. 150-174.

Hummert, Paul A. *Bernard Shaw's Marxian Romance*. 1973. Pp. 13, 16-25.

MARY SHELLEY

Frankenstein, 1818

Aldiss, Brian W. *Billion Year Spree*. 1973. Pp. 20-30.

Aldiss, Brian W. "*The Billion Year Spree*: I. Origin of the Species." *Extrapolation*, 14 (1973), 178-185.

Bloom, Harold. *The Ringers in the Tower*. 1971. Pp. 119-129.

Breitinger, Eckhard. *Der Tod im englischen Roman*. 1971. Pp. 41-44.

Cameron, Kenneth Neill. *Romantic Rebels*. 1973. Pp. 72-75.

Cude, Wilfred. "Mary Shelley's Modern Prometheus: A Study in the Ethics of Scientific Creativity." *Dalhousie Review*, 52 (1972), 212-225.

Glut, Donald F. *The Frankenstein Legend*. 1973. Pp. 12-25.

Höhne, Horst. "Mary Shelleys *Frankenstein*: Komplexität eines poetischen Bildes und das ideologische Dilemma romantischer Dichtung." *Zeitschrift für Anglistik und Amerikanistik*, 22 (1974), 267-285.

Kiely, Robert. *The Romantic Novel in England*. 1972. Pp. 155-173.

Levine, George. *"Frankenstein* and the Tradition of Realism." *Novel*, 7 (1973), 14-30.

Palacio, Jean de. *Mary Shelley dans son oeuvre*. 1969. Pp. 572-585.

Seeber, Hans Ulrich. *Wandlungen der Form*. 1970. Pp. 204-207.

Small, Christopher. *Ariel Like a Harpy*. 1972.

Swingle, L. J. "Frankenstein's Monster and Its Romantic Relatives: Problems of Knowledge in English Romanticism." *Texas Studies in Literature and Language*, 15 (1973), 51-65.

The Last Man, 1826

Aldiss, Brian W. *Billion Year Spree*. 1973. Pp. 31-34.

Aldiss, Brian W. *"The Billion Year Spree*: I. Origin of the Species." *Extrapolation*, 14 (1973), 186-189.

Cameron, Kenneth Neill. *Romantic Rebels*. 1973. Pp. 75-78.

Palacio, Jean de. *Mary Shelley dans son oeuvre*. 1969. Pp. 585-592.

Valperga, 1823

Cameron, Kenneth Neill. *Romantic Rebels*. 1973. Pp. 78-80.

PERCY BYSSHE SHELLEY

Zastrozzi, 1810

Breitinger, Eckhard. *Der Tod im englischen Roman*. 1971. Pp. 36-38.

PHILIP SIDNEY

Arcadia, 1598

Bergbusch, Martin. "Rebellion in the *New Arcadia.*" *Philological Quarterly*, 53 (1974), 29-41.

Cluett, Robert. "Arcadia Wired: Preliminaries to an Electronic Investigation of the Prose Style of Philip Sidney." *Language and Style*, 7 (1974), 119-135.

Dana, Margaret E. "Heroic and Pastoral: Sidney's *Arcadia* as Masquerade." *Comparative Literature*, 25 (1973), 308-320.

Davis, Walter R. *Idea and Act*. 1969. Pp. 62-71.

Greenblatt, Stephen J. "Sidney's *Arcadia* and the Mixed Mode." *Studies in Philology*, 70 (1973), 269-278.

Hamilton, A. C. "Sidney's *Arcadia* as Prose Fiction: Its Relation to Its Sources." *English Literary Renaissance*, 2:1 (1972), 29-60.

Kimbrough, Robert. *Sir Philip Sidney*. 1971. Pp. 68-88, 125-143.

Lawry, Jon S. *Sidney's Two Arcadias*. 1972. Pp. 14-289.

Otten, Kurt. *Der englische Roman*. 1971. Pp. 26-30.

Parker, Robert W. "Terentian Structure and Sidney's Original *Arcadia.*" *English Literary Renaissance*, 2:1 (1972), 61-78.

Schleiner, Winfried. "Differences of Theme and Structure of the Erona Episode in the *Old* and *New Arcadia.*" *Studies in Philology*, 70 (1973), 377-391.

Toliver, Harold E. *Pastoral Forms and Attitudes.* 1971. Pp. 45-62.

Turner, Myron. "The Disfigured Face of Nature: Image and Metaphor in the Revised *Arcadia.*" *English Literary Renaissance*, 2:1 (1972), 116-135.

ALAN SILLITOE

The Death of William Posters, 1965

Nardella, Anna Ryan. "The Existential Dilemmas of Alan Sillitoe's Working-Class Heroes." *Studies in the Novel*, 5 (1973), 473-478.

Penner, Allen Richard. *Alan Sillitoe.* 1972. Pp. 115-123.

The General, 1960

Penner, Allen Richard. *Alan Sillitoe.* 1972. Pp. 92-98.

Key to the Door, 1961

Penner, Allen Richard. *Alan Sillitoe.* 1972. Pp. 99-113.

Saturday Night and Sunday Morning, 1958

Craig, David. *The Real Foundations.* 1973. Pp. 270-285.

Gray, Nigel. *The Silent Majority.* 1973. Pp. 103-132.

Kahrmann, Bernd. *Die idyllische Szene.* 1969. Pp. 66-70.

Lefranc, M. "Alan Sillitoe: An Interview by M. Lefranc." *Etudes Anglaises*, 26 (1973), 39-48.

Meckier, Jerome. "Looking Back in Anger: The Success of a Collapsing Stance." *Dalhousie Review*, 52 (1972), 51-53.

Nardella, Anna Ryan. "The Existential Dilemmas of Alan Sillitoe's Working-Class Heroes." *Studies in the Novel*, 5 (1973), 469-473.

Penner, Allen Richard. *Alan Sillitoe.* 1972. Pp. 73-89.

Schleussner, Bruno. *Der neopikareske Roman.* 1969. Pp. 154-161.

A Start in Life, 1970

Watrin, Jany. "Alan Sillitoe's *A Start in Life.*" *Revue des Langues Vivantes*, 38 (1972), 508-516.

A Tree on Fire, 1967

Nardella, Anna Ryan. "The Existential Dilemmas of Alan Sillitoe's Working-Class Heroes." *Studies in the Novel*, 5 (1973), 478-481.

Penner, Allen Richard. *Alan Sillitoe.* 1972. Pp. 126-133.

ANDREW SINCLAIR

Gog, 1967

    Bergonzi, Bernard. *The Situation of the Novel*. 1971. Pp. 76-79.

MAY SINCLAIR

The Allinghams, 1927

    Boll, Theophilus E. M. *Miss May Sinclair*. 1973. Pp. 293-297.

Anne Severn and the Fieldings, 1922

    Boll, Theophilus E. M. *Miss May Sinclair*. 1973. Pp. 276-278.

Arnold Waterlow, 1924

    Boll, Theophilus E. M. *Miss May Sinclair*. 1973. Pp. 282-286.
    Buckley, Jerome Hamilton. *Season of Youth*. 1974. Pp. 257-262.

Audrey Craven, 1897

    Boll, Theophilus E. M. *Miss May Sinclair*. 1973. Pp. 164-168.

The Combined Maze, 1913

    Boll, Theophilus E. M. *Miss May Sinclair*. 1973. Pp. 222-225.

The Creators, 1910

    Boll, Theophilus E. M. *Miss May Sinclair*. 1973. Pp. 199-208.

A Cure of Souls, 1924

    Boll, Theophilus E. M. *Miss May Sinclair*. 1973. Pp. 278-281.

The Divine Fire, 1904

    Boll, Theophilus E. M. *Miss May Sinclair*. 1973. Pp. 177-190.

Far End, 1926

    Boll, Theophilus E. M. *Miss May Sinclair*. 1973. Pp. 290-293.

The Flaw in the Crystal, 1912

    Boll, Theophilus E. M. *Miss May Sinclair*. 1973. Pp. 220-222.

The Helpmate, 1907

    Boll, Theophilus E. M. *Miss May Sinclair*. 1973. Pp. 190-195.

History of Anthony Waring, 1927

    Boll, Theophilus E. M. *Miss May Sinclair*. 1973. Pp. 297-300.

Kitty Tailleur, 1908

    Boll, Theophilus E. M. *Miss May Sinclair*. 1973. Pp. 197-199.

Life and Death of Harriett Frean, 1922

> Boll, Theophilus E. M. *Miss May Sinclair*. 1973. Pp. 273-276.

Mary Olivier, 1919

> Boll, Theophilus E. M. *Miss May Sinclair*. 1973. Pp. 239-245.
> Buckley, Jerome Hamilton. *Season of Youth*. 1974. Pp. 255-259.

Mr. and Mrs. Nevill Tyson, 1898

> Boll, Theophilus E. M. *Miss May Sinclair*. 1973. Pp. 169-172.

Mr. Waddington of Wyck, 1921

> Boll, Theophilus E. M. *Miss May Sinclair*. 1973. Pp. 270-273.

The Rector of Wyck, 1925

> Boll, Theophilus E. M. *Miss May Sinclair*. 1973. Pp. 286-290.

The Romantic, 1920

> Boll, Theophilus E. M. *Miss May Sinclair*. 1973. Pp. 245-248.

Tasker Jevons, 1916

> Boll, Theophilus E. M. *Miss May Sinclair*. 1973. Pp. 229-234.

The Three Sisters, 1914

> Boll, Theophilus E. M. *Miss May Sinclair*. 1973. Pp. 225-229.

The Tree of Heaven, 1917

> Boll, Theophilus E. M. *Miss May Sinclair*. 1973. Pp. 234-239.

OSBERT SITWELL

The Man Who Lost Himself, 1929

> Keppler, C. F. *The Literature of the Second Self*. 1972. Pp. 177-181.

CHARLOTTE SMITH

The Banished Man, 1794

> Vooys, Sijna de. *The Psychological Element*. 1966. Pp. 20-23.

The Old Manor House, 1793

> Breitinger, Eckhard. *Der Tod im englischen Roman*. 1971. Pp. 134-136.

TOBIAS SMOLLETT

The History and Adventures of an Atom, 1769

> Warner, John M. "Smollett's Development as a Novelist." *Novel*, 5 (1972), 157-158.

Ferdinand Count Fathom, 1753

Boucé, Paul-Gabriel. *Les Romans de Smollett.* 1971. Pp. 200-225.
Brooks, Douglas. *Number and Pattern.* 1973. Pp. 135-141.
Cozza, Andrea. *Tobias Smollett.* 1970. Pp. 161-174.
Giddings, Robert. *The Tradition of Smollett.* 1967. Pp. 118-126.
Preston, Thomas R. "Disenchanting the Man of Feeling: Smollett's *Ferdinand Count Fathom*," in Larry S. Champion, ed., *Quick Springs of Sense.* 1974. Pp. 223-238.
Treadwell, T. O. "The Two Worlds of *Ferdinand Count Fathom*," in G. S. Rousseau and P.-G. Boucé, eds., *Tobias Smollett.* 1971. Pp. 131-153.
Warner, John M. "Smollett's Development as a Novelist." *Novel*, 5 (1972), 155-156.

Humphry Clinker, 1771

Bertrand, Claude-Jean. "Humphry Clinker, a 'So-Called Methodist.' " *Bulletin de la Faculté des Lettres de Strasbourg*, 47 (1969), 189-202.
Boucé, Paul-Gabriel. *Les Romans de Smollett.* 1971. Pp. 243-298, 381-389.
Brooks, Douglas. *Number and Pattern.* 1973. Pp. 144-153.
Copeland, Edward. "*Humphry Clinker:* A Comic Pastoral Poem in Prose?" *Texas Studies in Literature and Language*, 16 (1974), 493-501.
Cozza, Andrea. *Tobias Smollett.* 1970. Pp. 253-288.
Donovan, Robert Alan. *The Shaping Vision.* 1966. Pp. 118-139.
Folkenflik, Robert. "Self and Society: Comic Union in *Humphry Clinker*." *Philological Quarterly*, 53 (1974), 195-204.
Franke, Wolfgang. "Smollett's *Humphry Clinker* as a 'Party Novel.' " *Studies in Scottish Literature*, 9 (1971-1972), 97-106.
Gassman, Byron. "The Economy of *Humphry Clinker*," in G. S. Rousseau and P.-G. Boucé, eds., *Tobias Smollett.* 1971. Pp. 155-168.
Gassman, Byron. "*Humphry Clinker* and the Two Kingdoms of George III." *Criticism*, 16 (1974), 95-108.
Giddings, Robert. *The Tradition of Smollett.* 1967. Pp. 140-150.
Göller, Karl Heinz. *"Romance" und "novel."* 1972. Pp. 96-100.
Iser, Wolfgang. *The Implied Reader.* 1974. Pp. 57-80.
Kronenberger, Louis, W. G. Rogers, and George D. Crothers. "*Humphry Clinker*," in George D. Crothers, ed., *Invitation to Learning.* 1966. Pp. 45-52.
Pannill, Linda. "Some Patterns of Imagery in *Humphry Clinker*." *Thoth*, 13 (1973), 37-43.
Schlüter, Kurt. "Smollett: The Expedition of *Humphry Clinker*," in Franz K. Stanzel, ed., *Der englische Roman.* 1969. Vol. I, 270-311.
Siebert, Donald T., Jr. "The Role of the Senses in *Humphry Clinker*." *Studies in the Novel*, 6 (1974), 17-26.
Staeck, Wolfgang. " 'Novelty' als Gestaltungsprinzip bei Smollett:

Ein Beitrag zur Interpretation seiner Sonderlingsfiguren." *German-isch-Romanische Monatsschrift*, 24 (1974), 76-86.
Warner, John M. "The Interpolated Narratives in the Fiction of Fielding and Smollett: An Epistemological View." *Studies in the Novel*, 5 (1973), 279-280.
Warner, John M. "Smollett's Development as a Novelist." *Novel*, 5 (1972), 158-161.

Peregrine Pickle, 1751

Boucé, Paul-Gabriel. *Les Romans de Smollett*. 1971. Pp. 177-193.
Brooks, Douglas. *Number and Pattern*. 1973. Pp. 128-135.
Cozza, Andrea. *Tobias Smollett*. 1970. Pp. 129-159.
Giddings, Robert. *The Tradition of Smollett*. 1967. Pp. 97-118.
Paulson, Ronald. "The Pilgrimage and the Family: Structures in the Novels of Fielding and Smollett," in G. S. Rousseau and P.-G. Boucé, eds., *Tobias Smollett*. 1971. Pp. 57-78.
Rousseau, G. S. "Pineapples, Pregnancy, Pica, and *Peregrine Pickle*," in G. S. Rousseau and P.-G. Boucé, eds., *Tobias Smollett*. 1971. Pp. 79-109.
Spacks, Patricia Meyer. "Early Fiction and the Frightened Male." *Novel*, 8 (1974), 7-8.
Stevick, Philip. "Smollett's Picaresque Games," in G. S. Rousseau and P.-G. Boucé, eds., *Tobias Smollett*. 1971. Pp. 111-130.
Warner, John M. "The Interpolated Narratives in the Fiction of Fielding and Smollett: An Epistemological View." *Studies in the Novel*, 5 (1973), 276-279.
Warner, John M. "Smollett's Development as a Novelist." *Novel*, 5 (1972), 152-155.

Roderick Random, 1748

Boucé, Paul-Gabriel. *Les Romans de Smollett*. 1971. Pp. 158-177.
Brooks, Douglas. *Number and Pattern*. 1973. Pp. 123-127.
Cozza, Andrea. *Tobias Smollett*. 1970. Pp. 55-95.
Fredman, Alice Green. "The Picaresque in Decline: Smollett's First Novel," in John H. Middendorf, ed., *English Writers*. 1971. Pp. 189-207.
Giddings, Robert. *The Tradition of Smollett*. 1967. Pp. 83-97.
Göller, Karl Heinz. *"Romance" und "novel."* 1972. Pp. 94-96.
Greiner, Walter F. *Studien zur Entstehung der englischen Romantheorie*. 1969. Pp. 224-230.
Highsmith, James Milton. "Smollett's Nancy Williams: A Mirror for Maggie." *English Miscellany*, 23 (1972), 113-123.
Stevick, Philip. "Smollett's Picaresque Games," in G. S. Rousseau and P.-G. Boucé, eds., *Tobias Smollett*. 1971. Pp. 111-130.
Warner, John M. "Smollett's Development as a Novelist." *Novel*, 5 (1972), 150-152.
Wolff, Erwin. *Der englische Roman*. 1968. Pp. 105-114.

Sir Lancelot Greaves, 1762

>Boucé, Paul-Gabriel. *Les Romans de Smollett*. 1971. Pp. 225-239.
>Cozza, Andrea. *Tobias Smollett*. 1970. Pp. 174-182.
>Giddings, Robert. *The Tradition of Smollett*. 1967. Pp. 127-139.
>Warner, John M. "Smollett's Development as a Novelist." *Novel*, 5
>(1972), 156-157.

C. P. SNOW

The Affair, 1960

>Graves, Nora C. *The Two Culture Theory*. 1971. Pp. 51-54.
>Karl, Frederick R. *C. P. Snow*. 1963. Pp. 136-153.

The Conscience of the Rich, 1958

>Graves, Nora C. *The Two Culture Theory*. 1971. Pp. 32-34.
>Karl, Frederick R. *C. P. Snow*. 1963. Pp. 117-135.

Corridors of Power, 1964

>Graves, Nora C. *The Two Culture Theory*. 1971. Pp. 54-57.
>Pérez Minik, Domingo. *Introducción a la novela inglesa actual*. 1968.
>Pp. 165-172.

Death Under Sail, 1932

>Graves, Nora C. *The Two Culture Theory*. 1971. Pp. 13-15.

Homecomings, 1956

>Graves, Nora C. *The Two Culture Theory*. 1971. Pp. 41-43.
>Karl, Frederick R. *C. P. Snow*. 1963. Pp. 101-116.

Last Things, 1970

>Bonnet, Jacky. "*Last Things*: Snow's Refusal of Man's Tragic Indi-
>vidual Condition." *Langues Modernes*, 66 (1972), 302-304.
>Bradbury, Malcolm. *Possibilities*. 1973. Pp. 203-210.
>Graves, Nora C. *The Two Culture Theory*. 1971. Pp. 63-66.

The Light and the Dark, 1947

>Graves, Nora C. *The Two Culture Theory*. 1971. Pp. 34-37.
>Karl, Frederick R. *C. P. Snow*. 1963. Pp. 52-66.

The Masters, 1951

>Graves, Nora C. *The Two Culture Theory*. 1971. Pp. 38-40.
>Karl, Frederick R. *C. P. Snow*. 1963. Pp. 67-82.

New Lives for Old, 1933

>Graves, Nora C. *The Two Culture Theory*. 1971. Pp. 15-19.

The New Men, 1954

Graves, Nora C. *The Two Culture Theory*. 1971. Pp. 45-51.
Karl, Frederick R. *C. P. Snow*. 1963. Pp. 83-100.
Seehase, Georg. "Humanistische Möglichkeiten im kritischen Real-
ismus von Charles Percy Snow." *Zeitschrift für Anglistik und
Amerikanistik*, 20 (1972), 127-128.

The Search, 1934

Graves, Nora C. *The Two Culture Theory*. 1971. Pp. 19-24.

The Sleep of Reason, 1968

Graves, Nora C. *The Two Culture Theory*. 1971. Pp. 57-63.

Strangers and Brothers, 1940-1970

Ashton, Thomas L. "Realism and the Chronicle: C. P. Snow's *Cinéma
Vérité.*" *South Atlantic Quarterly*, 72 (1973), 516-527.
Graves, Nora C. *The Two Culture Theory*. 1971. Pp. 30-32.
Karl, Frederick R. *C. P. Snow*. 1963. Pp. 28-43.
Morris, Robert K. *Continuance and Change*. 1972. Pp. 93-122.
Schrey, Helmut. *Didaktik des zeitgenössischen englischen Romans*.
1970. Pp. 81-90.
Thale, Jerome. *C. P. Snow*. 1964. Pp. 43-115.

Time of Hope, 1949

Graves, Nora C. *The Two Culture Theory*. 1971. Pp. 26-29.
Karl, Frederick R. *C. P. Snow*. 1963. Pp. 41-51.

SOMERVILLE AND ROSS

The Big House of Inver, 1925

Cronin, John. *Somerville and Ross*. 1972. Pp. 89-91.
Fehlmann, Guy. *Somerville et Ross*. 1970. Pp. 173-185, 275-281.

Dan Russel the Fox, 1911

Cronin, John. *Somerville and Ross*. 1972. Pp. 69-72.

An Enthusiast, 1921

Fehlmann, Guy. *Somerville et Ross*. 1970. Pp. 285-292.

An Irish Cousin, 1889

Fehlmann, Guy. *Somerville et Ross*. 1970. Pp. 200-204.

Mount Music, 1919

Cronin, John. *Somerville and Ross*. 1972. Pp. 78-84.
Fehlmann, Guy. *Somerville et Ross*. 1970. Pp. 167-171, 341-348.

Naboth's Vineyard, 1891

> Fehlmann, Guy. *Somerville et Ross*. 1970. Pp. 331-335.

The Real Charlotte, 1894

> Cronin, John. *Somerville and Ross*. 1972. Pp. 39-46.
> Fehlmann, Guy. *Somerville et Ross*. 1970. Pp. 299-304, 312-329.

The Silver Fox, 1898

> Cronin, John. *Somerville and Ross*. 1972. Pp. 46-49.

MURIEL SPARK

The Bachelors, 1960

> Kemp, Peter. *Muriel Spark*. 1974. Pp. 59-70.
> Stubbs, Patricia. *Muriel Spark*. 1973. Pp. 15-17.

The Ballad of Peckham Rye, 1960

> Kemp, Peter. *Muriel Spark*. 1974. Pp. 48-59.
> Stubbs, Patricia. *Muriel Spark*. 1973. Pp. 12-15.

The Comforters, 1957

> Dobie, Ann B., and Carl Wooton. "Spark and Waugh: Similarities by Coincidence." *Midwest Quarterly*, 13 (1972), 423-434.
> Kemp, Peter. *Muriel Spark*. 1974. Pp. 17-29.
> Lodge, David. *The Novelist at the Crossroads*. 1971. Pp. 121-122.
> Stubbs, Patricia. *Muriel Spark*. 1973. Pp. 5-6.

The Driver's Seat, 1970

> Bradbury, Malcolm. "Muriel Spark's Fingernails." *Critical Quarterly*, 14 (1972), 247-250.
> Bradbury, Malcolm. *Possibilities*. 1973. Pp. 252-255.
> Kemp, Peter. *Muriel Spark*. 1974. Pp. 122-130.
> Richmond, Velma B. "The Darkening Vision of Muriel Spark." *Critique* (Atlanta), 15:1 (1973), 76-80.

The Girls of Slender Means, 1963

> Kemp, Peter. *Muriel Spark*. 1974. Pp. 84-96.
> Stubbs, Patricia. *Muriel Spark*. 1973. Pp. 24-25.

The Hothouse by the East River, 1973

> Kemp, Peter. *Muriel Spark*. 1974. Pp. 141-158.

The Mandelbaum Gate, 1965

> Kemp, Peter. *Muriel Spark*. 1974. Pp. 24-26, 97-112.
> Stubbs, Patricia. *Muriel Spark*. 1973. Pp. 25-32.

Sudrann, Jean. "Hearth and Horizon: Changing Concepts of the 'Domestic' Life of the Heroine." *Massachusetts Review*, 14 (1973), 250-255.

Swinden, Patrick. *Unofficial Selves*. 1973. Pp. 225-230.

Memento Mori, 1959

Kemp, Peter. *Muriel Spark*. 1974. Pp. 38-48.
Stubbs, Patricia. *Muriel Spark*. 1973. Pp. 7-12.

Not to Disturb, 1971

Bradbury, Malcolm. "Muriel Spark's Fingernails." *Critical Quarterly*, 14 (1972), 241-250.
Kemp, Peter. *Muriel Spark*. 1974. Pp. 130-140.
Richmond, Velma B. "The Darkening Vision of Muriel Spark." *Critique* (Atlanta), 15:1 (1973), 80-85.

The Prime of Miss Jean Brodie, 1961

Kemp, Peter. *Muriel Spark*. 1974. Pp. 71-84.
Laffin, Garry S. "Muriel Spark's Portrait of the Artist as a Young Girl." *Renascence*, 24 (1972), 213-223.
Lodge, David. *The Novelist at the Crossroads*. 1971. Pp. 123-144.
Stubbs, Patricia. *Muriel Spark*. 1973. Pp. 17-24.

The Public Image, 1968

Bradbury, Malcolm. "Muriel Spark's Fingernails." *Critical Quarterly*, 14 (1972), 241-250.
Kemp, Peter. *Muriel Spark*. 1974. Pp. 115-122.
Richmond, Velma B. "The Darkening Vision of Muriel Spark." *Critique* (Atlanta), 15:1 (1973), 72-76.

Robinson, 1958

Kemp, Peter. *Muriel Spark*. 1974. Pp. 29-37.
Stubbs, Patricia. *Muriel Spark*. 1973. Pp. 6-7.

JAMES STEPHENS

Deirdre, 1923

McFate, Patricia Ann. "*Deirdre* and 'The Wooing of Becfola.'" *Papers in Language and Literature Supplement*, Fall 1972, pp. 165-171.

LAURENCE STERNE

A Sentimental Journey, 1768

Brissenden, R. F. *Virtue in Distress*. 1974. Pp. 218-242.
Gassenmeier, Michael. *Der Typus des "man of feeling."* 1972. Pp. 82-102.

Koppel, Gene. "Fulfillment Through Frustration: Some Aspects of Sterne's Art of the Incomplete in *A Sentimental Journey.*" *Studies in the Novel*, 2 (1970), 168-172.

Stonys, Juozas. "Psychological Analysis in Laurence Sterne's Works." *Literatura* (Vilnius), 12 (1969), 52-65.

White, F. Eugene. "Sterne's Quiet Journey of the Heart: Unphilosophic Projection of Enlightened Benevolence." *Enlightenment Essays*, 2 (1971), 103-110.

Wolff, Erwin. *Der englische Roman*. 1968. Pp. 100-103.

Tristram Shandy, 1760-1767

Alter, Robert. "Sterne and the Nostalgia for Reality." *Far-Western Forum*, 1 (1974), 1-21.

Anderson, Howard. "Answers to the Author of *Clarissa*: Theme and Narrative Technique in *Tom Jones* and *Tristram Shandy.*" *Philological Quarterly*, 51 (1972), 859-873.

Banerjee, Chinmoy. "*Tristram Shandy* and the Association of Ideas." *Texas Studies in Literature and Language*, 15 (1973), 693-706.

Battestin, Martin C. *The Providence of Wit*. 1974. Pp. 241-269.

Berger, Dieter A. "Das gezielte Missverständnis: Kommunikationsprobleme in Laurence Sternes *Tristram Shandy.*" *Poetica*, 5 (1972), 329-347.

Bradbury, Malcolm. *Possibilities*. 1973. Pp. 35-40.

Brady, Frank. "*Tristram Shandy*: Sexuality, Morality, and Sensibility." *Eighteenth-Century Studies*, 4 (1970), 41-56.

Brienza, Susan D. "Volume VII of *Tristram Shandy*: A Dance of Life." *University of Dayton Review*, 10 (Summer 1974), 59-62.

Brissenden, R. F. *Virtue in Distress*. 1974. Pp. 187-217.

Brooks, Douglas. *Number and Pattern*. 1973. Pp. 160-176.

Burton, Dolores M. "Intonation Patterns of Sermons in Seven Novels." *Language and Style*, 3 (1970), 208-210, 217-218.

Cash, Arthur. "Voices Sonorous and Cracked: Sterne's Pulpit Oratory," in Larry S. Champion, ed., *Quick Springs of Sense*. 1974. Pp. 197-208.

Columbus, Thomas M. "Tristram's Dance with Death: Volume VII of *Tristram Shandy.*" *University of Dayton Review*, 8 (Fall 1971), 3-15.

Columbus, Thomas M. "Postscriptum: 'A Dance *with* Death; A Dance *of* Life." *University of Dayton Review*, 10 (Summer 1974), 63.

Doherty, F. "Bayle and *Tristram Shandy*: 'Stage-Loads of Chymical Nostrums and Peripatetic Lumber.'" *Neophilologus*, 58 (1974), 339-348.

Donovan, Robert Alan. *The Shaping Vision*. 1966. Pp. 89-117.

Fabian, Bernhard. "Sterne: *Tristram Shandy*," in Franz K. Stanzel, ed., *Der englische Roman*. 1969. Vol. I, 232-269.

Gassenmeier, Michael. "Tristrams Onkel Toby: Ein 'Man of Feeling' aus ironischer Distanz." *Anglia*, 88 (1970), 509-518.

Gassenmeier, Michael. *Der Typus des "man of feeling."* 1972. Pp. 58-81, 168-175.

Golden, Morris. "Sterne's Journeys and Sallies." *Studies in Burke and His Time*, 16 (1974), 47-62.

Hauff, Jürgen, Albrecht Heller, Bernd Hüppauf, Lothar Köhn, and Klaus-Peter Philippi. *Methodendiskussion.* 1972. Pp. 134-136.

Hay, John A. "Rhetoric and Historiography: Tristram Shandy's First Nine Kalendar Months," in R. F. Brissenden, ed., *Studies in the Eighteenth Century.* 1973. Pp. 73-91.

Hilský, Martin. "A Note on the Style of *Tristram Shandy.*" *Prague Studies in English*, 14 (1971), 41-55.

Holtz, William V. *Image and Immortality.* 1970. Pp. 19-157.

Jones, Joseph R. "Two Notes on Sterne: Spanish Sources; the Hinde Tradition—Sterne's Debt to Cervantes and Fernández de Avellaneda." *Revue de Littérature Comparée*, 46 (1972), 437-444.

Kahler, Erich. *The Inward Turn of Narrative.* 1973. Pp. 178-199.

Lamb, Jonathan. " 'Uniting and Reconciling Every Thing': Book-Wit in *Tristram Shandy.*" *Southern Review* (Adelaide), 7 (1974), 236-245.

Lanham, Richard A. *"Tristram Shandy."* 1973. Pp. 19-167.

Madson, Peter. *Romanens Form.* 1973. Pp. 12-54.

Maskell, Duke. "Locke and Sterne, or Can Philosophy Influence Literature?" *Essays in Criticism*, 23 (1973), 22-39.

Mellown, Elgin W. "Narrative Technique in *Tristram Shandy.*" *Papers on Language and Literature*, 9 (1973), 263-270.

Meyer, Herman. *The Poetics of Quotation.* 1968. Pp. 72-93.

Michalopoulos, André, Harding Le May, and George D. Crothers. *"Tristram Shandy,"* in George D. Crothers, ed., *Invitation to Learning.* 1966. Pp. 54-60.

Miller, Norbert. *Der empfindsame Erzähler.* 1968. Pp. 258-278, 431-442.

New, Melvyn. "The Dunce Revisited: Colley Cibber and Tristram Shandy." *South Atlantic Quarterly*, 72 (1973), 547-559.

New, Melvyn. *Laurence Sterne.* 1970. Pp. 73-205.

New, Melvyn. "Laurence Sterne and Henry Baker's *The Microscope Made Easy.*" *Studies in English Literature, 1500-1900*, 10 (1970), 591-604.

Nuttall, A. D. *A Common Sky.* 1974. Pp. 45-91.

Otten, Kurt. *Der englische Roman.* 1971. Pp. 84-89.

Primeau, Ronald. " 'Betwixt Your Own and Your Reader's Conception': Limitations of Language in *Tristram Shandy.*" *CEA Critic*, 35 (May 1973), 20-21.

Rolle, Dietrich. *Fielding und Sterne.* 1963. Pp. 15-19, 31-41, 44-48, 73-82, 88-92, 99-105, 115-120, 125-130, 147-153, 169-171, 179-185.

Rubin, Louis D., Jr. "Don Quixote and Selected Progeny: Or, the Journey-man as Outsider." *Southern Review* (Baton Rouge), 10 (1974), 38-43.

Sallé, Jean-Claude. "A State of Warfare: Some Aspects of Time and Chance in *Tristram Shandy*," in Larry S. Champion, ed., *Quick Springs of Sense*. 1974. Pp. 211-220.

Segal, Ora. "On the Difficulties of Novel-Writing: A Reading of *Tristram Shandy*." *Hebrew University Studies in Literature*, 1 (1973), 132-158.

Seltzer, Alvin J. *Chaos in the Novel*. 1974. Pp. 29-51.

Spacks, Patricia Meyer. "Early Fiction and the Frightened Male." *Novel*, 8 (1974), 12-14.

Stanzel, Franz Karl. "*Tristram Shandy* und die Klima Theorie." *Germanisch-Romanische Monatsschrift*, 21 (1971), 16-28.

Stewart, Jack F. "Sterne's Absurd Comedy." *University of Windsor Review*, 5 (1970), 81-95.

Stonys, Juozas. "Psychological Analysis in Laurence Sterne's Works." *Literatura* (Vilnius), 12 (1969), 51-68.

Wolff, Erwin. *Der englische Roman*. 1968. Pp. 83-99.

ROBERT LOUIS STEVENSON

The Black Arrow, 1888

Eigner, Edwin M. *Robert Louis Stevenson*. 1966. Pp. 66-76.
Saposnik, Irving S. *Robert Louis Stevenson*. 1974. Pp. 109-111.

Catriona, 1893

Saposnik, Irving S. *Robert Louis Stevenson*. 1974. Pp. 116-117.

The Ebb-Tide, 1894

Eigner, Edwin M. *Robert Louis Stevenson*. 1966. Pp. 214-218.
Saposnik, Irving S. *Robert Louis Stevenson*. 1974. Pp. 131-134.

Kidnapped, 1886

Dölvers, Horst. *Der Erzähler Robert Louis Stevenson*. 1969. Pp. 137-141.
Eigner, Edwin M. *Robert Louis Stevenson*. 1966. Pp. 80-83.
Saposnik, Irving S. *Robert Louis Stevenson*. 1974. Pp. 111-116.

The Master of Ballantrae, 1889

Dölvers, Horst. *Der Erzähler Robert Louis Stevenson*. 1969. Pp. 155-170.
Eigner, Edwin M. *Robert Louis Stevenson*. 1966. Pp. 171-193.
Saposnik, Irving S. *Robert Louis Stevenson*. 1974. Pp. 119-125.

Prince Otto, 1885

Dölvers, Horst. *Der Erzähler Robert Louis Stevenson*. 1969. Pp. 97-105.
Saposnik, Irving S. *Robert Louis Stevenson*. 1974. Pp. 117-119.

Treasure Island, 1883

　　Capey, A. C. "*Treasure Island* and the Young Reader." *Use of English*,
　　25 (1974), 228-238.
　　Dölvers, Horst. *Der Erzähler Robert Louis Stevenson*. 1969. Pp. 122-
　　123.
　　Robson, W. W. "The Sea Cook: A Study in the Art of Robert Louis
　　Stevenson," in B. S. Benedikz, ed., *On the Novel*. 1971. Pp. 57-74.
　　Saposnik, Irving S. *Robert Louis Stevenson*. 1974. Pp. 105-109.
　　Ward, Hayden W. " 'The Pleasure of Your Heart': *Treasure Island*
　　and the Appeal of Boys' Adventure Fiction." *Studies in the Novel*,
　　6 (1974), 304-317.

Weir of Hermiston, 1896

　　Eigner, Edwin M. *Robert Louis Stevenson*. 1966. Pp. 218-228.
　　Hannah, Barbara. *Striving Towards Wholeness*. 1971. Pp. 56-61,
　　64-71.
　　Saposnik, Irving S. *Robert Louis Stevenson*. 1974. Pp. 126-128.

The Wrecker, 1892

　　Eigner, Edwin M. *Robert Louis Stevenson*. 1966. Pp. 106-110.
　　Saposnik, Irving S. *Robert Louis Stevenson*. 1974. Pp. 129-131.

The Wrong Box, 1889

　　Saposnik, Irving S. *Robert Louis Stevenson*. 1974. Pp. 117-119.

BRAM STOKER

Dracula, 1897

　　Bentley, C. F. "The Monster in the Bedroom: Sexual Symbolism in
　　Bram Stoker's *Dracula*." *Literature and Psychology*, 22 (1972),
　　27-33.
　　Bierman, Joseph S. "*Dracula*: Prolonged Childhood Illness and the
　　Oral Triad." *American Imago*, 29 (1972), 186-198.
　　Gattegno, Jean. "Folie, croyance et fantastique dans *Dracula*."
　　Littérature, 8 (1972), 72-83.
　　MacGillivray, Royce. "*Dracula*: Bram Stoker's Spoiled Masterpiece."
　　Queen's Quarterly, 79 (1972), 518-527.
　　Stein, Gérard. "*Dracula* ou la circulation du *sans*." *Littérature*, 8
　　(1972), 84-99.

ELIZABETH STONE

William Langshaw, 1842

　　Melada, Ivan. *The Captain of Industry*. 1970. Pp. 115-117.

DAVID STOREY

This Sporting Life, 1960

   Gray, Nigel. *The Silent Majority*. 1973. Pp. 135-159.

FRANCIS STUART

Black List, Section H, 1971

   Natterstad, J. H. "Francis Stuart: At the Edge of Recognition." *Eire-Ireland*, 9:3 (1974), 82-85.

The Coloured Dome, 1933

   Natterstad, J. H. "Francis Stuart: At the Edge of Recognition." *Eire-Ireland*, 9:3 (1974), 72-74.

Pigeon Irish, 1932

   Natterstad, J. H. "Francis Stuart: At the Edge of Recognition." *Eire-Ireland*, 9:3 (1974), 72-74.

Pillar of Cloud, 1948

   Natterstad, J. H. "Francis Stuart: At the Edge of Recognition." *Eire-Ireland*, 9:3 (1974), 77-78.

Redemption, 1949

   Natterstad, J. H. "Francis Stuart: At the Edge of Recognition." *Eire-Ireland*, 9:3 (1974), 78-81.

JONATHAN SWIFT

Gulliver's Travels, 1726

   Beauchamp, Gorman. "Gulliver's Return to the Cave: Plato's *Republic* and Book IV of *Gulliver's Travels*." *Michigan Academician*, 7 (1974), 201-209.
   Bony, Alain. "Call Me Gulliver." *Poétique*, 14 (1973), 197-209.
   Bryan, Margaret B. "Swift's Use of the Looking-Glass in *Gulliver's Travels*." *Connecticut Review*, 8 (1974), 90-94.
   Byrd, Max. *Visits to Bedlam*. 1974. Pp. 83-87.
   Carnochan, W. B. *Lemuel Gulliver's Mirror for Man*. 1968. Pp. 1-181.
   Clayborough, Arthur. *The Grotesque in English Literature*. 1965. Pp. 112-157.
   Clifford, James L. "Gulliver's Fourth Voyage: 'Hard' and 'Soft' Schools of Interpretation," in Larry S. Champion, ed., *Quick Springs of Sense*. 1974. Pp. 33-47.
   Cohan, Steven M. "Gulliver's Fiction." *Studies in the Novel*, 6 (1974), 7-16.

Colwell, C. Carter. *The Tradition of British Literature*. 1971. Pp. 218-224, 232-236.

Davis, Herbert. "Swift's Use of Irony," in Earl Miner, ed., *Stuart and Georgian Moments*. 1972. Pp. 231-238.

Donoghue, Denis. *Jonathan Swift*. 1969. Pp. 14-16, 19-21, 69-74, 160-187.

Dudley, Edward, and Maximillian E. Novak, eds., *The Wild Man Within*. 1972. Pp. 211-216.

Ehrenpreis, Irvin. *Literary Meaning and Augustan Values*. 1974. Pp. 94-109.

Elliott, Robert C. *The Shape of Utopia*. 1970. Pp. 52-67.

Fabian, Bernhard. "*Gulliver's Travels* als Satire." *Poetica*, 3 (1970), 426-434.

Fitzgerald, Robert P. "The Structure of *Gulliver's Travels*." *Studies in Philology*, 71 (1974), 247-263.

Golden, Morris. *The Self Observed*. 1972. Pp. 49-52.

Greene, Donald. "The Education of Lemuel Gulliver," in Peter Hughes and David Williams, eds., *The Varied Pattern*. 1971. Pp. 3-20.

Grubb, Daniel S. "Another Gulliver?" *Studies in the Humanities*, 4 (1974), 3-9.

Harlow, Benjamin C. "Houyhnhnmland: A Utopian Satire." *McNeese Review*, 13 (1962), 44-58.

Hodgart, Matthew. *Satire*. 1969. Pp. 67-71.

Jones, Myrddin. "Swift, Harrington and Corruption in England." *Philological Quarterly*, 53 (1974), 59-70.

Kahler, Erich. *The Inward Turn of Narrative*. 1973. Pp. 116-131.

Kallich, Martin. *The Other End of the Egg*. 1970. Pp. 1-94.

Kern, Edith. "Black Humor: The Pockets of Lemuel Gulliver and Samuel Beckett," in Melvin J. Friedman, ed., *Samuel Beckett Now*. 1970. Pp. 90-95.

Kettle, Arnold. "Einführung in die englische Romanliteratur," in Viktor Žmegač, ed., *Marxistische Literaturkritik*. 1970. Pp. 227-232.

Knowles, A. S., Jr. "Defoe, Swift, and Fielding: Notes on the Retirement Theme," in Larry S. Champion, ed., *Quick Springs of Sense*. 1974. Pp. 123-126.

Lawlis, Merritt. "Swift's Use of Narrative: The Third Chapter of the Voyage to Lilliput." *Journal of English and Germanic Philology*, 72 (1973), 1-16.

Lee, Jae Num. *Swift and Scatological Satire*. 1971. Pp. 98-120.

Maresca, Thomas E. *Epic to Novel*. 1974. Pp. 167-177.

Morris, John N. "Wishes as Horses: A Word for the Houyhnhnms." *Yale Review*, 62 (1973), 355-371.

Otten, Kurt. *Der englische Roman*. 1971. Pp. 58-61.

Patterson, Anne. "Swift's Irony and Cartesian Man." *Midwest Quarterly*, 15 (1974), 338-351.

Philmus, Robert M. "The Language of Utopia." *Studies in the Literary Imagination*, 6 (Fall 1973), 66-74.

Piper, William Bowman. "The Sense of *Gulliver's Travels.*" *Rice University Studies*, 61 (Winter 1975), 75-106.

Probyn, Clive T. "Gulliver and the Relativity of Things: A Commentary on Method and Mode, with a Note on Smollett." *Renaissance and Modern Studies*, 18 (1974), 63-74.

Probyn, Clive T. "Man, Horse and Drill: Temple's *Essay on Popular Discontents* and Gulliver's Fourth Voyage." *English Studies*, 55 (1974), 358-360.

Probyn, Clive T. "Swift and Linguistics: The Context Behind Lagado and Around the Fourth Voyage." *Neophilologus*, 58 (1974), 425-437.

Pullen, Charles H. "Gulliver: Student of Nature." *Dalhousie Review*, 51 (1971), 77-89.

Pyle, Fitzroy. "Yahoo: Swift and the Asses." *Ariel*, 3:2 (1972), 64-69.

Rawson, C. J. *Gulliver and the Gentle Reader.* 1973. Pp. 1-32.

Rexroth, Kenneth. *The Elastic Retort.* 1973. Pp. 55-58.

Rogers, J. P. W. "Swift, Walpole, and the Rope-Dancers." *Papers on Language and Literature*, 8 (1972), 159-171.

Rogers, Pat. "Gulliver and the Engineers." *Modern Language Review*, 70 (1975), 260-270.

Ross, Angus. "The Social Circumstances of Several Remote Nations of the World," in Brian Vickers, ed., *The World of Jonathan Swift.* 1968. Pp. 220-232.

Rovere, Richard, Louis Kronenberger, and Lyman Bryson. "*Gulliver's Travels,*" in George D. Crothers, ed., *Invitation to Learning.* 1966. Pp. 16-25.

Ryley, Robert M. "Gulliver, Flimnap's Wife, and the Critics." *Studies in the Literary Imagination*, 5 (Fall 1972), 53-63.

Schachterle, Lance. "The First Key to *Gulliver's Travels.*" *Revue des Langues Vivantes*, 38 (1972), 37-45.

Seeber, Hans Ulrich. *Wandlungen der Form.* 1970. Pp. 78-98.

Steele, Peter. "Terminal Days Among the Houyhnhnms." *Southern Review* (Adelaide), 4 (1971), 227-236.

Swaim, Kathleen M. *A Reading of "Gulliver's Travels."* 1972.

Tuveson, Ernest. "Swift: The View from Within the Satire," in H. James Jensen and Malvin R. Zirker, eds., *The Satirist's Art.* 1972. Pp. 70-85.

Uphaus, Robert W. "*Gulliver's Travels, A Modest Proposal,* and the Problematical Nature of Meaning." *Papers on Language and Literature*, 10 (1974), 268-276.

Vickers, Brian. "The Satiric Structure of *Gulliver's Travels* and More's *Utopia,*" in Brian Vickers, ed., *The World of Jonathan Swift.* 1968. Pp. 240-257.

Ward, David. *Jonathan Swift.* 1973. Pp. 121-183.

Wilding, Michael. "The Politics of *Gulliver's Travels,*" in R. F. Brissenden, ed., *Studies in the Eighteenth Century.* 1973. Pp. 303-322.

Zimmerman, Everett. "Gulliver the Preacher." *Publications of the*

Modern Language Association, 89 (1974), 1024-1032.
Zimmerman, Lester F. "Lemuel Gulliver," in David P. French, ed., *Jonathan Swift*. 1967. Pp. 61-73.

ALGERNON CHARLES SWINBURNE

Lesbia Brandon, 1952

Cassidy, John A. *Algernon C. Swinburne*. 1964. Pp. 106-112.
Fletcher, Ian. *Swinburne*. 1973. Pp. 43-44.
Fuller, Jean Overton. *Swinburne*. 1968. Pp. 125-142, 167-171.

Love's Cross Currents, 1901

Cassidy, John A. *Algernon C. Swinburne*. 1964. Pp. 106-112.
Fletcher, Ian. *Swinburne*. 1973. Pp. 41-43.
Fuller, Jean Overton. *Swinburne*. 1968. Pp. 71-79.

PHILIP MEADOWS TAYLOR

Tara, 1863

Viswanathan, K. *India in English Fiction*. 1971. Pp. 31-49.

WILLIAM MAKEPEACE THACKERAY

Catherine, 1840

Cabot, Frederick C. "The Two Voices in Thackeray's *Catherine*." *Nineteenth-Century Fiction*, 28 (1974), 404-416.
Hollingsworth, Keith. *The Newgate Novel*. 1963. Pp. 148-159.
Rawlins, Jack P. *Thackeray's Novels*. 1974. Pp. 71-83.
Wheatley, James H. *Patterns in Thackeray's Fiction*. 1969. Pp. 41-44.

Denis Duval, 1864

Sutherland, J. A. *Thackeray at Work*. 1974. Pp. 110-132.

Henry Esmond, 1852

Bledsoe, Robert. "*Sibi Constet*: The Goddess of Castlewood and the Goddess of Walcote." *Studies in the Novel*, 5 (1973), 211-219.
Donovan, Robert Alan. *The Shaping Vision*. 1966. Pp. 193-205.
Hagan, John. "'Bankruptcy of His Heart': The Unfulfilled Life of Henry Esmond." *Nineteenth-Century Fiction*, 27 (1972), 293-316.
Harden, Edgar F. "Esmond and the Search for Self." *Yearbook of English Studies*, 3 (1973), 181-195.
Hardy, Barbara. *The Exposure of Luxury*. 1972. Pp. 45-49, 83-86, 96-102, 114-117, 178-188.
Iser, Wolfgang. *The Implied Reader*. 1974. Pp. 123-135.
McMaster, Juliet. *Thackeray*. 1971. Pp. 87-125, 204-207.
Rawlins, Jack P. *Thackeray's Novels*. 1974. Pp. 187-233.

Rogers, Katharine M. "The Pressure of Convention on Thackeray's Women." *Modern Language Review*, 67 (1972), 259-260.

Slerca, Lea. *"Henry Esmond e Le Confessioni di un Italiano,"* in Claudio Gorlier, ed., *Studi e ricerche.* 1971. Pp. 217-232.

Sutherland, J. A. *Thackeray at Work.* 1974. Pp. 56-73.

Sutherland, John. "Thackeray's Patchwork: A Note on the Composition of the Eleventh Chapter of *Henry Esmond." Yearbook of English Studies,* 1 (1971), 141-148.

Wheatley, James H. *Patterns in Thackeray's Fiction.* 1969. Pp. 106-109.

Williams, Ioan. *The Realist Novel.* 1974. Pp. 156-168.

Lovel the Widower, 1860

Rogers, Katharine M. "The Pressure of Convention on Thackeray's Women." *Modern Language Review*, 67 (1972), 261.

The Luck of Barry Lyndon, 1844

McMaster, Juliet. *Thackeray.* 1971. Pp. 187-191.

Wheatley, James H. *Patterns in Thackeray's Fiction.* 1969. Pp. 49-53.

The Newcomes, 1854-1855

Hardy, Barbara. *The Exposure of Luxury.* 1972. Pp. 146-155, 168-171.

McMaster, Juliet. *Thackeray.* 1971. Pp. 127-176, 207-211.

McMaster, R. D. "The Pygmalion Motif in *The Newcomes." Nineteenth-Century Fiction,* 29 (1974), 22-39.

Phillipps, K. C. "Thackeray's Proper Names." *Neuphilologische Mitteilungen,* 75 (1974), 446-451.

Rawlins, Jack P. *Thackeray's Novels.* 1974. Pp. 91-111.

Rogers, Katharine M. "The Pressure of Convention on Thackeray's Women." *Modern Language Review*, 67 (1972), 260.

Sutherland, J. A. *Thackeray at Work.* 1974. Pp. 74-85.

Wheatley, James H. *Patterns in Thackeray's Fiction.* 1969. Pp. 114-119.

Pendennis, 1849-1850

Buckley, Jerome Hamilton. *Season of Youth.* 1974. Pp. 28-30.

Harden, Edgar F. "Theatricality in *Pendennis." Ariel,* 4:4 (1973), 74-94.

Hardy, Barbara. *The Exposure of Luxury.* 1972. Pp. 37-45, 86-94, 132-146, 171-178.

McMaster, Juliet. *Thackeray.* 1971. Pp. 51-86, 195-203.

Phillipps, K. C. "Thackeray's Proper Names." *Neuphilologische Mitteilungen,* 75 (1974), 445-450.

Rogers, Katharine M. "The Pressure of Convention on Thackeray's Women." *Modern Language Review*, 67 (1972), 259.

Sutherland, J. A. *Thackeray at Work.* 1974. Pp. 45-55.

Wheatley, James H. *Patterns in Thackeray's Fiction.* 1969. Pp. 135-145.

Wildman, John Hazard. "Thackeray's Wickedest Woman," in Thomas

Austin Kirby and William John Olive, eds., *Essays in Honor of Esmond Linworth Marilla*. 1970. Pp. 253-258.

Philip, 1862

McMaster, Juliet. *Thackeray*. 1971. Pp. 215-220.
Rawlins, Jack P. *Thackeray's Novels*. 1974. Pp. 187-233.
Rogers, Katharine M. "The Pressure of Convention on Thackeray's Women." *Modern Language Review*, 67 (1972), 261-262.

Rebecca and Rowena, 1850

Rogers, Katharine M. "The Pressure of Convention on Thackeray's Women." *Modern Language Review*, 67 (1972), 257.

Vanity Fair, 1848

Dibon, Anne-Marie. "Form and Value in the French and English 19th-Century Novel." *Modern Language Notes*, 87 (1972), 894-898.
Fairchild, Hoxie, Virgilia Peterson, and Lyman Bryson. "*Vanity Fair*," in George D. Crothers, ed., *Invitation to Learning*. 1966. Pp. 126-134.
Halperin, John. *Egoism and Self-Discovery*. 1974. Pp. 33-45.
Hardy, Barbara. *The Exposure of Luxury*. 1972. Pp. 23-37, 50-67, 71-79, 102-114, 126-131, 162-168.
Higdon, David Leon. "Pipkins and Kettles in *Vanity Fair*." *Victorian Newsletter*, No. 45 (1974), 25-26.
Hollingsworth, Keith. *The Newgate Novel*. 1963. Pp. 204-215.
Iser, Wolfgang. *The Implied Reader*. 1974. Pp. 101-120.
Krump, Jacqueline. "No Better Satires: Thackeray's Use of Letters in *Vanity Fair*." *Research Studies*, 39 (1971), 284-296.
Lemon, Lee T. "The Hostile Universe: A Developing Pattern in Nineteenth-Century Fiction," in George Goodin, ed., *The English Novel*. 1972. Pp. 8-10.
Lougy, Robert E. "Vision and Satire: The Warped Looking Glass in *Vanity Fair*." *Publications of the Modern Language Association*, 90 (1975), 256-269.
Lozes, Jean. "Le Snob et le gentleman." *Caliban*, 8 (1971), 40-47.
McDonald, Walter R. "*Vanity Fair*: A Note on Comic Exposé." *CEA Critic*, 34 (November 1971), 36.
McMaster, Juliet. *Thackeray*. 1971. Pp. 1-49, 191-195.
Moler, Kenneth L. "Evelina in Vanity Fair: Becky Sharp and Her Patrician Heroes." *Nineteenth-Century Fiction*, 27 (1972), 171-181.
Otten, Kurt. *Der englische Roman*. 1971. Pp. 140-145.
Paris, Bernard J. *A Psychological Approach*. 1974. Pp. 71-132.
Phillipps, K. C. "Thackeray's Proper Names." *Neuphilologische Mitteilungen*, 75 (1974), 444-452.
Rawlins, Jack P. *Thackeray's Novels*. 1974. Pp. 1-35.
Reinhold, Heinz. "Thackeray: *Vanity Fair*," in Franz K. Stanzel, ed., *Der englische Roman*. 1969. Vol. II, 71-111.

Rogers, Katharine M. "The Pressure of Convention on Thackeray's Women." *Modern Language Review*, 67 (1972), 257-259.

Sutherland, J. A. "The Expanding Narrative of *Vanity Fair.*" *Journal of Narrative Technique*, 3 (1973), 149-169.

Sutherland, J. A. "The Handling of Time in *Vanity Fair.*" *Anglia*, 89 (1971), 349-356.

Sutherland, J. A. *Thackeray at Work*. 1974. Pp. 11-44.

Swanson, Roger M. "*Vanity Fair*: The Double Standard," in George Goodin, ed., *The English Novel*. 1972. Pp. 126-144.

Wheatley, James H. *Patterns in Thackeray's Fiction*. 1969. Pp. 56-93.

The Virginians, 1858-1859

Hardy, Barbara. *The Exposure of Luxury*. 1972. Pp. 155-159.

McMaster, Juliet. *Thackeray*. 1971. Pp. 211-215.

Rawlins, Jack P. *Thackeray's Novels*. 1974. Pp. 187-233.

Rogers, Katharine M. "The Pressure of Convention on Thackeray's Women." *Modern Language Review*, 67 (1972), 260-261.

Sutherland, J. A. *Thackeray at Work*. 1974. Pp. 86-109.

DYLAN THOMAS

Adventures in the Skin Trade, 1955

Korg, Jacob. *Dylan Thomas*. 1965. Pp. 172-174.

WILLIAM EDWARDS TIREBUCK

Miss Grace of All Souls, 1895

Keating, P. J. *The Working Classes*. 1971. Pp. 235-239.

J. R. R. TOLKIEN

The Fellowship of the Ring, 1954

Ohlmarks, Ake. *Sagan om Tolkien*. 1972. Pp. 52-58.

The Hobbit, 1937

Kocher, Paul H. *Master of Middle-Earth*. 1972. Pp. 19-33.

Miller, David M. "Hobbits: Common Lens for Heroic Experience." *Tolkien Journal*, No. 11 (1970), 11-15.

Ohlmarks, Ake. *Sagan om Tolkien*. 1972. Pp. 101-108.

Ready, William. *The Tolkien Relation*. 1968. Pp. 75-89.

Verch, Maria. "Zur Wiederaufnahme der Gattung des Rätsels in J. R. R. Tolkiens *The Hobbit.*" *Germanisch-Romanische Monatsschrift*, 24 (1974), 360-365.

The Lord of the Rings, 1966

Aldiss, Brian W. *Billion Year Spree.* 1973. Pp. 265-269.

Auden, W. H. "Good and Evil in *The Lord of the Rings.*" *Tolkien Journal,* 3:1 (1967), 5-8.

Barbour, Douglas. "'The Shadow of the Past': History in Middle Earth." *University of Windsor Review,* 8 (1972), 35-42.

Boswell, George W. "Tolkien as *Littérateur.*" *South Central Bulletin,* 32 (1972), 188-197.

Callahan, Patrick J. "Animism and Magic in Tolkien's *The Lord of the Rings.*" *Riverside Quarterly,* 4 (1971), 240-249.

Clausen, Christopher. "*Lord of the Rings* and 'The Ballad of the White Horse.'" *South Atlantic Bulletin,* 39 (1974), 10-16.

Ellmann, Mary. "Growing Up Hobbitic." *New American Review,* No. 2 (1968), 217-229.

Ellwood, Gracia Fay. "The Good Guys and the Bad Guys." *Tolkien Journal,* No. 10 (1969), 9-11.

Ellwood, Gracia Fay. *Good News from Tolkien's Middle Earth.* 1970. Pp. 27-43, 92-142.

Evans, Robley. *J. R. R. Tolkien.* 1971. Pp. 22-202.

Friedman, Barton R. "Fabricating History: Narrative Strategy in *The Lord of the Rings.*" *Clio,* 2 (1973), 123-144.

Gottlieb, Stephen A. "An Interpretation of Gollum." *Tolkien Journal,* No. 14 (1970-1971), 11-12.

Hartlaub, Geno. "Der Herr der Ringe." *Neue Rundschau,* 82 (1971), 383-386.

Helms, Randel. "Orc: The Id in Blake and Tolkien." *Literature and Psychology,* 20 (1970), 31-35.

Kocher, Paul H. *Master of Middle-Earth.* 1972. Pp. 34-160.

Levitin, Alexis. "The Genre of *The Lord of the Rings.*" *Tolkien Journal,* No. 11 (1970), 4-8.

Levitin, Alexis. "Power in *The Lord of the Rings.*" *Tolkien Journal,* No. 13 (1970), 11-14.

Miller, David M. "Hobbits: Common Lens for Heroic Experience." *Tolkien Journal,* No. 11 (1970), 11-15.

Moorman, Charles W. "Heroism in *The Lord of the Rings.*" *Southern Quarterly,* 11 (1972), 29-39.

Ohlmarks, Ake. *Sagan om Tolkien.* 1972. Pp. 186-216.

Orjollet, Jean-François. "J. R. R. Tolkien: Syllogistique du merveilleux." *Littérature,* 8 (1972), 41-52.

"The Peril of the World." *Tolkien Journal,* No. 15 (1972), 16-17.

Randolph, Burr. "The Singular Incompetence of the Volar." *Tolkien Journal,* No. 9 (1968), 11-13.

Ready, William. *The Tolkien Relation.* 1968. Pp. 93-131.

Sale, Roger. *Modern Heroism.* 1973. Pp. 197-239.

Scott, Nan C. "War and Pacifism in *The Lord of the Rings.*" *Tolkien Journal,* No. 15 (1972), 23-30.

Sirridge, Mary. "J. R. R. Tolkien and Fairy Tale Truth." *British Journal of Aesthetics*, 15 (1975), 81-92.

Sister Pauline, C. S. M. "Mysticism in *The Ring.*" *Tolkien Journal*, No. 10 (1969), 12-14.

Wojcik, Jan, S. J. "Samwise—Halfwise? or Who Is the Hero of *The Lord of the Rings?*" *Tolkien Journal*, 3:2 (1967), 16-18.

Wright, Marjorie Evelyn. "The Vision of Cosmic Order in the Oxford Mythmakers," in Charles A. Huttar, ed., *Imagination and the Spirit.* 1971. Pp. 263-266, 271-272, 274-275.

Zgorzelski, Andrzej. "Time Setting in J. R. R. Tolkien's *The Lord of the Rings.*" *Zagadnienia Rodzajow Literackich*, 13 (1971), 91-99.

The Return of the King, 1955

Ohlmarks, Ake. *Sagan om Tolkien.* 1972. Pp. 25-31.

BROWNE PHELAN TONNA

Helen Fleetwood, 1841

Cazamian, Louis. *The Social Novel in England.* 1973. Pp. 237-240.

Melada, Ivan. *The Captain of Industry.* 1970. Pp. 95-103.

ANTHONY TROLLOPE

The American Senator, 1877

apRoberts, Ruth. "Trollope's One World." *South Atlantic Quarterly*, 68 (1969), 463-477.

Hennessey, James Pope. *Anthony Trollope.* 1971. Pp. 344-350.

Polhemus, Robert M. *The Changing World.* 1968. Pp. 209-211.

Barchester Towers, 1857

Davey, Jocelyn, Pierre Szamek, and Lyman Bryson. "*Barchester Towers*," in George D. Crothers, ed., *Invitation to Learning.* 1966. Pp. 136-143.

Hennedy, Hugh L. *Unity in Barsetshire.* 1971. Pp. 37-55.

Lombardo, Agostino. *Ritratto di Enobarbo.* 1971. Pp. 262-273.

Polhemus, Robert M. *The Changing World.* 1968. Pp. 35-50.

The Belton Estate, 1866

Polhemus, Robert M. *The Changing World.* 1968. Pp. 124-128.

The Bertrams, 1859

Polhemus, Robert M. *The Changing World.* 1968. Pp. 60-63.

Can You Forgive Her?, 1864

Hennessey, James Pope. *Anthony Trollope.* 1971. Pp. 254-257.

Levine, George. "Can You Forgive Him? Trollope's *Can You Forgive*

Her? and the Myth of Realism." *Victorian Studies*, 18 (1974), 5-30.

McMaster, Juliet. " 'The Meaning of Words and the Nature of Things': Trollope's *Can You Forgive Her?" Studies in English Literature, 1500-1900*, 14 (1974), 603-618.

Polhemus, Robert M. *The Changing World*. 1968. Pp. 102-111.

Castle Richmond, 1860

Hennedy, Hugh L. "Love and Famine, Family and Country in Trollope's *Castle Richmond." Eire-Ireland*, 7:4 (1972), 48-66.

Polhemus, Robert M. *The Changing World*. 1968. Pp. 63-65.

Wittig, E. W. "Trollope's Irish Fiction." *Eire-Ireland*, 9:3 (1974), 105-109.

The Claverings, 1867

Polhemus, Robert M. *The Changing World*. 1968. Pp. 113-120.

Cousin Henry, 1879

Hennessey, James Pope. *Anthony Trollope*. 1971. Pp. 360-364.

Polhemus, Robert M. *The Changing World*. 1968. Pp. 231-236.

Doctor Thorne, 1858

Hennedy, Hugh L. *Unity in Barsetshire*. 1971. Pp. 56-70.

Melada, Ivan. *The Captain of Industry*. 1970. Pp. 166-171.

Polhemus, Robert M. *The Changing World*. 1968. Pp. 52-58.

Dr. Wortle's School, 1881

Slakey, Roger L. "Trollope's Case for Moral Imperative." *Nineteenth-Century Fiction*, 28 (1973), 308-309.

The Duke's Children, 1880

Johnson, P. Hansford. "Trollope's Young Women," in B. S. Benedikz, ed., *On the Novel*. 1971. Pp. 20-22.

Polhemus, Robert M. *The Changing World*. 1968. Pp. 219-231.

The Eustace Diamonds, 1872

Hennessey, James Pope. *Anthony Trollope*. 1971. Pp. 300-305.

Polhemus, Robert M. *The Changing World*. 1968. Pp. 172-177.

An Eye for an Eye, 1879

Hennessey, James Pope. *Anthony Trollope*. 1971. Pp. 364-366.

Wittig, E. W. "Trollope's Irish Fiction." *Eire-Ireland*, 9:3 (1974), 115-118.

The Fixed Period, 1882

Skilton, David. "*The Fixed Period*: Anthony Trollope's Novel of 1980." *Studies in the Literary Imagination*, 6 (Fall 1973), 39-50.

Framley Parsonage, 1861

    Glavin, John J. "Trollope's 'Most Natural English Girl.' " *Nineteenth-Century Fiction*, 28 (1974), 477-485.
    Halperin, John. *Egoism and Self-Discovery*. 1974. Pp. 61-78.
    Hennedy, Hugh L. *Unity in Barsetshire*. 1971. Pp. 71-89.
    Polhemus, Robert M. *The Changing World*. 1968. Pp. 65-76.

He Knew He Was Right, 1869

    Polhemus, Robert M. *The Changing World*. 1968. Pp. 163-167.

Is He Popenjoy?, 1878

    Hennessey, James Pope. *Anthony Trollope*. 1971. Pp. 337-344.

John Caldigate, 1879

    Hennessey, James Pope. *Anthony Trollope*. 1971. Pp. 314-318.

The Kellys and the O'Kellys, 1848

    Polhemus, Robert M. *The Changing World*. 1968. Pp. 19-20.
    Wittig, E. W. "Trollope's Irish Fiction." *Eire-Ireland*, 9:3 (1974), 102-104.

Kept in the Dark, 1882

    Hennessey, James Pope. *Anthony Trollope*. 1971. Pp. 375-379.

Lady Anna, 1874

    Hennessey, James Pope. *Anthony Trollope*. 1971. Pp. 310-314.

The Landleaguers, 1883

    Wittig, E. W. "Trollope's Irish Fiction." *Eire-Ireland*, 9:3 (1974), 109-115.

The Last Chronicle of Barset, 1867

    Corsa, Helen Storm. " 'The Cross-Grainedness of Men': The Rev. Josiah Crawley—Trollope's Study of a Paranoid Personality." *Hartford Studies in Literature*, 5 (1973), 160-172.
    Fredman, Alice Green. *Anthony Trollope*. 1971. Pp. 17-21.
    Harvey, G. M. "Heroes in Barsetshire." *Dalhousie Review*, 52 (1972), 458-468.
    Hennedy, Hugh L. *Unity in Barsetshire*. 1971. Pp. 105-124.
    Hennessey, James Pope. *Anthony Trollope*. 1971. Pp. 272-277.
    Page, Norman. "Trollope's Conversational Mode." *English Studies in Africa*, 15 (1972), 33-37.
    Polhemus, Robert M. *The Changing World*. 1968. Pp. 129-146.

Linda Tressel, 1868

    West, William A. "The Anonymous Trollope." *Ariel*, 5:1 (1974), 46-64.

The Macdermotts of Ballycloran, 1847

Hennessey, James Pope. *Anthony Trollope*. 1971. Pp. 106-108.
Polhemus, Robert M. *The Changing World*. 1968. Pp. 11-18.
Wittig, E. W. "Significant Revisions in Trollope's *The Macdermotts of Ballycloran.*" *Notes and Queries*, 20 (1973), 90-91.
Wittig, E. W. "Trollope's Irish Fiction." *Eire-Ireland*, 9:3 (1974), 98-102.

Miss Mackenzie, 1865

Polhemus, Robert M. *The Changing World*. 1968. Pp. 112-113.

Mr. Scarborough's Family, 1883

Fredman, Alice Green. *Anthony Trollope*. 1971. Pp. 30-32.
Hennessey, James Pope. *Anthony Trollope*. 1971. Pp. 380-383.
Polhemus, Robert M. *The Changing World*. 1968. Pp. 240-242.
Slakey, Roger L. "Trollope's Case for Moral Imperative." *Nineteenth-Century Fiction*, 28 (1973), 309-320.

Nina Balatka, 1867

Blinderman, Charles. "The Servility of Dependence: The Dark Lady in Trollope," in Susan Koppelman Cornillon, ed., *Images of Women in Fiction*. 1973. Pp. 63-66.
Polhemus, Robert M. *The Changing World*. 1968. Pp. 128-129.
West, William A. "The Anonymous Trollope." *Ariel*, 5:1 (1974), 46-64.

An Old Man's Love, 1884

Hennessey, James Pope. *Anthony Trollope*. 1971. Pp. 383-385.

Orley Farm, 1862

Hennessey, James Pope. *Anthony Trollope*. 1971. Pp. 244-246.
Polhemus, Robert M. *The Changing World*. 1968. Pp. 76-88.
Slakey, Roger L. "Trollope's Case for Moral Imperative." *Nineteenth-Century Fiction*, 28 (1973), 307-308.

Phineas Finn, 1869

Brown, Beatrice Curtis. *Anthony Trollope*. 1969. Pp. 76-78.
Polhemus, Robert M. *The Changing World*. 1968. Pp. 150-163.

Phineas Redux, 1874

Polhemus, Robert M. *The Changing World*. 1968. Pp. 178-185.

The Prime Minister, 1876

apRoberts, Ruth. *The Moral Trollope*. 1971. Pp. 134-147.
Fredman, Alice Green. *Anthony Trollope*. 1971. Pp. 22-26.
Halperin, John. "Politics, Palmerston, and Trollope's Prime Minister." *Clio*, 3 (1974), 187-218.

Hennessey, James Pope. *Anthony Trollope*. 1971. Pp. 328-331.
Klingler, Helmut. "Varieties of Failure: The Significance of Trollope's *The Prime Minister.*" *English Miscellany*, 23 (1972), 167-183.
Polhemus, Robert M. *The Changing World*. 1968. Pp. 197-214.

Rachel Ray, 1863

Polhemus, Robert M. *The Changing World*. 1968. Pp. 98-101.

Ralph the Heir, 1871

Polhemus, Robert M. *The Changing World*. 1968. Pp. 170-172.

The Small House at Allington, 1864

Hennedy, Hugh L. *Unity in Barsetshire*. 1971. Pp. 90-104.
Polhemus, Robert M. *The Changing World*. 1968. Pp. 91-98.

The Three Clerks, 1858

Brown, Beatrice Curtis. *Anthony Trollope*. 1969. Pp. 94-99.
Polhemus, Robert M. *The Changing World*. 1968. Pp. 51-52.
Snow, C. P. "Trollope: The Psychological Stream," in B. S. Benedikz, ed., *On the Novel*. 1971. Pp. 3-16.

La Vendée, 1850

Polhemus, Robert M. *The Changing World*. 1968. Pp. 20-22.

The Warden, 1855

apRoberts, Ruth. *The Moral Trollope*. 1971. Pp. 34-42.
Haskin, Dayton, S. J. "Awakening Moral Conscience: Trollope as Teacher in *The Warden.*" *Cithara*, 13:1 (1973), 42-52.
Heilman, Robert B. "Trollope's *The Warden*: Structure, Tone, Genre," in Thomas Austin Kirby and William John Olive, eds., *Essays in Honor of Esmond Linworth Marilla*. 1970. Pp. 210-229.
Hennedy, Hugh L. *Unity in Barsetshire*. 1971. Pp. 21-36.
Hennessey, James Pope. *Anthony Trollope*. 1971. Pp. 146-149.
Lombardo, Agostino. *Ritratto di Enobarbo*. 1971. Pp. 249-262.
Moran, Charles. "On Teaching Trollope in the 'Seventies." *CEA Critic*, 35 (January 1973), 28-29.
Pickering, Samuel F., Jr. "Trollope's Poetics and Authorial Intrusion in *The Warden* and *Barchester Towers.*" *Journal of Narrative Technique*, 3 (1973), 135-138.
Polhemus, Robert M. *The Changing World*. 1968. Pp. 25-34.

The Way We Live Now, 1875

apRoberts, Ruth. *The Moral Trollope*. 1971. Pp. 166-173.
Brown, Beatrice Curtis. *Anthony Trollope*. 1969. Pp. 58-60.
Fredman, Alice Green. *Anthony Trollope*. 1971. Pp. 26-29.
Hewitt, Douglas. *The Approach to Fiction*. 1972. Pp. 13-42.
Polhemus, Robert M. *The Changing World*. 1968. Pp. 187-197.

FRANCES TROLLOPE

Michael Armstrong, 1840

> Cazamian, Louis. *The Social Novel in England.* 1973. Pp. 235-237.
> Melada, Ivan. *The Captain of Industry.* 1970. Pp. 90-95.

JOHN WAIN

Hurry on Down, 1953

> Schleussner, Bruno. *Der neopikareske Roman.* 1969. Pp. 117-122.

The Smaller Sky, 1967

> Kahrmann, Bernd. *Die idyllische Szene.* 1969. Pp. 59-61.

Strike the Father Dead, 1962

> Meckier, Jerome. "Looking Back in Anger: The Success of a Collapsing Stance." *Dalhousie Review*, 52 (1972), 50-51.

HORACE WALPOLE

The Castle of Otranto, 1765

> Göller, Karl Heinz. *"Romance" und "novel."* 1972. Pp. 214-217.
> Kallich, Martin. *Horace Walpole.* 1971. Pp. 92-104.
> Kiely, Robert. *The Romantic Novel in England.* 1972. Pp. 27-42.
> Lévy, Maurice. *Le Roman "gothique" anglais.* 1968. Pp. 96-131.
> Otten, Kurt. *Der englische Roman.* 1971. Pp. 101-104.
> Poenicke, Klaus. " 'Schönheit im Schosse des Schreckens': Raumgefüge und Menschenbild im englischen Schauerroman." *Archiv für das Studium der Neueren Sprachen und Literaturen*, 207 (1970), 1-3.
> Solomon, Stanley J. "Subverting Propriety as a Pattern of Irony in Three Eighteenth-Century Novels: *The Castle of Otranto, Vathek,* and *Fanny Hill." Erasmus Review*, 1 (1971), 108-112.

HUGH WALPOLE

Above the Dark Circus, 1931

> Steele, Elizabeth. *Hugh Walpole.* 1972. Pp. 100-102.

The Blind Man's House, 1941

> Steele, Elizabeth. *Hugh Walpole.* 1972. Pp. 113-115.

The Bright Pavilions, 1940

> Steele, Elizabeth. *Hugh Walpole.* 1972. Pp. 131-134.

Captain Nicholas, 1934

> Steele, Elizabeth. *Hugh Walpole.* 1972. Pp. 64-66.

The Captives, 1920

    Steele, Elizabeth. *Hugh Walpole*. 1972. Pp. 80-82.

The Cathedral, 1922

    Steele, Elizabeth. *Hugh Walpole*. 1972. Pp. 73-77.

The Dark Forest, 1916

    Caillol, Robert. "Aspect du récit dans *The Dark Forest* du Hugh Walpole," in *Récit et roman*. 1972. Pp. 75-77.
    Steele, Elizabeth. *Hugh Walpole*. 1972. Pp. 55-58.

The Duchess of Wrexe, 1914

    Steele, Elizabeth. *Hugh Walpole*. 1972. Pp. 95-96.

Farthing Hall, 1929

    Steele, Elizabeth. *Hugh Walpole*. 1972. Pp. 117-119.

Fortitude, 1913

    Steele, Elizabeth. *Hugh Walpole*. 1972. Pp. 42-45.

The Fortress, 1932

    Steele, Elizabeth. *Hugh Walpole*. 1972. Pp. 124-125.

The Green Mirror, 1918

    Steele, Elizabeth. *Hugh Walpole*. 1972. Pp. 61-63.

Hans Frost, 1929

    Steele, Elizabeth. *Hugh Walpole*. 1972. Pp. 45-48.

Harmer John, 1926

    Steele, Elizabeth. *Hugh Walpole*. 1972. Pp. 84-85.

The Inquisitor, 1935

    Steele, Elizabeth. *Hugh Walpole*. 1972. Pp. 85-87.

John Cornelius, 1937

    Steele, Elizabeth. Hugh Walpole. 1972. Pp. 48-50.

The Joyful Delaneys, 1938

    Steele, Elizabeth. *Hugh Walpole*. 1972. Pp. 102-104.

Judith Paris, 1931

    Steele, Elizabeth. *Hugh Walpole*. 1972. Pp. 122-124.

Katherine Christian, 1944

    Steele, Elizabeth. *Hugh Walpole*. 1972. Pp. 134-135.

The Killer and the Slain, 1942

> Materassi, Mario. "Sul nuovo romanzo inglese dell' orrore: Il Pipistrello nel frigorifero." *Il Ponte*, 28 (1972), 660-662.
>
> Steele, Elizabeth. *Hugh Walpole*. 1972. Pp. 69-71.

Maradick at Forty, 1910

> Steele, Elizabeth. *Hugh Walpole*. 1972. Pp. 30-33.

Mr. Perrin and Mr. Traill, 1911

> Steele, Elizabeth. *Hugh Walpole*. 1972. Pp. 33-38.

The Old Ladies, 1924

> Steele, Elizabeth. *Hugh Walpole*. 1972. Pp. 89-91.

Portrait of a Man with Red Hair, 1925

> Steele, Elizabeth. *Hugh Walpole*. 1972. Pp. 82-84.

A Prayer for My Son, 1936

> Steele, Elizabeth. *Hugh Walpole*. 1972. Pp. 66-67.

The Prelude to Adventure, 1912

> Steele, Elizabeth. *Hugh Walpole*. 1972. Pp. 77-79.

Rogue Herries, 1930

> Steele, Elizabeth. *Hugh Walpole*. 1972. Pp. 119-122.

The Sea Tower, 1939

> Steele, Elizabeth. *Hugh Walpole*. 1972. Pp. 67-69.

The Secret City, 1919

> Steele, Elizabeth. *Hugh Walpole*. 1972. Pp. 58-61.

Vanessa, 1933

> Steele, Elizabeth. *Hugh Walpole*. 1972. Pp. 125-126.

Wintersmoon, 1928

> Steele, Elizabeth. *Hugh Walpole*. 1972. Pp. 104-106.

The Wooden Horse, 1909

> Steele, Elizabeth. *Hugh Walpole*. 1972. Pp. 28-30.

The Young Enchanted, 1921

> Steele, Elizabeth. *Hugh Walpole*. 1972. Pp. 98-100.

MRS. HUMPHRY WARD

David Grieve, 1892

  Colby, Vineta. *The Singular Anomaly*. 1970. Pp. 145-150.

Helbeck of Bannisdale, 1898

  Colby, Vineta. *The Singular Anomaly*. 1970. Pp. 150-153.

Marcella, 1894

  Vooys, Sijna de. *The Psychological Element*. 1966. Pp. 111-114

Robert Elsmere, 1888

  Colby, Vineta. *The Singular Anomaly*. 1970. Pp. 136-144.

Sir George Tressady, 1896

  Vooys, Sijna de. *The Psychological Element*. 1966. Pp. 114-116.

KEITH WATERHOUSE

Billy Liar, 1959

  Gray, Nigel. *The Silent Majority*. 1973. Pp. 49-72.
  Schleussner, Bruno. *Der neopikareske Roman*. 1969. Pp. 129-135.

EVELYN WAUGH

Black Mischief, 1932

  Browning, Gordon. "Silenus' Wheel: Static and Dynamic Characters
    in the Satiric Fiction of Evelyn Waugh." *Cithara*, 14:1 (1974), 18-21.
  Cook, William J., Jr. *Masks, Modes, and Morals*. 1971. Pp. 101-122.
  Deschner, Karlheinz. "Evelyn Waugh," in Otto Mann, ed., *Christliche
    Dichter*. 1968. Pp. 243-244.
  Giraudoux, Jean. "Jean Giraudoux's 'Preface' to the French Edition of
    Waugh's *Black Mischief*." *Evelyn Waugh Newsletter*, 8:1 (1974),
    6-7.
  Kernan, Alvin B. *The Plot of Satire*. 1965. Pp. 160-163.
  Wyss, Kurt O. *Pikareske Thematik*. 1973. Pp. 85-93.

Brideshead Revisited, 1945

  Burzynska, Joanna. "Funkcje plaszczyzn czasowych w *Brideshead
    Revisited* Evelyna Waugh." *Kwartalnik Neofilologiczny*, 20 (1973),
    265-275.
  Cook, William J., Jr. *Masks, Modes, and Morals*. 1971. Pp. 193-235.
  Deschner, Karlheinz. "Evelyn Waugh," in Otto Mann, ed., *Christliche
    Dichter*. 1968. Pp. 247-250.
  Gill, Richard. *Happy Rural Seat*. 1972. Pp. 211-216.

Hynes, Joseph. "Varieties of Death Wish: Evelyn Waugh's Central Theme." *Criticism*, 14 (1972), 69-72.

Kahrmann, Bernd. *Die idyllische Szene*. 1969. Pp. 62-65.

Kellogg, Gene. *The Vital Tradition*. 1970. Pp. 108-110.

Lodge, David. *Evelyn Waugh*. 1971. Pp. 28-34.

Wyss, Kurt O. *Pikareske Thematik*. 1973. Pp. 154-163.

Decline and Fall, 1928

Browning, Gordon. "Silenus' Wheel: Static and Dynamic Characters in the Satiric Fiction of Evelyn Waugh." *Cithara*, 14:1 (1974), 13-17.

Cook, William J., Jr. *Masks, Modes, and Morals*. 1971. Pp. 61-82.

Farr, D. Paul. "The Success and Failure of *Decline and Fall*." *Etudes Anglaises*, 24 (1971), 257-270.

Friedmann, Thomas. "*Decline and Fall* and the Satirist's Responsibility." *Evelyn Waugh Newsletter*, 6:2 (1972), 3-8.

Johnson, J. J. "Counterparts: The Classic and the Modern 'Pervigilium Veneris.'" *Evelyn Waugh Newsletter*, 8:3 (1974), 7-8.

Kernan, Alvin B. *The Plot of Satire*. 1965. Pp. 154-158, 166-167.

Lodge, David. *Evelyn Waugh*. 1971. Pp. 16-19.

McAleer, Edward C. "*Decline and Fall* as Imitation." *Evelyn Waugh Newsletter*, 7:3 (1973), 1-4.

Wyss, Kurt O. *Pikareske Thematik*. 1973. Pp. 66-77.

A Handful of Dust, 1934

Browning, Gordon, "Silenus' Wheel: Static and Dynamic Characters in the Satiric Fiction of Evelyn Waugh." *Cithara*, 14:1 (1974), 21-22.

Cook, William J., Jr. *Masks, Modes, and Morals*. 1971. Pp. 122-144.

Davis, Murray. "Title and Theme in *A Handful of Dust*." *Evelyn Waugh Newsletter*, 6:2 (1972), 1.

Deschner, Karlheinz. "Evelyn Waugh," in Otto Mann, ed., *Christliche Dichter*. 1968. Pp. 245-247.

Firchow, Peter E. "In Search of *A Handful of Dust*: The Literary Background of Evelyn Waugh's Novel." *Journal of Modern Literature*, 2 (1971), 79-84.

Gill, Richard. *Happy Rural Seat*. 1972. Pp. 155-160.

Kellogg, Gene. *The Vital Tradition*. 1970. Pp. 104-107.

Kernan, Alvin B. *The Plot of Satire*. 1965. Pp. 163-166.

Lodge, David. *Evelyn Waugh*. 1971. Pp. 25-28.

Ulanov, Barry. "The Ordeal of Evelyn Waugh," in Melvin J. Friedman, ed., *The Vision Obscured*. 1970. Pp. 84-87.

Wyss, Kurt O. *Pikareske Thematik*. 1973. Pp. 104-113.

Helena, 1950

Wyss, Kurt O. *Pikareske Thematik*. 1973. Pp. 163-167.

The Loved One, 1948

Browning, Gordon. "Silenus' Wheel: Static and Dynamic Characters in

the Satiric Fiction of Evelyn Waugh." *Cithara*, 14:1 (1974), 22-24.
Lodge, David. *Evelyn Waugh*. 1971. Pp. 36-37.
Wyss, Kurt O. *Pikareske Thematik*. 1973. Pp. 127-133.

Men at Arms, 1952

Cook, William J., Jr. *Masks, Modes, and Morals*. 1971. Pp. 238-271.
Coppieters, R. "A Linguistic Analysis of a Corpus of Quoted Speech in Evelyn Waugh's Trilogy *The Sword of Honour*." *Studia Germanica Gandensia*, 11 (1969), 95-138.

Officers and Gentlemen, 1955

Cook, William J., Jr. *Masks, Modes, and Morals*. 1971. Pp. 271-296.

The Ordeal of Gilbert Pinfold, 1957

Dobie, Ann B., and Carl Wooton. "Spark and Waugh: Similarities by Coincidence." *Midwest Quarterly*, 13 (1972), 423-434.
Heath, Jeffrey M. "Apthorpe Placatus?" *Ariel*, 5:1 (1974), 5-24.
Lodge, David. "The Arrogance of Evelyn Waugh." *Critic*, 30:5 (1972), 63-70.
Lodge, David. *Evelyn Waugh*. 1971. Pp. 37-39.

Put Out More Flags, 1942

Cook, William J., Jr. *Masks, Modes, and Morals*. 1971. Pp. 165-192.
Wyss, Kurt O. *Pikareske Thematik*. 1973. Pp. 93-102.

Scoop, 1938

Blayac, Alain. "Technique and Meaning in *Scoop*: Is *Scoop* a Modern Fairy-Tale?" *Evelyn Waugh Newsletter*, 6:3 (1972), 1-8.
Cook, William J., Jr. *Masks, Modes, and Morals*. 1971. Pp. 148-165.
Wyss, Kurt O. *Pikareske Thematik*. 1973. Pp. 114-120.

Scott-King's Modern Europe, 1947

Wyss, Kurt O. *Pikareske Thematik*. 1973. Pp. 121-127.

Sword of Honour, 1965

Coppieters, R. "A Linguistic Analysis of a Corpus of Quoted Speech in Evelyn Waugh's Trilogy *The Sword of Honour*." *Studia Germanica Gandensia*, 11 (1969), 87-138.
Gill, Richard. *Happy Rural Seat*. 1972. Pp. 216-222.
Hynes, Joseph. "Varieties of Death Wish: Evelyn Waugh's Central Theme." *Criticism*, 14 (1972), 72-77.
Lodge, David. *Evelyn Waugh*. 1971. Pp. 39-45.
Russell, John. "The War Trilogies of Anthony Powell and Evelyn Waugh." *Modern Age*, 16 (1972), 289-300.
Wilson, B. W. "*Sword of Honour*: The Last Crusade." *English*, 23 (1974), 87-93.
Wyss, Kurt O. *Pikareske Thematik*. 1973. Pp. 134-150.

Unconditional Surrender, 1961

> Cook, William J., Jr. *Masks, Modes, and Morals.* 1971. Pp. 297-337.
> Coppieters, R. "A Linguistic Analysis of a Corpus of Quoted Speech in Evelyn Waugh's Trilogy *The Sword of Honour." Studia Germanica Gandensia,* 11 (1969), 95-138.

Vile Bodies, 1930

> Browning, Gordon. "Silenus' Wheel: Static and Dynamic Characters in the Satiric Fiction of Evelyn Waugh." *Cithara,* 14:1 (1974), 17-18.
> Cook, William J., Jr. *Masks, Modes, and Morals.* 1971. Pp. 82-99.
> Heath, Jeffrey M. "*Vile Bodies*: A Revolution in Film Art." *Evelyn Waugh Newsletter,* 8:3 (1974), 2-7.
> Kernan, Alvin B. *The Plot of Satire.* 1965. Pp. 158-160.
> Lodge, David. *Evelyn Waugh.* 1971. Pp. 20-22.
> Meckier, Jerome. "Evelyn Waugh: Satire and Symbol." *Georgia Review,* 27 (1973), 166-174.
> Wyss, Kurt O. *Pikareske Thematik.* 1971. Pp. 77-84.

MARY WEBB

Precious Bane, 1924

> Hannah, Barbara. *Striving Towards Wholeness.* 1971. Pp. 73-104.

DENTON WELCH

In Youth Is Pleasure, 1944

> Phillips, Robert. *Denton Welch.* 1974. Pp. 72-85.

Maiden Voyage, 1943

> Phillips, Robert. *Denton Welch.* 1974. Pp. 46-71.

A Voice Through a Cloud, 1950

> Phillips, Robert. *Denton Welch.* 1974. Pp. 108-116.

H. G. WELLS

Ann Veronica, 1909

> Chapple, J. A. V. *Documentary and Imaginative Literature.* 1970. Pp. 263-265.
> Dickson, Lovat. *H. G. Wells.* 1969. Pp. 158-163.

Boon, 1915

> Dickson, Lovat. *H. G. Wells.* 1969. Pp. 238-259.

The First Men in the Moon, 1901

> Chapple, J. A. V. *Documentary and Imaginative Literature*. 1970.
> Pp. 272-278.
> Suvin, Darko. "Wells as the Turning Point of the SF Tradition."
> *Minnesota Review*, No. 4 (Spring 1975), 111-112.
> Williamson, Jack. *H. G. Wells*. 1973. Pp. 111-119.
> Woodcock, George. "The Darkness Violated by Light: A Revisionist
> View of H. G. Wells." *Malahat Review*, No. 26 (1973), 154-156.

The Food of the Gods, 1904

> Williamson, Jack. *H. G. Wells*. 1973. Pp. 39-43.

The History of Mr. Polly, 1910

> Bellamy, William. *The Novels of Wells, Bennett, and Galsworthy*.
> 1971. Pp. 136-143.
> Dessner, Lawrence Jay. "H. G. Wells, *Mr. Polly*, and the Uses of Art."
> *English Literature in Transition*, 16 (1973), 121-134.
> Fido, Martin. "Mr. Biswas and Mr. Polly." *Ariel*, 5:4 (1974), 30-37.
> Newell, Kenneth B. *Structure in Four Novels*. 1968. Pp. 84-100.
> Shenfield, Margaret. "Mr. Biswas and Mr. Polly." *English*, 23 (1974),
> 95-100.

In the Days of the Comet, 1906

> Bellamy, William. *The Novels of Wells, Bennett, and Galsworthy*.
> 1971. Pp. 116-127.
> Müllenbrock, Heinz-Joachim. *Literatur und Zeitgeschichte*. 1967.
> Pp. 85-92.
> Williamson, Jack. *H. G. Wells*. 1973. Pp. 43-45.

The Invisible Man, 1897

> Suvin, Darko. "Wells as the Turning Point of the SF Tradition."
> *Minnesota Review*, No. 4 (Spring 1975), 110.
> Williamson, Jack. *H. G. Wells*. 1973. Pp. 83-88.

The Island of Dr. Moreau, 1896

> Aldiss, Brian W. *Billion Year Spree*. 1973. Pp. 121-125.
> Dickson, Lovat. *H. G. Wells*. 1969. Pp. 66-69.
> Suvin, Darko. "Wells as the Turning Point of the SF Tradition."
> *Minnesota Review*, No. 4 (Spring 1975), 110.
> Vernier, Jean-Pierre. *H. G. Wells et son temps*. 1971. Pp. 129-135.
> Williamson, Jack. *H. G. Wells*. 1973. Pp. 74-82.
> Woodcock, George. "The Darkness Violated by Light: A Revisionist
> View of H. G. Wells." *Malahat Review*, No. 26 (1973), 150-151.

Kipps, 1905

> Bellamy, William. *The Novels of Wells, Bennett, and Galsworthy*.
> 1971. Pp. 127-132.

Dickson, Lovat. *H. G. Wells.* 1969. Pp. 147-149.
Newell, Kenneth B. *Structure in Four Novels.* 1968. Pp. 42-72.

Love and Mr. Lewisham, 1900

Newell, Kenneth B. *Structure in Four Novels.* 1968. Pp. 13-41.
Vernier, Jean-Pierre. *H. G. Wells et son temps.* 1971. Pp. 147-151.

Marriage, 1912

Vernier, Jean-Pierre. *H. G. Wells et son temps.* 1971. Pp. 308-311.

Men Like Gods, 1923

Woodcock, George. "The Darkness Violated by Light: A Revisionist View of H. G. Wells." *Malahat Review*, No. 26 (1973), 158-159.

Mr. Britling Sees It Through, 1916

Dickson, Lovat. *H. G. Wells.* 1969. Pp. 261-265.
Vernier, Jean-Pierre. *H. G. Wells et son temps.* 1971. Pp. 358-363.

A Modern Utopia, 1905

Müllenbrock, Heinz-Joachim. *Literatur und Zeitgeschichte.* 1967. Pp. 73-79.
Vernier, Jean-Pierre. *H. G. Wells et son temps.* 1971. Pp. 197-206.

The New Machiavelli, 1910

Dickson, Lovat. *H. G. Wells.* 1969. Pp. 187-194.
Vernier, Jean-Pierre. *H. G. Wells et son temps.* 1971. Pp. 294-300.

The Sea Lady, 1902

Dickson, Lovat. *H. G. Wells.* 1969. Pp. 107-110.

The Time Machine, 1895

Bellamy, William. *The Novels of Wells, Bennett, and Galsworthy.* 1971. Pp. 51-70.
Connely, Wayne C. "H. G. Wells' *The Time Machine*: Its Neglected Mythos." *Riverside Quarterly*, 5 (1972), 178-191.
Dickson, Lovat. *H. G. Wells.* 1969. Pp. 62-64.
Harris, Mason. "Science Fiction as the Dream and Nightmare of Progress." *West Coast Review*, 9 (April 1975), 6-8.
Suvin, Darko. "*The Time Machine* versus *Utopia* as a Structural Model for Science Fiction." *Comparative Literature Studies*, 10 (1973), 334-352.
Suvin, Darko. "Wells as the Turning Point of the SF Tradition." *Minnesota Review*, No. 4 (Spring 1975), 108-109.
Vernier, Jean-Pierre. *H. G. Wells et son temps.* 1971. Pp. 118-125.
Williamson, Jack. *H. G. Wells.* 1973. Pp. 51-55.
Woodcock, George. "The Darkness Violated by Light: A Revisionist View of H. G. Wells." *Malahat Review*, No. 26 (1973), 148-150.

Tono-Bungay, 1909

Bellamy, William. *The Novels of Wells, Bennett, and Galsworthy.* 1971. Pp. 132-136.

Bergonzi, Bernard. *The Turn of a Century.* 1973. Pp. 72-95.

Bradbury, Malcolm. *The Social Context.* 1971. Pp. 50-52.

Buckley, Jerome Hamilton. *Season of Youth.* 1974. Pp. 186-203.

Dickson, Lovat. *H. G. Wells.* 1969. Pp. 155-157.

Gill, Richard. *Happy Rural Seat.* 1972. Pp. 100-108.

Herbert, Lucille. "*Tono-Bungay*: Tradition and Experiment." *Modern Language Quarterly*, 33 (1972), 140-155.

Newell, Kenneth B. *Structure in Four Novels.* 1968. Pp. 73-83.

Vernier, Jean-Pierre. *H. G. Wells et son temps.* 1971. Pp. 278-283.

The War in the Air, 1908

Müllenbrock, Heinz-Joachim. *Literatur und Zeitgeschichte.* 1967. Pp. 95-104.

The War of the Worlds, 1898

Suvin, Darko. "Wells as the Turning Point of the SF Tradition." *Minnesota Review*, No. 4 (Spring 1975), 110-111.

Williamson, Jack. *H. G. Wells.* 1973. Pp. 55-62.

Woodcock, George. "The Darkness Violated by Light: A Revisionist View of H. G. Wells." *Malahat Review*, No. 26 (1973), 151-153.

When the Sleeper Wakes, 1899

Vernier, Jean-Pierre. *H. G. Wells et son temps.* 1971. Pp. 140-143.

Williamson, Jack. *H. G. Wells.* 1973. Pp. 106-110.

The Wonderful Visit, 1895

Vernier, Jean-Pierre. *H. G. Wells et son temps.* 1971. Pp. 125-128.

The World Set Free, 1914

Dickson, Lovat. *H. G. Wells.* 1969. Pp. 228-230.

Müllenbrock, Heinz-Joachim. *Literatur und Zeitgeschichte.* 1967. Pp. 212-215.

THOMAS MARTIN WHEELER

Sunshine and Shadow, 1849-1850

Seehase, Georg. "*Sunshine and Shadow* and the Structure of Chartist Fiction." *Zeitschrift für Anglistik und Amerikanistik*, 21 (1973), 127-134.

REBECCA WEST

The Birds Fall Down, 1966

> Kobler, Turner S. "The Eclecticism of Rebecca West." *Critique* (Atlanta), 13:2 (1971), 44-48.
> Wolfe, Peter. *Rebecca West*. 1971. Pp. 114-129.

The Fountain Overflows, 1957

> Kobler, Turner S. "The Eclecticism of Rebecca West." *Critique* (Atlanta), 13:2 (1971), 40-44.
> Wolfe, Peter. *Rebecca West*. 1971. Pp. 99-114.

Harriet Hume, 1929

> Kobler, Turner S. "The Eclecticism of Rebecca West." *Critique* (Atlanta), 13:2 (1971), 36-48.
> Wolfe, Peter. *Rebecca West*. 1971. Pp. 42-46.

The Judge, 1922

> Kobler, Turner S. "The Eclecticism of Rebecca West." *Critique* (Atlanta), 13:2 (1971), 34-36.
> Wolfe, Peter. *Rebecca West*. 1971. Pp. 35-42.

The Return of the Soldier, 1918

> Kobler, Turner S. "The Eclecticism of Rebecca West." *Critique* (Atlanta), 13:2 (1971), 32-34.
> Wolfe, Peter. *Rebecca West*. 1971. Pp. 31-35.

The Thinking Reed, 1936

> Kobler, Turner S. "The Eclecticism of Rebecca West." *Critique* (Atlanta), 13:2 (1971), 38-40.
> Wolfe, Peter. *Rebecca West*. 1971. Pp. 46-55.
> Wolfer, Verena Elsbeth. *Rebecca West*. 1972. Pp. 101-156.

T. H. WHITE

The Candle in the Wind, 1958

> Crane, John K. *T. H. White*. 1974. Pp. 112-122.

Darkness at Pemberley, 1932

> Crane, John K. *T. H. White*. 1974. Pp. 37-42.

Dead Mr. Nixon, 1931

> Crane, John K. *T. H. White*. 1974. Pp. 31-37.

Earth Stopped, 1934

> Crane, John K. *T. H. White*. 1974. Pp. 59-62.

The Elephant and the Kangaroo, 1948

Crane, John K. *T. H. White*. 1974. Pp. 134-141.

Farewell Victoria, 1933

Crane, John K. *T. H. White*. 1974. Pp. 52-58.

First Lesson, 1932

Crane, John K. *T. H. White*. 1974. Pp. 46-51.

Gone to Ground, 1935

Crane, John K. *T. H. White*. 1974. Pp. 62-65.

The Ill-Made Knight, 1941

Crane, John K. *T. H. White*. 1974. Pp. 99-112.

The Master, 1957

Crane, John K. *T. H. White*. 1974. Pp. 168-172.

Mistress Masham's Repose, 1947

Crane, John K. *T. H. White*. 1974. Pp. 123-134.

The Once and Future King, 1958

Crane, John K. *T. H. White*. 1974. Pp. 75-122.
Swanson, Donald R. "The Uses of Tradition: King Arthur in the Modern World." *CEA Critic*, 36 (March 1974), 19-21.

The Sword in the Stone, 1938

Crane, John K. *T. H. White*. 1974. Pp. 75-85.

They Winter Abroad, 1932

Crane, John K. *T. H. White*. 1974. Pp. 42-46.

The Witch in the Wood, 1940

Crane, John K. *T. H. White*. 1974. Pp. 86-99.

WILLIAM HALE WHITE

The Autobiography of Mark Rutherford, 1881

McCraw, Harry Wells. "Two Novelists of Despair: James Anthony Froude and William Hale White." *Southern Quarterly*, 13 (1974), 21-51.
Merton, Stephen. *Mark Rutherford*. 1967. Pp. 42-61.

Catharine Furze, 1893

Merton, Stephen. *Mark Rutherford*. 1967. Pp. 103-119.

Clara Hopgood, 1896

    Hughes, Linda K. "Madge and Clara Hopgood: William Hale White's
    Spinozan Sisters." *Victorian Studies*, 18 (1974), 57-75.
    Merton, Stephen. *Mark Rutherford*. 1967. Pp. 120-134.

Mark Rutherford's Deliverance, 1885

    Merton, Stephen. *Mark Rutherford*. 1967. Pp. 62-74.

Miriam's Schooling, 1890

    Merton, Stephen. *Mark Rutherford*. 1967. Pp. 89-102.

The Revolution in Tanner's Lane, 1887

    Merton, Stephen. *Mark Rutherford*. 1967. Pp. 75-88.
    Vooys, Sijna de. *The Psychological Element*. 1966. Pp. 121-129.

RICHARD WHITEING

No. 5 John Street, 1899

    Vooys, Sijna de. *The Psychological Element*. 1966. Pp. 146-154.

OSCAR WILDE

The Picture of Dorian Gray, 1891

    Altieri, Charles. "Organic and Humanist Models in Some English
    Bildungsroman." *Journal of General Education*, 23 (1971), 221-227.
    Fernandez, Diane. "Oscar Wilde et le masque." *Lettres Nouvelles*,
    March 1971, pp. 147-148.
    Goetsch, Paul. *Die Romankonzeption in England*. 1967. Pp. 201-205.
    Haefner, Gerhard. "Elemente der Prosa Oscar Wildes in *The Picture
    of Dorian Gray:* Ein Beitrag zur ästhetischen Bewegung in England."
    Neusprachliche Mitteilungen aus Wissenschaft und Praxis, 24
    (1971), 32-37.
    Keefe, Robert. "Artist and Model in *The Picture of Dorian Gray*."
    Studies in the Novel, 5 (1973), 63-70.
    Keppler, C. F. *The Literature of the Second Self*. 1972. Pp. 79-82.
    Murray, Isabel. "Some Elements in the Composition of *The Picture
    of Dorian Gray*." *Durham University Journal*, 64 (1972), 220-231.
    Nassar, Christopher S. *Into the Demon Universe*. 1974. Pp. 37-72.
    Pappas, John J. "The Flower and the Beast: A Study of Oscar Wilde's
    Antithetical Attitudes Toward Nature and Man in *The Picture of
    Dorian Gray*." *English Literature in Transition*, 15 (1972), 37-48.
    Rogers, Robert. *A Psychoanalytic Study*. 1970. Pp. 22-23.
    San Juan, Epifanio, Jr. *The Art of Oscar Wilde*. 1967. Pp. 49-73.
    Sullivan, Kevin. *Oscar Wilde*. 1972. Pp. 14-21.
    Thomalla, Ariane. *Die "femme fragile."* 1972. Pp. 91-93.

CHARLES WILLIAMS

All Hallows' Eve, 1945

Boies, J. J. "Existential Exchange in the Novels of Charles Williams." *Renascence*, 26 (1974), 226-228.
Holder, Robert C. "Art and the Artist in the Fiction of Charles Williams." *Renascence*, 27 (1975), 81-87.

Descent into Hell, 1937

Boies, J. J. "Existential Exchange in the Novels of Charles Williams." *Renascence*, 26 (1974), 220-226.
Holder, Robert C. "Art and the Artist in the Fiction of Charles Williams." *Renascence*, 27 (1975), 81-87.

Many Dimensions, 1931

Bolling, Douglass. "Imagery of Light and Darkness in Charles Williams' *Many Dimensions*." *Ball State University Forum*, 14 (Autumn 1973), 69-73.

ANGUS WILSON

Anglo-Saxon Attitudes, 1956

Riddell, Edwin. "The Humanist Character in Angus Wilson." *English*, 21 (1972), 45-53.
Schultze, Bruno. "Das Bild der Wirklichkeit in den Romanen Angus Wilsons." *Die Neueren Sprachen*, 72 (1973), 211-217.

Hemlock and After, 1952

Riddell, Edwin. "The Humanist Character in Angus Wilson." *English*, 21 (1972), 45-53.
Schrey, Helmut. *Didaktik des zeitgenössischen englischen Romans.* 1970. Pp. 50-53.
Wogatzky, Karin. *Angus Wilson.* 1971. Pp. 16-120.

Late Call, 1964

Riddell, Edwin. "The Humanist Character in Angus Wilson." *English*, 21 (1972), 45-53.

The Middle Age of Mrs. Eliot, 1958

Fletcher, John. "Women in Crisis: Louise and Mrs. Eliot." *Critical Quarterly*, 15 (1973), 157-170.
Riddell, Edwin. "The Humanist Character in Angus Wilson." *English*, 21 (1972), 45-53.

No Laughing Matter, 1967

Bradbury, Malcolm. *Possibilities.* 1973. Pp. 219-230.

Kums, Guido. "Reality in Fiction: *No Laughing Matter.*" *English Studies*, 53 (1972), 523-531.

Riddell, Edwin. "The Humanist Character in Angus Wilson." *English*, 21 (1972), 45-53.

The Old Men at the Zoo, 1961

Bergonzi, Bernard. *The Situation of the Novel.* 1971. Pp. 154-157.

Schultze, Bruno. "Das Bild der Wirklichkeit in den Romanen Angus Wilsons." *Die Neueren Sprachen*, 72 (1973), 212-220.

Riddell, Edwin. "The Humanist Character in Angus Wilson." *English*, 21 (1972), 45-53.

COLIN WILSON

Ritual in the Dark, 1960

Pérez Minik, Domingo. *Introducción a la novela inglesa actual.* 1968. Pp. 252-256.

P. G. WODEHOUSE

Love Among the Chickens, 1906

French, R. B. D. *P. G. Wodehouse.* 1966. Pp. 31-36.

Mike, 1909

French, R. B. D. *P. G. Wodehouse.* 1966. Pp. 37-42.

Psmith in the City, 1910

French, R. B. D. *P. G. Wodehouse.* 1966. Pp. 42-45.

Something Fresh, 1915

French, R. B. D. *P. G. Wodehouse.* 1966. Pp. 54-60.

Thank You, Jeeves, 1934

Appia, Henry. "O Rare P. G. Wodehouse." *Etudes Anglaises*, 26 (1973), 22-34.

Boothroyd, Basil. "The Laughs," in Thelma Cazalet-Keir, ed., *Homage to P. G. Wodehouse.* 1973. Pp. 61-76.

Uneasy Money, 1917

French, R. B. D. *P. G. Wodehouse.* 1966. Pp. 67-68, 71, 75, 81-82.

The White Feather, 1907

French. R. B. D. *P. G. Wodehouse.* 1966. Pp. 24-27.

MRS. HENRY WOOD

Mrs. Halliburton's Troubles, 1862

    Melada, Ivan. *The Captain of Industry.* 1970. Pp. 181-185.

LEONARD SIDNEY WOOLF

The Village in the Jungle, 1913

    Gooneratne, Yasmine. "Leonard Woolf's 'Waste Land': *The Village in the Jungle.*" *Journal of Commonwealth Literature*, 7 (1972), 22-34.
    Medcalf, Stephen. "*The Village in the Jungle.*" *Adam*, 37 (1972), 75-79.

The Wise Virgins, 1914

    Gottlieb, Freema. "L. W.—The Creative Writer." *Adam*, 37 (1972), 66-70.

VIRGINIA WOOLF

Between the Acts, 1941

    Alexander, Jean. *The Venture of Form.* 1974. Pp. 200-220.
    Bazin, Nancy Topping. *Virginia Woolf.* 1973. Pp. 191-222.
    Brewster, Dorothy. *Virginia Woolf.* 1962. Pp. 151-160.
    Daiches, David. *Virginia Woolf.* 1963. Pp. 121-129.
    Fleishman, Avrom. *Virginia Woolf.* 1975. Pp. 202-219.
    Fox, Stephen D. "The Fish Pond as Symbolic Center in *Between the Acts.*" *Modern Fiction Studies*, 18 (1972), 467-473.
    Gill, Richard. *Happy Rural Seat.* 1972. Pp. 199-202.
    Guiguet, Jean. *Virginia Woolf.* 1965. Pp. 319-329.
    Heine, Elizabeth. "The Significance of Structure in the Novels of E. M. Forster and Virginia Woolf." *English Literature in Transition*, 16 (1973), 301-302.
    Johnson, Manly. *Virginia Woolf.* 1973. Pp. 103-113.
    Kelley, Alice van Buren. *The Novels of Virginia Woolf.* 1973. Pp. 225-250.
    McLaurin, Allen. *Virginia Woolf.* 1973. Pp. 49-59.
    Naremore, James. "The 'Orts and Fragments' in *Between the Acts.*" *Ball State University Forum*, 14 (Winter 1973), 59-69.
    Naremore, James. *The World Without a Self.* 1973. Pp. 219-239.
    Quick, Jonathan R. "The Shattered Moment: Form and Crisis in *Mrs. Dalloway* and *Between the Acts.*" *Mosaic*, 7 (Spring 1974), 135-136.
    Schaefer, Josephine O'Brien. *The Three-Fold Nature of Reality.* 1965. Pp. 186-199.

Shanahan, Mary Steussy. *"Between the Acts*: Virginia Woolf's Final
Endeavor in Art." *Texas Studies in Literature and Language*, 14
(1972), 123-138.
Stadtfeld, Frieder. "Virginia Woolfs letzter Roman: More Quintes-
sential Than the Others." *Anglia*, 91 (1973), 56-76.
Thakur, N. C. *The Symbolism of Virginia Woolf*. 1965. Pp. 141-164.

Jacob's Room, 1922

Alexander, Jean. *The Venture of Form*. 1974. Pp. 63-84.
Bazin, Nancy Topping. *Virginia Woolf*. 1973. Pp. 89-99.
Brewster, Dorothy. *Virginia Woolf*. 1962. Pp. 100-107.
Buckley, Jerome Hamilton. *Season of Youth*. 1974. Pp. 262-265.
Daiches, David. *Virginia Woolf*. 1963. Pp. 55-61.
Fleishman, Avrom. *Virginia Woolf*. 1975. Pp. 46-68.
Freedman, Ralph. *The Lyrical Novel*. 1963. Pp. 206-213.
Guiguet, Jean. *Virginia Woolf*. 1965. Pp. 214-227.
Johnson, Manly. *Virginia Woolf*. 1973. Pp. 42-49.
Kelley, Alice van Buren. *The Novels of Virginia Woolf*. 1973. Pp.
63-87.
McLaurin, Allen. *Virginia Woolf*. 1973. Pp. 124-127.
Morgenstern, Barry. "The Self-Conscious Narrator in *Jacob's Room*."
Modern Fiction Studies, 18 (1972), 351-361.
Rosenbaum, S. P. "The Philosophical Realism of Virginia Woolf," in
S. P. Rosenbaum, ed., *English Literature*. 1971. Pp. 326-331.
Rubenstein, Roberta. "The Evolution of an Image: Virginia Woolf and
the 'Globe of Life.'" *Antigonish Review*, No. 15 (1973), 44-46.
Schaefer, Josephine O'Brien. *The Three-Fold Nature of Reality*. 1965.
Pp. 67-81.
Thakur, N. C. *The Symbolism of Virginia Woolf*. 1965. Pp. 36-54.

Mrs. Dalloway, 1925

Alexander, Jean. *The Venture of Form*. 1974. Pp. 85-104.
Ames, Kenneth J. "Elements of Mock-Heroic in Virginia Woolf's
Mrs. Dalloway." *Modern Fiction Studies*, 18 (1972), 363-374.
Bazin, Nancy Topping. *Virginia Woolf*. 1973. Pp. 102-123.
Beja, Morris. *Epiphany in the Modern Novel*. 1971. Pp. 133-139.
Beker, Miroslav. "London as a Principle of Structure in *Mrs. Dallo-
way*." *Modern Fiction Studies*, 18 (1972), 375-385.
Brewster, Dorothy. *Virginia Woolf*. 1962. Pp. 107-114.
Dahl, Liisa. *Linguistic Features*. 1970. Pp. 42-53.
Daiches, David. *Virginia Woolf*. 1963. Pp. 61-78.
Dölle, Erika. *Experiment und Tradition*. 1971. Pp. 74-92.
Fleishman, Avrom. *Virginia Woolf*. 1975. Pp. 69-95.
Freedman, Ralph. *The Lyrical Novel*. 1963. Pp. 213-226.
Ghiselin, Brewster. "Virginia Woolf's Party." *Sewanee Review*, 80
(1972), 47-50.
Gillen, Francis. " 'I Am This, I Am That': Shifting Distance and Move-

ment in *Mrs. Dalloway." Studies in the Novel*, 4 (1972), 484-493.

Guiguet, Jean. *Virginia Woolf*. 1965. Pp. 227-260.

Heilbrun, Carolyn G. *Towards a Recognition of Androgyny*. 1973. Pp. 163-165.

Johnson, Manly. *Virginia Woolf*. 1973. Pp. 52-63.

Kelley, Alice van Buren. *The Novels of Virginia Woolf*. 1973. Pp. 88-113.

Lakshmi, Vijay. "Virginia Woolf and E. M. Forster: A Study of Their Critical Relations." *Literary Half-Yearly*, 12 (1971), 40-41.

McLaurin, Allen. *Virginia Woolf*. 1973. Pp. 38-44, 66-69, 149-157.

Mayoux, Jean-Jacques. "Le Pouvoir des images." *Quinzaine Littéraire*, No. 172 (1973), 12-16.

Miller, J. Hillis. "Virginia Woolf's All Souls' Day: The Omniscient Narrator in *Mrs. Dalloway*," in Melvin J. Friedman and John B. Vickery, eds., *The Shaken Realist*. 1970. Pp. 100-127.

Miroiu, Mihai. "Unity and Coherence in *Mrs. Dalloway." Analele Universitatii Bucuresti: Literatura Universala si Comparata*, 19:1, (1970), 117-121.

Mueller, William R. *Celebration of Life*. 1972. Pp. 189-206.

Naremore, James. *The World Without a Self*. 1973. Pp. 77-111.

Penner, Catherine S. "The Sacred Will in *Mrs. Dalloway." Thoth*, 12 (Winter 1972), 3-20.

Quick, Jonathan R. "The Shattered Moment: Form and Crisis in *Mrs. Dalloway* and *Between the Acts." Mosaic*, 7 (Spring 1974), 128-135.

Rachman, Shalom. "Clarissa's Attic: Virginia Woolf's *Mrs. Dalloway* Reconsidered." *Twentieth-Century Literature*, 18 (1972), 3-18.

Rosenbaum, S. P. "The Philosophical Realism of Virginia Woolf," in S. P. Rosenbaum, ed., *English Literature*. 1971. Pp. 331-337.

Ruotolo, Lucio P. *Six Existential Heroes*. 1973. Pp. 13-35.

Sakamoto, Tadanobu. "Virginia Woolf: 'Mrs. Dalloway in Bond Street' and *Mrs. Dalloway." Studies in English Literature* (Tokyo), English Number (1974), 75-88.

Samuels, Marilyn Schauer. "The Symbolic Functions of the Sun in *Mrs. Dalloway." Modern Fiction Studies*, 18 (1972), 387-399.

Schaefer, Josephine O'Brien. *The Three-Fold Nature of Reality*. 1965. Pp. 85-109.

Schlack, Beverly Ann. "A Freudian Look at Mrs. Dalloway." *Literature and Psychology*, 23 (1973), 49-58.

Shields, E. F. "Death and Individual Values in *Mrs. Dalloway." Queen's Quarterly*, 80 (1973), 79-89.

Swanston, Hamish F. G. "Virginia Woolf and the Corinthians." *New Blackfriars*, 54 (1973), 360-365.

Thakur, N. C. *The Symbolism of Virginia Woolf*. 1965. Pp. 55-71.

Walcutt, Charles Child. *Man's Changing Mask*. 1966. Pp. 297-298.

Wyatt, Jean M. "*Mrs. Dalloway*: Literary Allusion as Structural Metaphor." *Publications of the Modern Language Association*, 88 (1973), 440-451.

Night and Day, 1919

Alexander, Jean. *The Venture of Form*. 1974. Pp. 55-63.
Bazin, Nancy Topping. *Virginia Woolf*. 1973. Pp. 74-88.
Brewster, Dorothy. *Virginia Woolf*. 1962. Pp. 92-98.
Cumings, Melinda Feldt. "*Night and Day*: Virginia Woolf's Visionary Synthesis of Reality." *Modern Fiction Studies*, 18 (1972), 339-349.
Daiches, David. *Virginia Woolf*. 1963. Pp. 17-33.
Fleishman, Avrom. *Virginia Woolf*. 1975. Pp. 22-45.
Guiguet, Jean. *Virginia Woolf*. 1965. Pp. 206-214.
Johnson, Manly. *Virginia Woolf*. 1973. Pp. 33-38.
Kelley, Alice van Buren. *The Novels of Virginia Woolf*. 1973. Pp. 34-62.
McLaurin, Allen. *Virginia Woolf*. 1973. Pp. 32-37.
Schaefer, Josephine O'Brien. *The Three-Fold Nature of Reality*. 1965. Pp. 49-66.
Thakur, N. C. *The Symbolism of Virginia Woolf*. 1965. Pp. 11-35.

Orlando, 1928

Alexander, Jean. *The Venture of Form*. 1974. Pp. 127-146.
Brewster, Dorothy. *Virginia Woolf*. 1962. Pp. 120-124.
Daiches, David. *Virginia Woolf*. 1963. Pp. 97-103.
Fleishman, Avrom. *Virginia Woolf*. 1975. Pp. 135-149.
Gill, Richard. *Happy Rural Seat*. 1972. Pp. 197-199.
Guiguet, Jean. *Virginia Woolf*. 1965. Pp. 261-280.
Johnson, Manly. *Virginia Woolf*. 1973. Pp. 78-82.
Morgan, Ellen. "Humanbecoming: Form and Focus in the Neo-Feminist Novel," in Susan Koppelman Cornillon, ed., *Images of Women in Fiction*. 1973. Pp. 189-192.
Naremore, James. *The World Without a Self*. 1973. Pp. 190-218.
Rubenstein, Roberta. "*Orlando*: Virginia Woolf's Improvisations on a Russian Theme." *Forum for Modern Language Studies*, 9 (1973), 166-169.
Sakamoto, Tadanobu. "*Orlando*—What Happened in It." *Hiroshima Studies in English Language and Literature*, 19 (1972), 22-33.
Stewart, Jack F. "Historical Impressionism in *Orlando*." *Studies in the Novel*, 5 (1973), 71-85.
Thakur, N. C. *The Symbolism of Virginia Woolf*. 1965. Pp. 89-102.

To the Lighthouse, 1927

Alexander, Jean. *The Venture of Form*. 1974. Pp. 104-126.
Bazin, Nancy Topping. *Virginia Woolf*. 1973. Pp. 124-138.
Beja, Morris. *Epiphany in the Modern Novel*. 1971. Pp. 139-146.
Brewster, Dorothy. *Virginia Woolf*. 1962. Pp. 114-120.
Brower, Reuben A. "The Novel as Poem: Virginia Woolf Exploring a Critical Metaphor," in Morton W. Bloomfield, ed., *The Interpretation of Narrative*. 1970. Pp. 236-247.

Corsa, Helen Storm. "*To the Lighthouse*: Death, Mourning, and Transfiguration." *Literature and Psychology*, 21 (1971), 115-130.

Daiches, David. *Virginia Woolf.* 1963. Pp. 79-96.

Donovan, Josephine. "Feminist Style Criticism," in Susan Koppelman Cornillon, ed., *Images of Women in Fiction.* 1973. Pp. 349-352.

Fleishman, Avrom. *Virginia Woolf.* 1975. Pp. 96-134.

Freedman, Ralph. *The Lyrical Novel.* 1963. Pp. 226-243.

Gill, Richard. *Happy Rural Seat.* 1972. Pp. 195-197.

Hanquart, Evelyne. "Humanisme féministe ou humanisme au féminin? Une Lecture de l'oeuvre romanesque de Virginia Woolf et E. M. Forster." *Etudes Anglaises*, 26 (1973), 281-284.

Heilbrun, Carolyn G. *Towards a Recognition of Androgyny.* 1973. Pp. 156-163.

Heine, Elizabeth. "The Significance of Structure in the Novels of E. M. Forster and Virginia Woolf." *English Literature in Transition*, 16 (1973), 298-299, 304.

Hoffmann, A. C. "Subject and Object and the Nature of Reality: The Dialectic of *To the Lighthouse.*" *Texas Studies in Literature and Language*, 13 (1972), 691-703.

Jeffrey, David K. "*To the Lighthouse*: A Bergsonian Reading." *North Dakota Quarterly*, 42 (1974), 5-15.

Johnson, Manly. *Virginia Woolf.* 1973. Pp. 66-76.

Joyner, Nancy. "The Underside of the Butterfly: Lessing's Debt to Woolf." *Journal of Narrative Technique*, 4 (1974), 204-211.

Kelley, Alice van Buren. *The Novels of Virginia Woolf.* 1973. Pp. 114-143.

Leaska, Mitchell A. *Virginia Woolf's Lighthouse.* 1970. Pp. 47-164.

Little, Judith. "Heroism in *To the Lighthouse*," in Susan Koppelman Cornillon, ed., *Images of Women in Fiction.* 1973. Pp. 237-242.

McLaurin, Allen. *Virginia Woolf.* 1973. Pp. 177-206.

Mayoux, Jean-Jacques. "Le Pouvoir des images." *Quinzaine Littéraire*, No. 172 (1973), 13-16.

Naremore, James. *The World Without a Self.* 1973. Pp. 112-150.

Ottavi, Anne. "La Figure maternelle chez Colette et Virginia Woolf." *Annales de la Faculté des Lettres et Sciences Humaines de Nice*, 22 (1974), 181-191.

Pratt, Annis. "Sexual Imagery in *To the Lighthouse*: A New Feminist Approach." *Modern Fiction Studies*, 18 (1972), 417-431.

Rose, Phyllis. "Mrs. Ramsay and Mrs. Woolf." *Women's Studies*, 1 (1973), 199-216.

Rosenbaum, S. P. "The Philosophical Realism of Virginia Woolf," in S. P. Rosenbaum, ed., *English Literature.* 1971. Pp. 337-346.

Schaefer, Josephine O'Brien. *The Three-Fold Nature of Reality.* 1965. Pp. 110-136.

Seltzer, Alvin J. *Chaos in the Novel.* 1974. Pp. 120-140.

Spacks, Patricia Meyer. "Taking Care: Some Women Novelists." *Novel*, 6 (1972), 48-51.

Steiger, Klaus Peter. "Der Romananfang von Virginia Woolfs *To the Lighthouse.*" *Germanisch-Romanische Monatsschrift*, 23 (1973), 105-115.

Thakur, N. C. *The Symbolism of Virginia Woolf.* 1965. Pp. 72-88.

Walcutt, Charles Child. *Man's Changing Mask.* 1966. P. 297.

Whitehead, Lee M. "The Shawl and the Skull: Virginia Woolf's 'Magic Mountain.'" *Modern Fiction Studies*, 18 (1972), 401-415.

The Voyage Out, 1915

Alexander, Jean. *The Venture of Form.* 1974. Pp. 31-55.

Bazin, Nancy Topping. *Virginia Woolf.* 1973. Pp. 47-74.

Brewster, Dorothy. *Virginia Woolf.* 1962. Pp. 84-92.

Daiches, David. *Virginia Woolf.* 1963. Pp. 9-17.

Fleishman, Avrom. *Virginia Woolf.* 1975. Pp. 1-21.

Guiguet, Jean. *Virginia Woolf.* 1965. Pp. 197-206.

Heine, Elizabeth. "The Significance of Structure in the Novels of E. M. Forster and Virginia Woolf." *English Literature in Transition*, 16 (1973), 291-292, 294, 296.

Johnson, Manly. *Virginia Woolf.* 1973. Pp. 26-33.

Kelley, Alice van Buren. *The Novels of Virginia Woolf.* 1973. Pp. 7-33.

McLaurin, Allen. *Virginia Woolf.* 1973. Pp. 29-32, 85-86.

Naremore, James. *The World Without a Self.* 1973. Pp. 5-59.

Schaefer, Josephine O'Brien. *The Three-Fold Nature of Reality.* 1965. Pp. 33-48.

Thakur, N. C. *The Symbolism of Virginia Woolf.* 1965. Pp. 11-35.

The Waves, 1931

Alexander, Jean. *The Venture of Form.* 1974. Pp. 147-178.

Bazin, Nancy Topping. *Virginia Woolf.* 1973. Pp. 139-165.

Brandt, Magdalene. *Realismus und Realität.* 1968. Pp. 97-137.

Brewster, Dorothy. *Virginia Woolf.* 1962. Pp. 125-128.

Collins, Robert G. *Virginia Woolf's Black Arrows of Sensation.* 1962. Pp. 5-47.

Daiches, David. *Virginia Woolf.* 1963. Pp. 104-111.

Dölle, Erika. *Experiment und Tradition.* 1971. Pp. 92-119.

Fleishman, Avrom. *Virginia Woolf.* 1975. Pp. 150-171.

Freedman, Ralph. *The Lyrical Novel.* 1963. Pp. 244-268.

Gorsky, Susan. "'The Central Shadow': Characterization in *The Waves.*" *Modern Fiction Studies*, 18 (1972), 449-466.

Guiguet, Jean. *Virginia Woolf.* 1965. Pp. 280-302.

Heine, Elizabeth. "The Significance of Structure in the Novels of E. M. Forster and Virginia Woolf." *English Literature in Transition*, 16 (1973), 299-300.

Johnson, Manly. *Virginia Woolf.* 1973. Pp. 82-91.

Kelley, Alice van Buren. *The Novels of Virginia Woolf.* 1973. Pp. 144-199.

McLaurin, Allen. *Virginia Woolf.* 1973. Pp. 79-84, 128-148.

Mayoux, Jean-Jacques. "Le Pouvoir des images." *Quinzaine Littéraire*, No. 172 (1973), 13-16.

Naremore, James. *The World Without a Self.* 1973. Pp. 151-189.

Richardson, Robert O. "Point of View in Virginia Woolf's *The Waves.*" *Texas Studies in Literature and Language*, 14 (1973), 691-709.

Rosenbaum, S. P. "The Philosophical Realism of Virginia Woolf," in S. P. Rosenbaum, ed., *English Literature.* 1971. Pp. 347-355.

Rubenstein, Roberta. "The Evolution of an Image: Virginia Woolf and the 'Globe of Light.'" *Antigonish Review*, No. 15 (1973), 44-46.

Schaefer, Josephine O'Brien. *The Three-Fold Nature of Reality.* 1965. Pp. 137-164.

Shanahan, Mary Steussy. "The Artist and the Resolution of *The Waves.*" *Modern Language Quarterly*, 36 (1975), 54-74.

Snow, Lotus. "The Wreckful Siege: Disorder in *The Waves.*" *Research Studies*, 42 (1974), 71-80.

Stewart, J. I. M. "Notes for a Study of *The Waves*," in B. S. Benedikz, ed., *On the Novel.* 1971. Pp. 98-112.

Stewart, Jack F. "Existence and Symbol in *The Waves.*" *Modern Fiction Studies*, 18 (1972), 433-447.

Swanston, Hamish F. G. "Virginia Woolf and the Corinthians." *New Blackfriars*, 54 (1973), 360-365.

Thakur, N. C. *The Symbolism of Virginia Woolf.* 1965. Pp. 103-124.

Webb, Igor. " 'Things in Themselves': Virginia Woolf's *The Waves.*" *Modern Fiction Studies*, 17 (1971-1972), 570-573.

The Years, 1937

Alexander, Jean. *The Venture of Form.* 1974. Pp. 183-199.

Bazin, Nancy Topping. *Virginia Woolf.* 1973. Pp. 167-191.

Brewster, Dorothy. *Virginia Woolf.* 1962. Pp. 139-151.

Daiches, David. *Virginia Woolf.* 1963. Pp. 111-121.

Fleishman, Avrom. *Virginia Woolf.* 1975. Pp. 172-201.

Guiguet, Jean. *Virginia Woolf.* 1965. Pp. 302-319.

Johnson, Manly. *Virginia Woolf.* 1973. Pp. 94-103.

Kelley, Alice van Buren. *The Novels of Virginia Woolf.* 1973. Pp. 200-224.

McLaurin, Allen. *Virginia Woolf.* 1973. Pp. 158-165.

Radin, Grace. " 'I Am Not a Hero': Virginia Woolf and the First Version of *The Years.*" *Massachusetts Review*, 16 (1975), 195-208.

Schaefer, Josephine O'Brien. *The Three-Fold Nature of Reality.* 1965. Pp. 167-185.

Thakur, N. C. *The Symbolism of Virginia Woolf.* 1965. Pp. 125-140.

CHARLOTTE YONGE

The Clever Woman of the Family, 1865

> Dennis, Barbara. "The Two Voices of Charlotte Yonge." *Durham University Journal*, 65 (1973), 187-188.
> Stark, Myra C. "*The Clever Woman of the Family*—And What Happened to Her." *Mary Wollstonecraft Journal*, 2 (May 1974), 17-18.

The Daisy Chain, 1856

> Colby, Vineta. *Yesterday's Woman*. 1974. Pp. 189-193.
> Dennis, Barbara. "The Two Voices of Charlotte Yonge." *Durham University Journal*, 65 (1973), 181-185.
> Stark, Myra C. "*The Clever Woman of the Family*—And What Happened to Her." *Mary Wollstonecraft Journal*, 2 (May 1974), 15-17.

The Heir of Redclyffe, 1853

> Colby, Vineta. *Yesterday's Woman*. 1974. Pp. 193-201.
> Dennis, Barbara. "The Two Voices of Charlotte Yonge." *Durham University Journal*, 65 (1973), 181-185.

Hopes and Fears, 1860

> Dennis, Barbara. "The Two Voices of Charlotte Yonge." *Durham University Journal*, 65 (1973), 185-188.

FRANCIS BRETT YOUNG

The Black Diamond, 1921

> Leclaire, Jacques. *Un Témoin de l'avènement*. 1969. Pp. 140-144.

The City of Gold, 1939

> Leclaire, Jacques. *Un Témoin de l'avènement*. 1969. Pp. 274-281.

Dr. Bradley Remembers, 1939

> Leclaire, Jacques. *Un Témoin de l'avènement*. 1969. Pp. 161-167, 242-248.

Jim Redlake, 1930

> Leclaire, Jacques. *Un Témoin de l'avènement*. 1969. Pp. 61-70.

My Brother Jonathan, 1928

> Leclaire, Jacques. *Un Témoin de l'avènement*. 1969. Pp. 156-159.

This Little World, 1934

> Leclaire, Jacques. *Un Témoin de l'avènement*. 1969. Pp. 197-202.

Wistanlow, 1956

Leclaire, Jacques. *Un Témoin de l'avènement*. 1969. Pp. 235-239.

ISRAEL ZANGWILL

Children of the Ghetto, 1892

Adams, Elsie Bonita. *Israel Zangwill*. 1971. Pp. 52-63.
Winehouse, Bernard. "Israel Zangwill's *Children of the Ghetto*: A Literary History of the First Anglo-Jewish Best-Seller." *English Literature in Transition*, 16 (1973), 93-117.

Jinny the Carrier, 1919

Adams, Elsie Bonita. *Israel Zangwill*. 1971. Pp. 79-82.

The King of Schnorrers, 1894

Adams, Elsie Bonita. *Israel Zangwill*. 1971. Pp. 63-68.
Fisch, Harold. *The Dual Image*. 1971. Pp. 76-77.

The Mantle of Elijah, 1900

Adams, Elsie Bonita. *Israel Zangwill*. 1971. Pp. 75-79.

The Master, 1895

Adams, Elsie Bonita. *Israel Zangwill*. 1971. Pp. 68-75.

The Premier and the Painter, 1888

Adams, Elsie Bonita. *Israel Zangwill*. 1971. Pp. 40-46.

ANONYMOUS NOVELS

Dobsons Drie Bobbes, 1607

O'Brien, Avril S. "*Dobsons Drie Bobbes*: A Significant Contribution to the Development of Prose Fiction." *Studies in English Literature, 1500-1900*, 12 (1972), 55-70.

Lights and Shadows of English Life, 1855

Melada, Ivan. *The Captain of Industry*. 1970. Pp. 144-147.

Plebeians and Patricians, 1836

Melada, Ivan. *The Captain of Industry*. 1970. Pp. 34-40.

LIST OF BOOKS INDEXED

Abbott, H. Porter. *The Fiction of Samuel Beckett: Form and Effect*. Berkeley and Los Angeles: University of California Press, 1973.

Adam, Ian. *George Eliot*. New York: Humanities, 1969.

Adams, Elsie Bonita. *Bernard Shaw and the Aesthetes*. Columbus: Ohio State University Press, 1971.

Adams, Elsie Bonita. *Israel Zangwill*. New York: Twayne, 1971.

Adams, Robert M. *Proteus, His Lies, His Truth: Discussions of Literary Translation*. New York: Norton, 1973.

Adams, Robert Martin. *Surface and Symbol: The Consistency of James Joyce's "Ulysses."* New York: Oxford University Press, 1962.

Adelstein, Michael E. *Fanny Burney*. New York: Twayne, 1968.

Aitken, A. J., Angus McIntosh, and Hermann Pálsson, eds., *Edinburgh Studies in English and Scots*. London: Longman, 1971.

Aldiss, Brian W. *Billion Year Spree: The True History of Science Fiction*. New York: Doubleday, 1973.

Alexander, Jean. *The Venture of Form in the Novels of Virginia Woolf*. Port Washington, N.Y.: Kennikat, 1974.

Alldritt, Keith. *The Making of George Orwell: As Essay in Literary History*. New York: St. Martin's, 1969.

Allott, Miriam, ed. *Emily Brontë: "Wuthering Heights"—A Casebook*. London: Macmillan, 1970.

Alter, Robert. *Fielding and the Nature of the Novel*. Cambridge: Harvard University Press, 1968.

Alvarez, A. *Samuel Beckett*. New York: Viking, 1973.

Amis, Kingsley. *What Became of Jane Austen? and Other Questions*. New York: Harcourt Brace Jovanovich, 1971.

Andreach, Robert J. *The Slain and Resurrected God: Conrad, Ford, and the Christian Myth*. New York: New York University Press, 1970.

apRoberts, Ruth. *The Moral Trollope*. Athens: Ohio University Press, 1971.

Arnold, Armin. *James Joyce*. Rev. ed. New York: Ungar, 1969.

Aubert, Jacques. *Introduction à l'esthétique de James Joyce*. Paris: Didier, 1973.

Austin, Allan E. *Elizabeth Bowen*. New York: Twayne, 1971.

Autobiography, Biography, and the Novel: Papers Read at a Clark Library Seminar, May 13, 1972. Los Angeles: William Andrews Clark Memorial Library, University of California, Los Angeles, 1973.

Bäckman, Sven. *This Singular Tale: A Study of "The Vicar of Wakefield" and Its Literary Background*. Lund Studies in English, 40. Lund: Gleerup, 1971.

Baim, Joseph, Ann L. Hayes, and Robert J. Gangewere, eds. *In Honor of Austin Wright*. Pittsburgh: Carnegie-Mellon University Press, 1972.

Baine, Rodney M. *Thomas Holcroft and the Revolutionary Novel*. Athens: University of Georgia Press, 1965.

Baldanza, Frank. *Iris Murdoch*. New York: Twayne, 1974.

Baldanza, Frank. *Ivy Compton-Burnett*. New York: Twayne, 1964.

Ball, Donald L. *Samuel Richardson's Theory of Fiction*. De Proprietatibus Litterarum, Series Practica, 15. The Hague: Mouton, 1971.

Bareiss, Dieter. *Die Vierpersonenkonstellation im Roman: Strukturuntersuchungen zur Personenführung*. Europäische Hochschulschriften XIV, 1. Berne: Lang, 1969.

Barker, Dudley. *G. K. Chesterton: A Biography*. London: Constable, 1973.

Barker, Dudley. *Writer by Trade: A Portrait of Arnold Bennett*. New York: Atheneum, 1966.

Barnard, Robert. *Imagery and Theme in the Novels of Dickens*. Norwegian Studies in English, 17. New York: Humanities, 1974.

Barrett, William. *Time of Need: Forms of Imagination in the Twentieth Century*. New York: Harper and Row, 1972.

Bates, Ronald, and Harry J. Pollock, eds. *Litters from Aloft: Papers Delivered at the Second Canadian James Joyce Seminar, McMaster University*. University of Tulsa Monograph Series, 13. Tulsa: University of Tulsa Press, 1971.

Battestin, Martin C. *The Providence of Wit: Aspects of Form in Augustan Literature and the Arts*. Oxford: Clarendon, 1974.

Bauer, Gero, Franz K. Stanzel, and Franz Zaic, ed. *Festschrift Prof. Dr. Herbert Koziol zum siebzigsten Geburtstag*. Wiener Beiträge zur englischen Philologie, 75. Vienna: Braumüller, 1973.

Bazin, Nancy Topping. *Virginia Woolf and the Androgynous Vision*. New Brunswick: Rutgers University Press, 1973.

Beaty, Frederick L. *Light from Heaven: Love in British Romantic Literature*. DeKalb: Northern Illinois University Press, 1971.

Bedford, Sybille. *Aldous Huxley: A Biography*. 2 vols. London: Collins, and Chatto and Windus, 1973-1974.

Bedient, Calvin. *Architects of the Self: George Eliot, D. H. Lawrence, and E. M. Forster*. Berkeley and Los Angeles: University of California Press, 1972.

Beer, J. B. *The Achievement of E. M. Forster*. London: Chatto and Windus, 1962.

Beer, Patricia. *Reader, I Married Him: A Study of the Women Characters of Jane Austen, Charlotte Brontë, Elizabeth Gaskell and George Eliot*. London: Macmillan, 1974.

Begnal, Michael H. *Joseph Sheridan LeFanu*. Lewisburg, Pa.: Bucknell University Press, 1971.

Begnal, Michael H., and Grace Eckley. *Narrator and Character in "Finnegans Wake."* Lewisburg, Pa.: Bucknell University Press, 1975.

Begnal, Michael H., and Fritz Senn, eds. *A Conceptual Guide to "Finnegans Wake."* University Park: Pennsylvania State University Press, 1974.

Beja, Morris. *Epiphany in the Modern Novel*. Seattle: University of Washington Press, 1971.

Bell, Alan, ed. *Scott Bicentenary Essays: Selected Papers Read at the Sir Walter Scott Bicentenary Conference*. Edinburgh: Scottish Academic Press, 1973.

Bellamy, William. *The Novels of Wells, Bennett, and Galsworthy: 1890-1910.* New York: Barnes and Noble, 1971.

Benedikz, B. S., ed. *On the Novel: A Present for Walter Allen on His 60th Birthday from His Friends and Colleagues.* London: Dent, 1971.

Benjamin, Judy-Lynn, ed. *The Celtic Bull: Essays on James Joyce's "Ulysses."* University of Tulsa Monograph Series, 1. Tulsa: University of Tulsa Press, 1966.

Benkovitz, Miriam J. *Ronald Firbank: A Biography.* London: Weidenfeld and Nicolson, 1970.

Bensen, Alice R. *Rose Macaulay.* New York: Twayne, 1969.

Benstock, Bernard. *Joyce-Again's Wake: An Analysis of "Finnegans Wake."* Seattle: University of Washington Press, 1965.

Bentley, Phyllis. *The English Regional Novel.* New York: Haskell House, 1966.

Bergonzi, Bernard. *The Situation of the Novel.* Pittsburgh: University of Pittsburgh Press, 1971.

Bergonzi, Bernard. *The Turn of a Century: Essays on Victorian and Modern English Literature.* London: Macmillan, 1973.

Berthoff, Warner. *Fictions and Events: Essays in Criticism and Literary History.* New York: Dutton, 1971.

Biles, Jack I. *Talk: Conversations with William Golding.* New York: Harcourt Brace Jovanovich, 1970.

Bizám, Lenke. *Kritikai allegóriák Dickensről és Kafkáról.* Budapest: Akadémiai Kiadó, 1970.

Blake, Kathleen. *Play, Games, and Sport: The Literary Works of Lewis Carroll.* Ithaca: Cornell University Press, 1974.

Blamires, David. *David Jones: Artist and Writer.* Manchester: Manchester University Press, 1971.

Blamires, Harry. *The Bloomsday Book: A Guide Through Joyce's "Ulysses."* London: Methuen, 1966.

Blish, James. *More Issues at Hand: Critical Studies in Contemporary Science Fiction.* Chicago: Advent, 1970.

Bloom, Harold. *The Ringers in the Tower: Studies in Romantic Tradition.* Chicago: University of Chicago Press, 1971.

Bloom, Robert. *The Indeterminate World: A Study of the Novels of Joyce Cary.* Philadelphia: University of Pennsylvania Press, 1962.

Bloomfield, Morton W., ed. *The Interpretation of Narrative: Theory and Practice.* Cambridge: Harvard University Press, 1970.

Boardman, Gwenn R. *Graham Greene: The Aesthetics of Exploration.* Gainesville: University of Florida Press, 1971.

Boisdeffre, Pierre de. *Où va le roman?* Rev. ed. Paris: Editions Mondiales, 1972.

Boldereff, Frances M. *Hermes to His Son Thoth: Being Joyce's Use of Giordano Bruno in "Finnegans Wake."* Woodward, Pa.: Classic Non-Fiction Library, 1968.

Boll, Theophilus E. M. *Miss May Sinclair, Novelist: A Biographical and Critical Introduction.* Rutherford, N.J.: Fairleigh Dickinson University Press, 1973.

Bond, W. H., ed. *Eighteenth-Century Studies in Honor of Donald F. Hyde.* New York: Grolier Club, 1970.

Bonheim, Helmut. *Joyce's Benefictions.* Berkeley and Los Angeles: University of California Press, 1964.

Borrello, Alfred. *Gabriel Fielding.* New York: Twayne, 1974.

Boucé, Paul-Gabriel. *Les Romans de Smollett: Etude critique.* Paris: Didier, 1971.

Boyle, Ted E. *Brendan Behan.* New York: Twayne, 1969.

Boyle, Ted E. *Symbol and Meaning in the Fiction of Joseph Conrad.* The Hague: Mouton, 1965.

Bradbury, Malcolm. *Possibilities: Essays on the State of the Novel.* London: Oxford University Press, 1973.

Bradbury, Malcolm. *The Social Context of Modern English Literature.* New York: Schocken, 1971.

Brandabur, Edward. *A Scrupulous Meanness: A Study of Joyce's Early Work.* Urbana: University of Illinois Press, 1971.

Brander, Laurence. *E. M. Forster: A Critical Study.* London: Rupert Hart-Davis, 1968.

Brander, Laurence. *Aldous Huxley: A Critical Study.* Lewisburg, Pa.: Bucknell University Press, 1970.

Brandt, Magdalene. *Realismus und Realität im modernen Roman: Methodologische Untersuchungen zu Virginia Woolfs "The Waves."* Linguistica et Litteraria, 2. Bad Homburg: Max Gehlen, 1968.

Braudy, Leo. *Narrative Form in History and Fiction: Hume, Fielding and Gibbon.* Princeton: Princeton University Press, 1970.

Braun, Andrzej. *Sladami Conrada.* Warsaw: Czytelnik, 1972.

Breitinger, Eckhard. *Der Tod im englischen Roman um 1800: Untersuchungen zum englischen Schauerroman.* Göppinger Akademische Beiträge, 19. Göppingen: Kümmerle, 1971.

Brennan, Neil. *Anthony Powell.* New York: Twayne, 1974.

Brewster, Dorothy. *Virginia Woolf.* New York: New York University Press, 1962.

Brinkley, Richard. *Thomas Hardy as a Regional Novelist: With Special Reference to "The Return of the Native."* Monographs on the Life, Times and Works of Thomas Hardy, 49. St. Peter Port, Guernsey: Toucan Press, 1968.

Brissenden, R. F., ed. *Studies in the Eighteenth Century, II: Papers Presented at the Second David Nichol Smith Memorial Seminar, Canberra 1970.* Toronto: Toronto University Press, 1973.

Brissenden, R. F. *Virtue in Distress: Studies in the Novel of Sentiment from Richardson to Sade.* London: Macmillan, 1974.

Bronzwaer, W. J. M. *Tense in the Novel: An Investigation of Some Potentialities of Linguistic Criticism.* Groningen: Wolters-Noordhoff, 1970.

Brook, G. L. *The Language of Dickens.* London: Deutsch, 1970.

Brooks, Douglas. *Number and Pattern in the Eighteenth-Century Novel: Defoe, Fielding, Smollett and Sterne.* London: Routledge and Kegan Paul, 1973.

Brooks, Peter, ed. *The Child's Part*. New Haven: Yale University Press, 1969.

Brophy, Brigid. *Prancing Novelist: A Defence of Fiction in the Form of a Critical Biography in Praise of Ronald Firbank*. London: Macmillan, 1973.

Brophy, Elizabeth Bergen. *Samuel Richardson: The Triumph of Craft*. Knoxville: University of Tennessee Press, 1974.

Broughton, Bradford B., ed. *Twenty-Seven to One: A Potpourri of Humanistic Material Presented to Dr. Donald Gale Stillman*. Ogdensburg, N.Y.: Ryan, 1970.

Brower, Reuben A., ed. *Twentieth-Century Literature in Retrospect*. Cambridge: Harvard University Press, 1971.

Brown, Arthur Washburn. *Sexual Analysis of Dickens' Props*. New York: Emerson, 1971.

Brown, Beatrice Curtis. *Anthony Trollope*. 2nd ed. London: Barker, 1969.

Brown, Homer Obed. *James Joyce's Early Fiction: The Biography of a Form*. Cleveland: Case Western Reserve University Press, 1972.

Brown, Ivor. *Conan Doyle: A Biography of the Creator of Sherlock Holmes*. London: Hamish Hamilton, 1972.

Brown, Ivor. *J. B. Priestley*. London: Longmans, Green, 1957.

Brown, Lloyd W. *Bits of Ivory: Narrative Techniques in Jane Austen's Fiction*. Baton Rouge: Louisiana State University Press, 1973.

Brown, Malcolm. *The Politics of Irish Literature: From Thomas Davis to W. B. Yeats*. Seattle: University of Washington Press, 1972.

Buckley, Jerome Hamilton. *Season of Youth: The Bildungsroman from Dickens to Golding*. Cambridge: Harvard University Press, 1974.

Burgess, Anthony. *Joysprick: An Introduction to the Language of James Joyce*. London: Deutsch, 1973.

Burkhart, Charles. *Ada Leverson*. New York: Twayne, 1973.

Burkhart, Charles. *Charlotte Brontë: A Psychosexual Study of Her Novels*. London: Gollancz, 1973.

Burns, Wayne. *Charles Reade: A Study in Victorian Authorship*. New York: Bookman Associates, 1961.

Bush, Douglas. *Jane Austen*. New York: Collier, 1975.

Butler, Marilyn. *Maria Edgeworth: A Literary Biography*. Oxford: Clarendon, 1972.

Butt, John. *Pope, Dickens and Others: Essays and Addresses*. Edinburgh: Edinburgh University Press, 1969.

Butt, J., and I. F. Clarke, eds. *The Victorians and Social Protest: A Symposium*. Hamden, Conn.: Archon, 1973.

Byrd, Max. *Visits to Bedlam: Madness and Literature in the Eighteenth Century*. Columbia: University of South Carolina Press, 1974.

Calder, Angus, and Jenni Calder. *Scott*. New York: Arco, 1971.

Calder, Jenni. *Chronicles of Conscience: A Study of George Orwell and Arthur Koestler*. Pittsburgh: University of Pittsburgh Press, 1968.

Calder, Robert Lorin. *W. Somerset Maugham and the Quest for Freedom*. Garden City, N.Y.: Doubleday, 1973.

Cambon, Glauco. *La Lotta con Proteo*. Milan: Bompiani, 1963.

Cameron, Kenneth Neill, ed. *Romantic Rebels: Essays on Shelley and His Circle*. Cambridge: Harvard University Press, 1973.

Camilucci, Marcello. *Il Viaggiatore curioso: Testimonianze critiche*. Milan: Bietti, 1971.

Carey, John. *The Violent Effigy: A Study of Dickens' Imagination*. London: Faber and Faber, 1973.

Carnochan, W. B. *Lemuel Gulliver's Mirror for Man*. Berkeley and Los Angeles: University of California Press, 1968.

Carpenter, Richard. *Thomas Hardy*. New York: Twayne, 1964.

Cassell, Richard A. *Ford Madox Ford: A Study of His Novels*. Baltimore: Johns Hopkins Press, 1961.

Cassidy, John A. *Algernon C. Swinburne*. New York: Twayne, 1964.

Cavaliero, Glen. *John Cowper Powys: Novelist*. Oxford: Clarendon, 1973.

Cazalet-Keir, Thelma, ed. *Homage to P. G. Wodehouse*. London: Barrie and Jenkins, 1973.

Cazamian, Louis. *The Social Novel in England, 1830-1850: Dickens, Disraeli, Mrs. Gaskell, Kingsley*. Translated by Martin Fido. London: Routledge and Kegan Paul, 1973.

Champion, Larry S., ed. *Quick Springs of Sense: Studies in the Eighteenth Century*. Athens: University of Georgia Press, 1974.

Chapman, Robert T. *Wyndham Lewis: Fictions and Satires*. New York: Barnes and Noble, 1973.

Chapple, J. A. V. *Documentary and Imaginative Literature, 1880-1920*. New York: Barnes and Noble, 1970.

Charles Dickens and George Cruikshank: Papers Read at a Clark Library Seminar on May 9, 1970. Los Angeles: William Andrews Clark Memorial Library, University of California, Los Angeles, 1971.

Chatman, Seymour, ed. *Literary Style: A Symposium*. London: Oxford University Press, 1971.

Christiani, Dounia Bunis. *Scandinavian Elements of "Finnegans Wake."* Evanston: Northwestern University Press, 1965.

Clareson, Thomas D., ed. *SF: The Other Side of Realism—Essays on Modern Fantasy and Science Fiction*. Bowling Green, Ohio: Bowling Green University Popular Press, 1971.

Clarke, Colin. *River of Dissolution: D. H. Lawrence and English Romanticism*. New York: Barnes and Noble, 1969.

Clayborough, Arthur. *The Grotesque in English Literature*. Oxford: Clarendon, 1965.

Clipper, Lawrence J. *G. K. Chesterton*. New York: Twayne, 1974.

Cockshut, Anthony O. J. *The Achievement of Walter Scott*. New York: New York University Press, 1969.

Cohn, Ruby. *Samuel Beckett: The Comic Gamut*. New Brunswick: Rutgers University Press, 1962.

Colby, Vineta. *The Singular Anomaly: Women Novelists of the Nineteenth Century*. New York: New York University Press, 1970.

Colby, Vineta. *Yesterday's Woman: Domestic Realism in the English Novel*. Princeton: Princeton University Press, 1974.

Colby, Vineta, and Robert A. Colby. *The Equivocal Virtue: Mrs. Oliphant and the Victorian Literary Market Place*. Hamden, Conn.: Archon, 1966.

Coles, Robert. *Irony in the Mind's Life: Essays on Novels by James Agee, Elizabeth Bowen, and George Eliot*. Charlottesville: University Press of Virginia, 1974.

Collins, H. P. *John Cowper Powys: Old Earth-Man*. New York: October House, 1967.

Collins, R. G., ed. *The Novel and Its Changing Form*. Winnipeg: University of Manitoba Press, 1972.

Collins, Robert G. *Virginia Woolf's Black Arrows of Sensation: "The Waves."* Ilfracombe, England: Stockwell, 1962.

Colloms, Brenda. *Charles Kingsley: The Lion of Eversley*. New York: Barnes and Noble, 1975.

Colwell, C. Carter. *The Tradition of British Literature*. New York: Putnam's, 1971.

Conrad, Peter. *The Victorian Treasure-House*. London: Collins, 1973.

Cook, William J., Jr. *Masks, Modes, and Morals: The Art of Evelyn Waugh*. Rutherford, N.J.: Fairleigh Dickinson University Press, 1971.

Coolidge, Olivia. *The Three Lives of Joseph Conrad*. Boston: Houghton Mifflin, 1972.

Cooper, Christopher. *Conrad and the Human Dilemma*. New York: Barnes and Noble, 1970.

Cooper, Susan. *J. B. Priestley: Portrait of an Author*. New York: Harper and Row, 1971.

Cordell, Richard A. *Somerset Maugham: A Writer for All Seasons—A Biographical and Critical Study*. 2nd ed. Bloomington: Indiana University Press, 1969.

Cornillon, Susan Koppelman, ed. *Images of Women in Fiction: Feminist Perspectives*. Rev. ed. Bowling Green, Ohio: Bowling Green University Popular Press, 1973.

Costa, Richard Hauer. *Malcolm Lowry*. New York: Twayne, 1972.

Cowan, James C. *D. H. Lawrence's American Journey: A Study in Literature and Myth*. Cleveland: Case Western Reserve University Press, 1970.

Cox, C. B. *Joseph Conrad: The Modern Imagination*. Totowa, N.J.: Rowman and Littlefield, 1974.

Cox, C. B., and A. E. Dyson, eds. *The Twentieth-Century Mind: History, Ideas, and Literature in Britain*. 3 vols. London: Oxford University Press, 1972.

Cox, Homer T. *Henry Seton Merriman*. New York: Twayne, 1967.

Cozza, Andrea. *Tobias Smollett*. Biblioteca di Studi Inglesi, 19. Bari: Adriatica, 1970.

Craig, David. *The Real Foundations: Literature and Social Change*. London: Chatto and Windus, 1973.

Craik, W. A. *Elizabeth Gaskell and the English Provincial Novel*. London: Methuen, 1975.

Crane, John K. *T. H. White*. New York: Twayne, 1974.

Crews, Frederick C. *E. M. Forster: The Perils of Humanism*. Princeton: Princeton University Press, 1962.

Crinkley, Richmond. *Walter Pater: Humanist*. Lexington: University Press of Kentucky, 1970.

Cronin, John. *Somerville and Ross*. Lewisburg, Pa.: Bucknell University Press, 1972.

Cross, Richard K. *Flaubert and Joyce: The Rite of Fiction*. Princeton: Princeton University Press, 1971.

Crothers, George D., ed. *Invitation to Learning: English and American Novels*. New York: Basic Books, 1966.

Culler, Jonathan. *Structuralist Poetics: Structuralism, Linguistics and the Study of Literature*. London: Routledge and Kegan Paul, 1975.

Curtis, Anthony. *The Pattern of Maugham: A Critical Portrait*. London: Hamish Hamilton, 1974.

Curtius, E. R. *Essays on European Literature*. Translated by Michael Kowal. Princeton: Princeton University Press, 1973.

Cusac, Marian H. *Narrative Structure in the Novels of Sir Walter Scott*. De Proprietatibus Litterarum, Series Practica, 6. The Hague: Mouton, 1969.

Dabney, Ross H. *Love and Property in the Novels of Dickens*. Berkeley and Los Angeles: University of California Press, 1967.

Dahl, Liisa. *Linguistic Features of the Stream-of-Consciousness Techniques of James Joyce, Virginia Woolf and Eugene O'Neill*. Annales Universitatis Turkuensis, Series B, 116. Turku, Finland: Turun Yliopisto, 1970.

Daiches, David. *Virginia Woolf*. Rev. ed. New York: New Directions, 1963.

Daleski, Herman M. *Dickens and the Art of Analogy*. New York: Schocken, 1970.

Daleski, Herman M. *The Forked Flame: A Study of D. H. Lawrence*. Evanston: Northwestern University Press, 1965.

Dalton, Jack P., and Clive Hart, eds. *Twelve and a Tilly: Essays on the Occasion of the 25th Anniversary of "Finnegans Wake."* Evanston: Northwestern University Press, 1965.

Davis, Earle. *The Flint and the Flame: The Artistry of Charles Dickens*. Columbia: University of Missouri Press, 1963.

Davis, Walter R. *Idea and Act in Elizabethan Fiction*. Princeton: Princeton University Press, 1969.

Dawson, Carl. *Thomas Love Peacock*. London: Routledge and Kegan Paul, 1968.

Day, Douglas. *Malcolm Lowry: A Biography*. New York: Oxford University Press, 1973.

DeLaura, David J. *Hebrew and Hellene in Victorian England: Newman, Arnold, and Pater*. Austin: University of Texas Press, 1969.

Delavenay, Emile. *D. H. Lawrence and Edward Carpenter: A Study in Edwardian Transition*. New York: Taplinger, 1971.

Delavenay, Emile. *D. H. Lawrence: The Man and His Work—The Formative Years, 1885-1919*. London: Heinemann, 1972.

DeVitis, A. A. *Anthony Burgess*. New York: Twayne, 1972.

Devlin, David D. *The Author of Waverley: A Critical Study of Walter Scott*. Lewisburg, Pa.: Bucknell University Press, 1971.

Dick, Bernard F. *The Hellenism of Mary Renault*. Carbondale: Southern Illinois University Press, 1972.

Dick, Kay. *Friends and Friendship: Conversations and Reflections*. London: Sidgwick and Jackson, 1974.

Dickson, Lovat. *H. G. Wells: His Turbulent Life and Times*. New York: Atheneum, 1969.

Dietrich, R. F. *Portrait of the Artist as a Young Superman: A Study of Shaw's Novels*. Gainesville: University of Florida Press, 1969.

Dodson, Daniel B. *Malcolm Lowry*. New York: Columbia University Press, 1970.

Dölle, Erika. *Experiment und Tradition in der Prosa Virginia Woolfs*. Munich: Fink, 1971.

Dölvers, Horst. *Der Erzähler Robert Louis Stevenson: Interpretationen*. Berne: Francke, 1969.

Donoghue, Denis. *Jonathan Swift: A Critical Introduction*. London: Cambridge University Press, 1969.

Donovan, Frank. *Dickens and Youth*. New York: Dodd, Mead, 1968.

Donovan, Robert Alan. *The Shaping Vision: Imagination in the English Novel from Defoe to Dickens*. Ithaca: Cornell University Press, 1966.

Doody, Margaret Anne. *A Natural Passion: A Study of the Novels of Samuel Richardson*. Oxford: Clarendon, 1974.

Downes, David Anthony. *The Temper of Victorian Belief: Studies in the Religious Novels of Pater, Kingsley, and Newman*. New York:Twayne, 1972.

Doyle, Esther M., and Virginia Hastings Floyd, eds. *Studies in Interpretation*. Amsterdam: Rodopi, 1972.

Doyle, Paul A. *Sean O'Faolain*. New York: Twayne, 1968.

Dubu, Jean. *La Poétique de Graham Greene dans "La Puissance et la gloire."* Paris: Minard, 1972.

Dudley, Edward, and Maximillian E. Novak, eds. *The Wild Man Within: An Image in Western Thought from the Renaissance to Romanticism*. Pittsburgh: University of Pittsburgh Press, 1972.

Duerksen, Roland A. *Shelleyan Ideas in Victorian Literature*. The Hague: Mouton, 1966.

Dunleavy, Janet Egleston. *George Moore: The Artist's Vision, the Story-teller's Art*. Lewisburg, Pa.: Bucknell University Press, 1973.

Durant, Will, and Ariel Durant. *Interpretations of Life: A Survey of Contemporary Literature*. New York: Simon and Schuster, 1970.

Duytschaever, Joris. *James Joyce*. Ontmoetingen, 88. Bruges: de Brouwer, 1970.

Eaves, T. C. Duncan, and Ben D. Kimpel. *Samuel Richardson: A Biography*. Oxford: Clarendon, 1971.

Echeruo, Michael J. C. *Joyce Cary and the Novel of Africa*. New York: Longman, 1973.

Eckley, Grace. *Benedict Kiely*. New York: Twayne, 1972.

Egri, Peter. *Avantgardism and Modernity: A Comparison of James Joyce's "Ulysses" with Thomas Mann's "Der Zauberberg" and "Lotte in Weimar."* Translated by Paul Aston. University of Tulsa Monograph Series, 14. Tulsa: University of Tulsa Press, 1972.

Egri, Peter. *James Joyce és Thomas Mann: Dekadencia és Modernség*. Budapest: Akadémiai Kiadó, 1967.

Ehrenpreis, Irvin. *Literary Meaning and Augustan Values*. Charlottesville: University of Virginia Press, 1974.

Eigner, Edwin M. *Robert Louis Stevenson and Romantic Tradition*. Princeton: Princeton University Press, 1966.

Einbond, Bernard L. *Samuel Johnson's Allegory*. De Proprietatibus Litterarum, Series Practica, 24. The Hague: Mouton, 1971.

Elliott, Robert C. *The Shape of Utopia: Studies in a Literary Genre*. Chicago: University of Chicago Press, 1970.

Ellmann, Richard. *Ulysses on the Liffey*. New York: Oxford University Press, 1972.

Ellwood, Gracia Fay. *Good News from Tolkien's Middle Earth: Two Essays on the "Applicability" of "The Lord of the Rings."* Grand Rapids: Eerdmans, 1970.

Emrich, Wilhelm. *Polemik: Streitschriften, Pressefehden und kritische Essays um Prinzipien, Methoden und Masstäbe der Literaturkritik*. Frankfurt: Athenaum, 1968.

Engleberg, Edward. *The Unknown Distance: From Consciousness to Conscience—Goethe to Camus*. Cambridge: Harvard University Press, 1972.

Epstein, Edmund L. *The Ordeal of Stephen Dedalus: The Conflict of the Generations in James Joyce's "A Portrait of the Artist as a Young Man."* Carbondale: Southern Illinois University Press, 1971.

Epstein, Perle S. *The Private Labyrinth of Malcolm Lowry: "Under the Volcano" and "The Cabbala."* New York: Holt, Rinehart and Winston, 1969.

Epstein, William H. *John Cleland: Images of a Life*. New York: Columbia University Press, 1974.

Evans, Robley. *J. R. R. Tolkien*. New York: Warner Paperback Library, 1971.

Faurot, Ruth Marie. *Jerome K. Jerome*. New York: Twayne, 1974.

Federman, Raymond. *Journey to Chaos: Samuel Beckett's Early Fiction*. Berkeley and Los Angeles: University of California Press, 1965.

Fehlmann, Guy. *Somerville et Ross: Témoins de l'Irlande d'hier*. Publications de la Faculté des Lettres et Sciences Humaines de l'Université de Caen, 20. Caen, 1970.

Felstiner, John. *The Lies of Art: Max Beerbohm's Parody and Caricature*. New York: Knopf, 1972.

Felton, Felix. *Thomas Love Peacock*. London: Allen and Unwin, 1972.

Field, P. J. C. *Romance and Chronicle: A Study of Malory's Prose Style*. Bloomington: Indiana University Press, 1971.

Fietz, Lothar. *Menschenbild und Romanstruktur in Aldous Huxleys Ideenromanen.* Studien zur englischen Philologie, Neue Folge, 13. Tübingen: Niemeyer, 1969.

Finkelstein, Bonnie Blumenthal. *Forster's Women: Eternal Differences.* New York: Columbia University Press, 1975.

Firchow, Peter E. *Aldous Huxley: Satirist and Novelist.* Minneapolis: University of Minnesota Press, 1972.

Fisch, Harold. *The Dual Image: The Figure of the Jew in English and American Literature.* New York: Ktav, 1971.

Finney, Brian H. *"Since How It Is": A Study of Samuel Beckett's Later Fiction.* London: Covent Garden, 1972.

Fish, Stanley E. *Self-Consuming Artifacts: The Experience of Seventeenth-Century Literature.* Berkeley and Los Angeles: University of California Press, 1972.

Fleishman, Avrom. *A Reading of "Mansfield Park": An Essay in Critical Synthesis.* Minneapolis: University of Minnesota Press, 1967.

Fleishman, Avrom. *Virginia Woolf: A Critical Study.* Baltimore: Johns Hopkins Press, 1975.

Fletcher, Ian, ed. *Meredith Now: Some Critical Essays.* New York: Barnes and Noble, 1971.

Fletcher, Ian. *Swinburne.* Harlow: Longman for the British Council, 1973.

Fletcher, John. *The Novels of Samuel Beckett.* London: Chatto and Windus, 1964.

Foltinek, Herbert. *Vorstufen zum viktorianischen Realismus: Der englische Roman von Jane Austen bis Charles Dickens.* Wiener Beiträge zur englischen Philologie, 71. Vienna: Braumüller, 1968.

Fraser, George S. *Lawrence Durrell: A Study.* Rev. ed. London: Faber and Faber, 1973.

Frederick, John T. *William Henry Hudson.* New York: Twayne, 1972.

Fredman, Alice Green. *Anthony Trollope.* New York: Columbia University Press, 1971.

Freedman, Ralph. *The Lyrical Novel: Studies in Hermann Hesse, André Gide, and Virginia Woolf.* Princeton: Princeton University Press, 1963.

French, David P., ed. *Jonathan Swift: Tercentenary Essays.* University of Tulsa Monograph Series, 3. Tulsa: University of Tulsa Press, 1967.

French, R. B. D. *P. G. Wodehouse.* New York: Barnes and Noble, 1966.

Friedman, Alan Warren. *Lawrence Durrell and "The Alexandria Quartet": Art for Love's Sake.* Norman: University of Oklahoma Press, 1970.

Friedman, Melvin J., ed. *Samuel Beckett Now: Critical Approaches to His Novels, Poetry and Plays.* Chicago: University of Chicago Press, 1970.

Friedman, Melvin J., ed. *The Vision Obscured: Perceptions of Some Twentieth-Century Catholic Novelists.* New York: Fordham University Press, 1970.

Friedman, Melvin J., and John B. Vickery, eds. *The Shaken Realist: Essays in Modern Literature in Honor of Frederick J. Hoffman.* Baton Rouge: Louisiana State University Press, 1970.

Fuhrmann, Manfred, ed. *Terror und Spiel: Probleme der Mythenrezeption.*

Munich: Fink, 1971.

Fujita, Seiji. *Structure and Motif in "Middlemarch."* Tokyo: Hokuseido, 1969.

Fuller, Jean Overton. *Swinburne: A Critical Biography.* London: Chatto and Windus, 1968.

Furbank, P. N. *Samuel Butler (1835-1902).* Cambridge: Cambridge University Press, 1948.

Fussell, Paul. *Samuel Johnson and the Life of Writing.* New York: Harcourt Brace Jovanovich, 1971.

Garrett, Peter K. *Scene and Symbol from George Eliot to James Joyce: Studies in Changing Fictional Mode.* New Haven: Yale University Press, 1969.

Garzilli, Enrico. *Circles Without Center: Paths to the Discovery and Creation of Self in Modern Literature.* Cambridge: Harvard University Press, 1972.

Gassenmeier, Michael. *Der Typus des "man of feeling": Studien zum sentimentalen Roman des 18. Jahrhunderts in England.* Studien zur englischen Philologie, Neue Folge, 16. Tübingen: Niemeyer, 1972.

Geduld, Harry M. *Sir James Barrie.* New York: Twayne, 1971.

Gerstenberger, Donna. *Iris Murdoch.* Lewisburg, Pa.: Bucknell University Press, 1975.

Gibb, Jocelyn, ed. *Light on C. S. Lewis.* London: Bles, 1965.

Giddings, Robert. *The Tradition of Smollett.* London: Methuen, 1967.

Gifford, Don, with Robert J. Seidman. *Notes for Joyce: An Annotation of James Joyce's "Ulysses."* New York: Dutton, 1974.

Gill, Richard. *Happy Rural Seat: The English Country House and the Literary Imagination.* New Haven: Yale University Press, 1972.

Gillen, Charles H. *H. H. Munro (Saki).* New York: Twayne, 1969.

Gittings, Robert. *Young Thomas Hardy.* London: Heinemann, 1975.

Glasheen, Adaline. *A Second Census of "Finnegans Wake."* Evanston: Northwestern University Press, 1963.

Glicksberg, Charles I. *The Ironic Vision in Modern Literature.* The Hague: Nijhoff, 1969.

Glicksberg, Charles I. *Modern Literary Perspectivism.* Dallas: Southern Methodist University Press, 1970.

Glut, Donald F. *The Frankenstein Legend: A Tribute to Mary Shelley and Boris Karloff.* Metuchen, N.J.: Scarecrow, 1973.

Göller, Karl Heinz. *"Romance" und "novel": Die Anfänge des englischen Romans.* Sprache und Literatur: Regensburger Arbeiten zur Anglistik und Amerikanistik, 1. Regensburg: Carl, 1972.

Goetsch, Paul. *Die Romankonzeption in England, 1880-1910.* Anglistische Forschungen, 94. Heidelberg: Winter, 1967.

Gold, Joseph. *Charles Dickens: Radical Moralist.* Minneapolis: University of Minnesota Press, 1972.

Goldberg, Michael. *Carlyle and Dickens.* Athens: University of Georgia Press, 1972.

Goldberg, S. L. *The Classical Temper: A Study of James Joyce's "Ulys-*

ses." London: Chatto and Windus, 1961.

Golden, Morris. *Richardson's Characters.* Ann Arbor: University of Michigan Press, 1963.

Golden, Morris. *The Self Observed: Swift, Johnson, Wordsworth.* Baltimore: Johns Hopkins Press, 1972.

Goldknopf, David. *The Life of the Novel.* Chicago: University of Chicago Press, 1972.

Goodheart, Eugene. *The Cult of the Ego: The Self in Modern Literature.* Chicago: University of Chicago Press, 1968.

Goodheart, Eugene. *The Utopian Vision of D. H. Lawrence.* Chicago: University of Chicago Press, 1963.

Goodin, George, ed. *The English Novel in the Nineteenth Century: Essays on the Literary Mediation of Human Values.* Illinois Studies in Language and Literature, 63. Urbana: University of Illinois Press, 1972.

Gopnik, Irwin. *A Theory of Style and Richardson's "Clarissa."* De Proprietatibus Litterarum, Series Practica, 10. The Hague: Mouton, 1970.

Gordon, Ambrose, Jr. *The Invisible Tent: The War Novels of Ford Madox Ford.* Austin: University of Texas Press, 1964.

Gorlier, Claudio, ed. *Studi e ricerche di letteratura inglese e americana, II.* Milan: Cisalpino-Goliardica, 1971.

Gose, Elliott B., Jr. *Imagination Indulged: The Irrational in the Nineteenth-Century Novel.* Montreal: McGill-Queen's University Press, 1972.

Gransden, K. W. *E. M. Forster.* Rev. ed. Edinburgh: Oliver and Boyd, 1970.

Gray, Nigel. *The Silent Majority: A Study of the Working Class in Post-War British Fiction.* New York: Barnes and Noble, 1973.

Graves, Nora Calhoun. *The Two Culture Theory in C. P. Snow's Novels.* Hattiesburg: University and College Press of Mississippi, 1971.

Greaves, Margaret. *The Blazon of Honour: A Study in Renaissance Magnanimity.* New York: Barnes and Noble, 1964.

Greaves, Richard Lee. *John Bunyan.* Grand Rapids: Eerdmans, 1969.

Green, Roger Lancelyn, and Walter Hooper. *C. S. Lewis: A Biography.* London: Collins, 1974.

Greene, Donald J. *Samuel Johnson.* New York: Twayne, 1970.

Greenless, Ian. *Norman Douglas.* London: Longmans, Green, 1957.

Greiner, Walter F. *Studien zur Entstehung der englischen Romantheorie an der Wende zum 18. Jahrhundert.* Tübingen: Niemeyer, 1969.

Grillo, Virgil. *Charles Dickens' "Sketches by Boz": End in the Beginning.* Boulder: Colorado Associated University Press, 1974.

Gross, John. *James Joyce.* New York: Viking, 1970.

Guiguet, Jean. *Virginia Woolf and Her Works.* Translated by Jean Stewart. New York: Harcourt Brace and World, 1965.

Gurko, Leo. *The Two Lives of Joseph Conrad.* New York: Crowell, 1965.

Guthke, Karl S. *Die Mythologie der entgötterten Welt: Ein literarisches Thema von der Aufklärung bis zur Gegenwart.* Göttingen: Vandenhoeck and Ruprecht, 1971.

Hall, James. *Arnold Bennett: Primitivism and Taste.* Seattle: University of Washington Press, 1959.

Halper, Nathan. *The Early James Joyce.* New York: Columbia University Press, 1973.

Halperin, John. *Egoism and Self-Discovery in the Victorian Novel: Studies in the Ordeal of Knowledge in the Nineteenth Century.* New York: Burt Franklin, 1974.

Halperin, John. *The Language of Meditation: Four Studies in Nineteenth-Century Fiction.* Elms Court, England: Stockwell, 1973.

Hannah, Barbara. *Striving Towards Wholeness.* New York: Putnam's, 1971.

Harden, O. Elizabeth McWhorter. *Maria Edgeworth's Art of Prose Fiction.* The Hague: Mouton, 1971.

Hardwick, Elizabeth. *Seduction and Betrayal: Women and Literature.* New York: Random House, 1970.

Hardy, Barbara. *The Appropriate Form: An Essay on the Novel.* London: Athlone, 1964.

Hardy, Barbara. *The Exposure of Luxury: Radical Themes in Thackeray.* London: Owen, 1972.

Hardy, Barbara. *Rituals and Feeling in the Novels of George Eliot.* Swansea: University College of Swansea, 1973.

Harmon, Maurice. *Sean O'Faolain: A Critical Introduction.* Notre Dame: University of Notre Dame Press, 1966.

Hart, Clive. *James Joyce's "Ulysses."* Sydney: Sydney University Press, 1968.

Hart, Clive. *Structure and Motif in "Finnegans Wake."* Evanston: Northwestern University Press, 1962.

Hart, Clive, and David Hayman, eds. *James Joyce's "Ulysses": Critical Essays.* Berkeley and Los Angeles: University of California Press, 1974.

Hart, Francis R. *Scott's Novels: The Plotting of Historic Survival.* Charlottesville: University of Virginia Press, 1966.

Harvey, Lawrence E. *Samuel Beckett: Poet and Critic.* Princeton: Princeton University Press, 1970.

Harvey, W. J. *The Art of George Eliot.* New York: Oxford University Press, 1969.

Hassan, Ihab. *The Dismemberment of Orpheus: Towards a Postmodern Literature.* New York: Oxford University Press, 1971.

Hassan, Ihab. *Paracriticisms: Seven Speculations of the Times.* Urbana: University of Illinois Press, 1975.

Hatfield, Glenn W. *Henry Fielding and the Language of Irony.* Chicago: University of Chicago Press, 1968.

Hauff, Jürgen, Albrecht Heller, Bernd Hüppauf, Lothar Köhn, and Klaus-Peter Philippi. *Methodendiskussion: Arbeitsbuch zur Literaturwissenschaft.* Frankfurt: Fischer Athenäum, 1972.

Hayman, David. *"Ulysses": The Mechanics of Meaning.* Englewood Cliffs, N.J.: Prentice-Hall, 1970.

Hays, Peter L. *The Limping Hero: Grotesques in Literature.* New York: New York University Press, 1971.

Heilbrun, Carolyn G. *Christopher Isherwood.* New York: Columbia University Press, 1970.

Heilbrun, Carolyn G. *Towards a Recognition of Androgyny.* New York: Knopf, 1973.

Hennedy, Hugh L. *Unity in Barsetshire.* De Proprietatibus Litterarum, Series Practica, 28. The Hague: Mouton, 1971.

Hennessey, James Pope. *Anthony Trollope.* Boston: Little, Brown, 1971.

Hepburn, James G. *The Art of Arnold Bennett.* Bloomington: Indiana University Press, 1963.

Hewish, John. *Emily Brontë: A Critical and Biographical Study.* London: Macmillan, 1969.

Hewitt, Douglas. *The Approach to Fiction: Good and Bad Readings of Novels.* London: Longman, 1972.

Hienger, Jörg. *Literarische Zukunftsphantastik: Eine Studie über Science Fiction.* Göttingen: Vandenhoeck and Ruprecht, 1971.

Highet, Gilbert. *Explorations.* New York: Oxford University Press, 1971.

Hirshberg, Edgar W. *George Henry Lewes.* New York: Twayne, 1970.

Hochman, Baruch. *Another Ego: The Changing View of Self and Society in the Work of D. H. Lawrence.* Columbia: University of South Carolina Press, 1970.

Hodgart, Matthew. *Satire.* New York: McGraw-Hill, 1969.

Hodges, Robert R. *The Dual Heritage of Joseph Conrad.* The Hague: Mouton, 1967.

Hoffman, Fredrick J. *The Imagination's New Beginning: Theology and Modern Literature.* University of Notre Dame Ward-Phillips Lectures in English Language and Literature, 1. Notre Dame: University of Notre Dame Press, 1967.

Hoffmann, Charles G. *Ford Madox Ford.* New York: Twayne, 1967.

Hogan, Robert. *Eimar O'Duffy.* Lewisburg, Pa.: Bucknell University Press, 1972.

Hollingsworth, Keith. *The Newgate Novel (1830-1847): Bulwer, Ainsworth, Dickens, and Thackeray.* Detroit: Wayne State University Press, 1963.

Hollis, Christopher. *The Mind of Chesterton.* Coral Gables: University of Miami Press, 1970.

Holtz, William V. *Image and Immortality: A Study of "Tristram Shandy."* Providence: Brown University Press, 1970.

Hooker, Jeremy. *John Cowper Powys.* Cardiff: University of Wales Press, 1973.

Hornback, Bert G. *"Noah's Arkitecture": A Study of Dickens's Mythology.* Athens: Ohio University Press, 1972.

Hopkins, Robert H. *The True Genius of Oliver Goldsmith.* Baltimore: Johns Hopkins Press, 1969.

Howe, Irving. *A World More Attractive: A View of Modern Literature and Politics.* New York: Horizon, 1963.

Hughes, Peter, and David Williams, eds. *The Varied Pattern: Studies in the 18th Century*. Toronto: Hakkert, 1971.

Humfrey, Belinda, ed. *Essays on John Cowper Powys*. Cardiff: University of Wales Press, 1972.

Hummert, Paul A. *Bernard Shaw's Marxian Romance*. Lincoln: University of Nebraska Press, 1973.

Huttar, Charles A., ed. *Imagination and the Spirit: Essays in Literature and the Christian Faith Presented to Clyde S. Kilby*. Grand Rapids: Eerdmans, 1971.

Inglis, Fred. *An Essential Discipline: An Introduction to Literary Criticism*. London: Methuen, 1968.

Inniss, Kenneth. *D. H. Lawrence's Bestiary: A Study of His Use of Animal Trope and Symbol*. De Proprietatibus Litterarum, Series Practica, 30. The Hague: Mouton, 1971.

Irwin, Michael. *Henry Fielding: The Tentative Realist*. Oxford: Clarendon, 1967.

Iser, Wolfgang, ed. *Henry Fielding und der englische Roman des 18. Jahrhunderts*. Wege der Forschung, 161. Darmstadt: Wissenschaftliche Buchgesellschaft, 1972.

Iser, Wolfgang. *The Implied Reader: Patterns of Communication in Prose Fiction from Bunyan to Beckett*. Baltimore: Johns Hopkins Press, 1974.

Iser, Wolfgang, and Fritz Schalk, eds. *Dargestellte Geschichte in der europäischen Literatur des 19. Jahrhunderts*. Studien zur Philosophie und Literatur des neunzehnten Jahrhunderts, 7. Frankfurt: Klostermann, 1970.

Jacobsen, Josephine, and William R. Mueller. *The Testament of Samuel Beckett*. New York: Hill and Wang, 1964.

Jacquet, Claude. *Joyce et Rabelais: Aspects de la création verbale dans "Finnegans Wake."* Paris: Didier, 1972.

James, E. Anthony. *Daniel Defoe's Many Voices: A Rhetorical Study of Prose Style and Literary Method*. Amsterdam: Rodopi, 1972.

Janvier, Ludovic. *Pour Samuel Beckett*. Paris: Minuit, 1966.

Jeffares, A. Norman, ed. *Scott's Mind and Art*. New York: Barnes and Noble, 1970.

Jensen, H. James, and Malvin R. Zirker, Jr., eds. *The Satirist's Art*. Bloomington: Indiana University Press, 1972.

Johnson, Edgar. *Sir Walter Scott: The Great Unknown*. 2 vols. New York: Macmillan, 1970.

Johnson, Manly. *Virginia Woolf*. New York: Ungar, 1973.

Jones, Peter. *Philosophy and the Novel: Philosophical Aspects of "Middlemarch," "Anna Karenina," "The Brothers Karamazov," "A la recherche du temps" and of the Methods of Criticism*. Oxford: Clarendon, 1975.

Kahler, Erich. *The Inward Turn of Narrative*. Translated by Richard and Clara Winston. Princeton: Princeton University Press, 1973.

Kahrmann, Bernd. *Die idyllische Szene im zeitgenössischen englischen Roman*. Bad Homburg: Max Gehlen, 1969.

Kinkead-Weekes, Mark. *Samuel Richardson: Dramatic Novelist.* London: Methuen, 1973.

Kirby, Thomas Austin, and William John Olive, eds. *Essays in Honor of Esmond Linworth Marilla.* Baton Rouge: Louisiana State University Press, 1970.

Klotz, Volker. *Die erzählte Stadt: Ein Sujet als Herausforderung des Romans von Lesage bis Döblin.* Munich: Hanser, 1969.

Knoepflmacher, U. C. *George Eliot's Early Novels: The Limits of Realism.* Berkeley and Los Angeles: University of California Press, 1968.

Kocher, Paul H. *Master of Middle-Earth: The Fiction of J. R. R. Tolkien.* Boston: Houghton Mifflin, 1972.

Konigsberg, Ira. *Samuel Richardson and the Dramatic Novel.* Lexington: University of Kentucky Press, 1968.

Kotzin, Michael C. *Dickens and the Fairy Tale.* Bowling Green, Ohio: Bowling Green University Popular Press, 1972.

Korg, Jacob. *Dylan Thomas.* New York: Twayne, 1965.

Korg, Jacob. *George Gissing: A Critical Biography.* Seattle: University of Washington Press, 1963.

Korshin, Paul J., ed. *Studies in Change and Revolution: Aspects of English Intellectual History, 1640-1800.* Menston, England: Scolar, 1972.

Kramer, Dale. *Charles Robert Maturin.* New York: Twayne, 1973.

Kreutzer, Eberhard. *Sprache und Spiel im "Ulysses" von James Joyce.* Studien zur englischen Literatur, 2. Bonn: Bouvier, 1969

Kroeber, Karl. *Styles in Fictional Structure: The Art of Jane Austen, Charlotte Brontë, George Eliot.* Princeton: Princeton University Press, 1971.

Kubal, David L. *Outside the Whale: George Orwell's Art and Politics.* Notre Dame: University of Notre Dame Press, 1972.

Lagercrantz, Olof. *Att finnas till: En Studie i James Joyces Roman "Odysseus."* Stockholm: Wahlström and Widstrand, 1970.

Lanham, Richard A. *"Tristram Shandy": The Games of Pleasure.* Berkeley and Los Angeles: University of California Press, 1973.

Lary, N. M. *Dostoevsky and Dickens: A Study of Literary Influence.* London: Routledge and Kegan Paul, 1973.

Lascelles, Mary. *Notions and Facts: Collected Criticism and Research.* Oxford: Clarendon, 1972.

Laurenson, Diana T., and Alan Swingewood. *The Sociology of Literature.* London: MacGibbon and Kee, 1971.

Lawry, Jon S. *Sidney's Two Arcadias: Pattern and Proceeding.* Ithaca: Cornell University Press, 1972.

Leaska, Mitchell A. *Virginia Woolf's Lighthouse: A Study in Critical Method.* New York: Columbia University Press, 1970.

Leavis, F. R., and Q. D. Leavis. *Dickens: The Novelist.* New York: Pantheon, 1970.

Lebowitz, Naomi. *Humanism and the Absurd in the Modern Novel.* Evanston: Northwestern University Press, 1971.

Leclaire, Jacques. *Un Témoin de l'avènement de l'Angleterre contemporaine: Francis Brett Young—L'Homme et l'oeuvre, 1884-1954*. Paris: Didier, 1969.

Lee, Jae Num. *Swift and Scatological Satire*. Albuquerque: University of New Mexico Press, 1971.

Lee, James W. *John Braine*. New York: Twayne, 1968.

Leimbach, Burkhard, and Karl-H. Löschen. *Fieldings "Tom Jones": Bürger und Aristokrat—Sozialethik als Indikator sozialgeschichtlicher Widersprüche*. Bonn: Bouvier, 1974.

Lerner, Laurence. *The Truthtellers: Jane Austen, George Eliot, D. H. Lawrence*. New York: Schocken, 1967.

LeRoy, Gaylord C., and Ursula Beitz, eds. *Preserve and Create: Essays in Marxist Literary Criticism*. New York: Humanities, 1973.

LeStourgeon, Diana E. *Rosamond Lehmann*. New York: Twayne, 1965.

Levin, Harry. *James Joyce: A Critical Introduction*. Rev. ed. New York: New Directions, 1960.

Levin, Milton. *Noel Coward*. New York: Twayne, 1968.

Levine, George R. *Henry Fielding and the Dry Mock: A Study of the Techniques of Irony in His Early Works*. The Hague: Mouton, 1967.

Levine, June Perry. *Creation and Criticism: "A Passage to India."* Lincoln: University of Nebraska Press, 1971.

Levine, Richard A. *Benjamin Disraeli*. New York: Twayne, 1968.

Lévy, Maurice. *Le Roman "gothique" anglais, 1764-1824*. Publications de la Faculté des Lettres et Sciences Humaines de Toulouse, Série A, 9. Toulouse, 1968.

Lid, R. W. *Ford Madox Ford: The Essence of His Art*. Berkeley and Los Angeles: University of California Press, 1964.

Liddell, Robert. *The Novels of I. Compton-Burnett*. London: Gollancz, 1955.

Lief, Ruth Ann. *Homage to Oceania: The Prophetic Vision of George Orwell*. Columbus: Ohio State University Press, 1969.

Liljegren, S. Bodvar. *Joseph Conrad as a "Prober of Feminine Hearts": Notes on the Novel "The Rescue."* Essays and Studies on English Language and Literature, 27. Upsala: Lundequistska, 1968.

Lindeman, Ralph D. *Norman Douglas*. New York: Twayne, 1965.

Link, Frederick M. *Aphra Behn*. New York: Twayne, 1968.

Lodge, David. *Evelyn Waugh*. New York: Columbia University Press, 1971.

Lodge, David. *Graham Greene*. New York: Columbia University Press, 1966.

Lodge, David. *The Novelist at the Crossroads and Other Essays on Fiction and Criticism*. Ithaca: Cornell University Press, 1971.

Logu, Pietro de. *La Narrativa di George Eliot*. Biblioteca di Studi Inglesi, 14. Bari: Adriatica, 1969.

Lombardo, Agostino. *Ritratto di Enobarbo: Saggi sulla letteratura inglese*. Pisa: Nistri-Lischi, 1971.

Lougy, Robert E. *Charles Robert Maturin*. Lewisburg, Pa.: Bucknell University Press, 1975.

Lucas, John, ed. *Literature and Politics in the Nineteenth Century*. London: Methuen, 1971.

Lucas, John. *The Melancholy Man: A Study of Dickens's Novels*. London: Methuen, 1970.

Lumiansky, R. M., and Herschel Baker, eds. *Critical Approaches to Six Major English Works: "Beowulf" Through "Paradise Lost."* Philadelphia: University of Pennsylvania Press, 1968.

Lyons, J. B. *James Joyce and Medicine*. Dublin: Dolmen, 1973.

McCrosson, Doris Ross. *Walter de la Mare*. New York: Twayne, 1966.

McDowell, Frederick P.W. *E. M. Forster*. New York: Twayne, 1969.

McElderry, Bruce R., Jr. *Max Beerbohm*. New York: Twayne, 1972.

McIntosh, Carey. *The Choice of Life: Samuel Johnson and the World of Fiction*. New Haven: Yale University Press, 1973.

McLaurin, Allen. *Virginia Woolf: The Echoes Enslaved*. London: Cambridge University Press, 1973.

McMaster, Juliet. *Thackeray: The Major Novels*. Toronto: University of Toronto Press, 1971.

MacShane, Frank. *The Life and Work of Ford Madox Ford*. New York: Horizon, 1965.

McVeagh, John. *Elizabeth Gaskell*. New York: Humanities, 1970.

Madden, David, ed. *Rediscoveries: Informal Essays in Which Well-Known Novelists Rediscover Neglected Works of Fiction by One of Their Favorite Authors*. New York: Crown, 1971.

Madsen, Peter. *Romanens form: En formel analyse af Sternes "Tristram Shandy."* Studier fra Sprog- og Oldtidsforskning, 283. Copenhagen: Gads, 1973.

Magalaner, Marvin, ed. *A James Joyce Miscellany*. 3rd series. Carbondale: Southern Illinois University Press, 1962.

Mahood, M. M. *Joyce Cary's Africa*. Boston: Houghton Mifflin, 1965.

Mann, Otto, ed. *Christliche Dichter im 20. Jahrhundert: Beiträge zur europäischen Literatur*. Rev. ed. Berne: Francke, 1968.

Mannheimer, Monica. *The Generations in Meredith's Novels*. Stockholm: Almqvist and Wiksell, 1972.

Manning, Sylvia Bank. *Dickens as Satirist*. New Haven: Yale University Press, 1971.

Mansell, Darrel. *The Novels of Jane Austen: An Interpretation*. London: Macmillan, 1973.

Maresca, Thomas E. *Epic to Novel*. Columbus: Ohio State University Press, 1974.

Marissel, André. *Samuel Beckett*. Paris: Editions Universitaires, 1963.

Marshall, William H. *Wilkie Collins*. New York: Twayne, 1970.

Mason, Michael. *James Joyce: "Ulysses."* London: Arnold, 1972.

May, Keith. *Aldous Huxley*. London: Elek, 1972.

Meier, Paul. *La Pensée utopique de William Morris*. Paris: Editions Sociales, 1972.

Meisel, Perry. *Thomas Hardy: The Return of the Repressed—A Study of the Major Fiction*. New Haven: Yale University Press, 1972.

zwischen dem Ende des 19. Jahrhunderts und dem Ausbruch des ersten Weltkrieges. Hamburg: de Gruyter, 1967.

Mueller, William R. *Celebration of Life: Studies in Modern Fiction.* New York: Sheed and Ward, 1972.

Murillo, L. A. *The Cyclical Night: Irony in James Joyce and Jorge Luis Borges.* Cambridge: Harvard University Press, 1968.

Murray, E. B. *Ann Radcliffe.* New York: Twayne, 1972.

Nahal, Chaman. *D. H. Lawrence: An Eastern View.* South Brunswick: A. S. Barnes, 1970.

Naik, M. K. *W. Somerset Maugham.* Norman: University of Oklahoma Press, 1966.

Nardin, Jane. *Those Elegant Decorums: The Concept of Propriety in Jane Austen's Novels.* Albany: State University of New York Press, 1973.

Naremore, James. *The World Without a Self: Virginia Woolf and the Novel.* New Haven: Yale University Press, 1973.

Nassar, Christopher S. *Into the Demon Universe: A Literary Exploration of Oscar Wilde.* New Haven: Yale University Press, 1974.

Negriolli, Claude. *La Symbolique de D.-H. Lawrence.* Paris: Presses Universitaires, 1970.

Neuhaus, Volker. *Typen multiperspektivischen Erzählens.* Literatur und Leben, Neue Folge, 13. Cologne: Bohlau, 1971.

Nevius, Blake. *Ivy Compton-Burnett.* New York: Columbia University Press, 1970.

New, Melvyn. *Laurence Sterne as Satirist: A Reading of "Tristram Shandy."* Gainesville: University of Florida Press, 1970.

New, William H. *Malcolm Lowry.* Toronto: McClelland and Stewart, 1971.

Newcomer, James. *Maria Edgeworth the Novelist, 1767-1849: A Bicentennial Study.* Fort Worth: Texas Christian University Press, 1967.

Newell, Kenneth B. *Structure in Four Novels by H. G. Wells.* The Hague: Mouton, 1968.

Nisbet, Ada, and Blake Nevius, eds. *Dickens Centennial Essays.* Berkeley and Los Angeles: University of California Press, 1971.

Novak, Maximillian E. *William Congreve.* New York: Twayne, 1971.

Nuttall, A. D. *A Common Sky: Philosophy and the Literary Imagination.* London: Chatto and Windus for Sussex University Press, 1974.

Ohlmarks, Ake. *Sagan om Tolkien.* Stockholm: Almqvist and Wiksell, 1972.

Ohmann, Carol. *Ford Madox Ford: From Apprentice to Craftsman.* Middletown, Conn.: Wesleyan University Press, 1964.

Omasreiter, Ria. *Naturwissenschaft und Literaturkritik im England des 18. Jahrhunderts.* Erlanger Beiträge zur Sprach- und Kunstwissenschaft, 41. Nuremberg: Carl, 1971.

Orel, Harold, and George J. Worth, eds. *The Nineteenth-Century Writer and His Audience.* Lawrence: University of Kansas Publications, 1969.

Ormond, Leonée. *George du Maurier.* Pittsburgh: University of Pittsburgh Press, 1969.

Otten, Kurt. *Der englische Roman: Vom 16. zum 19. Jahrhundert.* Grundlagen der Anglistik und Amerikanistik, 4. Berlin: Erich Schmidt, 1971.

Owens, Graham, ed. *George Moore's Mind and Art*. New York: Barnes and Noble, 1970.

Paci, Francesca Romana. *Vita e opere di James Joyce*. Bari: Laterza, 1968.

Page, Norman. *The Language of Jane Austen*. Oxford: Blackwell, 1972.

Pagliaro, Harold E., ed. *Studies in Eighteenth-Century Culture, Volume 2: Irrationalism in the Eighteenth Century*. Cleveland: Case Western Reserve University Press, 1972.

Palacio, Jean de. *Mary Shelley dans son oeuvre: Contribution aux études Shelleyennes*. Paris: Klincksieck, 1969.

Palmer, John A. *Joseph Conrad's Fiction: A Study in Literary Growth*. Ithaca: Cornell University Press, 1968.

Panichas, George A. *The Reverent Discipline: Essays in Literary Criticism and Culture*. Knoxville: University of Tennessee Press, 1973.

Paris, Bernard J. *A Psychological Approach to Fiction: Studies in Thackeray, Stendhal, George Eliot, Dostoevsky, and Conrad*. Bloomington: Indiana University Press, 1974.

Parisot, Henri, ed. *Lewis Carroll*. Paris: Herne, 1971.

Parr, Mary. *James Joyce: The Poetry of Conscience—A Study of "Ulysses."* Milwaukee: Inland, 1961.

Parry, Benita. *Delusions and Discoveries: Studies on India in the British Imagination, 1880-1930*. London: Lane, 1972.

Pastalosky, Rosa. *Henry Fielding y la tradición picaresca*. Buenos Aires: Solar/Hachette, 1970.

Penner, Allen Richard. *Alan Sillitoe*. New York: Twayne, 1972.

Pérez Minik, Domingo. *Introducción a la novela inglesa actual*. Textos Universitarios, 9. Madrid: Guadarrama, 1968.

Peters, Margot. *Charlotte Brontë: Style in the Novel*. Madison: University of Wisconsin Press, 1973.

Phillips, Robert. *Denton Welch*. New York: Twayne, 1974.

Pinion, F. B. *A Jane Austen Companion: A Critical Survey and Reference Book*. London: Macmillan, 1973.

Pochoda, Elizabeth T. *Arthurian Propaganda: "Le Morte Darthur" as an Historical Ideal of Life*. Chapel Hill: University of North Carolina Press, 1971.

Polhemus, Robert M. *The Changing World of Anthony Trollope*. Berkeley and Los Angeles: University of California Press, 1968.

Pollard, Arthur. *Mrs. Gaskell: Novelist and Biographer*. Cambridge: Harvard University Press, 1966.

Pritchard, R. E. *D. H. Lawrence: Body of Darkness*. Pittsburgh: University of Pittsburgh Press, 1971.

Pritchard, William H. *Wyndham Lewis*. New York: Twayne, 1968.

Pryce-Jones, David. *Graham Greene*. New York: Barnes and Noble, 1963.

Rafroidi, Patrick. *L'Irlande et le romantisme: La Littérature irlandaise-anglaise de 1789 à 1850 et sa place dans le mouvement occidental*. Paris: Editions Universitaires, 1972.

Rance, Nicholas. *The Historical Novel and Popular Politics in Nineteenth-*

Century England. London: Vision, 1975.

Rao, K. Bhaskara. *Rudyard Kipling's India*. Norman: University of Oklahoma Press, 1967.

Rawlins, Jack P. *Thackeray's Novels: A Fiction That Is True*. Berkeley and Los Angeles: University of California Press, 1974.

Rawson, C. J. *Gulliver and the Gentle Reader: Studies in Swift in Our Times*. London: Routledge and Kegan Paul, 1973.

Rawson, C. J. *Henry Fielding and the Augustan Ideal Under Stress*. London: Routledge and Kegan Paul, 1972.

Ready, William. *The Tolkien Relation: A Personal Inquiry*. Chicago: Regenery, 1968.

Récit et roman: Formes du roman anglais du XVIe au XX siècle. Paris: Didier, 1972.

Rees, Richard. *George Orwell: Fugitive from the Camp of Victory*. Carbondale: Southern Illinois University Press, 1961.

Reinhold, Heinz, ed. *Charles Dickens: Sein Werk im Lichte neuer deutscher Forschung*. Heidelberg: Winter, 1969.

Reis, Richard H. *George MacDonald*. New York: Twayne, 1972.

Rexroth, Kenneth. *The Elastic Retort: Essays in Literature and Ideas*. New York: Seabury, 1973.

Richetti, John J. *Popular Fiction Before Richardson: Narrative Patterns, 1700-1739*. Oxford: Clarendon, 1969.

Roberts, Gildas, ed. *Seven Studies in English*. Cape Town: Purnell, 1971.

Roberts, Mark. *The Tradition of Romantic Morality*. London: Macmillan, 1973.

Rogers, Robert. *A Psychoanalytic Study of the Double in Literature*. Detroit: Wayne State University Press, 1970.

Rolle, Dietrich. *Fielding und Sterne: Untersuchungen über die Funktion des Erzählers*. Neue Beiträge zur englischen Philologie, 2. Münster: Aschendorff, 1963.

Rose, Lois, and Stephen Rose. *The Shattered Ring: Science Fiction and the Quest for Making*. Richmond, Va.: Knox, 1970.

Rosenbaum, S. P., ed. *English Literature and British Philosophy: A Collection of Essays*. Chicago: University of Chicago Press, 1971.

Rosenfield, Claire. *Paradise of Snakes: An Archetypal Analysis of Conrad's Political Novels*. Chicago: University of Chicago Press, 1967.

Rosier, James L., ed. *Philological Essays: Studies in Old and Middle English Language and Literature in Honor of Herbert Dean Meritt*. Janua Linguarum, Series Major, 37. The Hague: Mouton, 1970.

Rousseau, G. S., and P.-G. Boucé, eds. *Tobias Smollett: Bicentennial Essays Presented to Lewis M. Knapp*. New York: Oxford University Press, 1971.

Rubin, Louis, D., Jr. *The Teller in the Tale*. Seattle: University of Washington Press, 1967.

Rubrecht, Werner Hermann. *Durrells "Alexandria Quartet": Struktur als Bezugssystem—Sichtung und Analyse*. Schweizer Anglistische Arbeiten, 72. Berne: Francke, 1972.

Ruotolo, Lucio P. *Six Existential Heroes: The Politics of Faith.* Cambridge: Harvard University Press, 1973.

Russell, John. *Henry Green: Nine Novels and an Unpacked Bag.* New Brunswick: Rutgers University Press, 1960.

Ryals, Clyde de L., ed., with the assistance of John Clubbe and Benjamin Franklin Fisher IV. *Nineteenth-Century Literary Perspectives: Essays in Honor of Lionel Stevenson.* Durham: Duke University Press, 1974.

Ryf, Robert S. *Henry Green.* New York: Columbia University Press, 1967.

Ryf, Robert S. *Joseph Conrad.* New York: Columbia University Press, 1970.

Sagar, Keith. *The Art of D. H. Lawrence.* London: Cambridge University Press, 1966.

Sale, Roger. *Modern Heroism: Essays on D. H. Lawrence, William Empson, and J. R. R. Tolkien.* Berkeley and Los Angeles: University of California Press, 1973.

San Juan, Epifanio, Jr. *The Art of Oscar Wilde.* Princeton: Princeton University Press, 1967.

Sanders, Scott. *D. H. Lawrence: The World of the Five Major Novels.* New York: Viking, 1973.

Saposnik, Irving S. *Robert Louis Stevenson.* New York: Twayne, 1974.

Saveson, John E. *Joseph Conrad: The Making of a Moralist.* Amsterdam: Rodopi, 1972.

Schaefer, Josephine O'Brien. *The Three-Fold Nature of Reality in the Novels of Virginia Woolf.* The Hague: Mouton, 1965.

Scheuerle, William H. *The Neglected Brother: A Study of Henry Kingsley.* Tallahassee: Florida State University Press, 1971.

Schleussner, Bruno. *Der neopikareske Roman: Pikareske Elemente in der Struktur moderner englischer Romane, 1950-1960.* Bonn: Bouvier, 1969.

Schneider, Ulrich. *Die Funktion der Zitate im "Ulysses" von James Joyce.* Studien zur englischen Literatur, 3. Bonn: Bouvier, 1970.

Schrey, Helmut. *Didaktik des zeitgenössischen englischen Romans: Versuch auf der Grenze von Literaturkritik und Fachdidaktik.* Wuppertal: Henn, 1970.

Scott, Nathan A. *Samuel Beckett.* New York: Hillary House, 1965.

Seeber, Hans Ulrich. *Wandlungen der Form in der literarischen Utopie: Studien zur Entfaltung des utopischen Romans in England.* Göppinger Akademische Beiträge, 13. Göppingen: Kümmerle, 1970.

Seltzer, Alvin J. *Chaos in the Novel: The Novel in Chaos.* New York: Schocken, 1974.

Senn, Fritz, ed. *New Light on Joyce from the Dublin Symposium.* Bloomington: Indiana University Press, 1972.

Shahane, V. A. *E. M. Forster: A Reassessment.* Delhi: Kitab Mahal, 1962.

Shahane, Vasant A. *Rudyard Kipling: Activist and Artist.* Carbondale: Southern Illinois University Press, 1973.

Sharps, John Geoffrey. *Mrs. Gaskell's Observation and Invention: A Study of Her Non-Biographical Works.* Fontwell, England: Linden, 1970.

Shesgreen, Sean. *Literary Portraits in the Novels of Henry Fielding.* De-Kalb: Northern Illinois University Press, 1972.

Shinagel, Michael. *Daniel Defoe and Middle-Class Gentility.* Cambridge: Harvard University Press, 1968.

Simpson, Hassell A. *Rumer Godden.* New York: Twayne, 1973.

Slade, Tony. *D. H. Lawrence.* London: Evans, 1969.

Small, Christopher. *Ariel Like a Harpy: Shelley, Mary and "Franken-stein."* London: Gollancz, 1972.

Smalley, Barbara. *George Eliot and Flaubert: Pioneers of the Modern Novel.* Athens: Ohio University Press, 1974.

Smith, Elton Edward, and Esther Greenwell Smith. *William Godwin.* New York: Twayne, 1965.

Smith, Eric. *Some Versions of the Fall: The Myth of the Fall of Man in English Literature.* London: Croom Helm, 1973.

Smith, Frank Glover. *D. H. Lawrence: "The Rainbow."* London: Arnold, 1971.

Smith, Grover. *Ford Madox Ford.* New York: Columbia University Press, 1972.

Southall, Raymond. *Literature and the Rise of Capitalism: Critical Essays Mainly on the Sixteenth and Seventeenth Centuries.* London: Lawrence and Wishart, 1973.

Southerington, F. R. *Hardy's Vision of Man.* London: Chatto and Windus, 1971.

Stallybrass, Oliver, ed. *Aspects of E. M. Forster: Essays and Recollections Written for His Ninetieth Birthday, January 1, 1969.* New York: Harcourt, Brace and World, 1969.

Stanzel, Franz K., ed. *Der englische Roman: Vom Mittelalter zur Moderne.* 2 vols. Düsseldorf: Basel, 1969.

Stanzel, Franz. *Narrative Situations in the Novel: "Tom Jones," "Moby-Dick," "The Ambassadors," "Ulysses."* Translated by James P. Pusack. Bloomington: Indiana University Press, 1971.

Steele, Elizabeth. *Hugh Walpole.* New York: Twayne, 1972.

Steinberg, Erwin R. *The Stream of Consciousness and Beyond in "Ulysses."* Pittsburgh: University of Pittsburgh Press, 1973.

Steinecke, Hartmut, ed. *Theorie und Technik des Romans im 20. Jahr-hundert.* Tübingen: Niemeyer, 1972.

Steinhoff, William. *George Orwell and the Origins of "1984."* Ann Arbor: University of Michigan Press, 1975.

Stern, J. P. *On Realism.* London: Routledge and Kegan Paul, 1973.

Stewart, J. I. M. *Rudyard Kipling.* New York: Dodd, Mead, 1966.

Stewart, J. I. M. *Thomas Hardy: A Critical Biography.* New York: Dodd, Mead, 1971.

Stoehr, Taylor. *Dickens: The Dreamer's Stance.* Ithaca: Cornell University Press, 1965.

Stone, Wilfred. *The Cave and the Mountain: A Study of E. M. Forster.* Stanford: Stanford University Press, 1966.

Stratford, Philip. *Faith and Fiction: Creative Process in Greene and*

Tompkins, J. M. S. *The Art of Rudyard Kipling*. London: Methuen, 1959.

Trilling, Lionel. *E. M. Forster*. 2nd ed. New York: New Directions, 1964.

Trilling, Lionel. *Sincerity and Authenticity*. Cambridge: Harvard University Press, 1972.

Two English Novelists: Aphra Behn and Anthony Trollope—Papers Read at a Clark Library Seminar, May 11, 1974. Los Angeles: William Andrews Clark Memorial Library, University of California, Los Angeles, 1975.

Van de Laar, Elisabeth Th. M. *The Inner Structure of "Wuthering Heights": A Study of an Imaginative Field*. The Hague: Mouton, 1969.

Van Kaam, Adrian, and Kathleen Healy. *The Demon and the Dove: Personality Growth Through Literature*. Pittsburgh: Duquesne University Press, 1967.

Varela Jácome, Benito. *Renovación de la novela en el siglo XX*. Barcelona: Destino, 1967.

Vernier, Jean-Pierre. *H. G. Wells et son temps*. Paris: Didier, 1971.

Vickers, Brian, ed. *The World of Jonathan Swift: Essays for the Tercenary*. Oxford: Blackwell, 1968.

Vickery, John B. *The Literary Impact of "The Golden Bough."* Princeton: Princeton University Press, 1973.

Vigar, Penelope. *The Novels of Thomas Hardy: Illusion and Reality*. London: Athlone, 1974.

Villgradter, Rudolf. *Die Darstellung des Bösen in den Romanen George Eliots*. Saarbrücken: Universitätsbibliothek, 1970.

Vinaver, Eugène. *The Rise of Romance*. New York: Oxford University Press, 1971.

Viswanathan, K. *India in English Fiction*. Waltair: Andhra University Press, 1971.

Vogt, Jochen, ed. *Der Kriminalroman*. Munich: Fink, 1971.

Vooys, Sijna de. *The Psychological Element in the English Sociological Novel of the Nineteenth Century*. New York: Haskell House, 1966.

Wagner, Geoffrey. *Five for Freedom: A Study of Feminism in Fiction*. London: Allen and Unwin, 1972.

Walcutt, Charles Child. *Man's Changing Mask: Modes and Methods of Characterization in Fiction*. Minneapolis: University of Minnesota Press, 1966.

Ward, David. *Jonathan Swift: An Introductory Essay*. London: Methuen, 1973.

Watson, Sara Ruth. *V. Sackville-West*. New York: Twayne, 1972.

Weatherhead, A. Kingsley. *A Reading of Henry Green*. Seattle: University of Washington Press, 1961.

Weber, Brom, ed. *Sense and Sensibility in Twentieth-Century Writing: A Gathering in Memory of William Van O'Connor*. Carbondale: Southern Illinois University Press, 1970.

Weigel, John A. *Lawrence Durrell*. New York: Twayne, 1965.

Weinstein, Arnold L. *Vision and Response in Modern Fiction*. Ithaca: Cornell University Press, 1974.

Weintraub, Stanley, and Philip Young, eds. *Directions in Literary Criticism: Contemporary Approaches to Literature.* University Park: Pennsylvania State University Press, 1973.

Welsh, Alexander. *The Hero of the Waverley Novels.* New Haven: Yale University Press, 1963.

Wheatley, James H. *Patterns in Thackeray's Fiction.* Cambridge: M. I. T. Press, 1969.

Whitbourn, Christine J., ed. *Knaves and Swindlers: Essays on the Picaresque Novel in Europe.* London: Oxford University Press for the University of Hull, 1974.

White, John J. *Mythology in the Modern Novel: A Study of Prefigurative Techniques.* Princeton: Princeton University Press, 1971.

White, R. J. *Thomas Hardy and History.* London: Macmillan, 1974.

Williams, Ioan. *The Realist Novel in England: A Study in Development.* London: Macmillan, 1974.

Williams, Merryn. *Thomas Hardy and Rural England.* New York: Macmillan, 1972.

Williams, Muriel Brittain. *Marriage: Fielding's Mirror of Morality.* University: University of Alabama Press, 1973.

Williamson, Jack. *H. G. Wells: Critic of Progress.* Baltimore: Mirage, 1973.

Wogatzky, Karin. *Angus Wilson: "Hemlock and After"—A Study in Ambiguity.* Schweizer Anglistische Arbeiten, 62. Berne: Francke, 1971.

Wolfe, Peter. *Mary Renault.* New York: Twayne, 1969.

Wolfe, Peter. *Graham Greene: The Entertainer.* Carbondale: Southern Illinois University Press, 1972.

Wolfe, Peter. *Rebecca West: Artist and Thinker.* Carbondale: Southern Illinois University Press, 1971.

Wolfer, Verena Elsbeth. *Rebecca West: Kunsttheorie und Romanschaffen.* Schweizer Anglistische Arbeiten, 66. Berne: Francke, 1972.

Wolff, Cynthia Griffin. *Samuel Richardson and the Eighteenth-Century Puritan Character.* Hamden, Conn.: Archon, 1972.

Wolff, Erwin. *Der englische Roman im 18. Jahrhundert: Wesen und Formen.* 2nd ed. Göttingen: Vandenhoeck and Ruprecht, 1968.

Wolff, Robert Lee. *Strange Stories and Other Explorations in Victorian Fiction.* Boston: Gambit, 1971.

Woodcock, George. *Dawn and the Darkest Hour: A Study of Aldous Huxley.* New York: Viking, 1972.

Woodcock, George. *The Crystal Spirit: A Study of George Orwell.* Boston: Little, Brown, 1966.

Wyss, Kurt O. *Pikareske Thematik im Romanwerk Evelyn Waughs.* Schweizer Anglistische Arbeiten, 77. Berne: Francke, 1973.

Yelton, Donald C. *Mimesis and Metaphor: An Inquiry into the Genesis and Scope of Conrad's Symbolic Imagery.* The Hague: Mouton, 1967.

Zeh, Dieter. *Studien zur Erzählkunst in den Romanen E. M. Forsters.* Frankfurt: Universitätsverlag, 1970.

Zéraffa, Michel. *Personne et personnage: Le Romanesque des années 1920 aux années 1950.* Paris: Klincksieck, 1969.

INDEX